NTED

WANTED

WA

DEAD OR ALIVE

KUMOKO

K **10,000,000**

So I'm a Spider, So What?

Art:
Asahiro Kakashi

Original Story:
Okina Baba

Character Design:
Tsukasa Kiryu

So I'm a Spider, So What?

#39-1   3

#39-2   17

#40-1   35

#40-2   51

#41-1   69

#41-2   87

#42   105

#43-1   121

#43-2   139

Bonus Short Comic:
Another Reincarnation #4   157

Bonus Short Story:
The Outside Food I Crave   173

CONTENTS

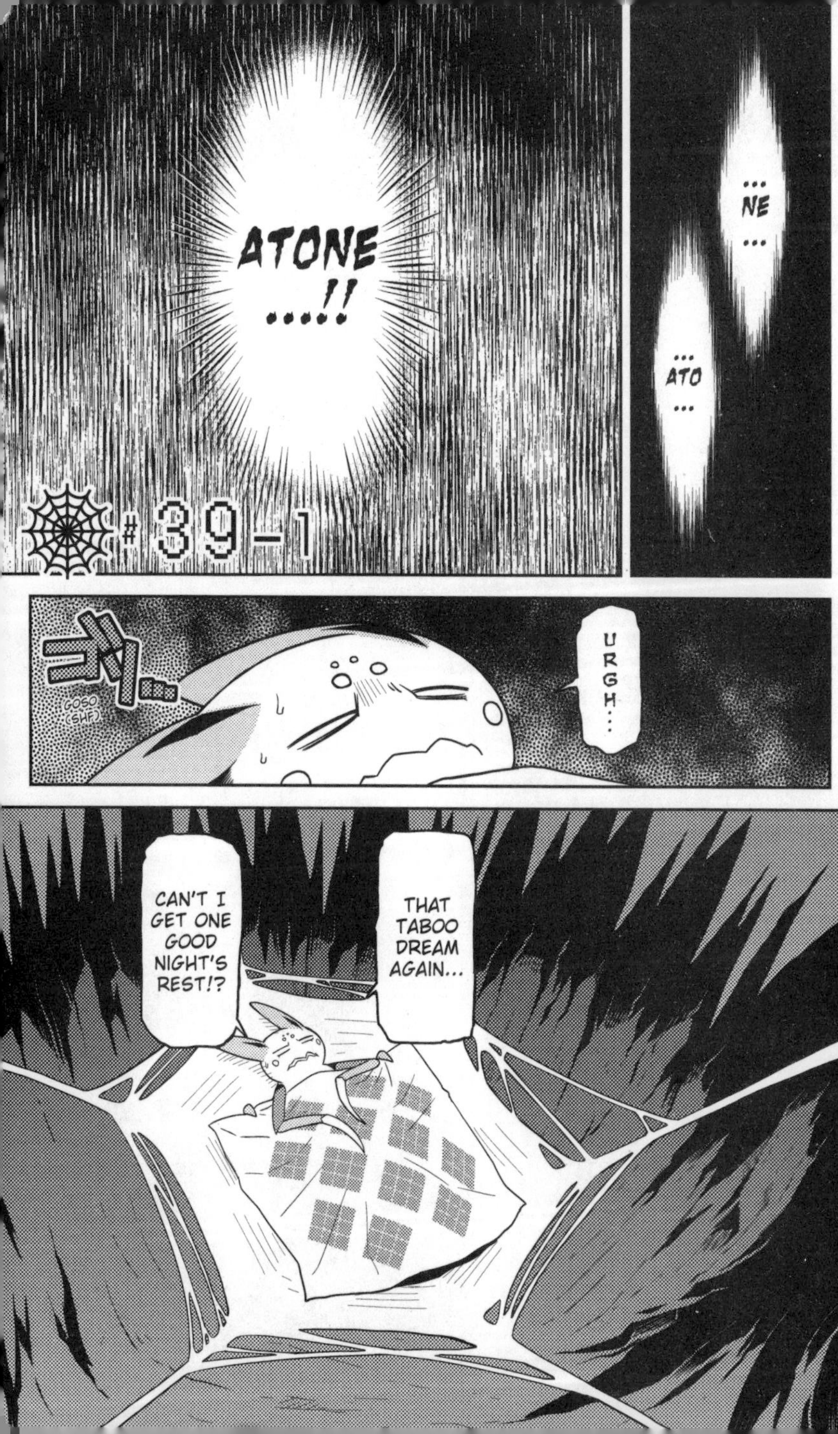

...NE...
...ATO...
ATONE ...!!
#39-1
URGH...
GOSO (SHF)
THAT TABOO DREAM AGAIN...
CAN'T I GET ONE GOOD NIGHT'S REST!?

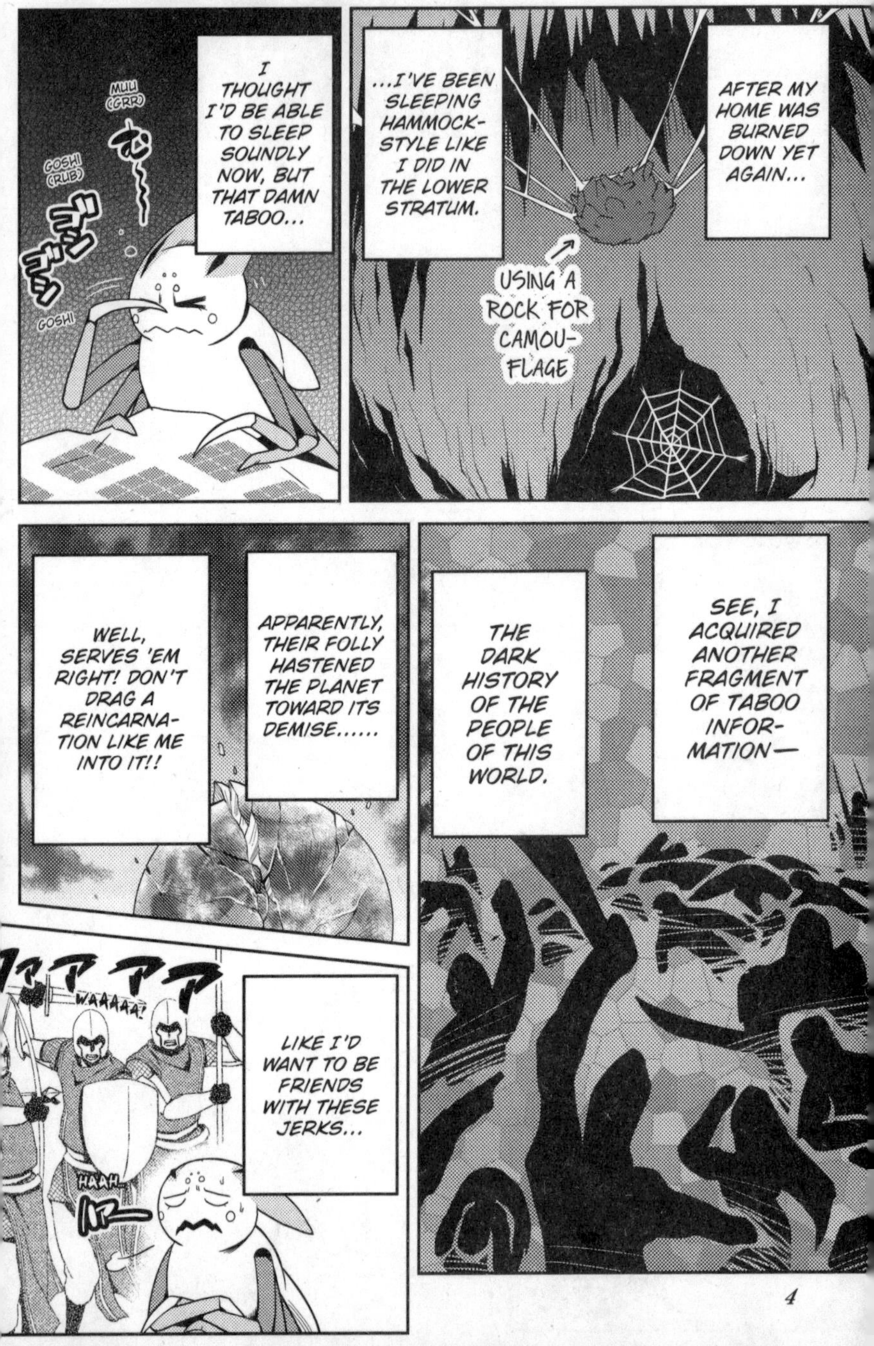
AFTER MY HOME WAS BURNED DOWN YET AGAIN...
...I'VE BEEN SLEEPING HAMMOCK-STYLE LIKE I DID IN THE LOWER STRATUM.
USING A ROCK FOR CAMOU-FLAGE
I THOUGHT I'D BE ABLE TO SLEEP SOUNDLY NOW, BUT THAT DAMN TABOO...
MUU (GRR)
GOSHI (RUB)
GOSHI
SEE, I ACQUIRED ANOTHER FRAGMENT OF TABOO INFOR-MATION—
THE DARK HISTORY OF THE PEOPLE OF THIS WORLD.
APPARENTLY, THEIR FOLLY HASTENED THE PLANET TOWARD ITS DEMISE......
WELL, SERVES 'EM RIGHT! DON'T DRAG A REINCARNA-TION LIKE ME INTO IT!!
WAAAAA!
LIKE I'D WANT TO BE FRIENDS WITH THESE JERKS...
HAAH...

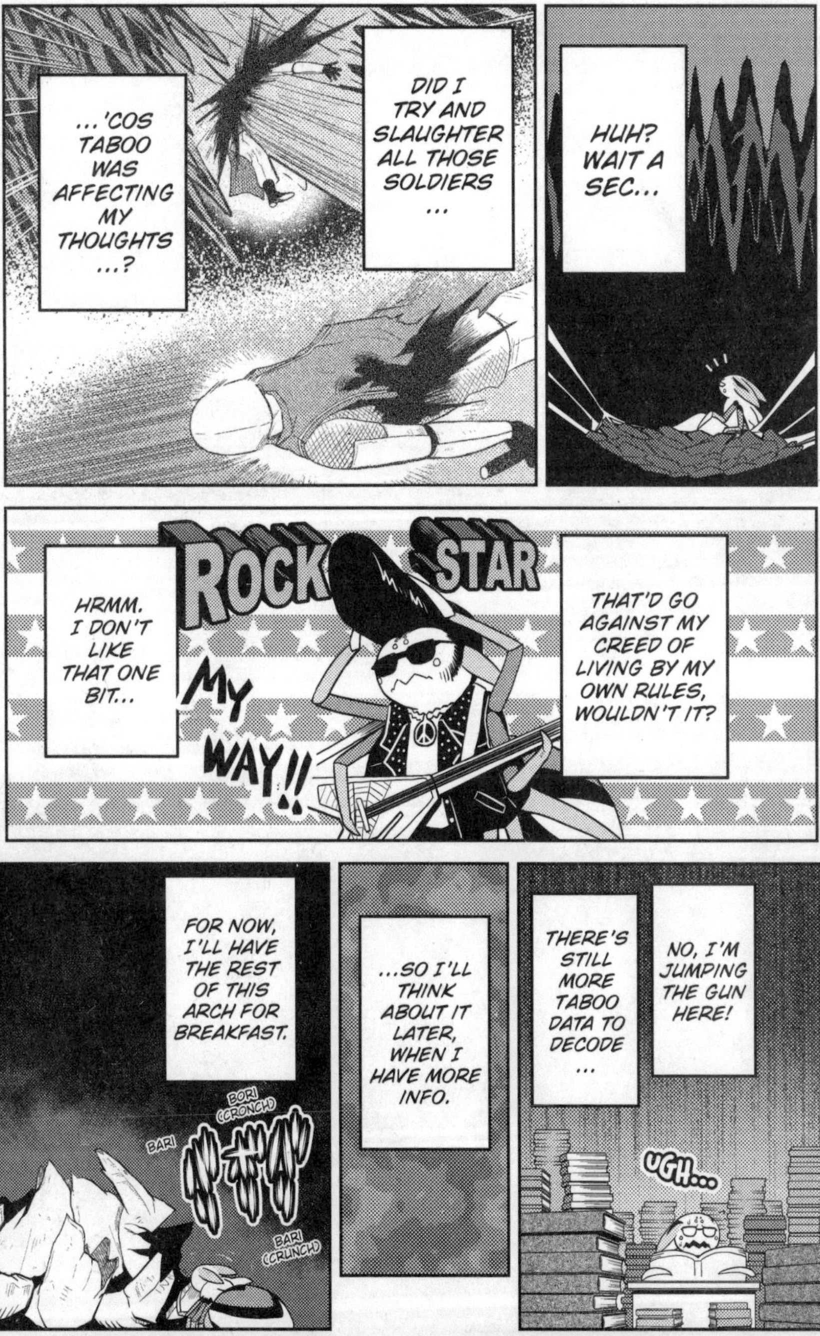
HUH? WAIT A SEC...
DID I TRY AND SLAUGHTER ALL THOSE SOLDIERS ...
...'COS TABOO WAS AFFECTING MY THOUGHTS ...?
ROCK STAR
THAT'D GO AGAINST MY CREED OF LIVING BY MY OWN RULES, WOULDN'T IT?
HRMM. I DON'T LIKE THAT ONE BIT...
MY WAY!!
NO, I'M JUMPING THE GUN HERE!
THERE'S STILL MORE TABOO DATA TO DECODE ...
UGH...
...SO I'LL THINK ABOUT IT LATER, WHEN I HAVE MORE INFO.
FOR NOW, I'LL HAVE THE REST OF THIS ARCH FOR BREAKFAST.
BORI (CRONCH)
BARI
BARI (CRUNCH)

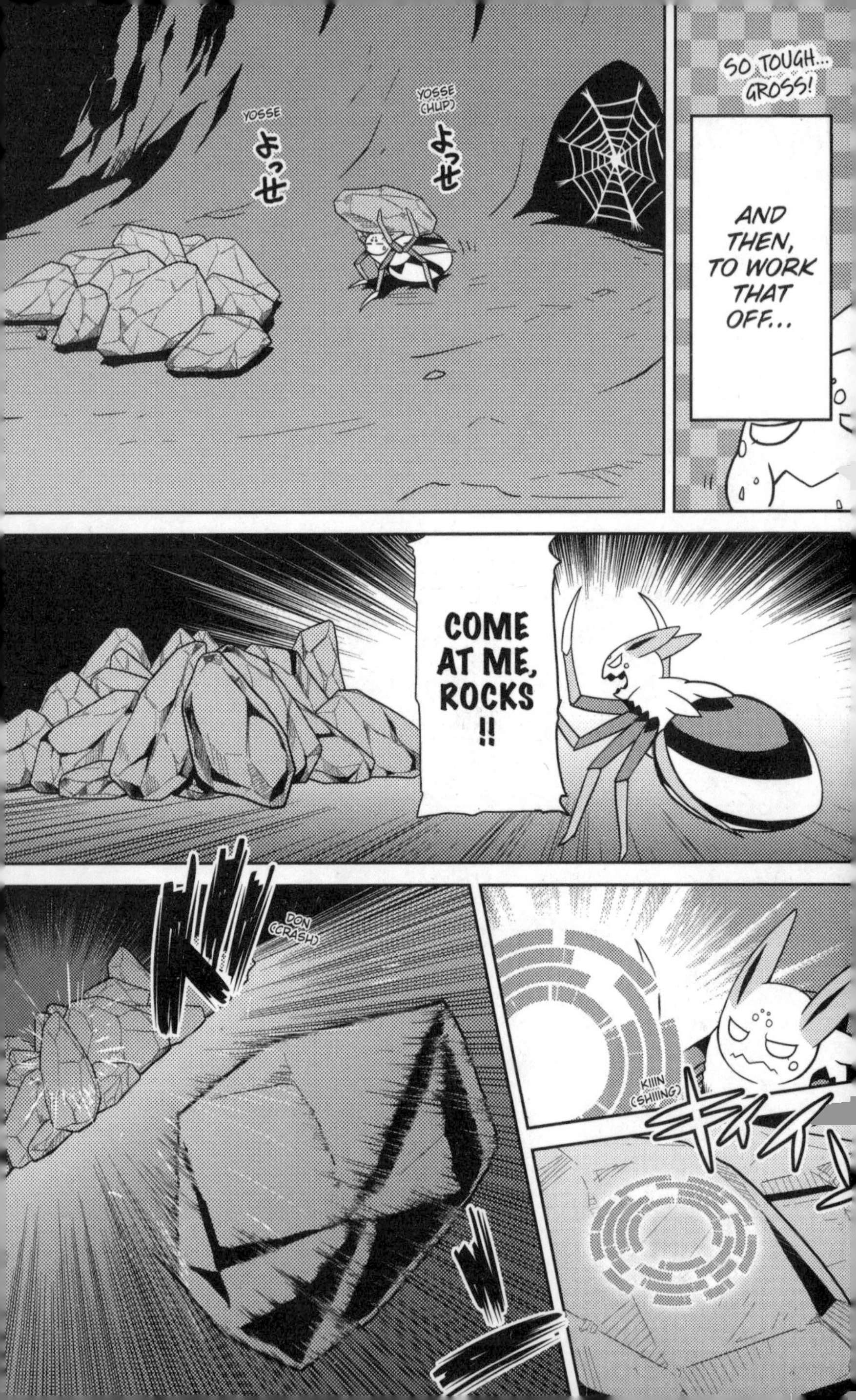
SO TOUGH... GROSS!
AND THEN, TO WORK THAT OFF...
YOSSE (HUP)
よっせ
YOSSE
よっせ
COME AT ME, ROCKS!!
KIIN (SHIIING)
DON (CRASH)

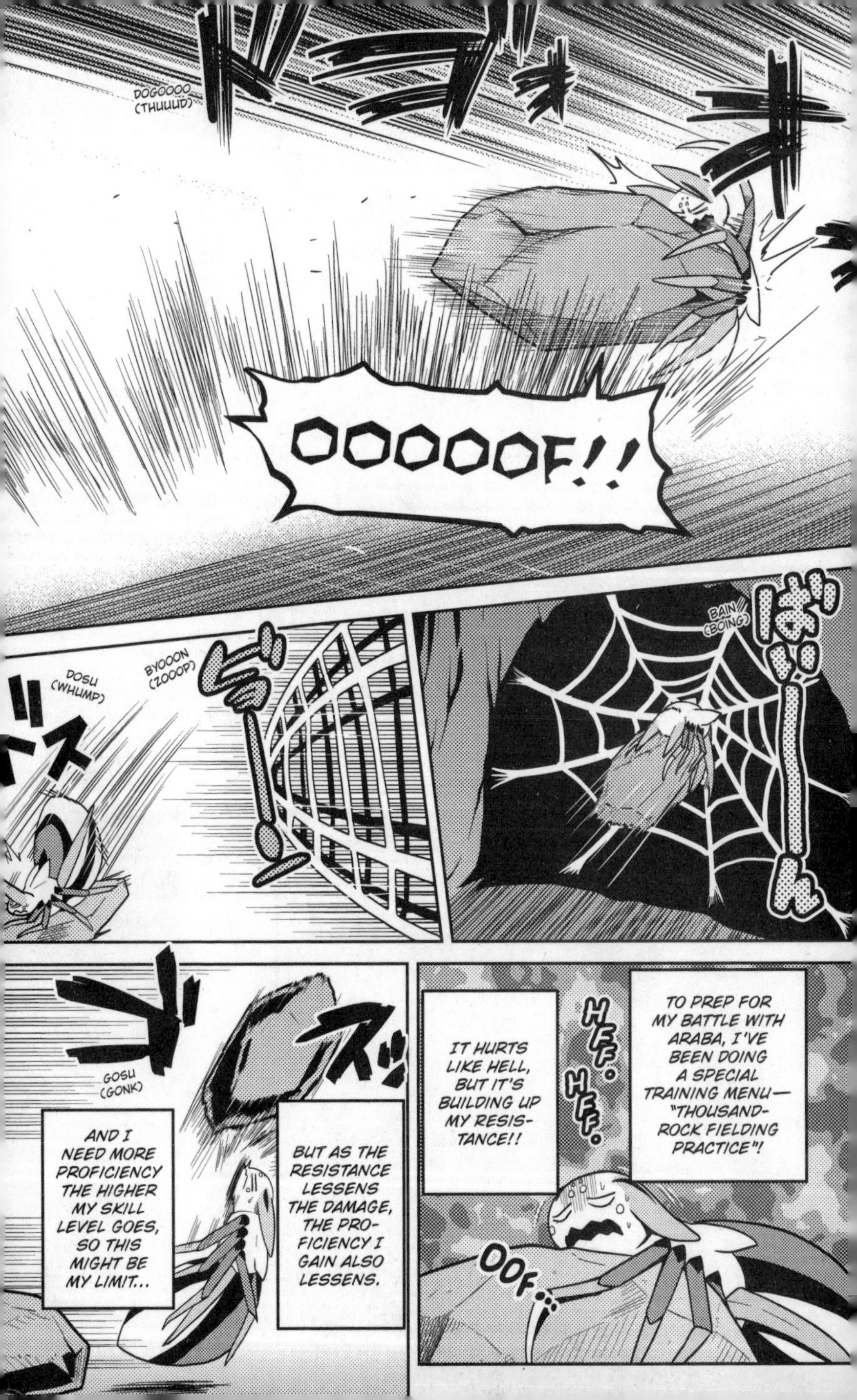
DOGOOOO
(THUUUD)
OOOOOF!!
BAIN
(BOING)
BYOOON
(ZOOOP)
DOSU
(WHUMP)
TO PREP FOR MY BATTLE WITH ARABA, I'VE BEEN DOING A SPECIAL TRAINING MENU—"THOUSAND-ROCK FIELDING PRACTICE"!
HFF. HFF.
IT HURTS LIKE HELL, BUT IT'S BUILDING UP MY RESIS-TANCE!!
OOF...
GOSU
(GONK)
BUT AS THE RESISTANCE LESSENS THE DAMAGE, THE PRO-FICIENCY I GAIN ALSO LESSENS.
AND I NEED MORE PROFICIENCY THE HIGHER MY SKILL LEVEL GOES, SO THIS MIGHT BE MY LIMIT...

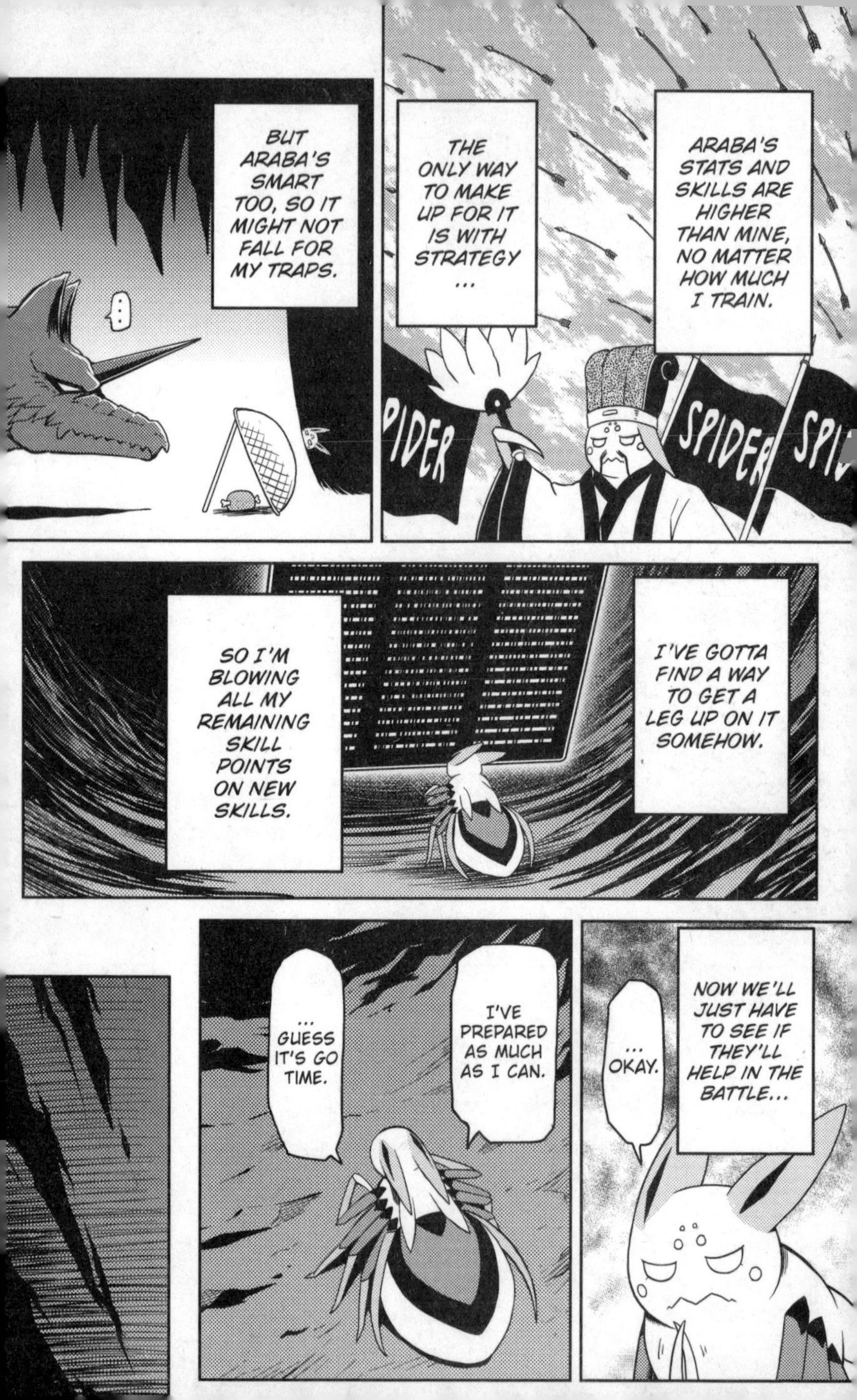
ARABA'S STATS AND SKILLS ARE HIGHER THAN MINE, NO MATTER HOW MUCH I TRAIN.
THE ONLY WAY TO MAKE UP FOR IT IS WITH STRATEGY...
BUT ARABA'S SMART TOO, SO IT MIGHT NOT FALL FOR MY TRAPS.
...
I'VE GOTTA FIND A WAY TO GET A LEG UP ON IT SOMEHOW.
SO I'M BLOWING ALL MY REMAINING SKILL POINTS ON NEW SKILLS.
NOW WE'LL JUST HAVE TO SEE IF THEY'LL HELP IN THE BATTLE...
...OKAY.
I'VE PREPARED AS MUCH AS I CAN.
...GUESS IT'S GO TIME.

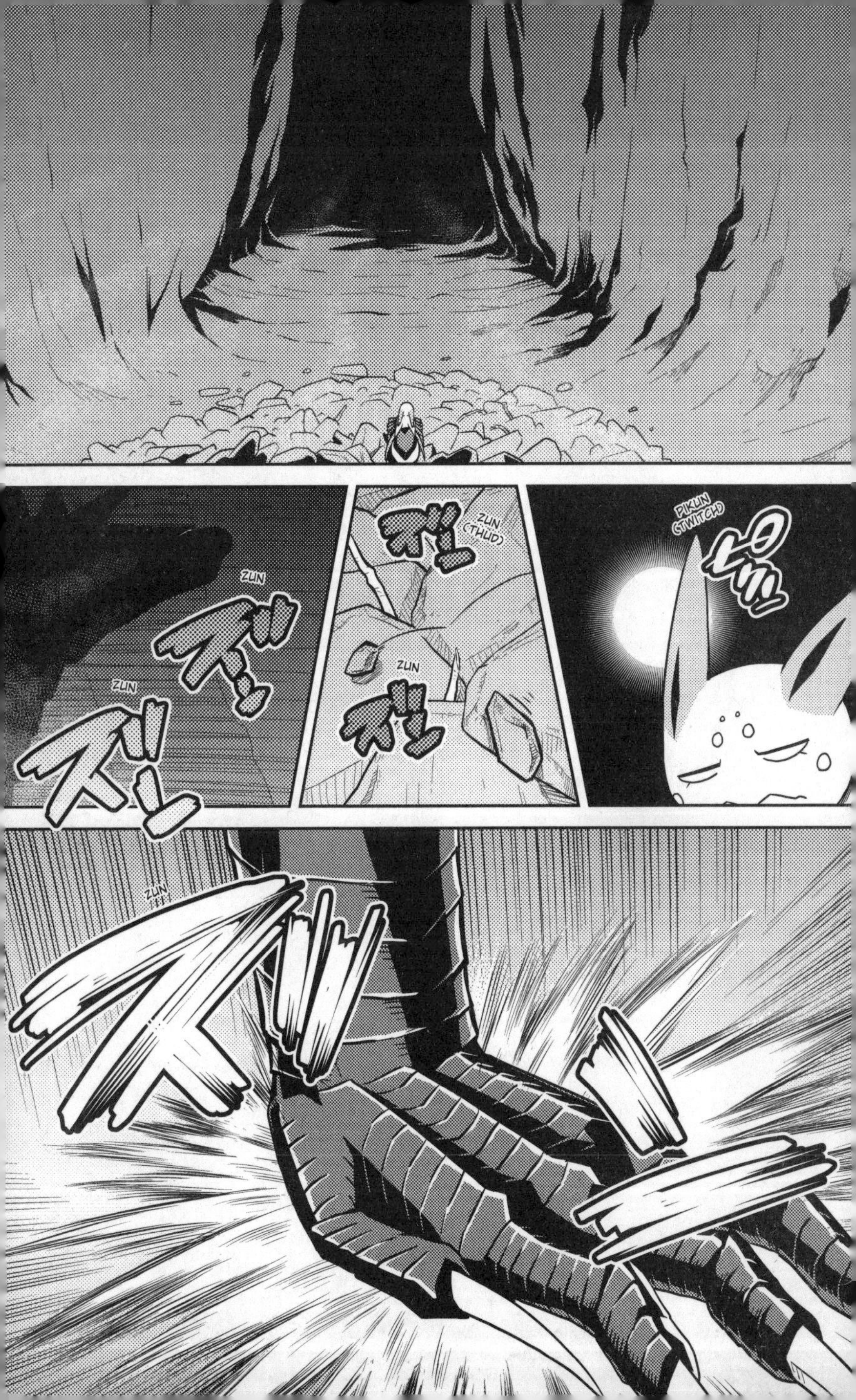
PIKUN
(TWITCH)
ZUN
(THUD)
ZUN
ZUN
ZUN
ZUN

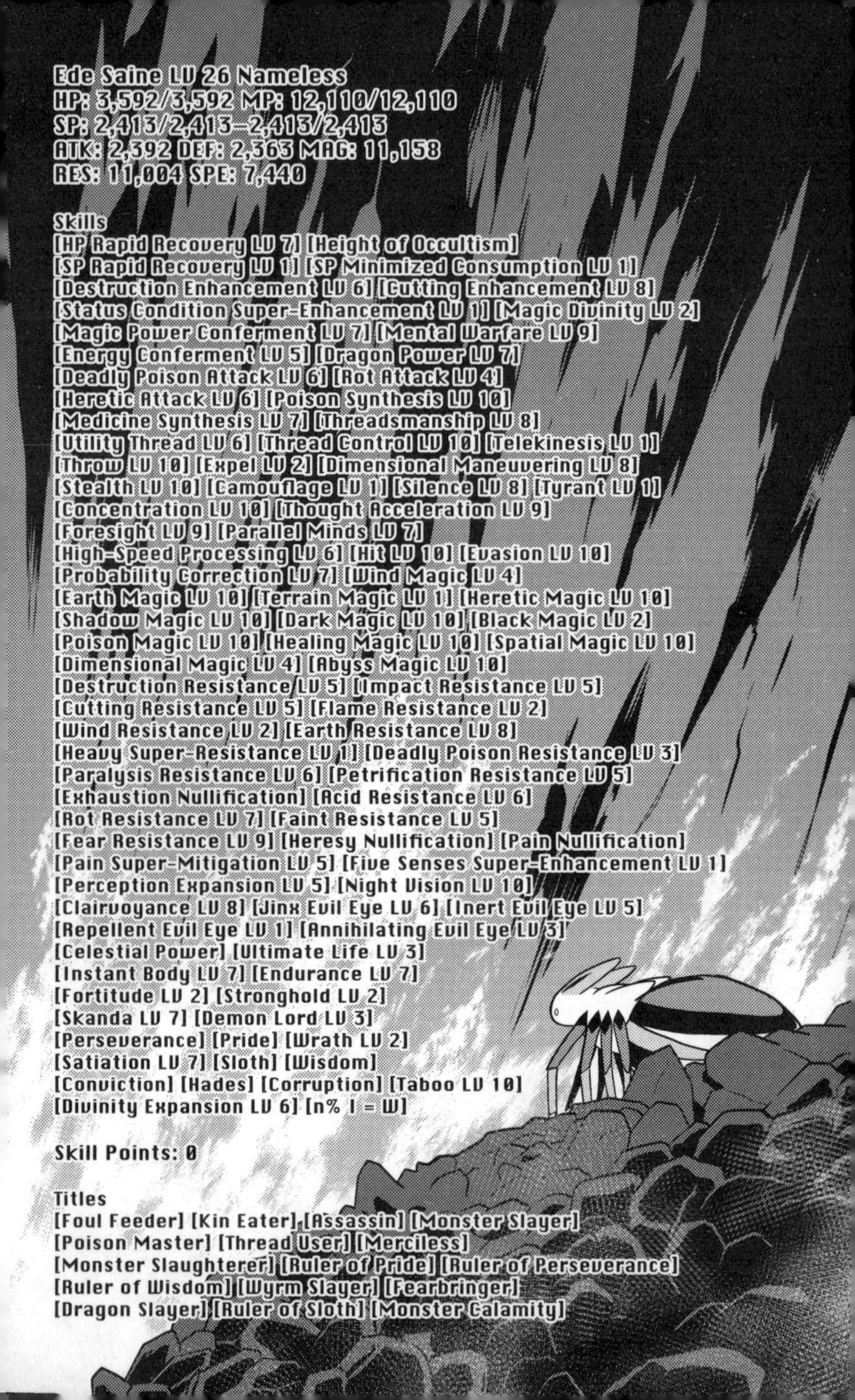

Ede Saine LV 26 Nameless
HP: 3,592/3,592 MP: 12,110/12,110
SP: 2,413/2,413–2,413/2,413
ATK: 2,392 DEF: 2,363 MAG: 11,158
RES: 11,004 SPE: 7,440

Skills
[HP Rapid Recovery LV 7] [Height of Occultism]
[SP Rapid Recovery LV 1] [SP Minimized Consumption LV 1]
[Destruction Enhancement LV 6] [Cutting Enhancement LV 8]
[Status Condition Super-Enhancement LV 1] [Magic Divinity LV 2]
[Magic Power Conferment LV 7] [Mental Warfare LV 9]
[Energy Conferment LV 5] [Dragon Power LV 7]
[Deadly Poison Attack LV 6] [Rot Attack LV 4]
[Heretic Attack LV 6] [Poison Synthesis LV 10]
[Medicine Synthesis LV 7] [Threadsmanship LV 8]
[Utility Thread LV 6] [Thread Control LV 10] [Telekinesis LV 1]
[Throw LV 10] [Expel LV 2] [Dimensional Maneuvering LV 8]
[Stealth LV 10] [Camouflage LV 1] [Silence LV 8] [Tyrant LV 1]
[Concentration LV 10] [Thought Acceleration LV 9]
[Foresight LV 9] [Parallel Minds LV 7]
[High-Speed Processing LV 6] [Hit LV 10] [Evasion LV 10]
[Probability Correction LV 7] [Wind Magic LV 4]
[Earth Magic LV 10] [Terrain Magic LV 1] [Heretic Magic LV 10]
[Shadow Magic LV 10] [Dark Magic LV 10] [Black Magic LV 2]
[Poison Magic LV 10] [Healing Magic LV 10] [Spatial Magic LV 10]
[Dimensional Magic LV 4] [Abyss Magic LV 10]
[Destruction Resistance LV 5] [Impact Resistance LV 5]
[Cutting Resistance LV 5] [Flame Resistance LV 2]
[Wind Resistance LV 2] [Earth Resistance LV 8]
[Heavy Super-Resistance LV 1] [Deadly Poison Resistance LV 3]
[Paralysis Resistance LV 6] [Petrification Resistance LV 5]
[Exhaustion Nullification] [Acid Resistance LV 6]
[Rot Resistance LV 7] [Faint Resistance LV 5]
[Fear Resistance LV 9] [Heresy Nullification] [Pain Nullification]
[Pain Super-Mitigation LV 5] [Five Senses Super-Enhancement LV 1]
[Perception Expansion LV 5] [Night Vision LV 10]
[Clairvoyance LV 8] [Jinx Evil Eye LV 6] [Inert Evil Eye LV 5]
[Repellent Evil Eye LV 1] [Annihilating Evil Eye LV 3]
[Celestial Power] [Ultimate Life LV 3]
[Instant Body LV 7] [Endurance LV 7]
[Fortitude LV 2] [Stronghold LV 2]
[Skanda LV 7] [Demon Lord LV 3]
[Perseverance] [Pride] [Wrath LV 2]
[Satiation LV 7] [Sloth] [Wisdom]
[Conviction] [Hades] [Corruption] [Taboo LV 10]
[Divinity Expansion LV 6] [n% I = W]

Skill Points: 0

Titles
[Foul Feeder] [Kin Eater] [Assassin] [Monster Slayer]
[Poison Master] [Thread User] [Merciless]
[Monster Slaughterer] [Ruler of Pride] [Ruler of Perseverance]
[Ruler of Wisdom] [Wyrm Slayer] [Fearbringer]
[Dragon Slayer] [Ruler of Sloth] [Monster Calamity]

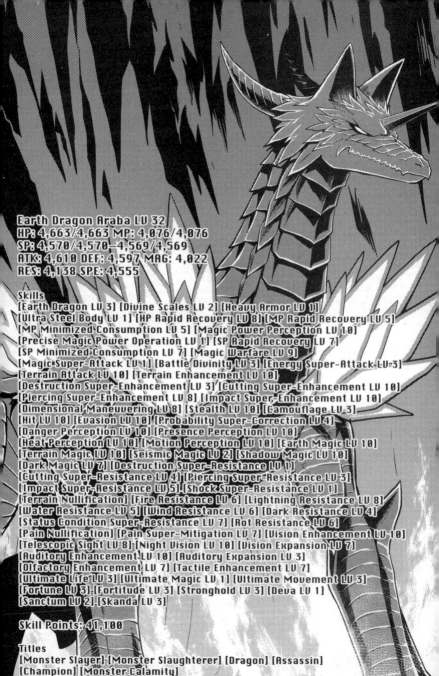

Earth Dragon Araba LV 32
HP: 4,663/4,663 MP: 4,076/4,076
SP: 4,570/4,570—4,569/4,569
ATK: 4,610 DEF: 4,597 MAG: 4,022
RES: 4,138 SPE: 4,555

Skills
[Earth Dragon LV 3] [Divine Scales LV 2] [Heavy Armor LV 1]
[Ultra Steel Body LV 1] [HP Rapid Recovery LV 8] [MP Rapid Recovery LV 5]
[MP Minimized Consumption LV 5] [Magic Power Perception LV 10]
[Precise Magic Power Operation LV 1] [SP Rapid Recovery LV 7]
[SP Minimized Consumption LV 7] [Magic Warfare LV 9]
[Magic Super-Attack LV 1] [Battle Divinity LV 3] [Energy Super-Attack LV 3]
[Terrain Attack LV 10] [Terrain Enhancement LV 10]
[Destruction Super-Enhancement LV 3] [Cutting Super-Enhancement LV 10]
[Piercing Super-Enhancement LV 8] [Impact Super-Enhancement LV 10]
[Dimensional Maneuvering LV 8] [Stealth LV 10] [Camouflage LV 3]
[Hit LV 10] [Evasion LV 10] [Probability Super-Correction LV 4]
[Danger Perception LV 10] [Presence Perception LV 10]
[Heat Perception LV 10] [Motion Perception LV 10] [Earth Magic LV 10]
[Terrain Magic LV 10] [Seismic Magic LV 2] [Shadow Magic LV 10]
[Dark Magic LV 7] [Destruction Super-Resistance LV 1]
[Cutting Super-Resistance LV 4] [Piercing Super-Resistance LV 3]
[Impact Super-Resistance LV 5] [Shock Super-Resistance LV 1]
[Terrain Nullification] [Fire Resistance LV 6] [Lightning Resistance LV 8]
[Water Resistance LV 5] [Wind Resistance LV 6] [Dark Resistance LV 4]
[Status Condition Super-Resistance LV 7] [Rot Resistance LV 6]
[Pain Nullification] [Pain Super-Mitigation LV 7] [Vision Enhancement LV 10]
[Telescopic Sight LV 8] [Night Vision LV 10] [Vision Expansion LV 7]
[Auditory Enhancement LV 10] [Auditory Expansion LV 3]
[Olfactory Enhancement LV 7] [Tactile Enhancement LV 7]
[Ultimate Life LV 3] [Ultimate Magic LV 1] [Ultimate Movement LV 3]
[Fortune LV 3] [Fortitude LV 3] [Stronghold LV 3] [Deva LV 1]
[Sanctum LV 2] [Skanda LV 3]

Skill Points: 41,100

Titles
[Monster Slayer] [Monster Slaughterer] [Dragon] [Assassin]
[Champion] [Monster Calamity]

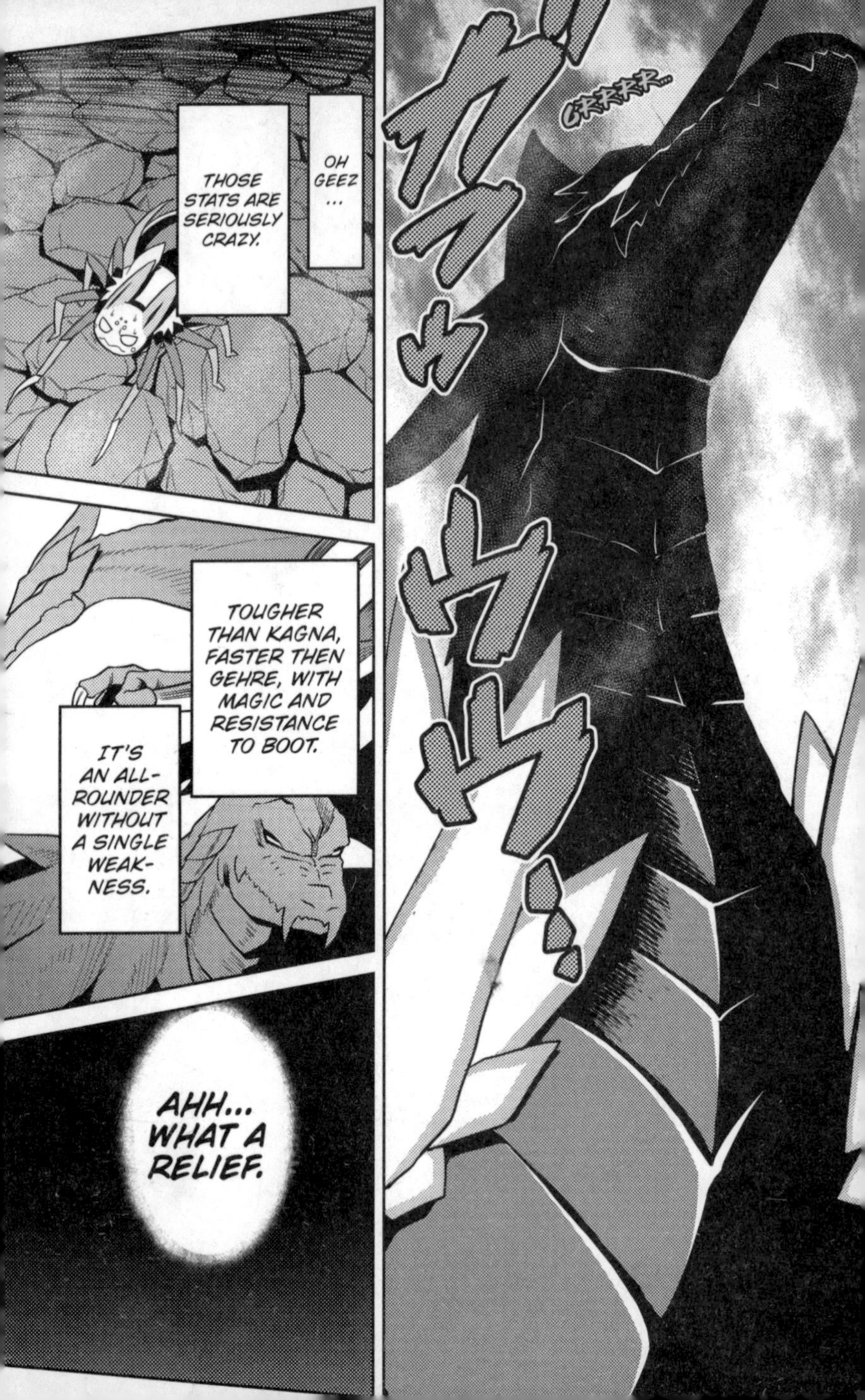
GRRRR...
OH GEEZ...
THOSE STATS ARE SERIOUSLY CRAZY.
TOUGHER THAN KAGNA, FASTER THEN GEHRE, WITH MAGIC AND RESISTANCE TO BOOT.
IT'S AN ALL-ROUNDER WITHOUT A SINGLE WEAK-NESS.
AHH... WHAT A RELIEF.

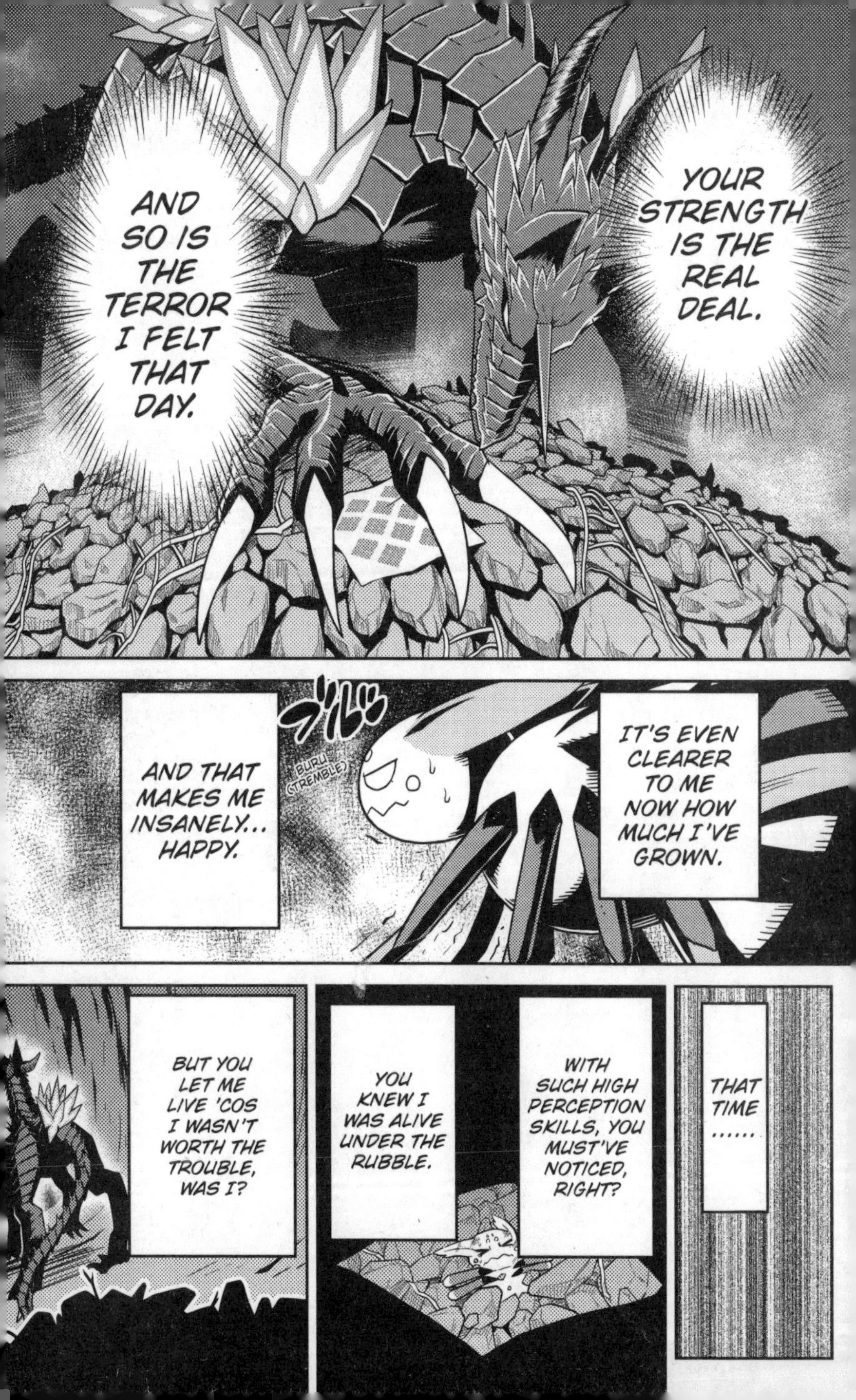
YOUR STRENGTH IS THE REAL DEAL.
AND SO IS THE TERROR I FELT THAT DAY.
IT'S EVEN CLEARER TO ME NOW HOW MUCH I'VE GROWN.
BURU (TREMBLE)
AND THAT MAKES ME INSANELY... HAPPY.
THAT TIME......
WITH SUCH HIGH PERCEPTION SKILLS, YOU MUST'VE NOTICED, RIGHT?
YOU KNEW I WAS ALIVE UNDER THE RUBBLE.
BUT YOU LET ME LIVE 'COS I WASN'T WORTH THE TROUBLE, WAS I?

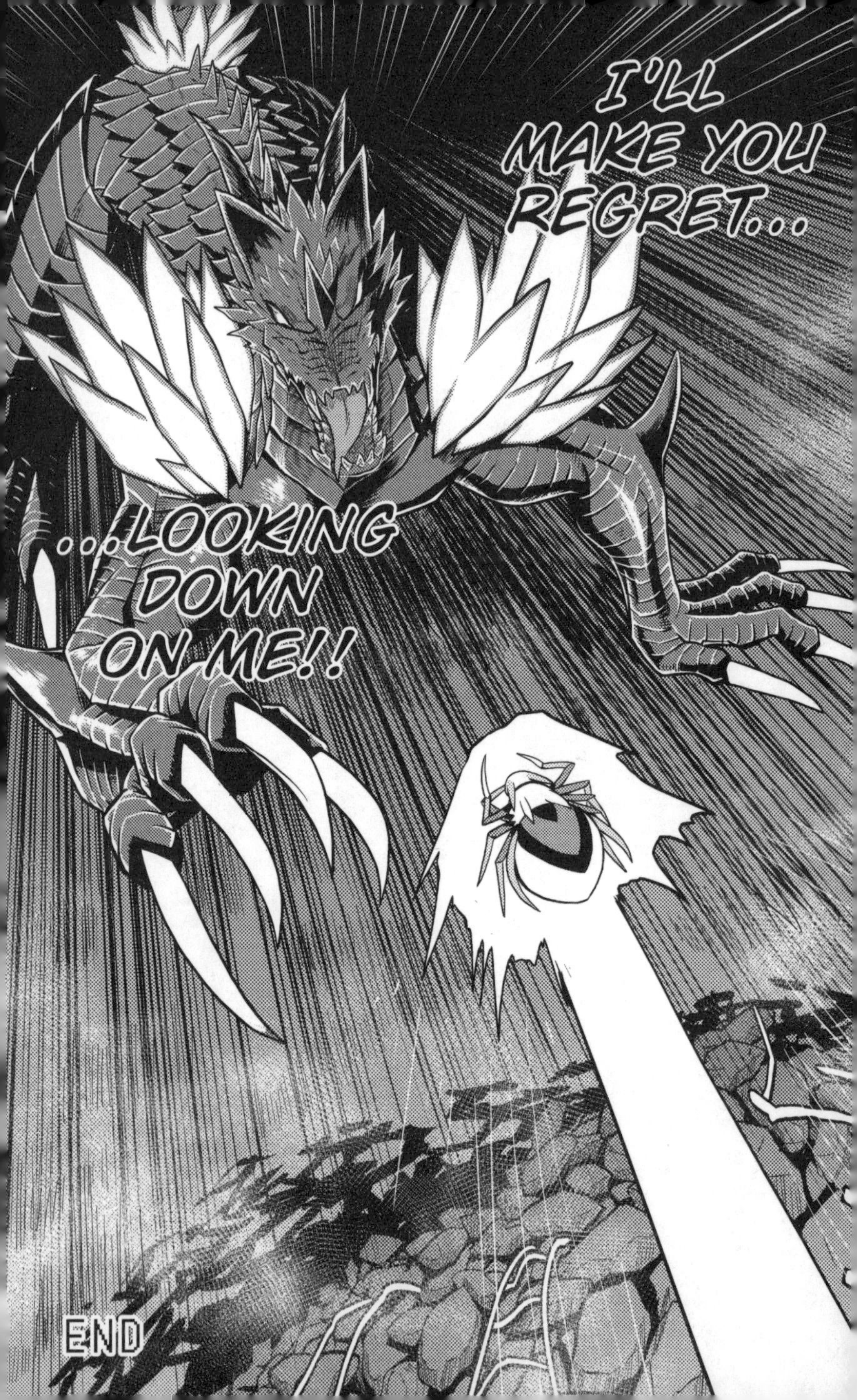
I'LL MAKE YOU REGRET...
...LOOKING DOWN ON ME!!
END

So I'm a Spider, So What?

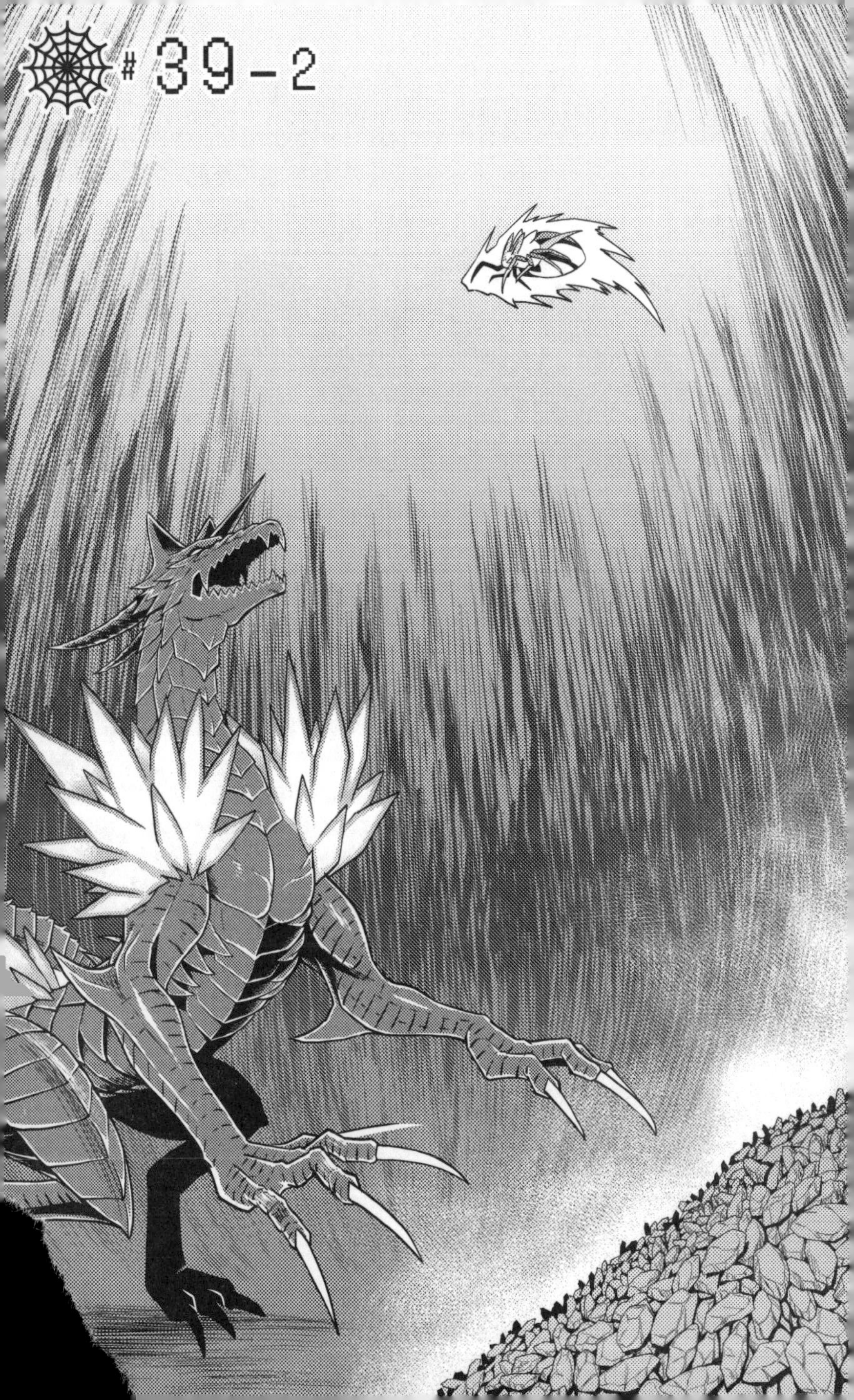
#39-2

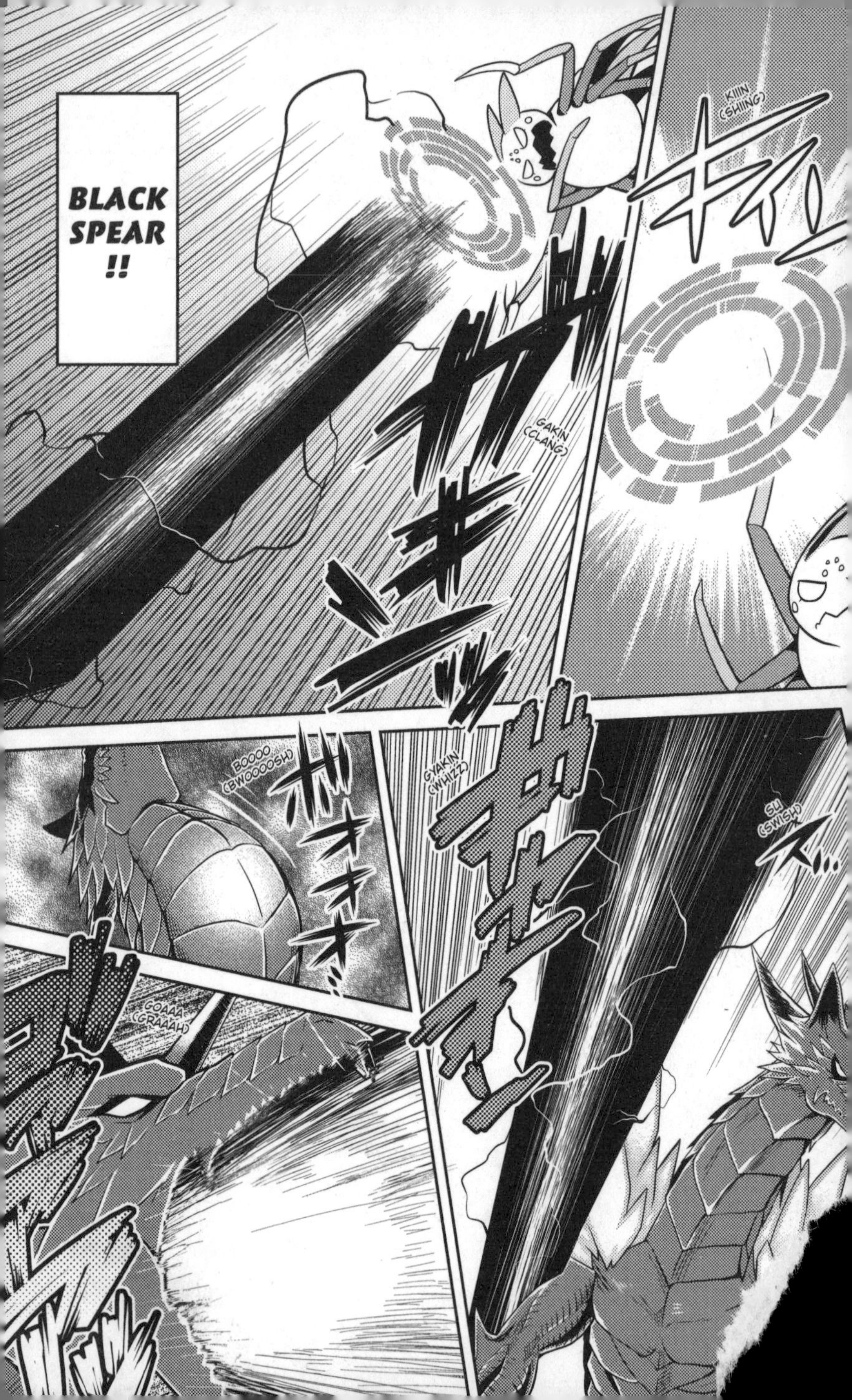
KIIN (SHIING)
BLACK SPEAR!!
GAKIN (CLANG)
SU (SWISH)
GYAKIN (WHIZZ)
BOOOO (BWOOOOSH)
GOAAA (GRAAAH)

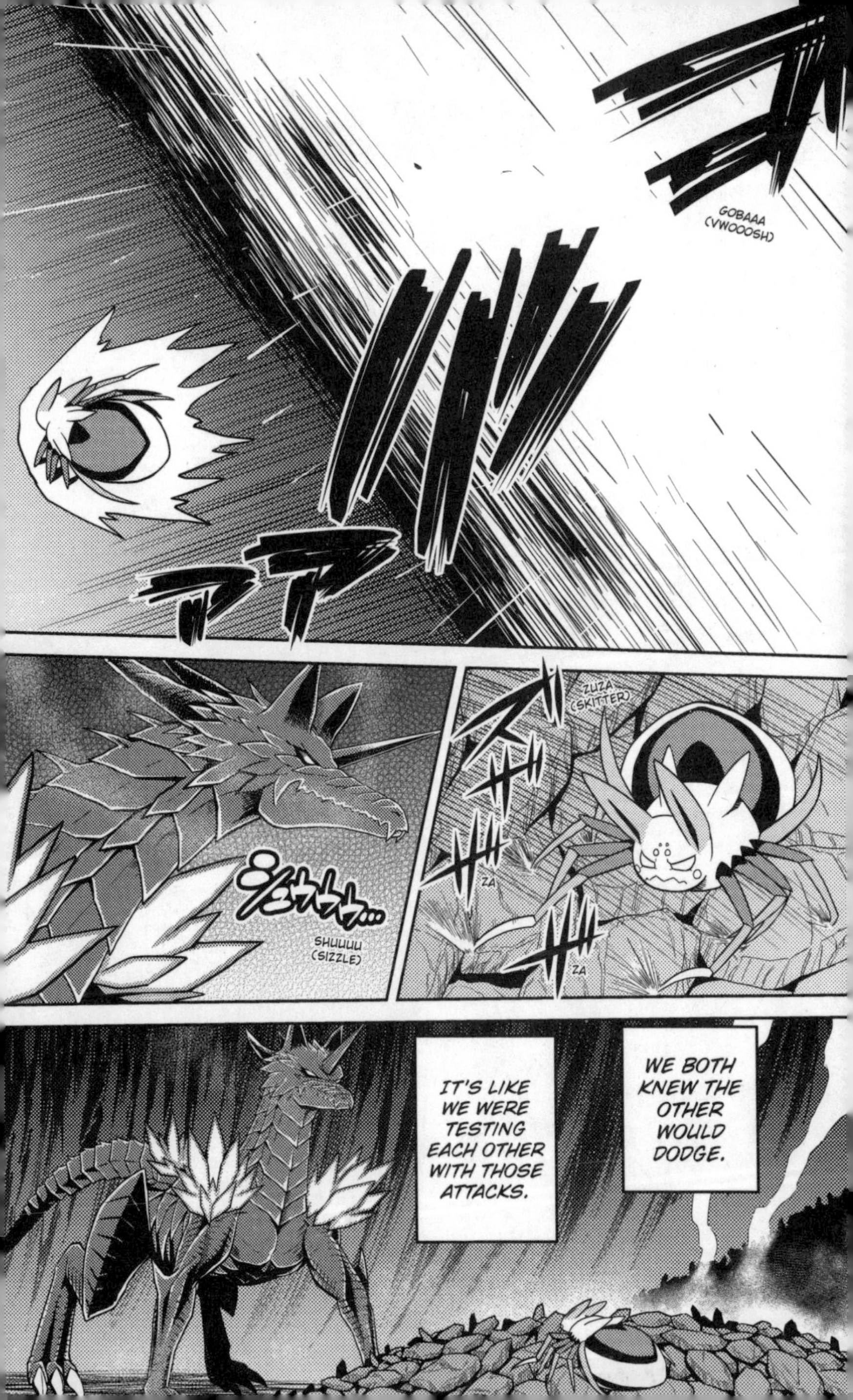
GOBAAA (VWOOOSH)
ZUZA (SKITTER)
ZA
ZA
SHUUUU (SIZZLE)
WE BOTH KNEW THE OTHER WOULD DODGE.
IT'S LIKE WE WERE TESTING EACH OTHER WITH THOSE ATTACKS.

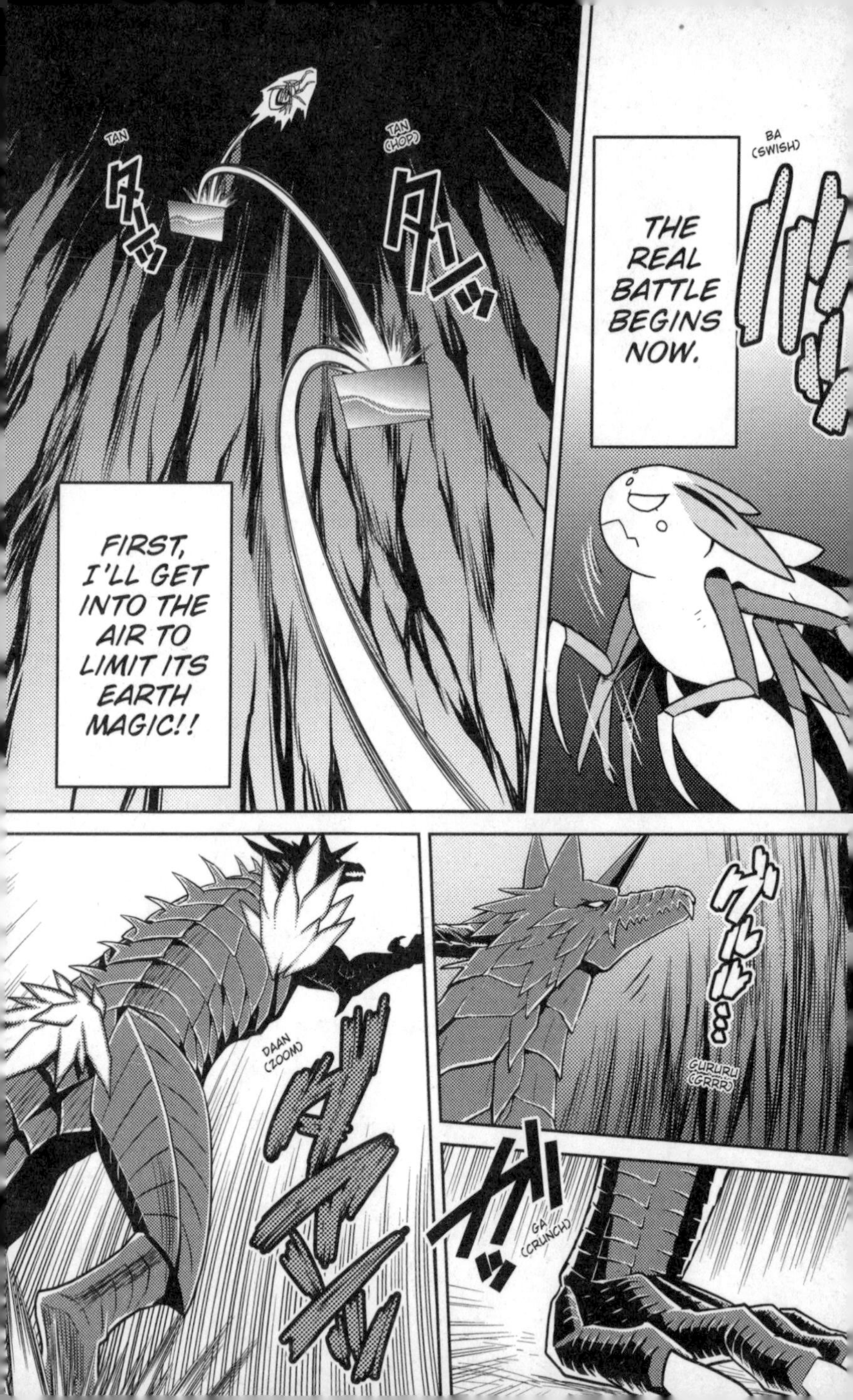
BA (SWISH)
THE REAL BATTLE BEGINS NOW.
TAN (HOP)
TAN
FIRST, I'LL GET INTO THE AIR TO LIMIT ITS EARTH MAGIC!!
GURURU (GRRR)
GA (CRUNCH)
DAAN (ZOOM)

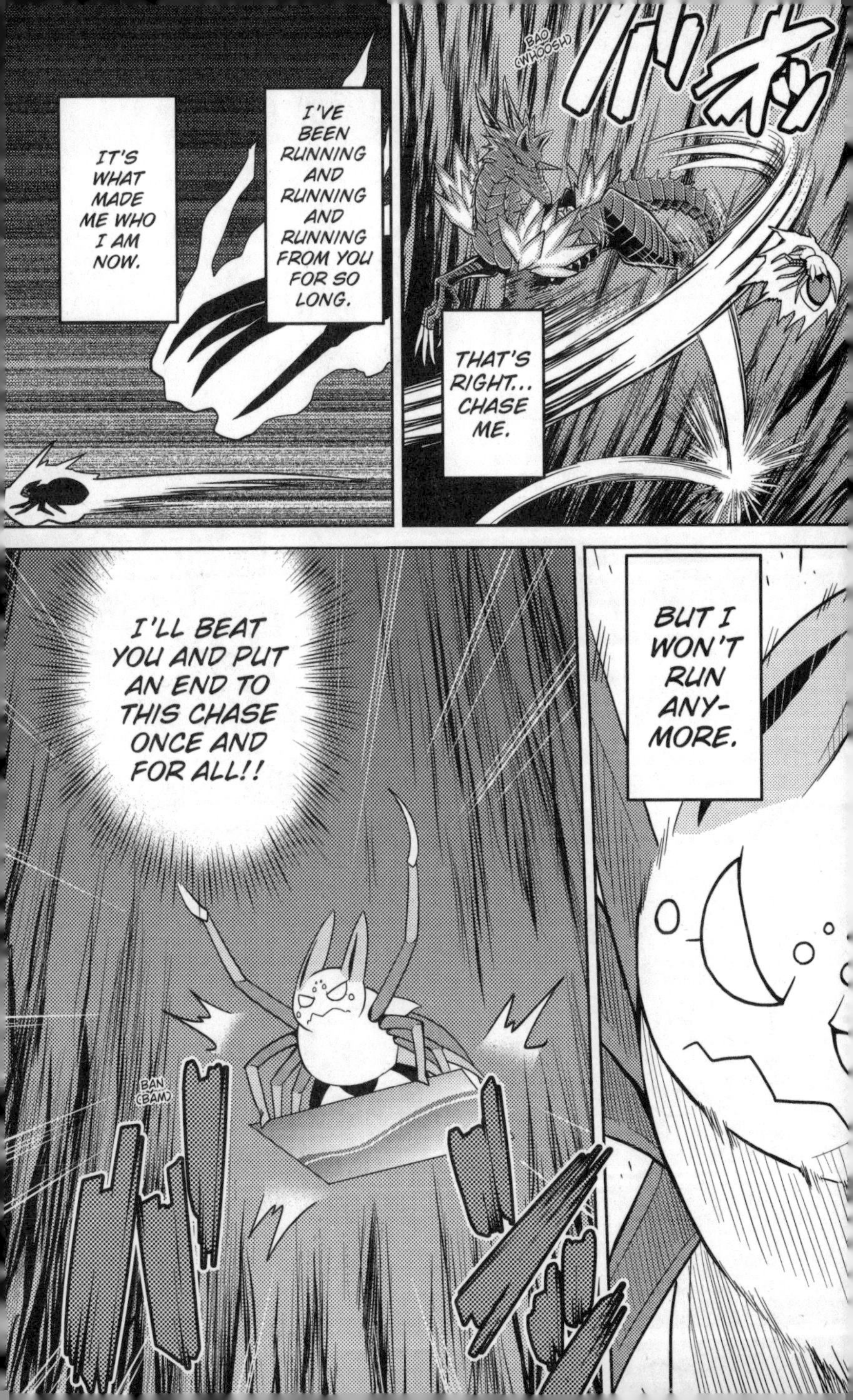
BAO (WHOOSH)
THAT'S RIGHT... CHASE ME.
I'VE BEEN RUNNING AND RUNNING AND RUNNING FROM YOU FOR SO LONG.
IT'S WHAT MADE ME WHO I AM NOW.
BUT I WON'T RUN ANY-MORE.
I'LL BEAT YOU AND PUT AN END TO THIS CHASE ONCE AND FOR ALL!!
BAN (BAM)

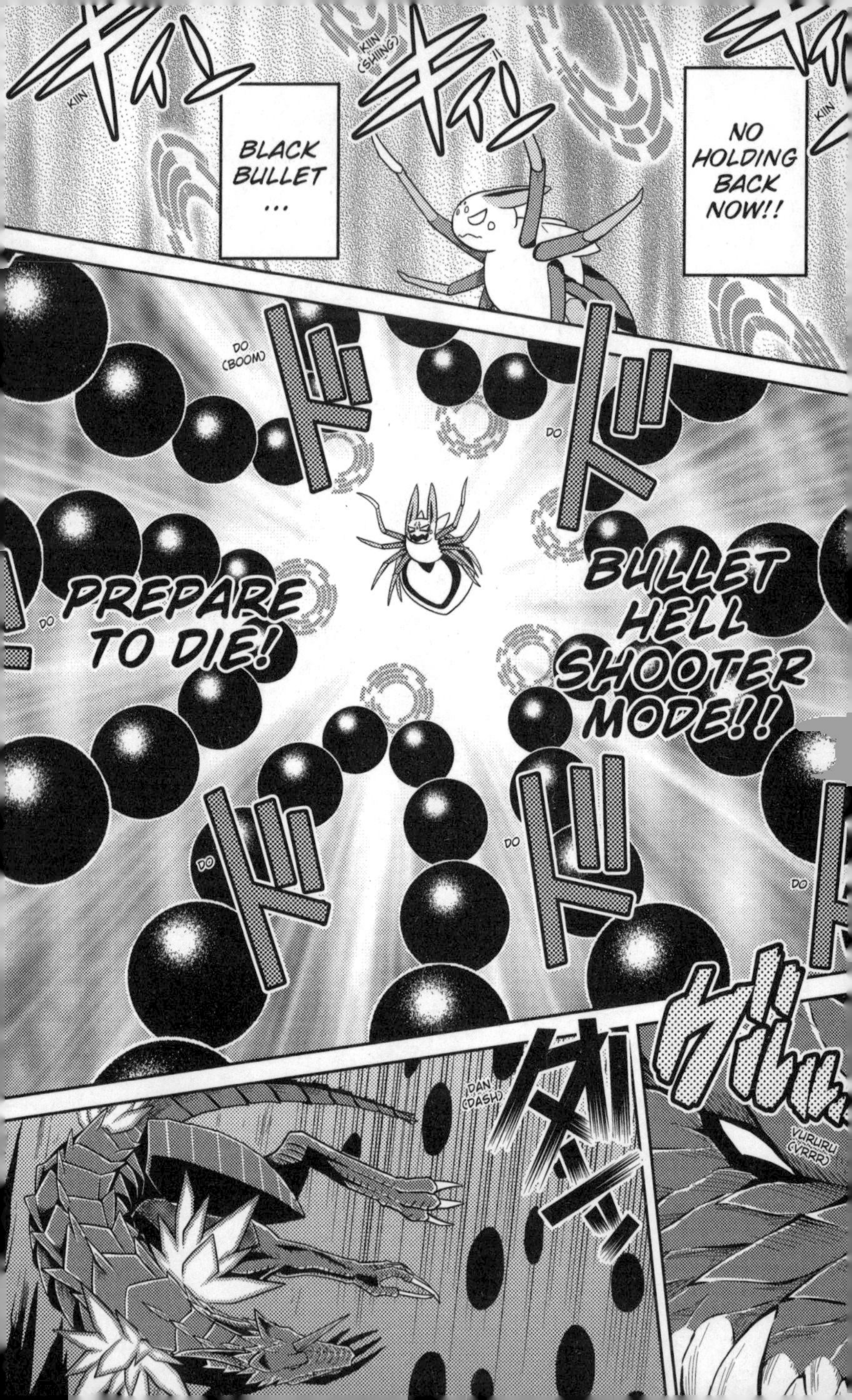
KIIN
NO HOLDING BACK NOW!!
KIIN (SHIING)
BLACK BULLET...
KIIN
DO
BULLET HELL SHOOTER MODE!!
DO
DO (BOOM)
PREPARE TO DIE!
DO
DO
DO
VURURU (VRRR)
DAN (DASH)

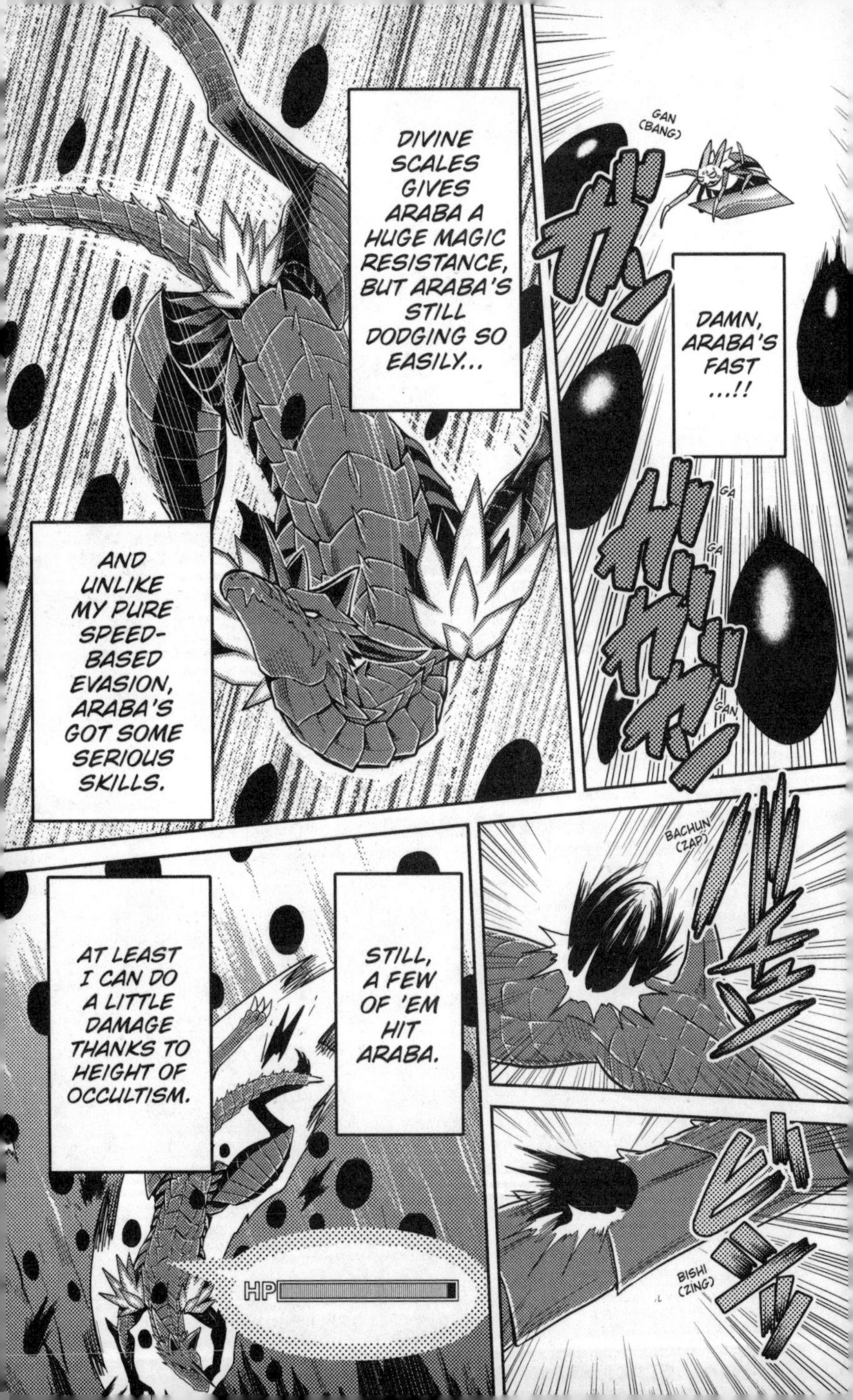
GAN (BANG)
DAMN, ARABA'S FAST ...!!
GA
GA
GAN
DIVINE SCALES GIVES ARABA A HUGE MAGIC RESISTANCE, BUT ARABA'S STILL DODGING SO EASILY...
AND UNLIKE MY PURE SPEED-BASED EVASION, ARABA'S GOT SOME SERIOUS SKILLS.
BACHUN (ZAP)
BISHI (ZING)
STILL, A FEW OF 'EM HIT ARABA.
AT LEAST I CAN DO A LITTLE DAMAGE THANKS TO HEIGHT OF OCCULTISM.
HP

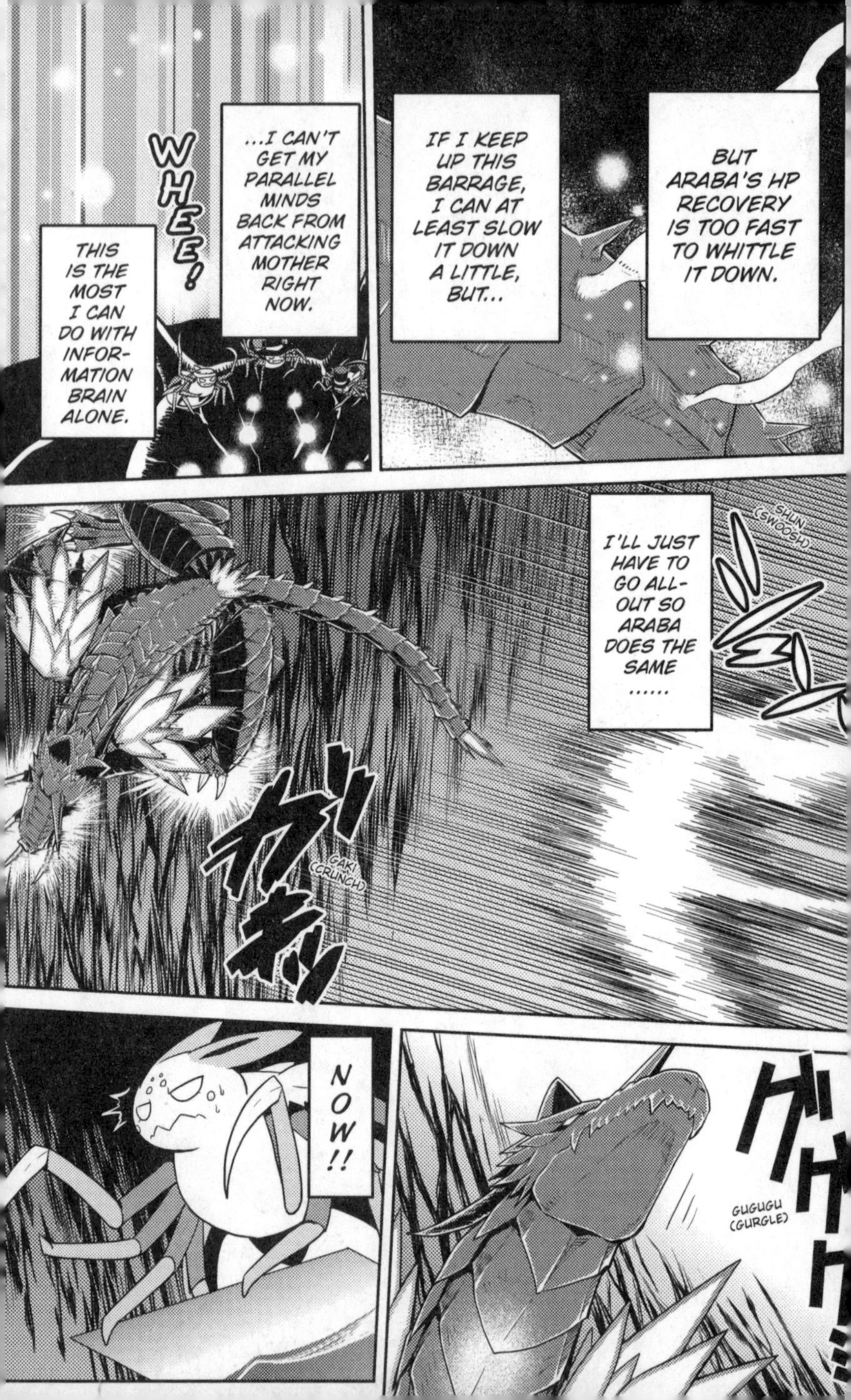
BUT ARABA'S HP RECOVERY IS TOO FAST TO WHITTLE IT DOWN.
IF I KEEP UP THIS BARRAGE, I CAN AT LEAST SLOW IT DOWN A LITTLE, BUT...
...I CAN'T GET MY PARALLEL MINDS BACK FROM ATTACKING MOTHER RIGHT NOW.
WHEE!
THIS IS THE MOST I CAN DO WITH INFOR-MATION BRAIN ALONE.
SHUN (SWOOSH)
I'LL JUST HAVE TO GO ALL-OUT SO ARABA DOES THE SAME ......
GAKI (CRUNCH)
GUGUGU (GURGLE)
NOW!!

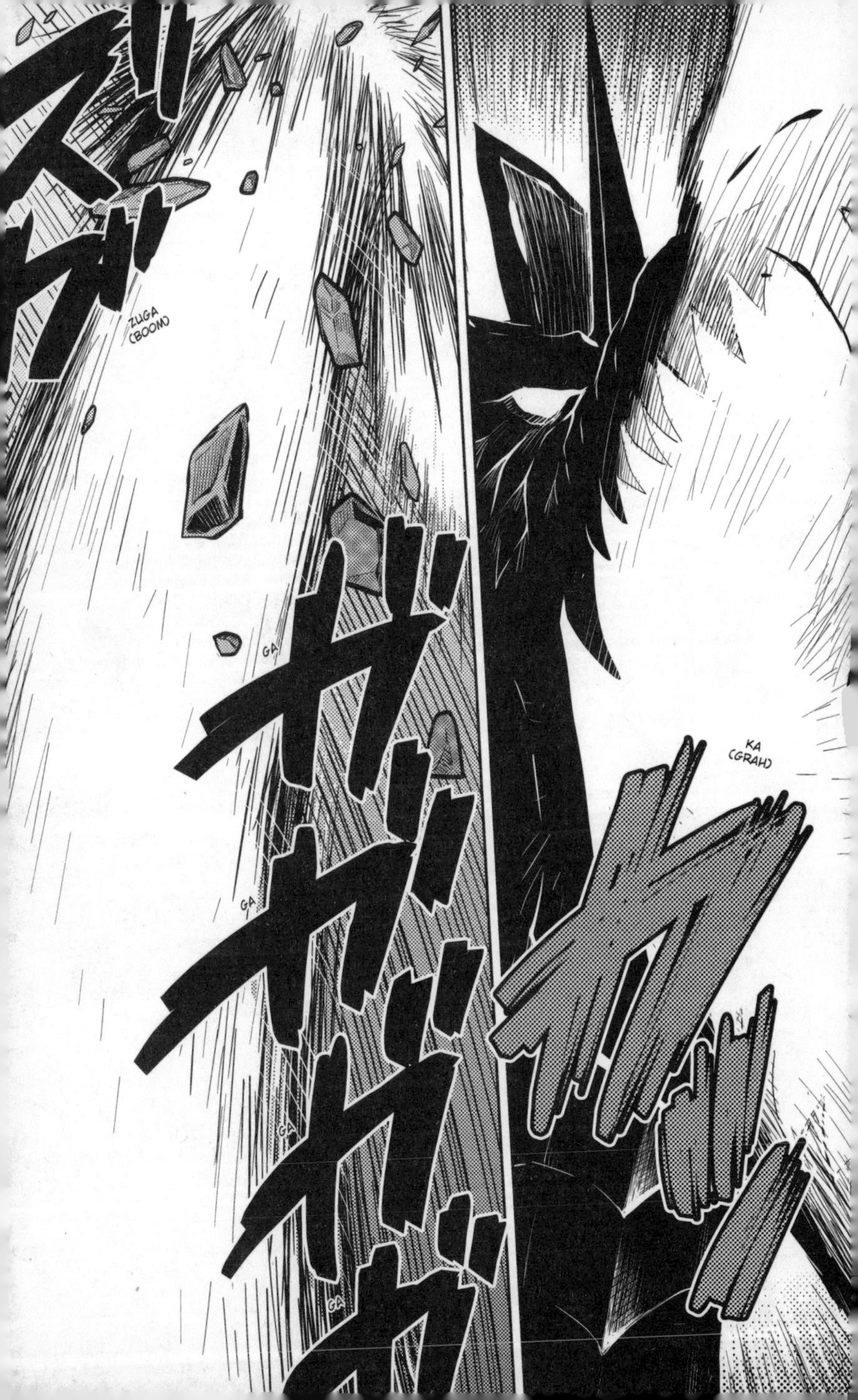
KA
(GRAH)
ZUGA
(BOOM)
GA
GA
GA
GA

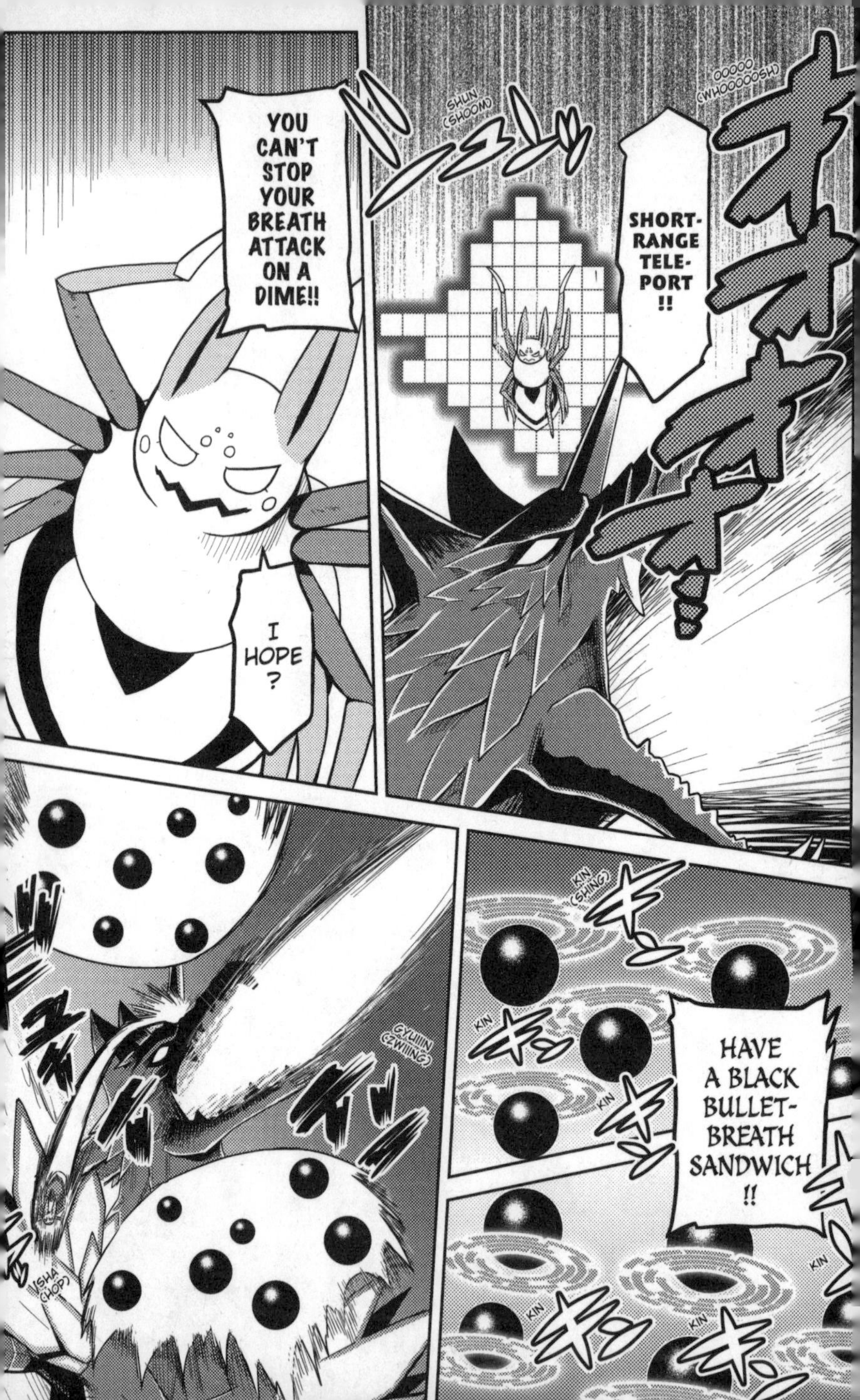

OOOOO (WHOOOOOSH)
SHORT-RANGE TELE-PORT!!
SHUN (SHOOM)
YOU CAN'T STOP YOUR BREATH ATTACK ON A DIME!!
I HOPE?
KIN (SHING)
HAVE A BLACK BULLET-BREATH SANDWICH!!
KIN
KIN
KIN
KIN
KIN
GYUIIIN (ZWIIING)
VSHA (HOP)

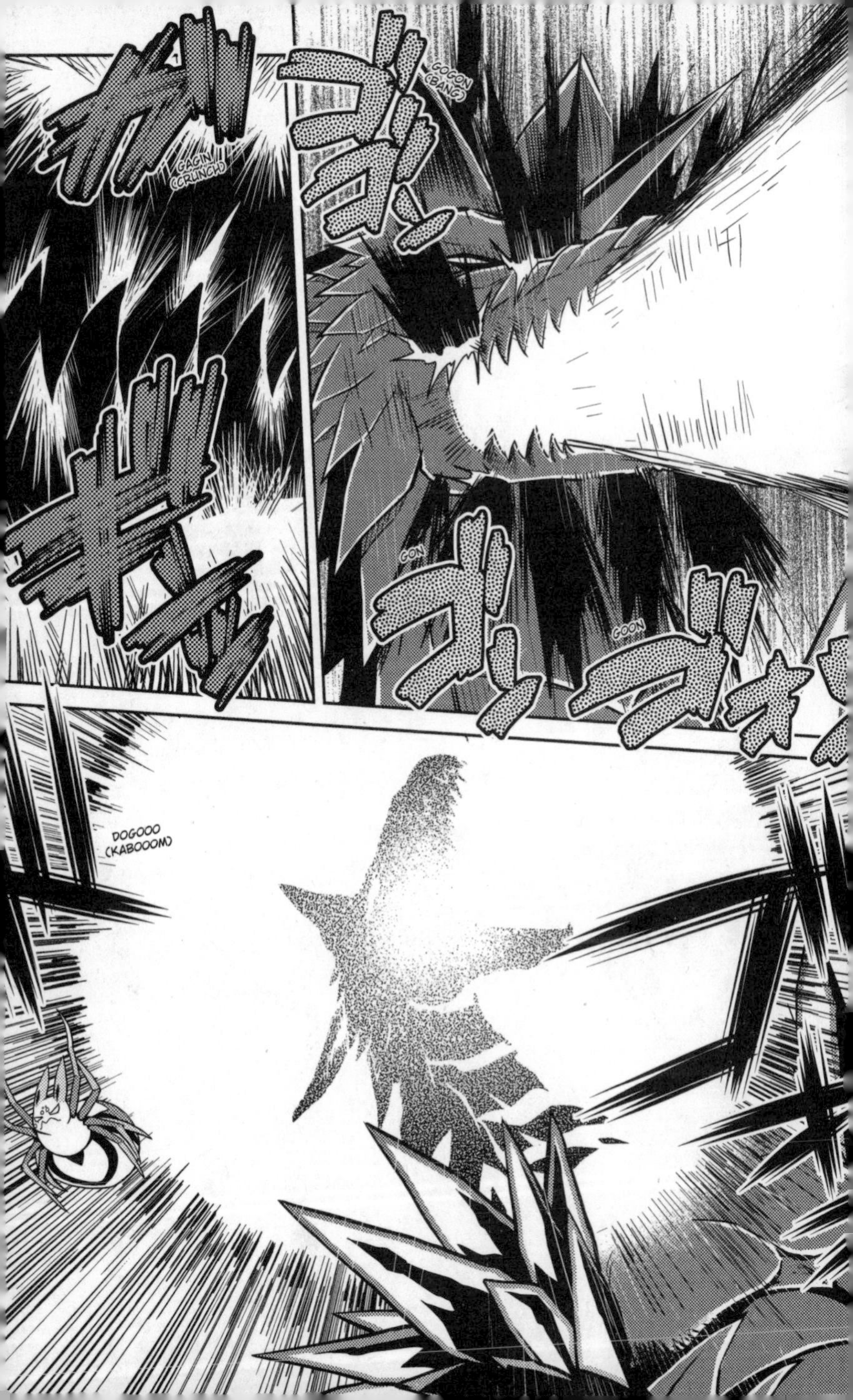
GOGON (BANG)
GON
GOON
GAGIN (CRUNCH)
DOGOOO (KABOOOM)

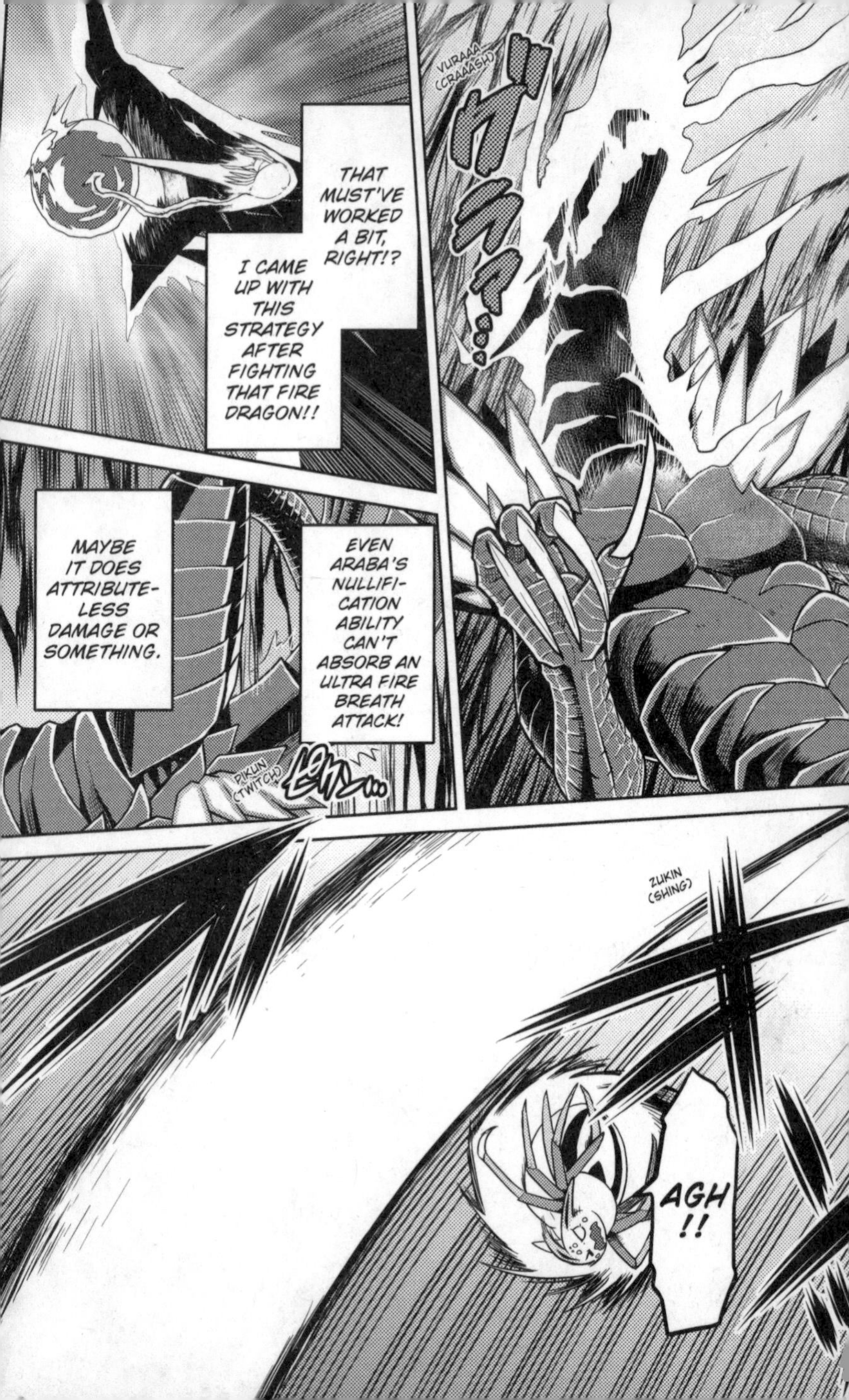
VURAAA (CRAAASH)
THAT MUST'VE WORKED A BIT, RIGHT!?
I CAME UP WITH THIS STRATEGY AFTER FIGHTING THAT FIRE DRAGON!!
EVEN ARABA'S NULLIFI-CATION ABILITY CAN'T ABSORB AN ULTRA FIRE BREATH ATTACK!
MAYBE IT DOES ATTRIBUTE-LESS DAMAGE OR SOMETHING.
PIKUN (TWITCH)
ZUKIN (SHING)
AGH !!

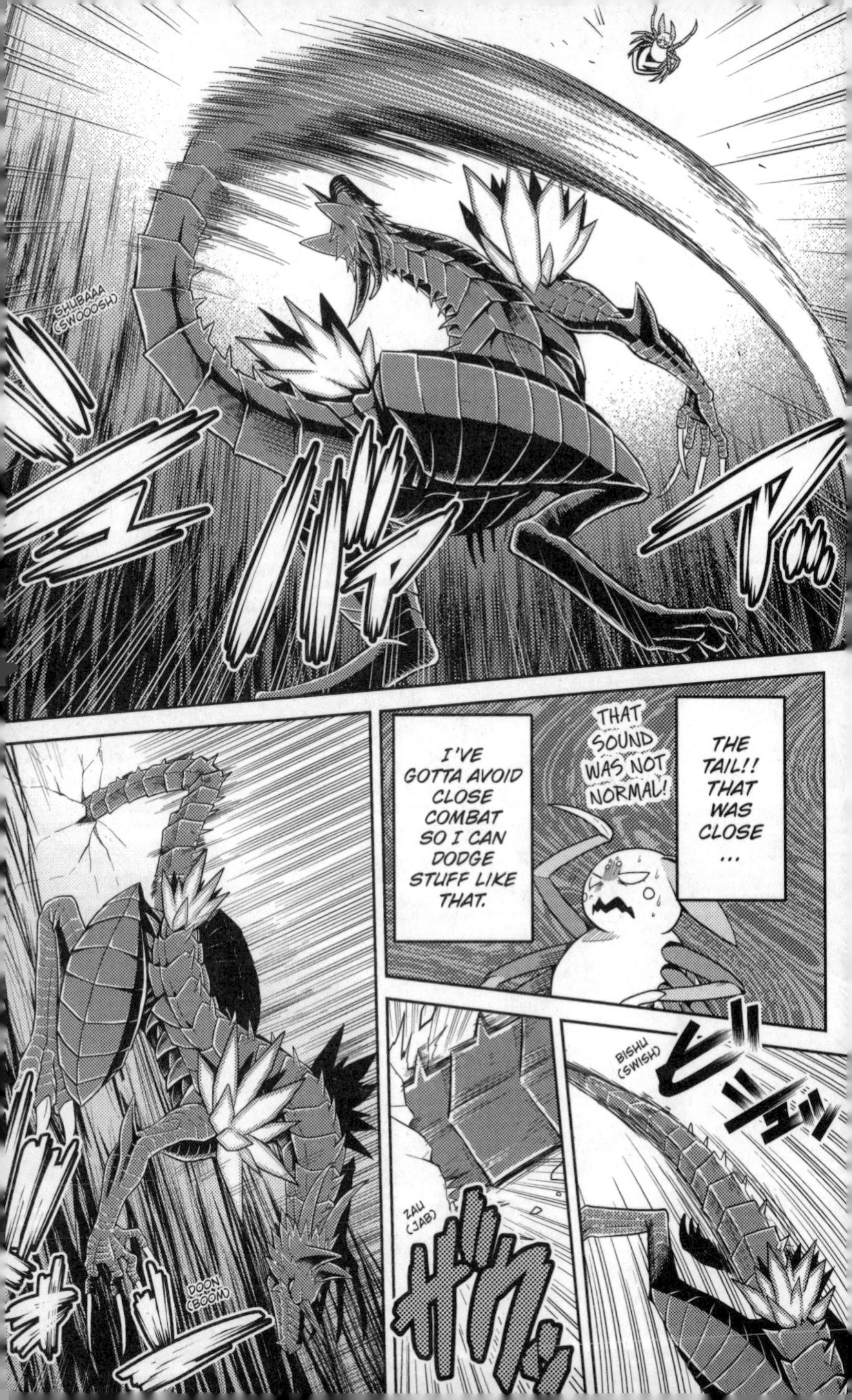
SHUBAAA (SWOOOSH)
THE TAIL!! THAT WAS CLOSE ...
THAT SOUND WAS NOT NORMAL!
I'VE GOTTA AVOID CLOSE COMBAT SO I CAN DODGE STUFF LIKE THAT.
BISHU (SWISH)
ZAU (JAB)
DOON (BOOM)

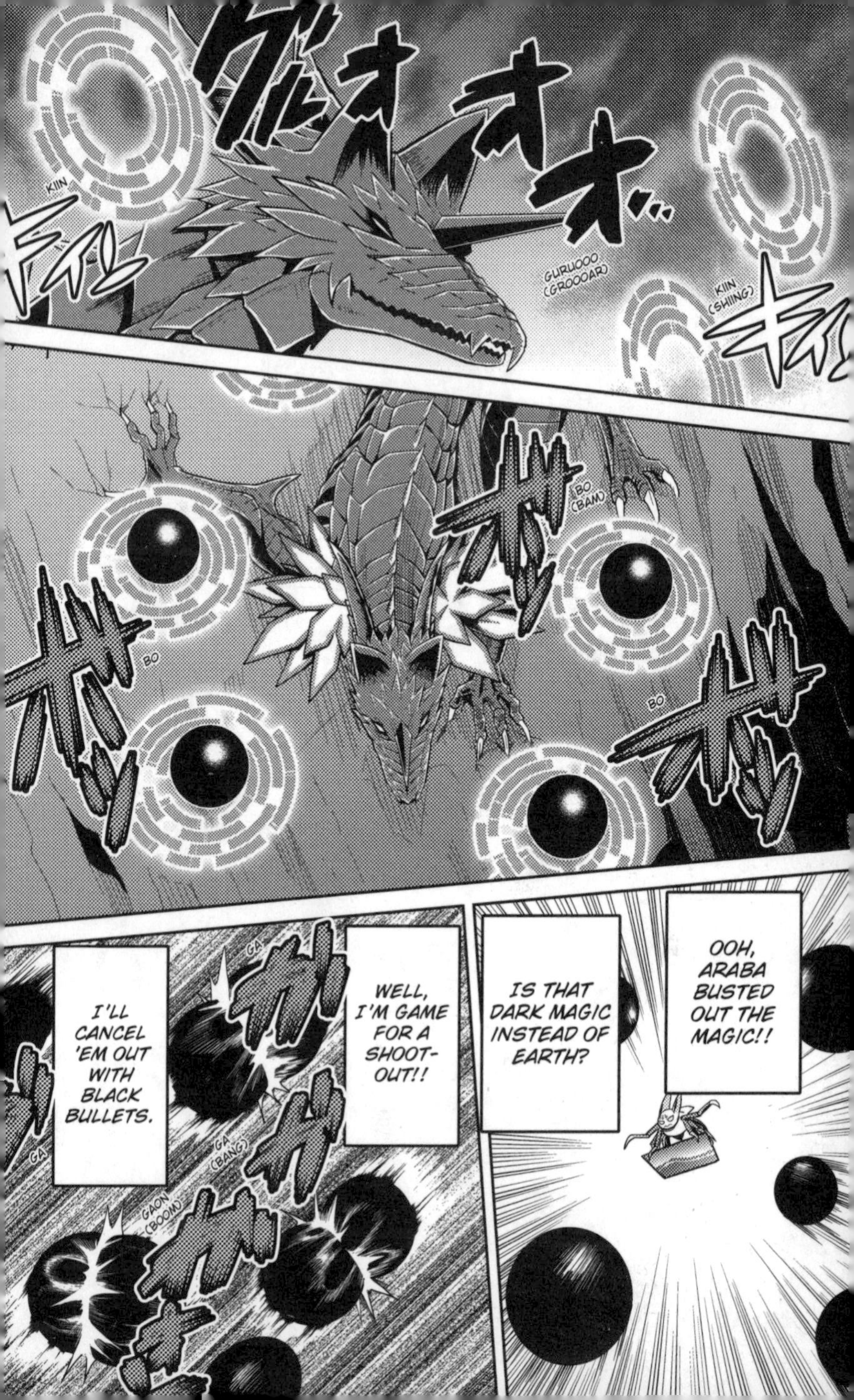
KIIN
(SHIING)
GURUOOO
(GROOOAR)
KIIN
BO
(BAM)
BO
BO
OOH, ARABA BUSTED OUT THE MAGIC!!
IS THAT DARK MAGIC INSTEAD OF EARTH?
WELL, I'M GAME FOR A SHOOT-OUT!!
I'LL CANCEL 'EM OUT WITH BLACK BULLETS.
GA
GA
(BANG)
GA
GAON
(BOOM)

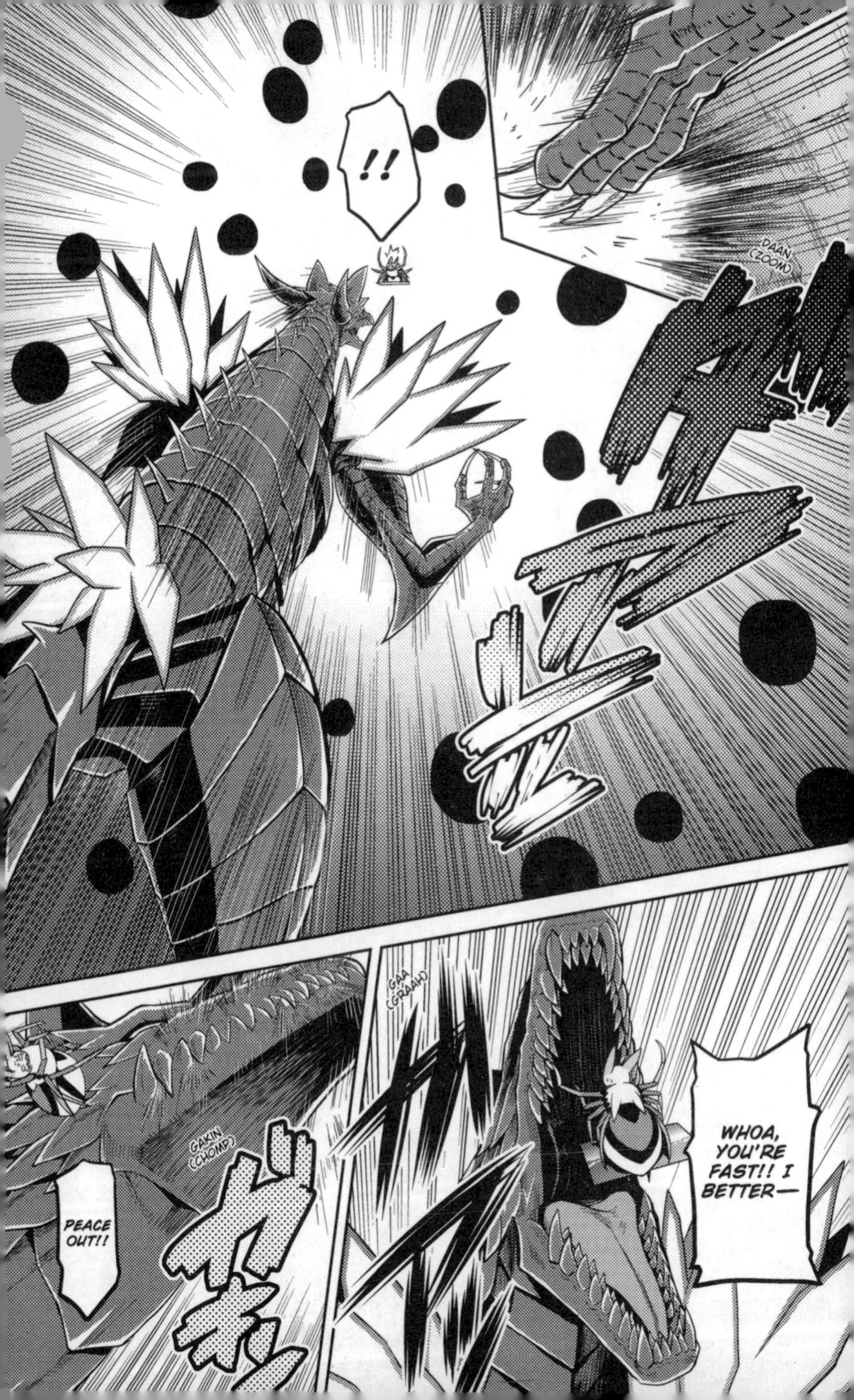
!!
DAAN (ZOOM)
WHOA, YOU'RE FAST!! I BETTER—
GAA (GRAAH)
GAKIN (CHOMP)
PEACE OUT!!

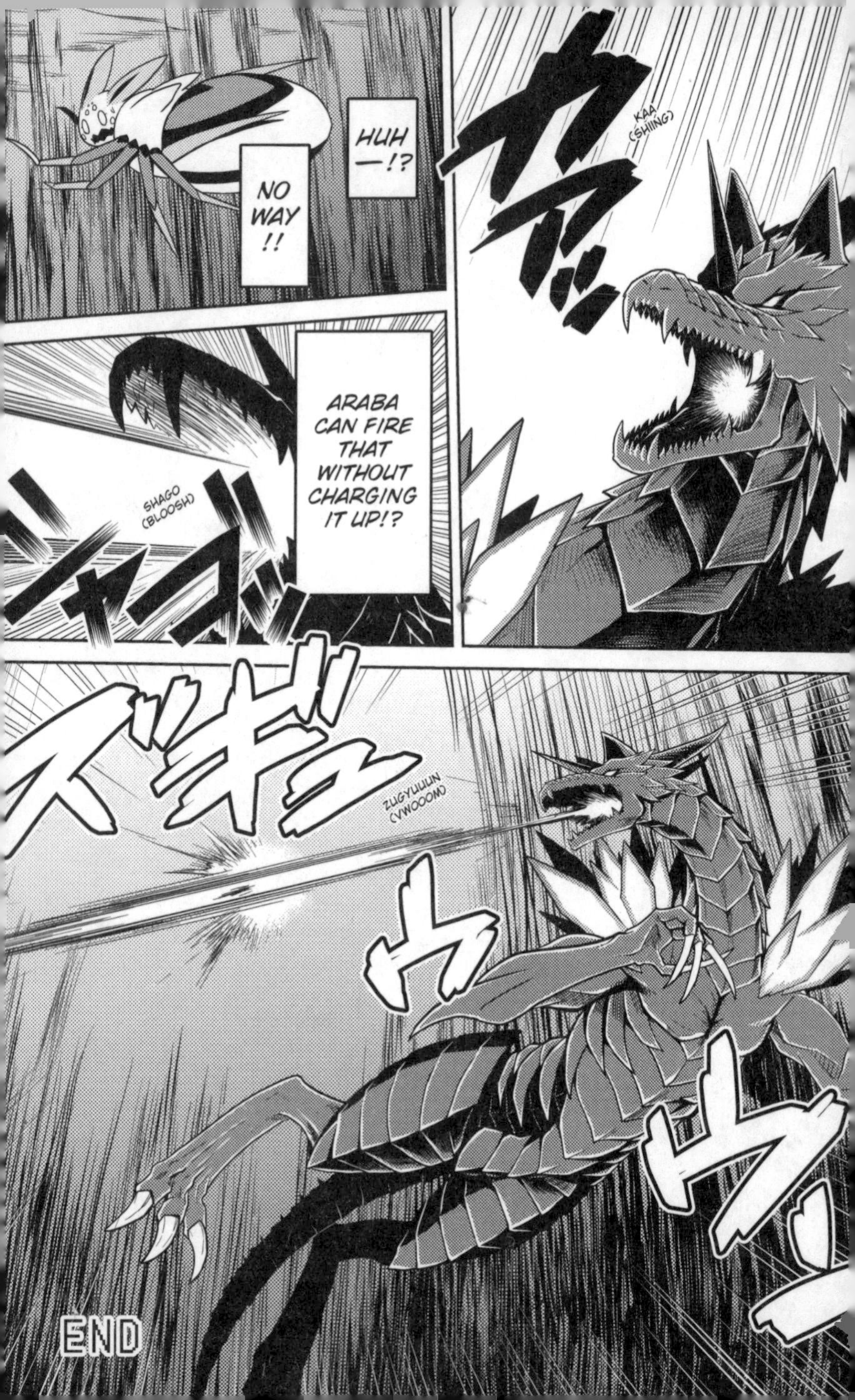
KAA
(SHIING)
HUH—!?
NO WAY!!
ARABA CAN FIRE THAT WITHOUT CHARGING IT UP!?
SHAGO
(BLOOSH)
ZUGYUUUN
(VWOOOM)
END

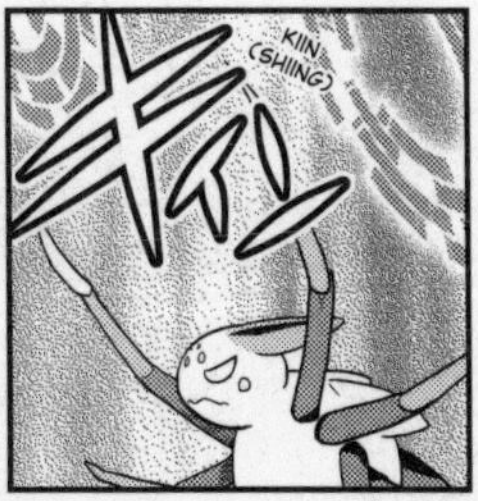
KIIN
(SHIING)

So I'm a Spider, So What?

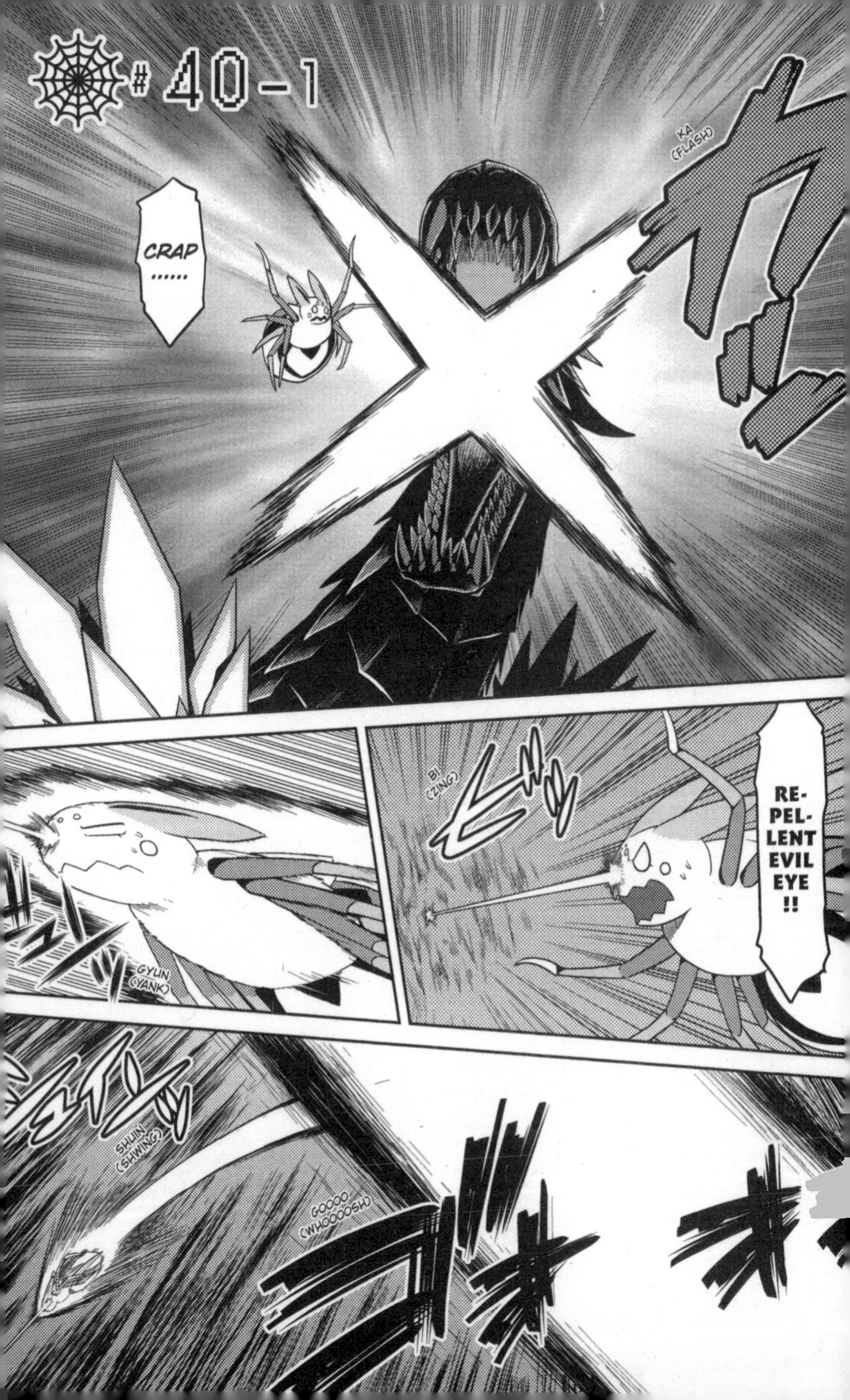
#40-1
KA (FLASH)
CRAP ......
REPEL-LENT EVIL EYE!!
BI (ZING)
GYUN (YANK)
GOOOO (WHOOOOSH)
SHUIN (SHWING)

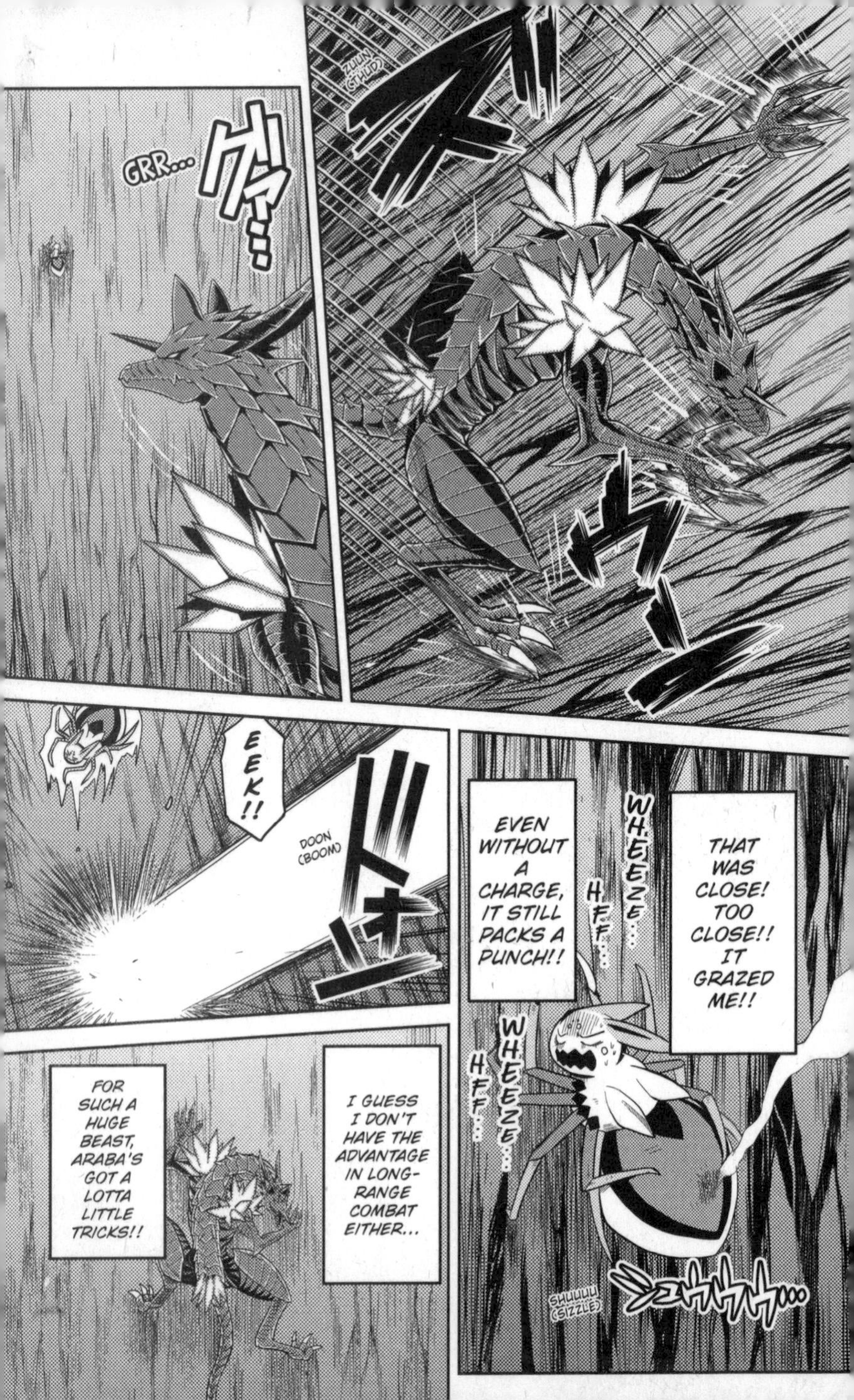
ZUUN (THUD)
GRR...
THAT WAS CLOSE! TOO CLOSE!! IT GRAZED ME!!
WHEEZE...
EVEN WITHOUT A CHARGE, IT STILL PACKS A PUNCH!!
HFF...
WHEEZE...
HFF...
SHUUUU (SIZZLE)
EEK!!
DOON (BOOM)
I GUESS I DON'T HAVE THE ADVANTAGE IN LONG-RANGE COMBAT EITHER...
FOR SUCH A HUGE BEAST, ARABA'S GOT A LOTTA LITTLE TRICKS!!

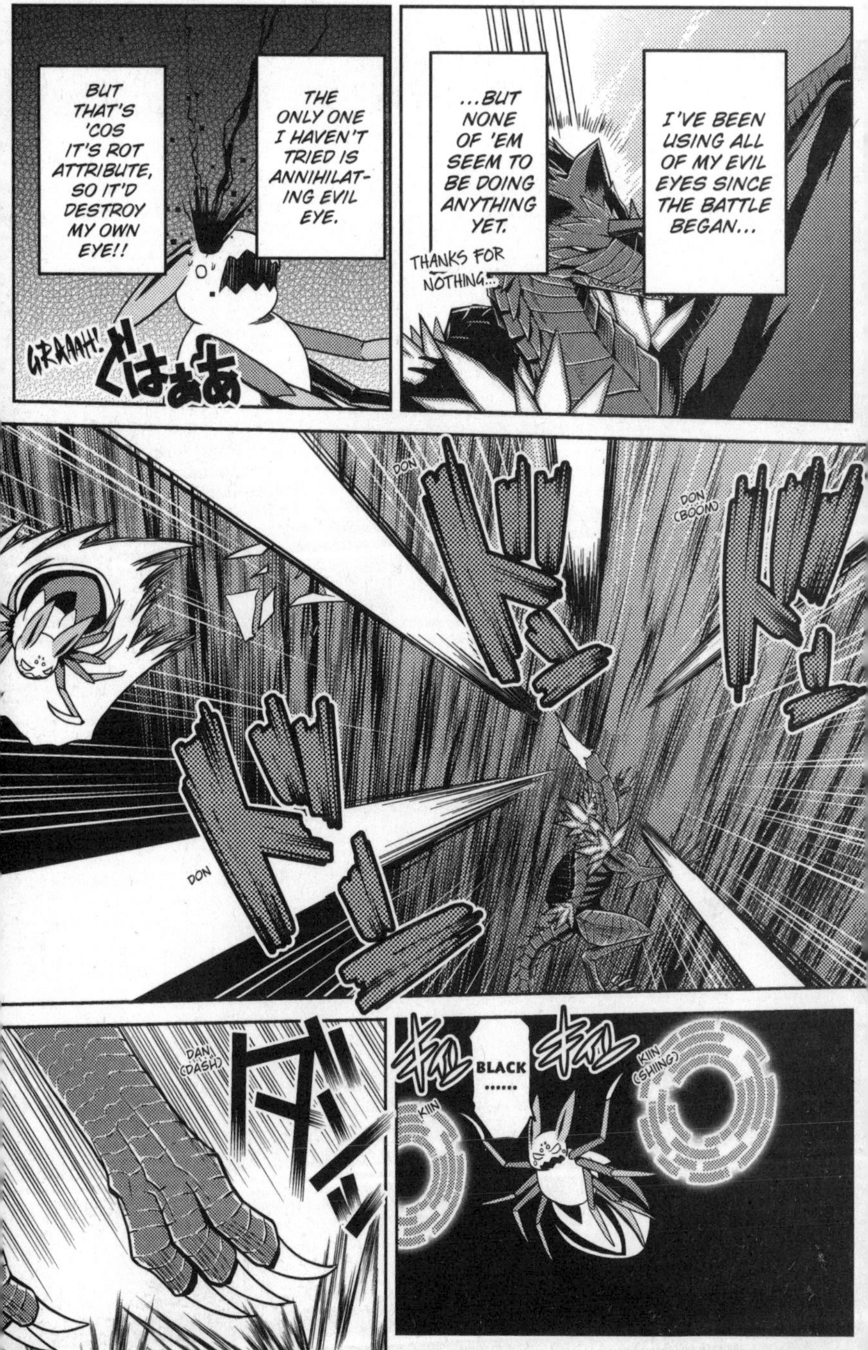
I'VE BEEN USING ALL OF MY EVIL EYES SINCE THE BATTLE BEGAN...
...BUT NONE OF 'EM SEEM TO BE DOING ANYTHING YET.
THANKS FOR NOTHING...
THE ONLY ONE I HAVEN'T TRIED IS ANNIHILATING EVIL EYE.
BUT THAT'S 'COS IT'S ROT ATTRIBUTE, SO IT'D DESTROY MY OWN EYE!!
GRAAAH! ぐはぁあ
DON (BOOM)
DON
DON
KIIN (SHIING)
BLACK.......
KIIN
DAN (DASH)

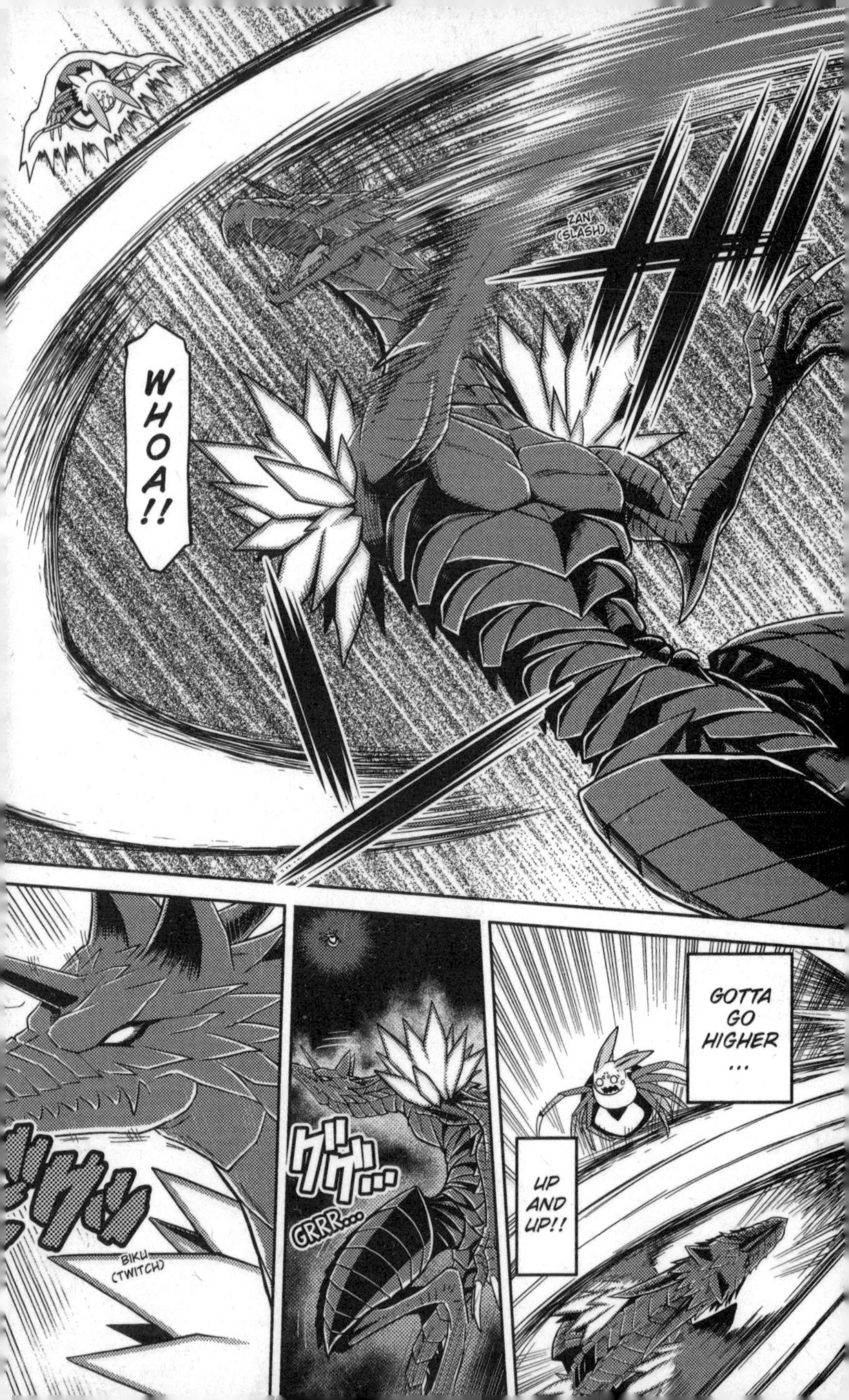
ZAN (SLASH)
WHOA!!
GOTTA GO HIGHER...
UP AND UP!!
GRRR...
BIKU (TWITCH)

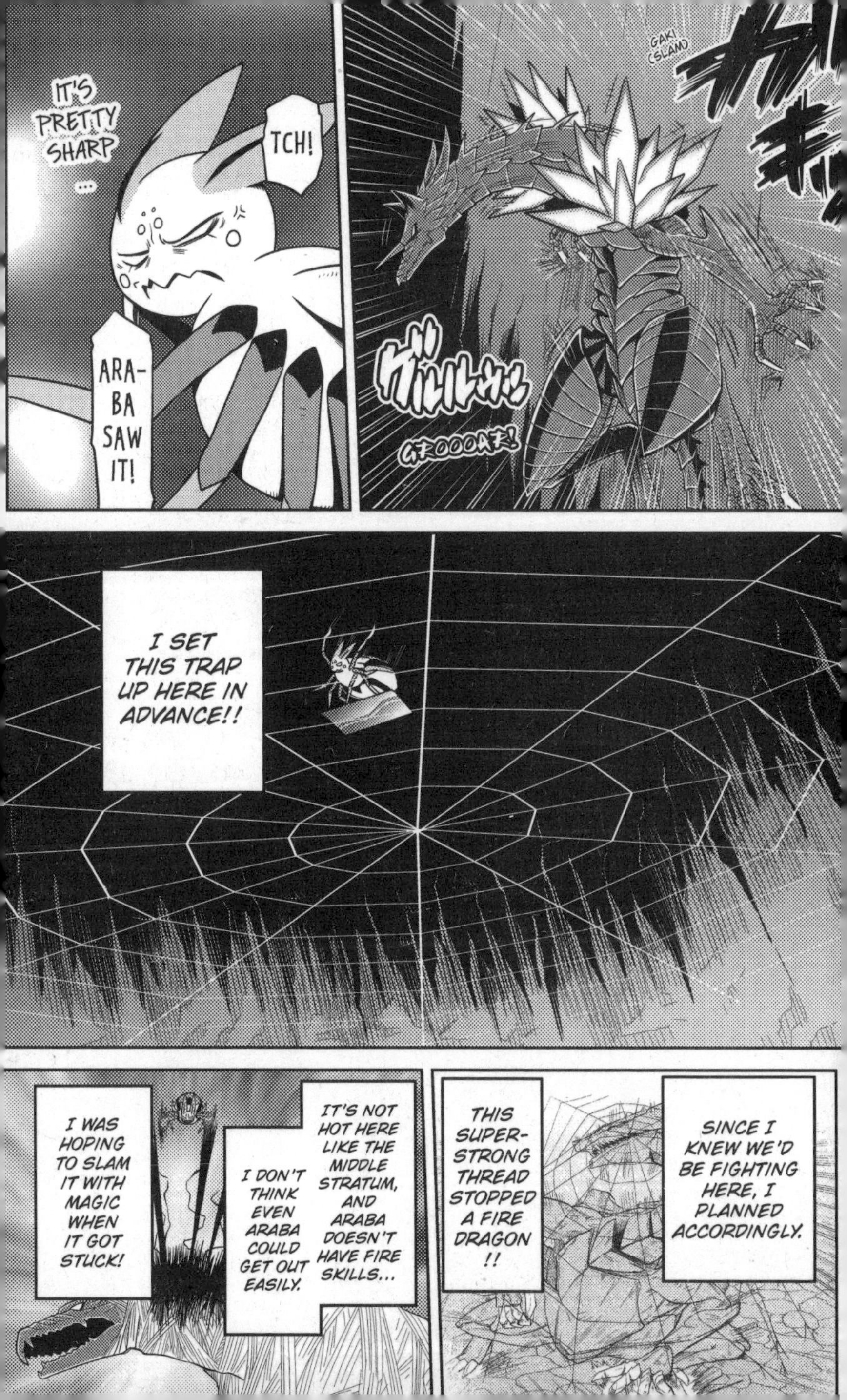
GAKI (SLAM)
GROOOAR!
TCH!
IT'S PRETTY SHARP...
ARA-BA SAW IT!
I SET THIS TRAP UP HERE IN ADVANCE!!
SINCE I KNEW WE'D BE FIGHTING HERE, I PLANNED ACCORDINGLY.
THIS SUPER-STRONG THREAD STOPPED A FIRE DRAGON!!
IT'S NOT HOT HERE LIKE THE MIDDLE STRATUM, AND ARABA DOESN'T HAVE FIRE SKILLS...
I DON'T THINK EVEN ARABA COULD GET OUT EASILY.
I WAS HOPING TO SLAM IT WITH MAGIC WHEN IT GOT STUCK!

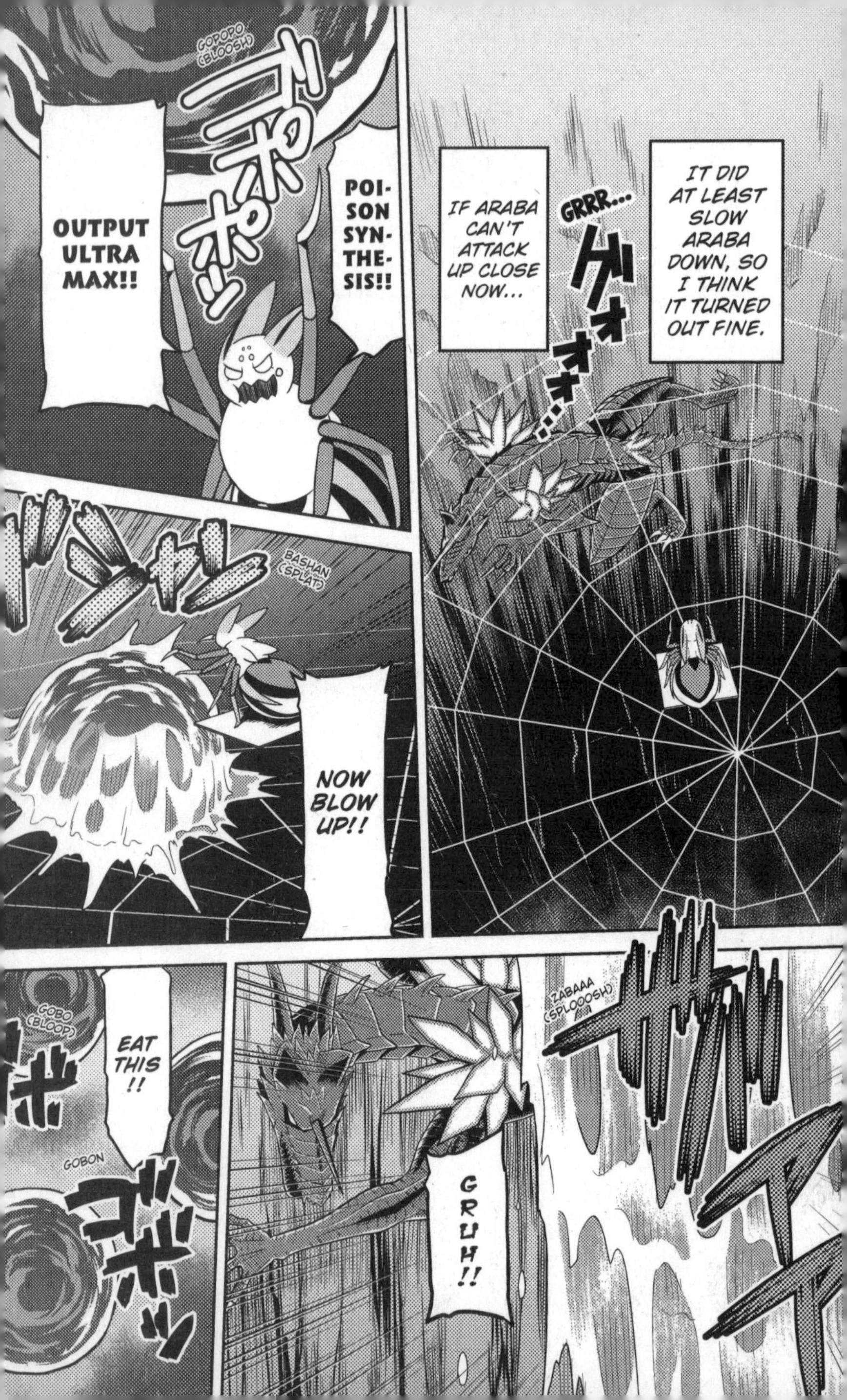
IT DID AT LEAST SLOW ARABA DOWN, SO I THINK IT TURNED OUT FINE.
GRRR...
IF ARABA CAN'T ATTACK UP CLOSE NOW...
GOPOPO (BLOOSH)
POI-SON SYN-THE-SIS!!
OUTPUT ULTRA MAX!!
BASHAN (SPLAT)
NOW BLOW UP!!
ZABAAA (SPLOOOSH)
GRUH!!
GOBO (BLOOP)
EAT THIS!!
GOBON

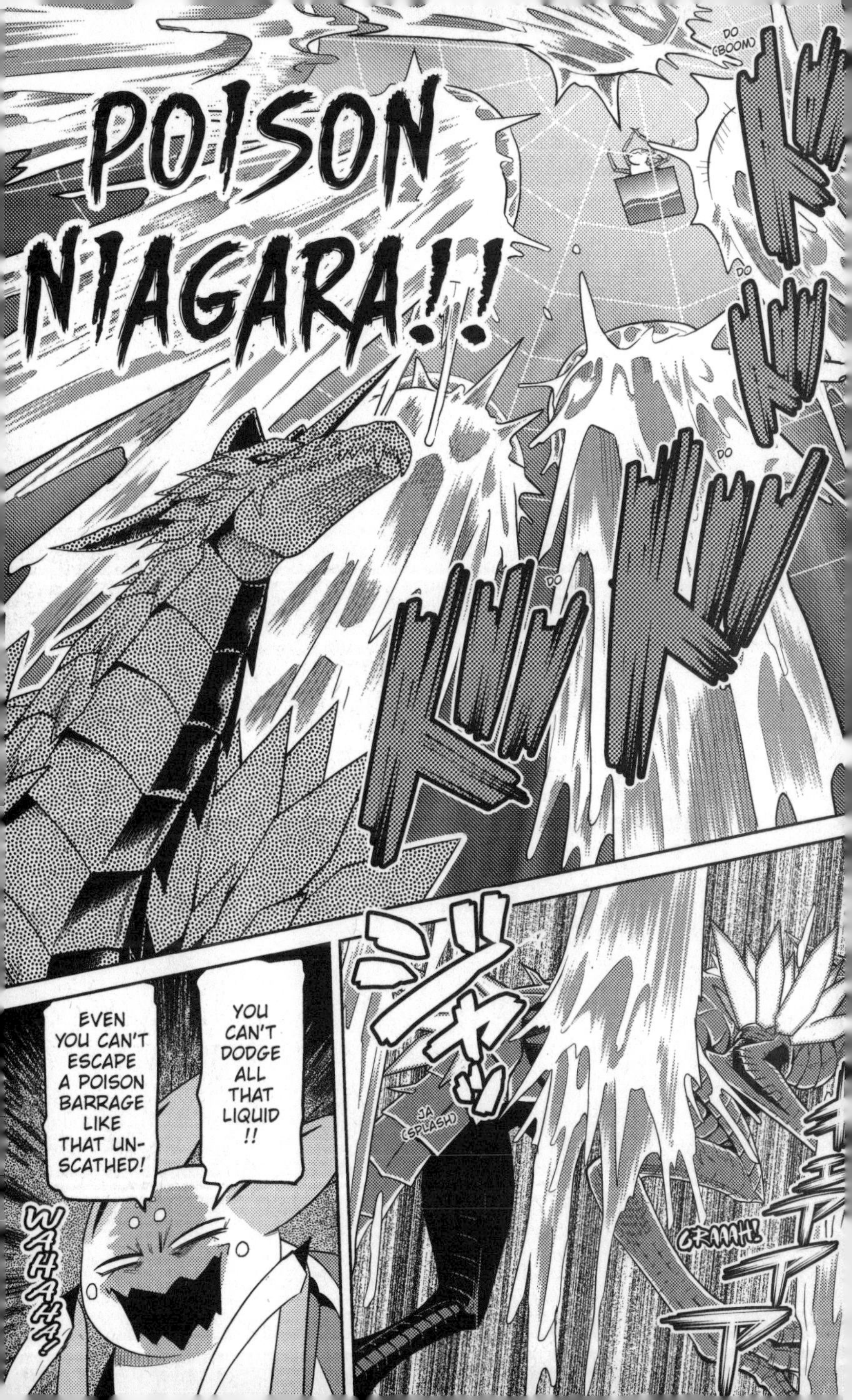
DO (BOOM)
DO
DO
POISON NIAGARA!!
DO
GRAAAH!
JA (SPLASH)
YOU CAN'T DODGE ALL THAT LIQUID!!
EVEN YOU CAN'T ESCAPE A POISON BARRAGE LIKE THAT UN-SCATHED!
WAHAHAHA!

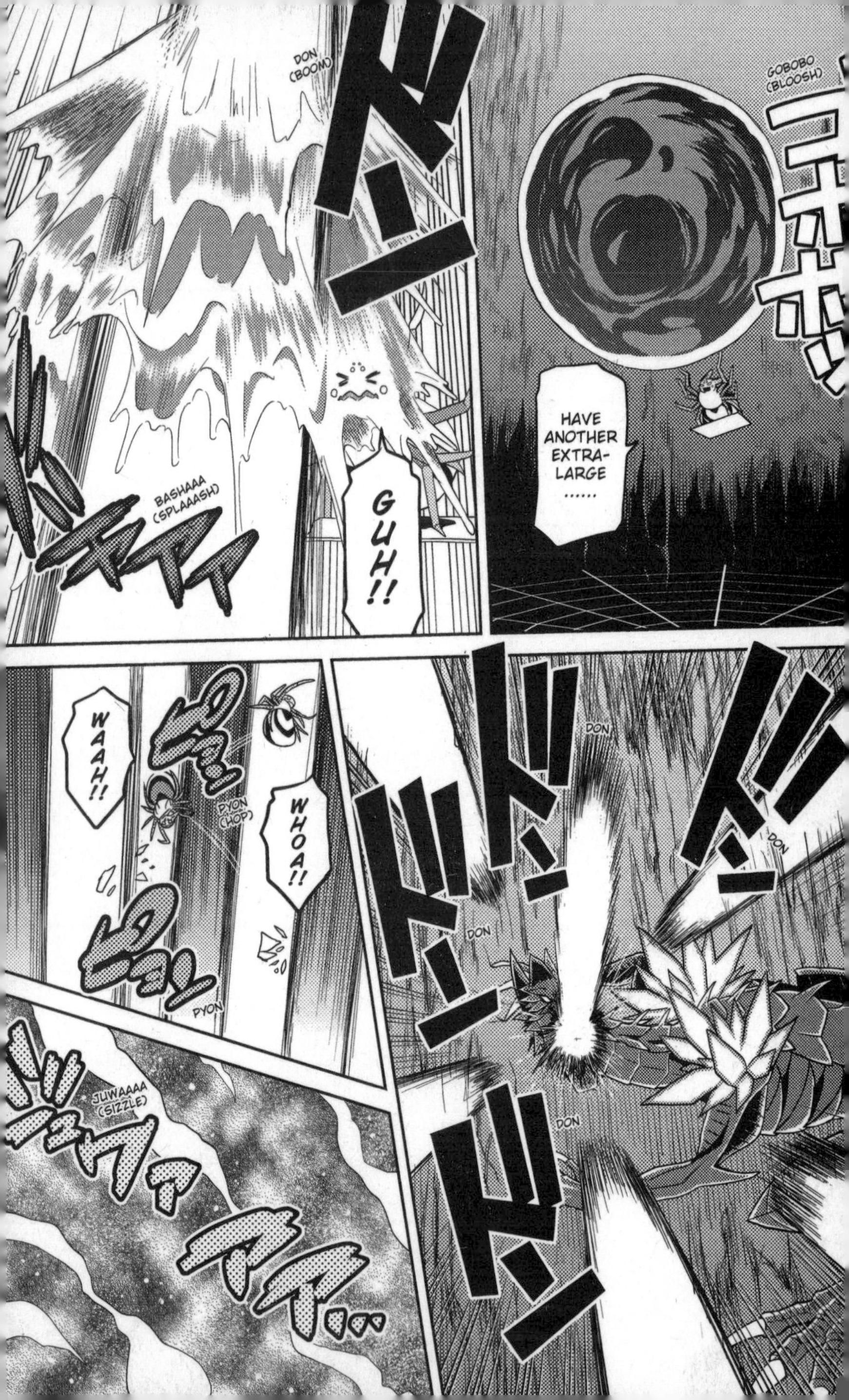
GOBOBO (BLOOSH)
HAVE ANOTHER EXTRA-LARGE......
DON (BOOM)
GUH!!
BASHAAA (SPLAAASH)
DON
DON
DON
DON
WHOA!!
WAAH!!
PYON (HOP)
PYON
JUWAAAA (SIZZLE)

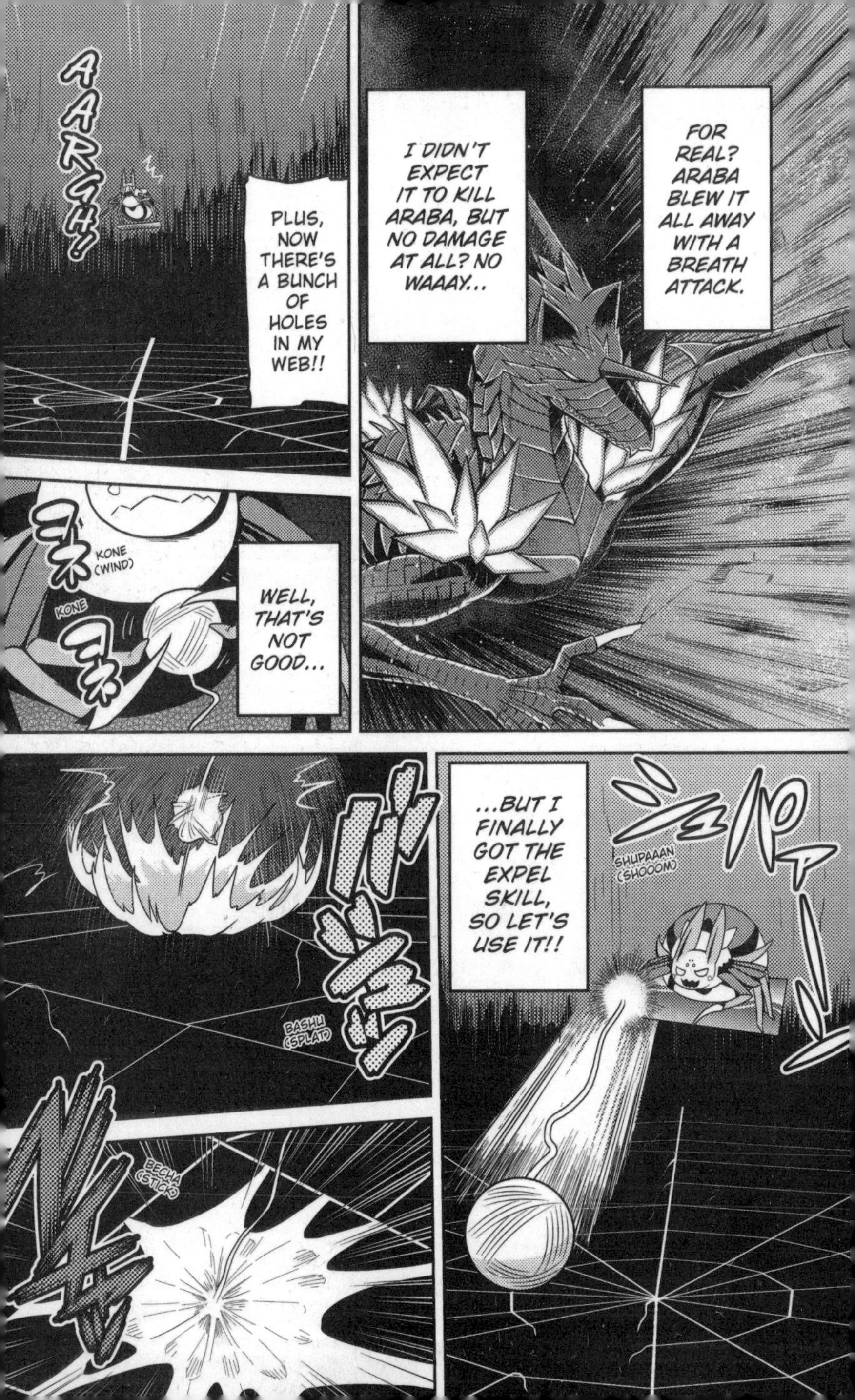
FOR REAL? ARABA BLEW IT ALL AWAY WITH A BREATH ATTACK.
I DIDN'T EXPECT IT TO KILL ARABA, BUT NO DAMAGE AT ALL? NO WAAAY...
PLUS, NOW THERE'S A BUNCH OF HOLES IN MY WEB!!
AARGH!
WELL, THAT'S NOT GOOD...
KONE (WIND)
KONE
...BUT I FINALLY GOT THE EXPEL SKILL, SO LET'S USE IT!!
SHUPAAAN (SHOOOM)
BASHU (SPLAT)
BECHA (STICK)

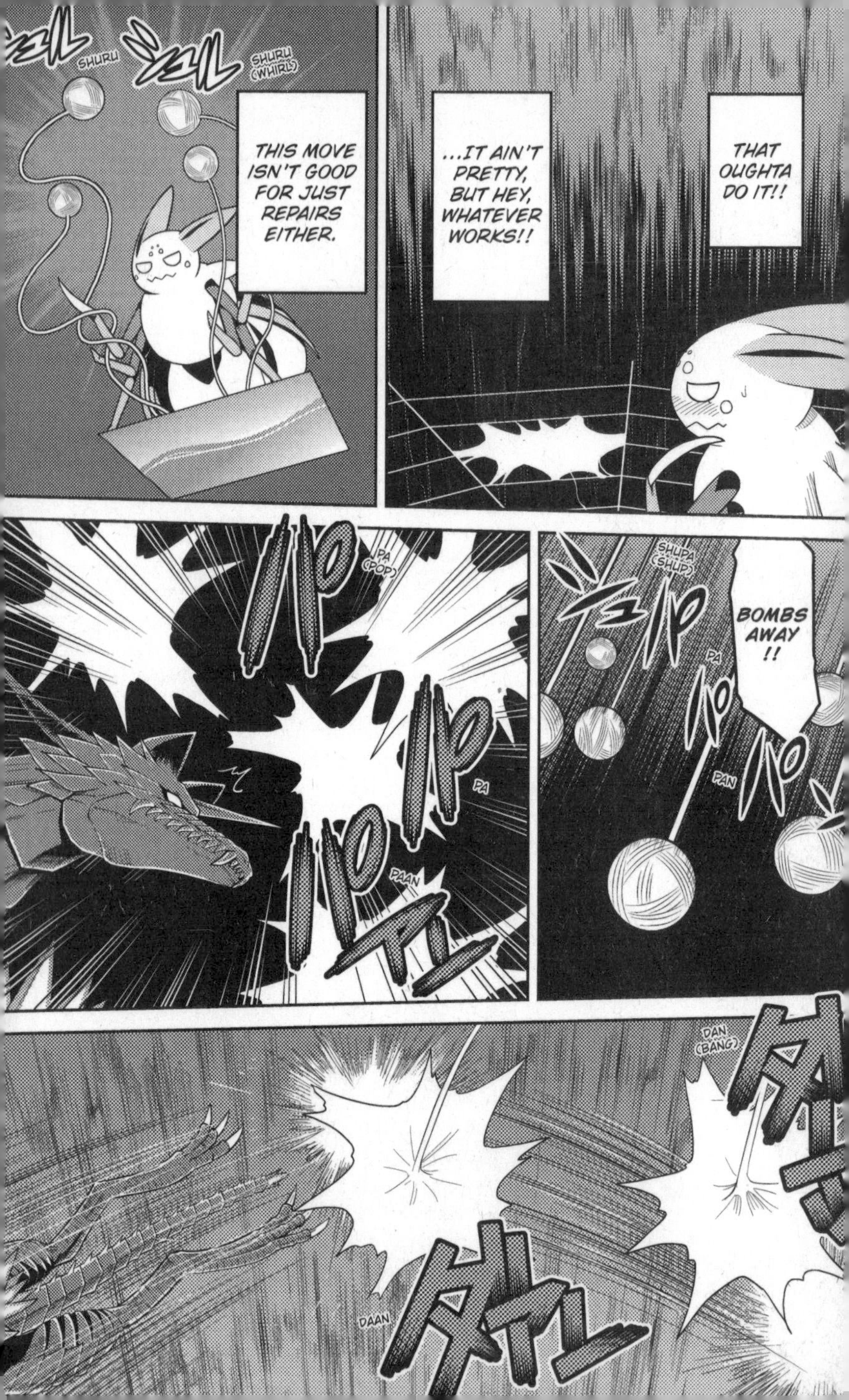
THAT OUGHTA DO IT!!
...IT AIN'T PRETTY, BUT HEY, WHATEVER WORKS!!
SHURU (WHIRL)
SHURU
THIS MOVE ISN'T GOOD FOR JUST REPAIRS EITHER.
BOMBS AWAY!!
SHUPA (SHUP)
PA
PAN
PA (POP)
PA
PAAN
DAN (BANG)
DAAN

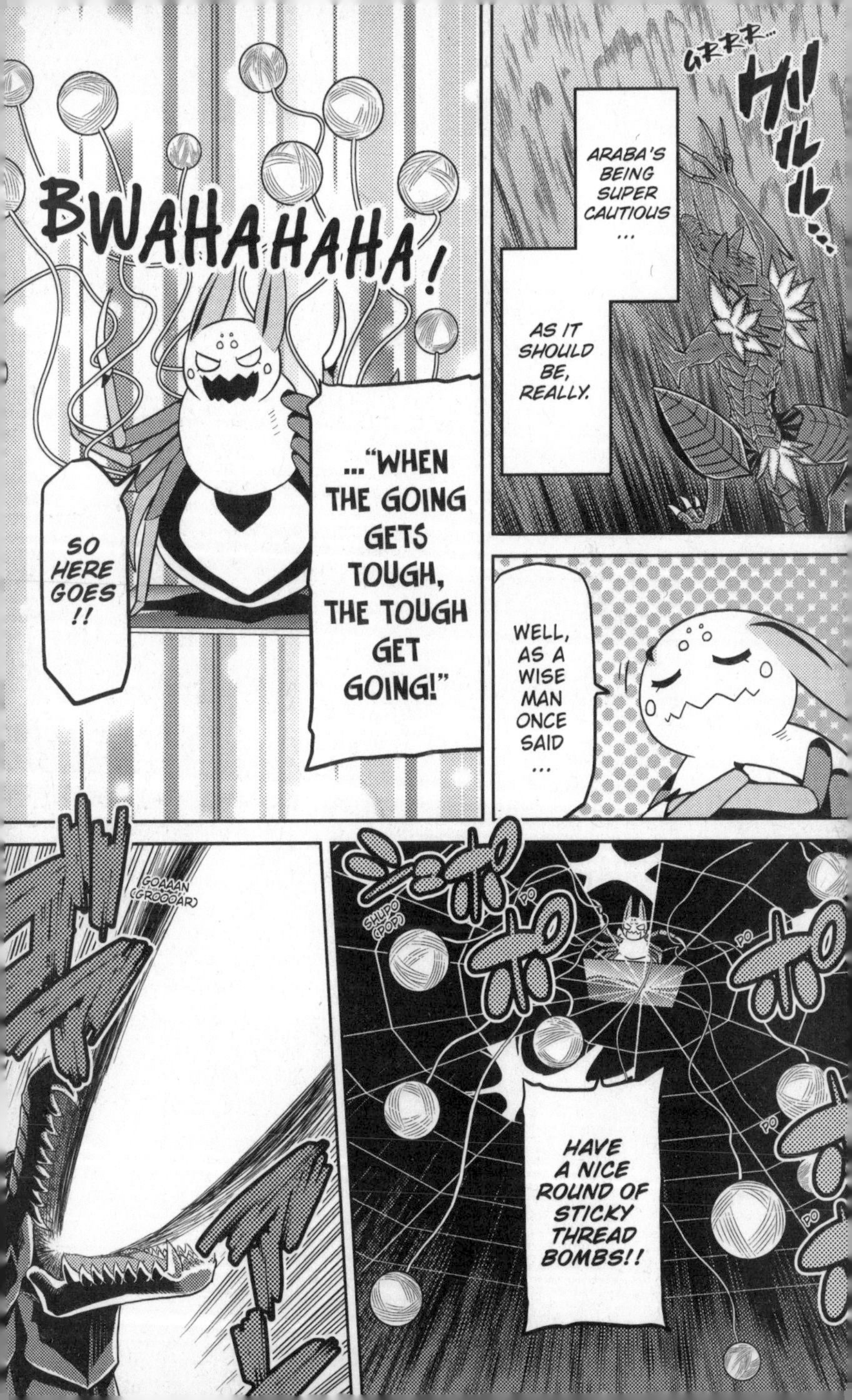
GRRRR...
ヴルル...
ARABA'S BEING SUPER CAUTIOUS ...
AS IT SHOULD BE, REALLY.
WELL, AS A WISE MAN ONCE SAID ...
BWAHAHAHAHA!
..."WHEN THE GOING GETS TOUGH, THE TOUGH GET GOING!"
SO HERE GOES!!
SHUPO (POP)
PO
PO
PO
PO
HAVE A NICE ROUND OF STICKY THREAD BOMBS!!
GOAAAN (GROOOAR)

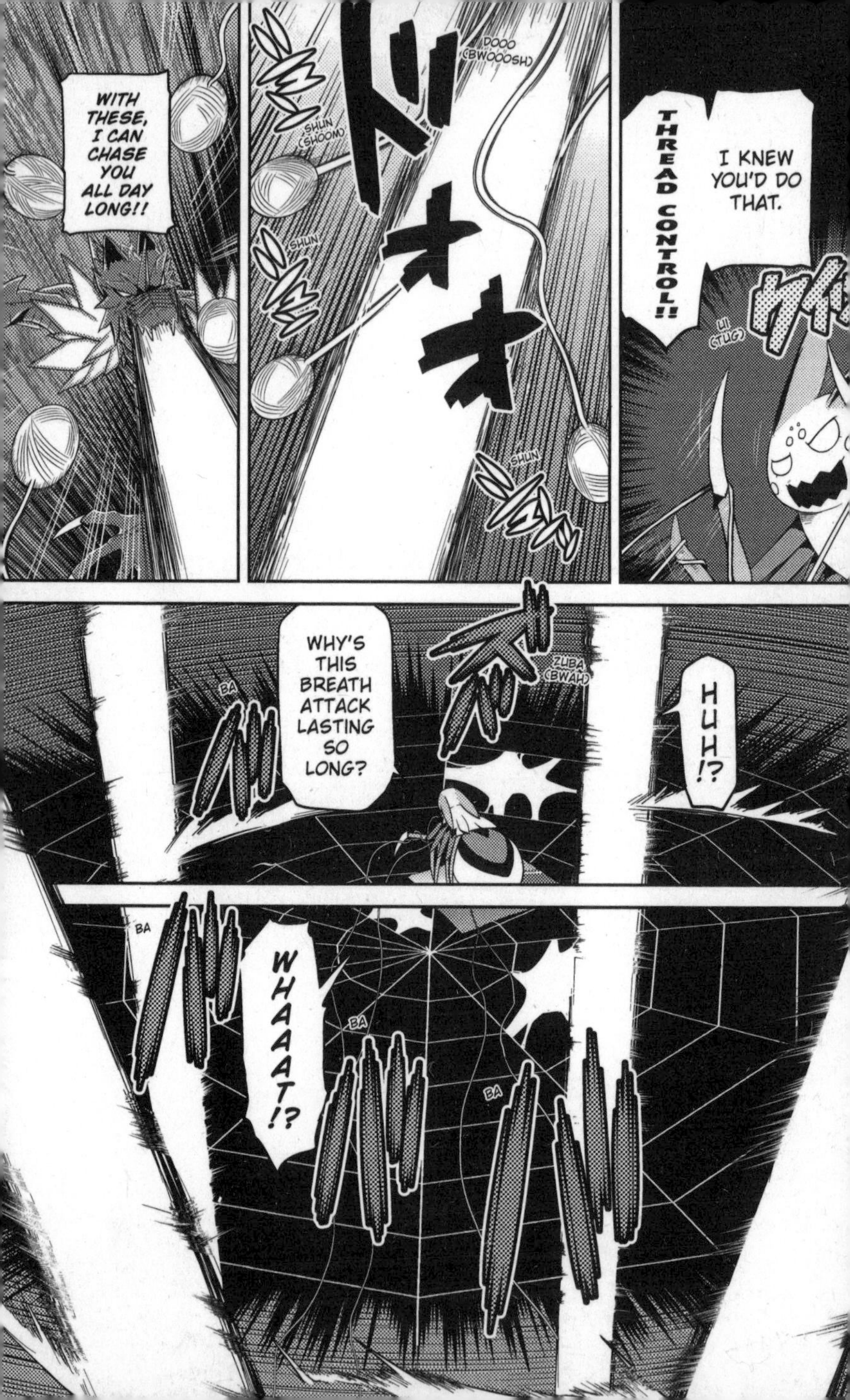
I KNEW YOU'D DO THAT.
THREAD CONTROL!!
UI (TUG)
DOOO (BWOOOSH)
SHUN (SHOOM)
SHUN
SHUN
WITH THESE, I CAN CHASE YOU ALL DAY LONG!!
HUH!?
ZUBA (BWAH)
WHY'S THIS BREATH ATTACK LASTING SO LONG?
BA
BA
WHAAAAT!?
BA
BA

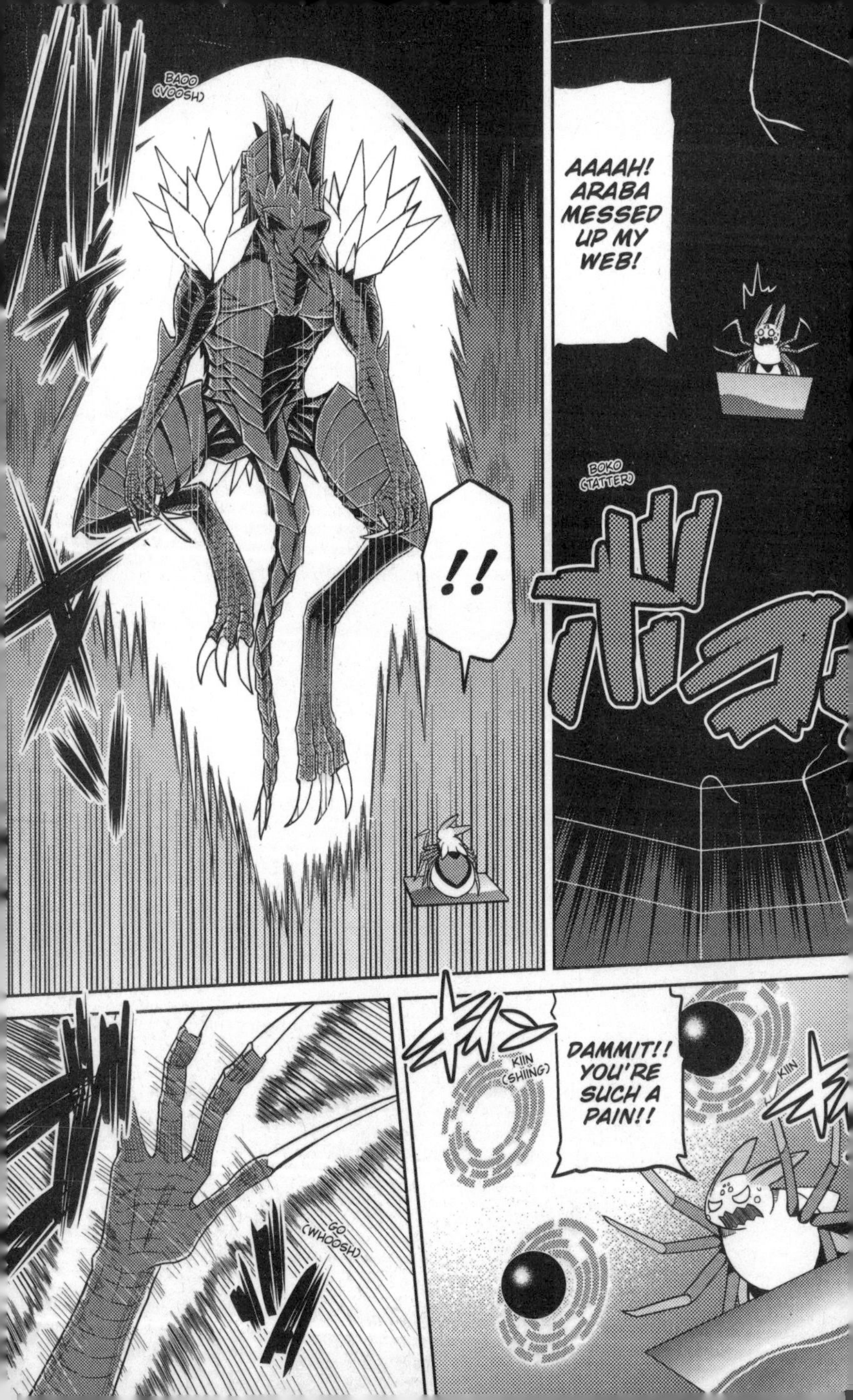
AAAAH! ARABA MESSED UP MY WEB!
BOKO (TATTER)
BAOO (VOOSH)
!!
KIIN
DAMMIT!! YOU'RE SUCH A PAIN!!
KIIN (SHIING)
GO (WHOOSH)

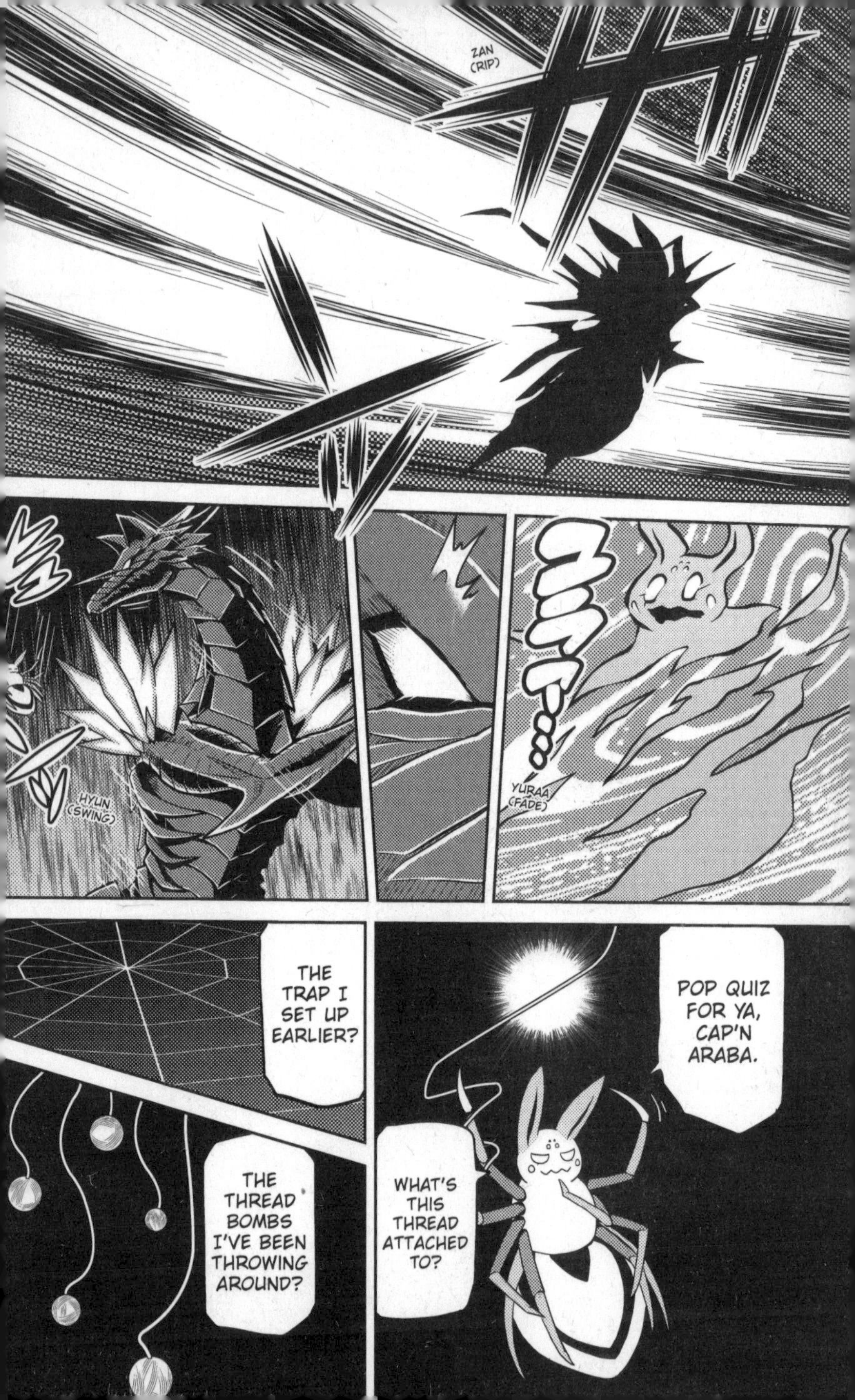
ZAN (RIP)
YURAA (FADE)
HYUN (SWING)
POP QUIZ FOR YA, CAP'N ARABA.
WHAT'S THIS THREAD ATTACHED TO?
THE TRAP I SET UP EARLIER?
THE THREAD BOMBS I'VE BEEN THROWING AROUND?

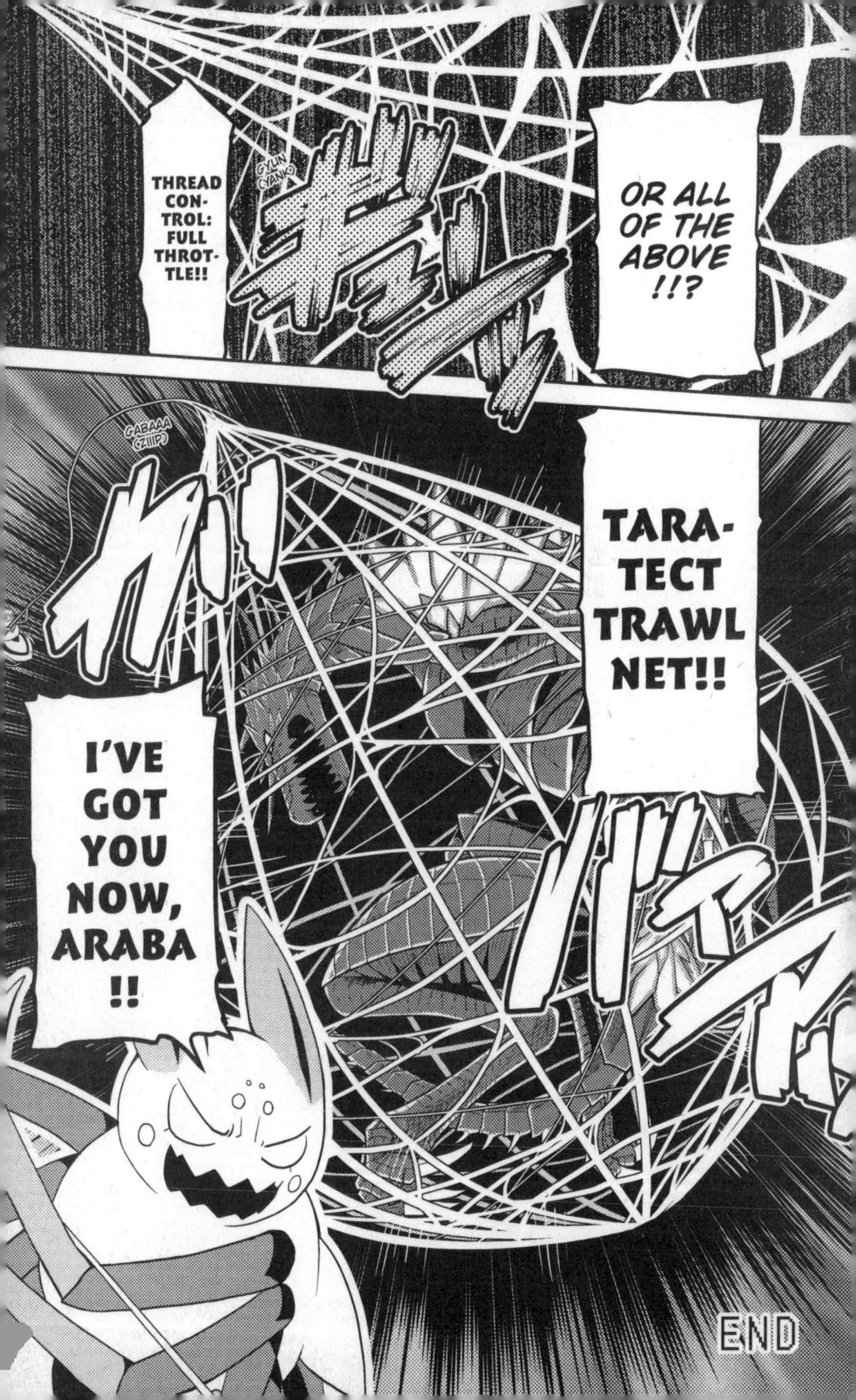
OR ALL OF THE ABOVE!!?
GYUN (YANK)
THREAD CONTROL: FULL THROTTLE!!
TARA-TECT TRAWL NET!!
GABAAA (ZIIIP)
I'VE GOT YOU NOW, ARABA!!
END

so I'm a Spider, so What?

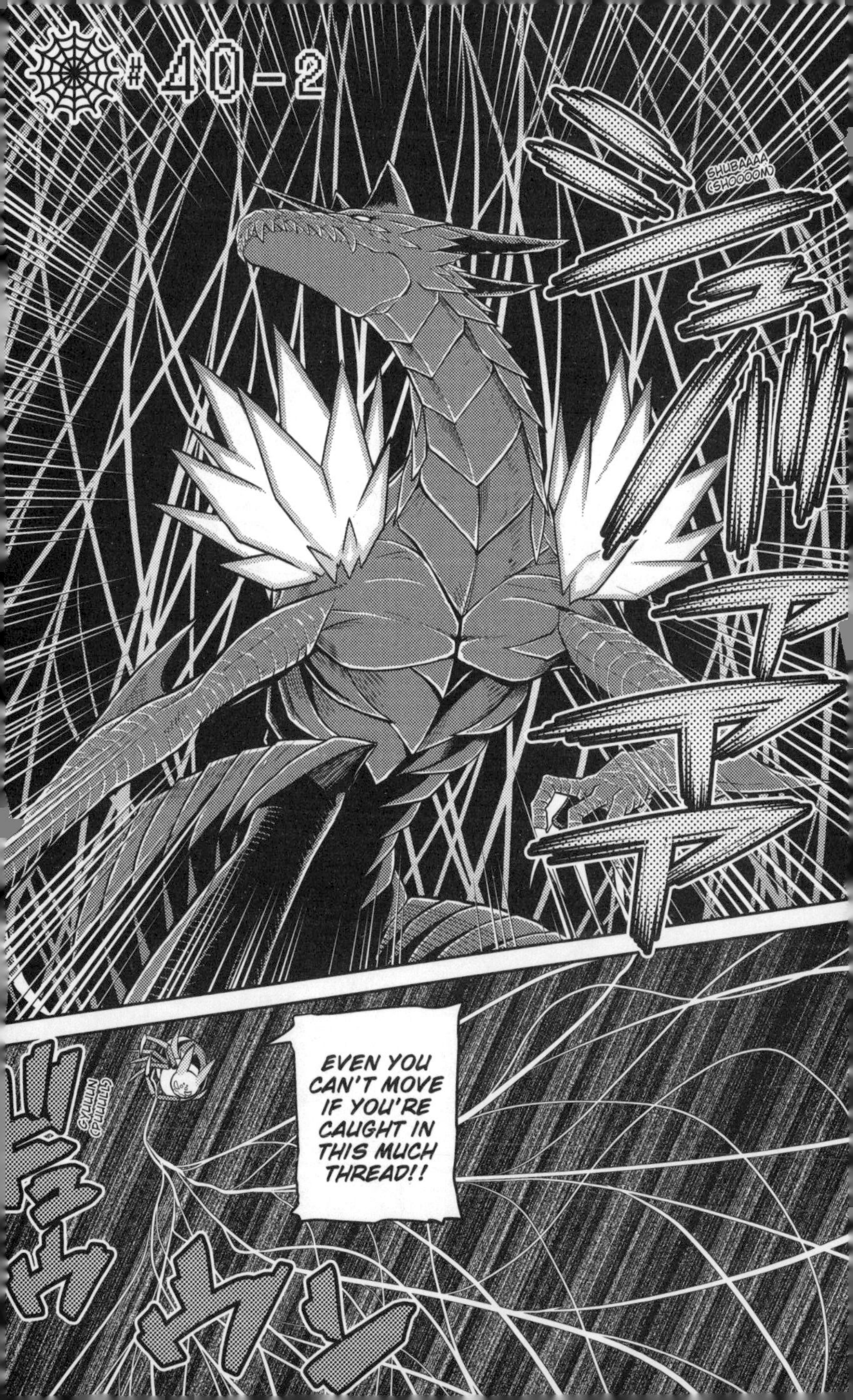
#40-2
SHUBAAAA (SHOOOOM)
GYUUUN (PUUULL)
EVEN YOU CAN'T MOVE IF YOU'RE CAUGHT IN THIS MUCH THREAD!!

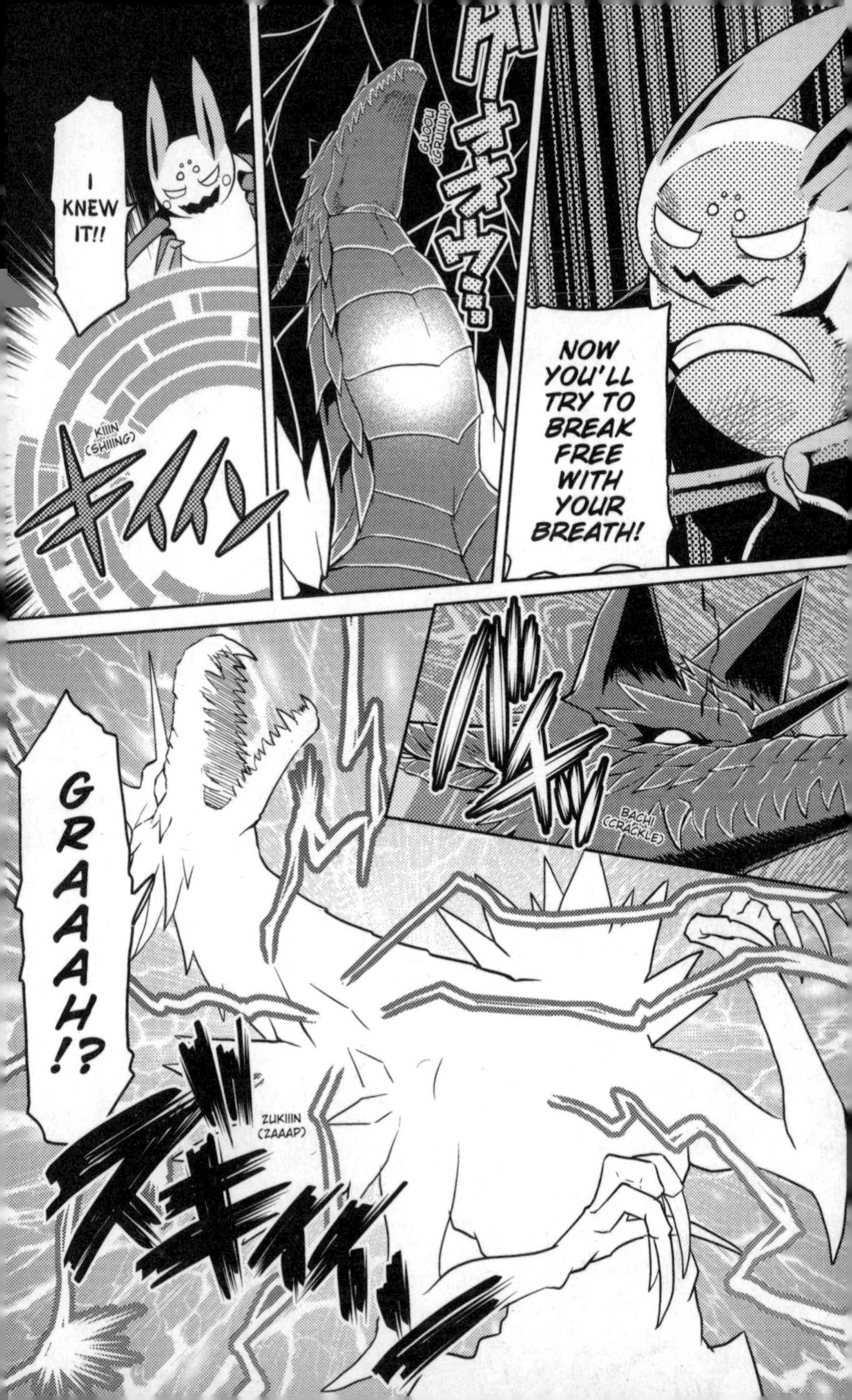
NOW YOU'LL TRY TO BREAK FREE WITH YOUR BREATH!
GUOOU (GRUUUH)
I KNEW IT!!
KIIIN (SHIIING)
BACHI (CRACKLE)
GRAAAAH!?
ZUKIIIN (ZAAAP)

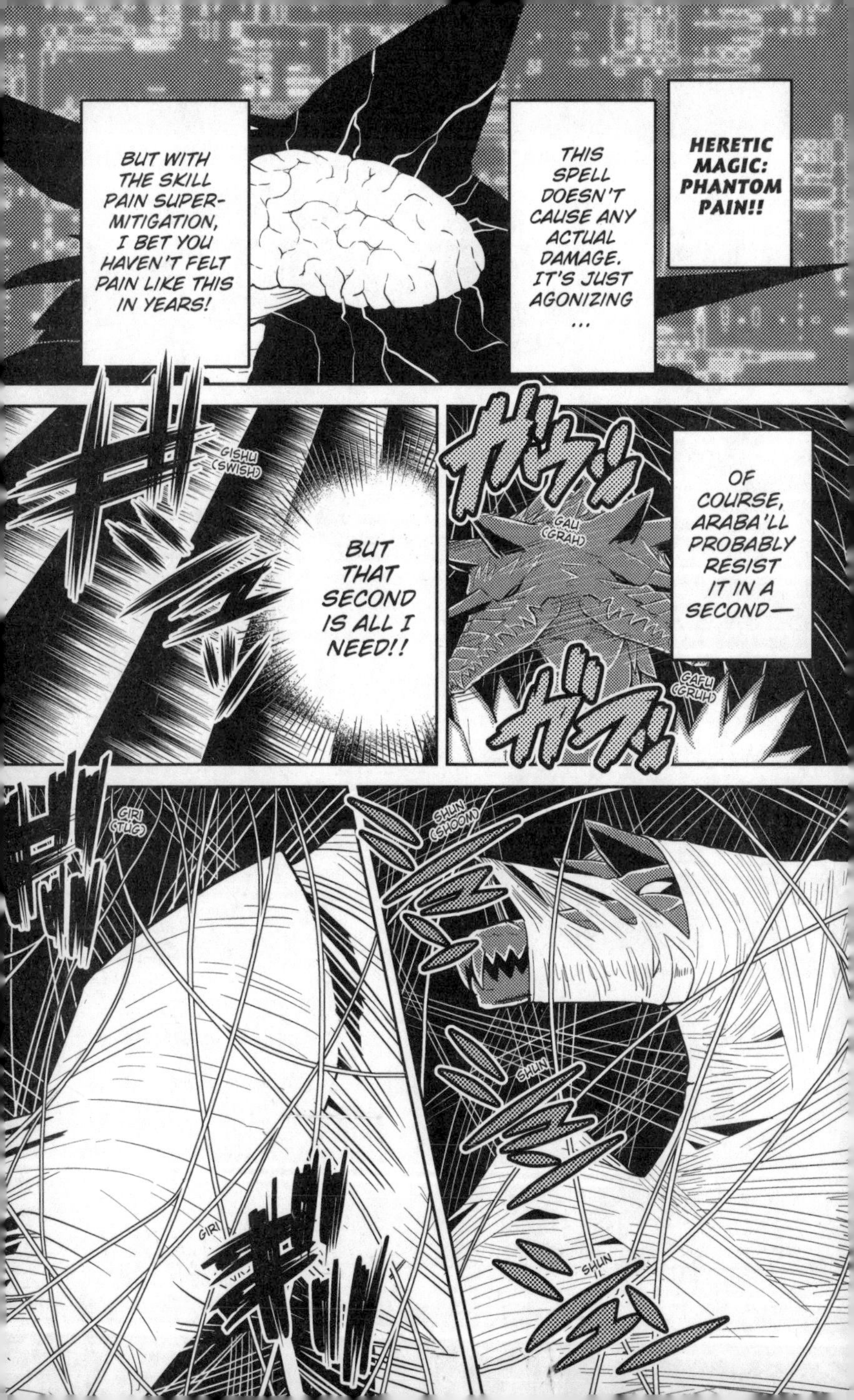
HERETIC MAGIC: PHANTOM PAIN!!
THIS SPELL DOESN'T CAUSE ANY ACTUAL DAMAGE. IT'S JUST AGONIZING ...
BUT WITH THE SKILL PAIN SUPER-MITIGATION, I BET YOU HAVEN'T FELT PAIN LIKE THIS IN YEARS!
OF COURSE, ARABA'LL PROBABLY RESIST IT IN A SECOND—
GAU (GRAH)
GAFU (GRUH)
GISHU (SWISH)
BUT THAT SECOND IS ALL I NEED!!
SHUN (SHOOM)
GIRI (TUG)
SHUN
GIRI
SHUN

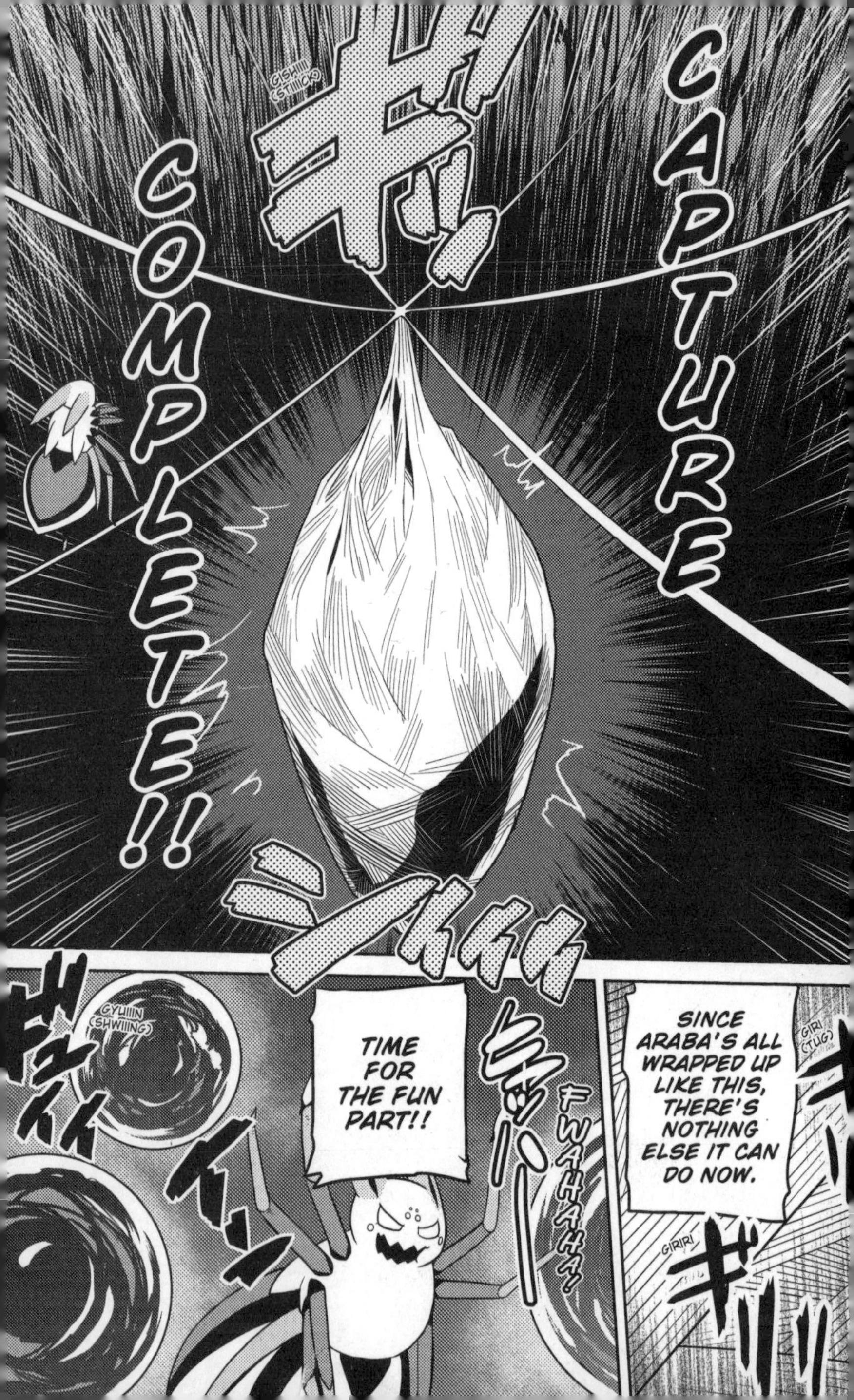
GISHIII (STIIICK)
CAPTURE
COMPLETE!!
SINCE ARABA'S ALL WRAPPED UP LIKE THIS, THERE'S NOTHING ELSE IT CAN DO NOW.
GIRI (TUG)
GIRIRI
TIME FOR THE FUN PART!!
FWAHAHA!
GYUIIIN (SHWIIING)

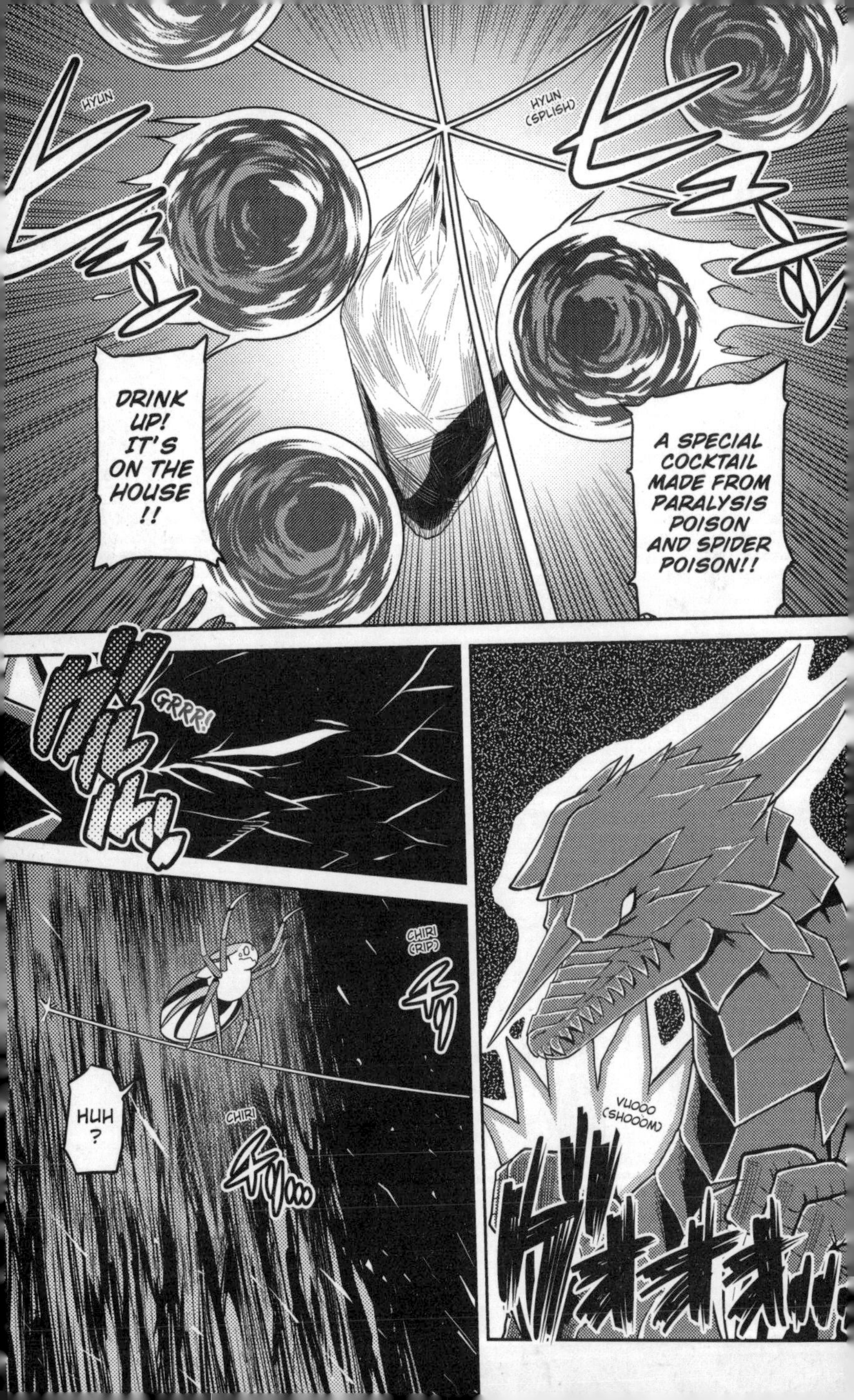
HYUN (SPLISH)
HYUN
A SPECIAL COCKTAIL MADE FROM PARALYSIS POISON AND SPIDER POISON!!
DRINK UP! IT'S ON THE HOUSE!!
VUOOO (SHOOOM)
GRRR!
CHIRI (RIP)
HUH?
CHIRI

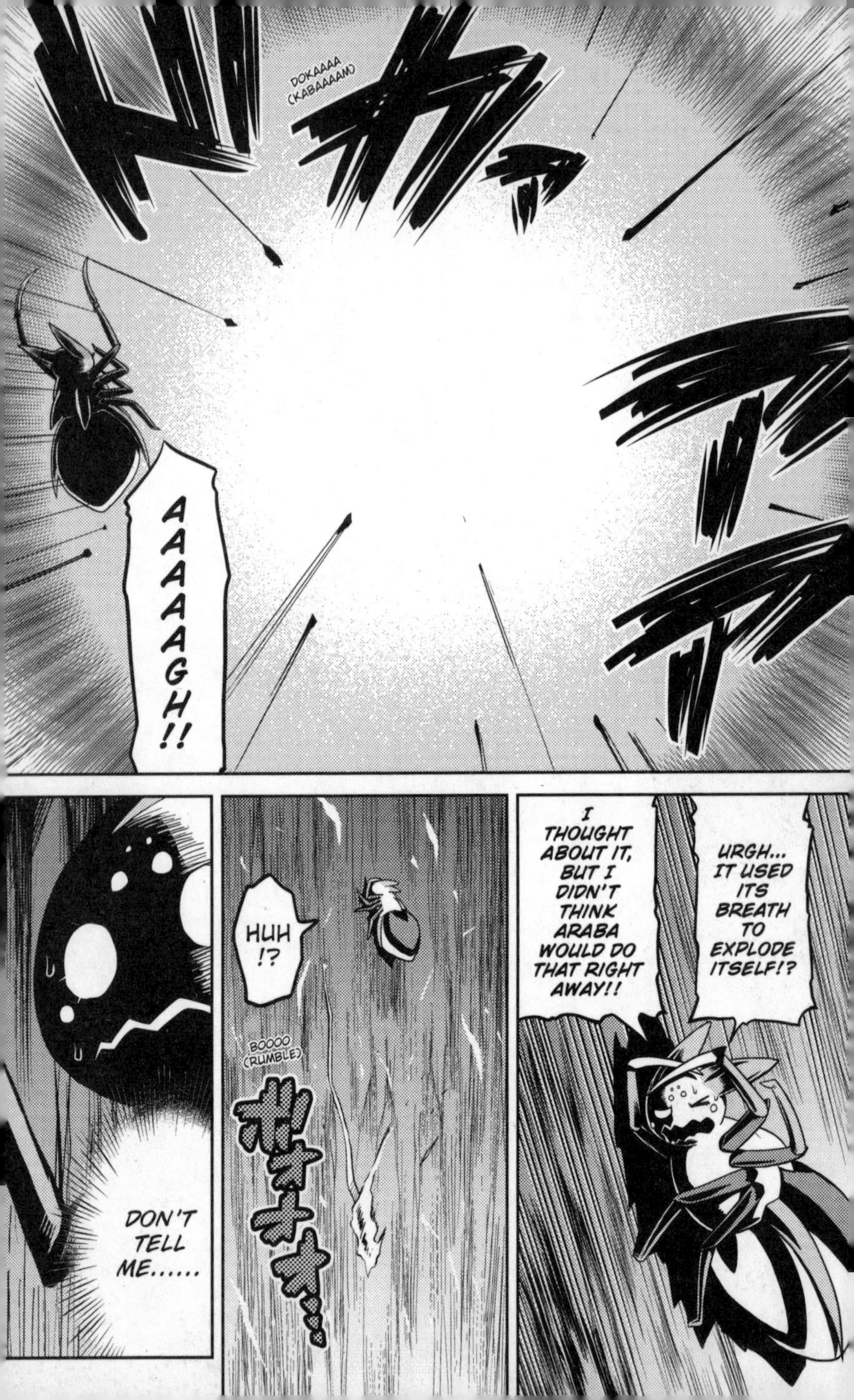
DOKAAAA (KABAAAAM)
AAAAAAGH!!
URGH... IT USED ITS BREATH TO EXPLODE ITSELF!?
I THOUGHT ABOUT IT, BUT I DIDN'T THINK ARABA WOULD DO THAT RIGHT AWAY!!
HUH!?
BOOOO (RUMBLE)
DON'T TELL ME......

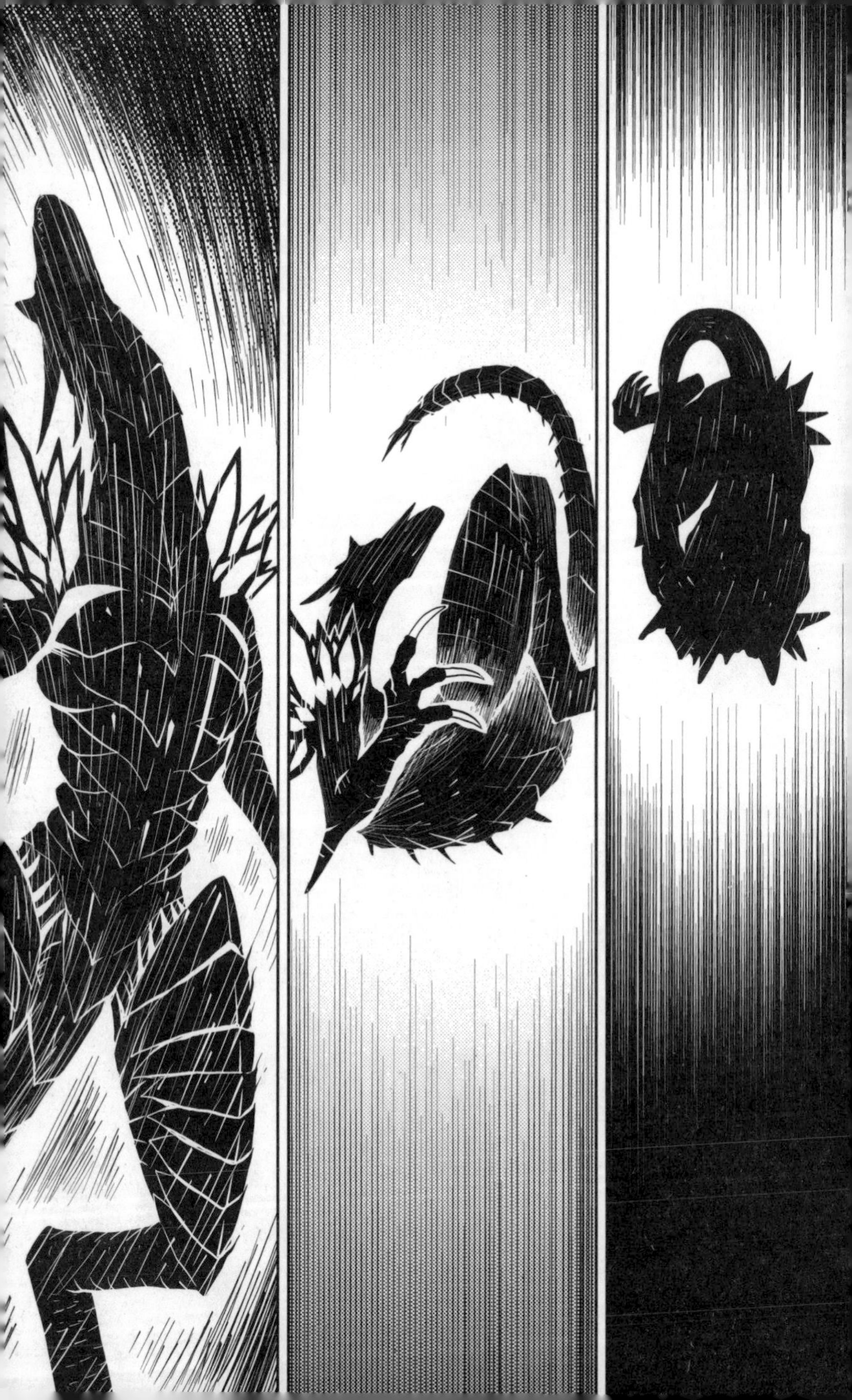

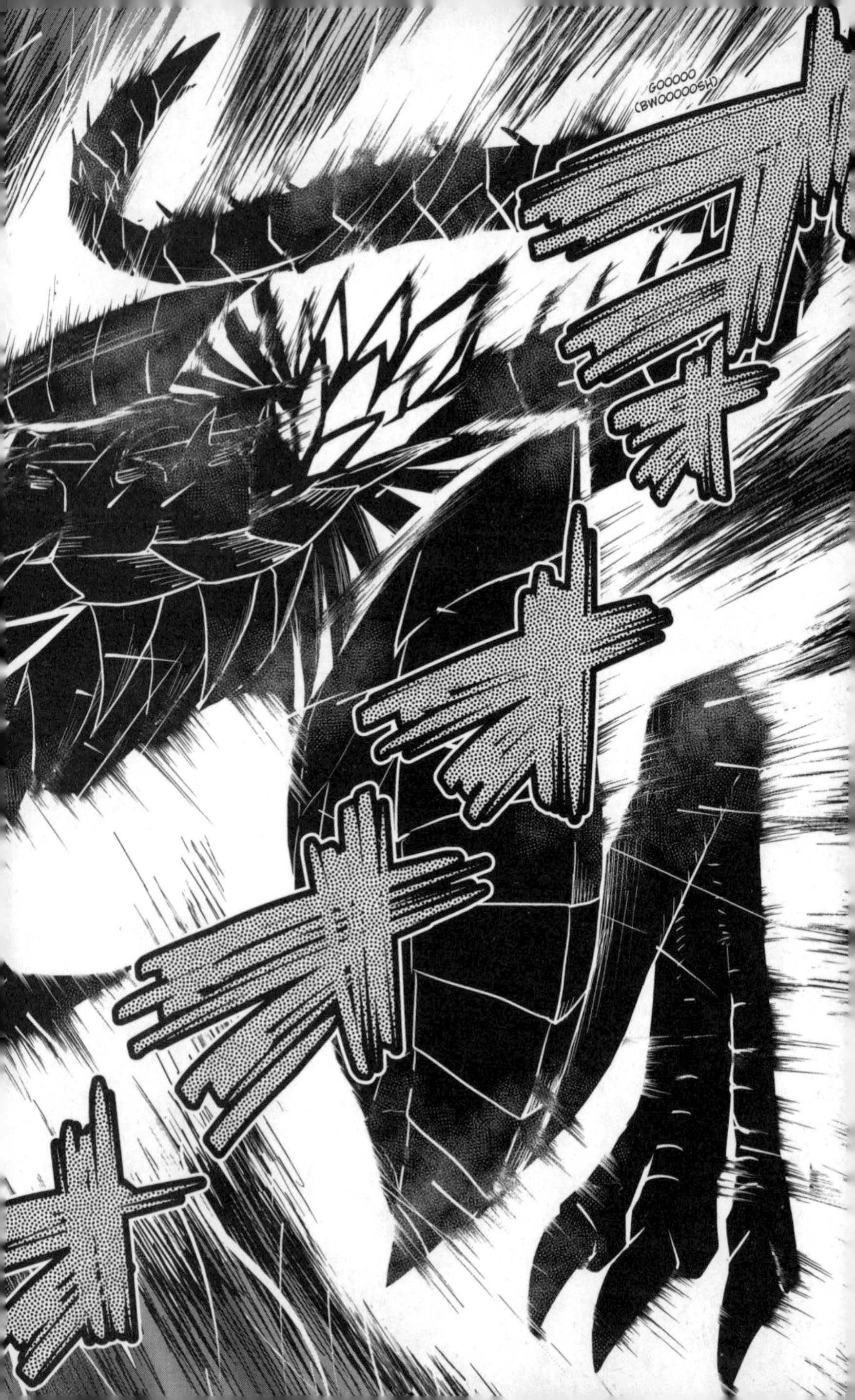
GOOOOO
(BWOOOOOSH)

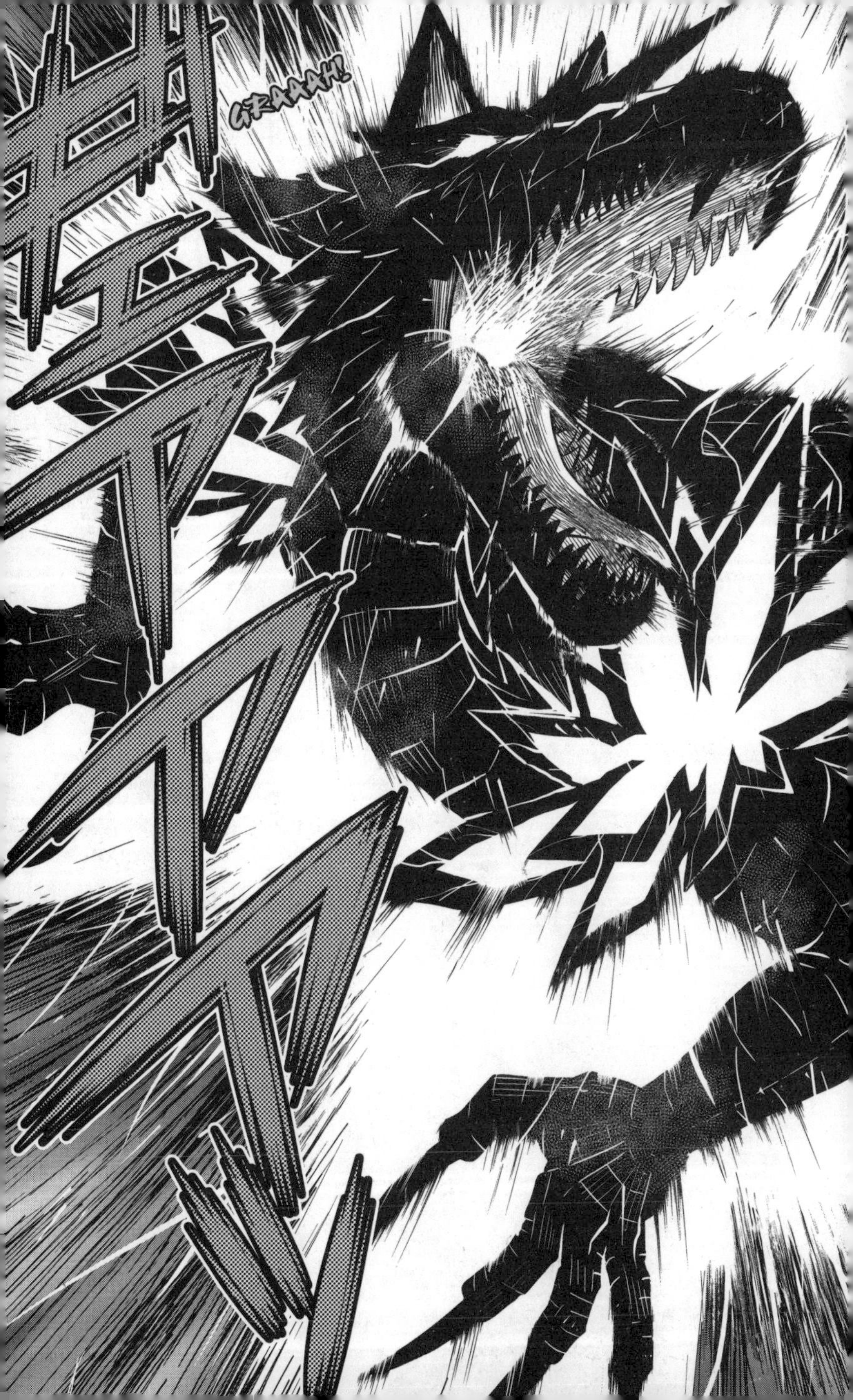
GRAAAH!

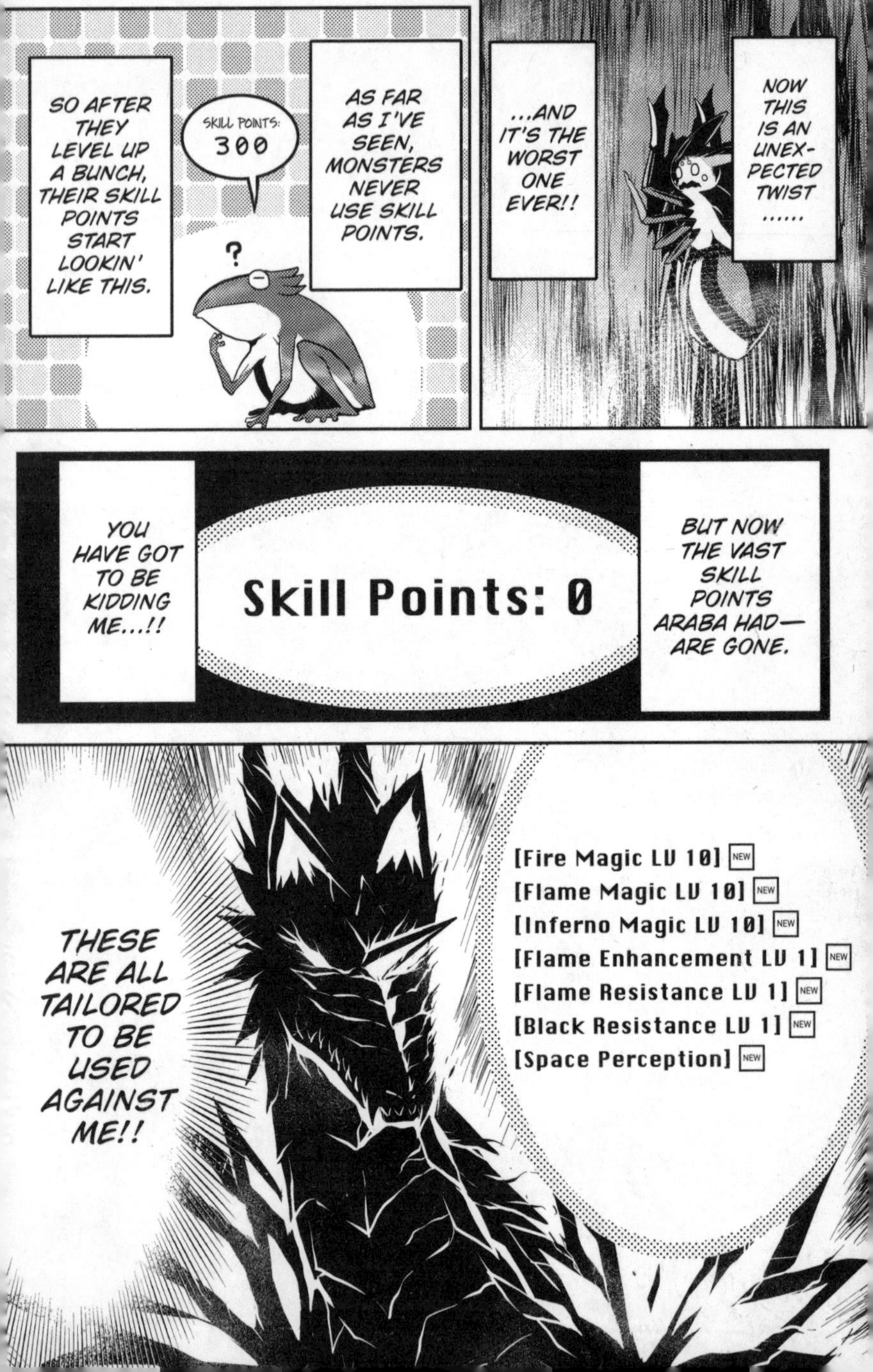
NOW THIS IS AN UNEXPECTED TWIST......
...AND IT'S THE WORST ONE EVER!!
AS FAR AS I'VE SEEN, MONSTERS NEVER USE SKILL POINTS.
SO AFTER THEY LEVEL UP A BUNCH, THEIR SKILL POINTS START LOOKIN' LIKE THIS.
SKILL POINTS: 300
?
BUT NOW THE VAST SKILL POINTS ARABA HAD—ARE GONE.
Skill Points: 0
YOU HAVE GOT TO BE KIDDING ME...!!
[Fire Magic LV 10] NEW
[Flame Magic LV 10] NEW
[Inferno Magic LV 10] NEW
[Flame Enhancement LV 1] NEW
[Flame Resistance LV 1] NEW
[Black Resistance LV 1] NEW
[Space Perception] NEW
THESE ARE ALL TAILORED TO BE USED AGAINST ME!!

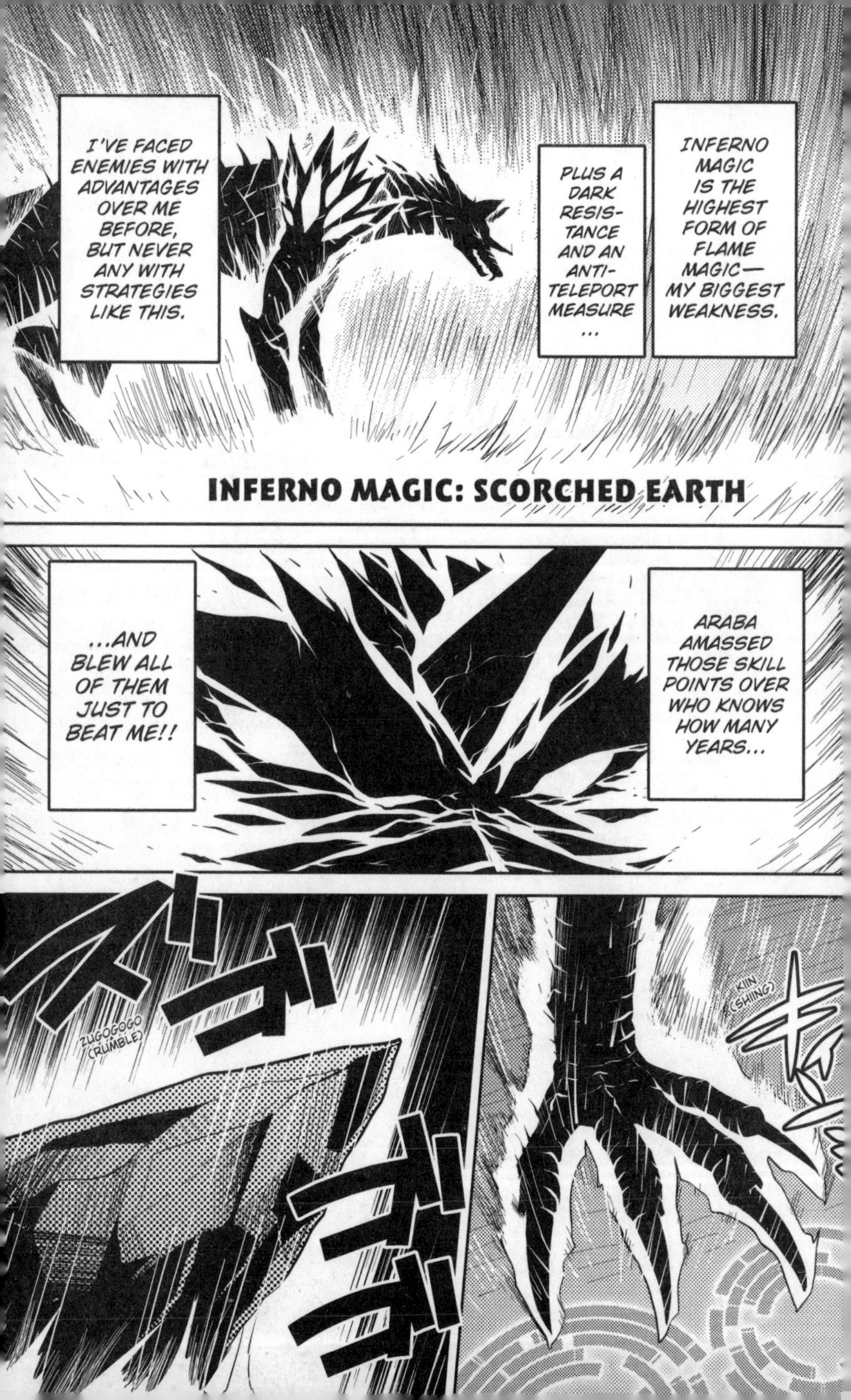
INFERNO MAGIC IS THE HIGHEST FORM OF FLAME MAGIC— MY BIGGEST WEAKNESS.
PLUS A DARK RESIS-TANCE AND AN ANTI-TELEPORT MEASURE …
I'VE FACED ENEMIES WITH ADVANTAGES OVER ME BEFORE, BUT NEVER ANY WITH STRATEGIES LIKE THIS.
INFERNO MAGIC: SCORCHED EARTH
ARABA AMASSED THOSE SKILL POINTS OVER WHO KNOWS HOW MANY YEARS…
…AND BLEW ALL OF THEM JUST TO BEAT ME!!
KIIN (SHIING)
ZUGOGOGO (RUMBLE)

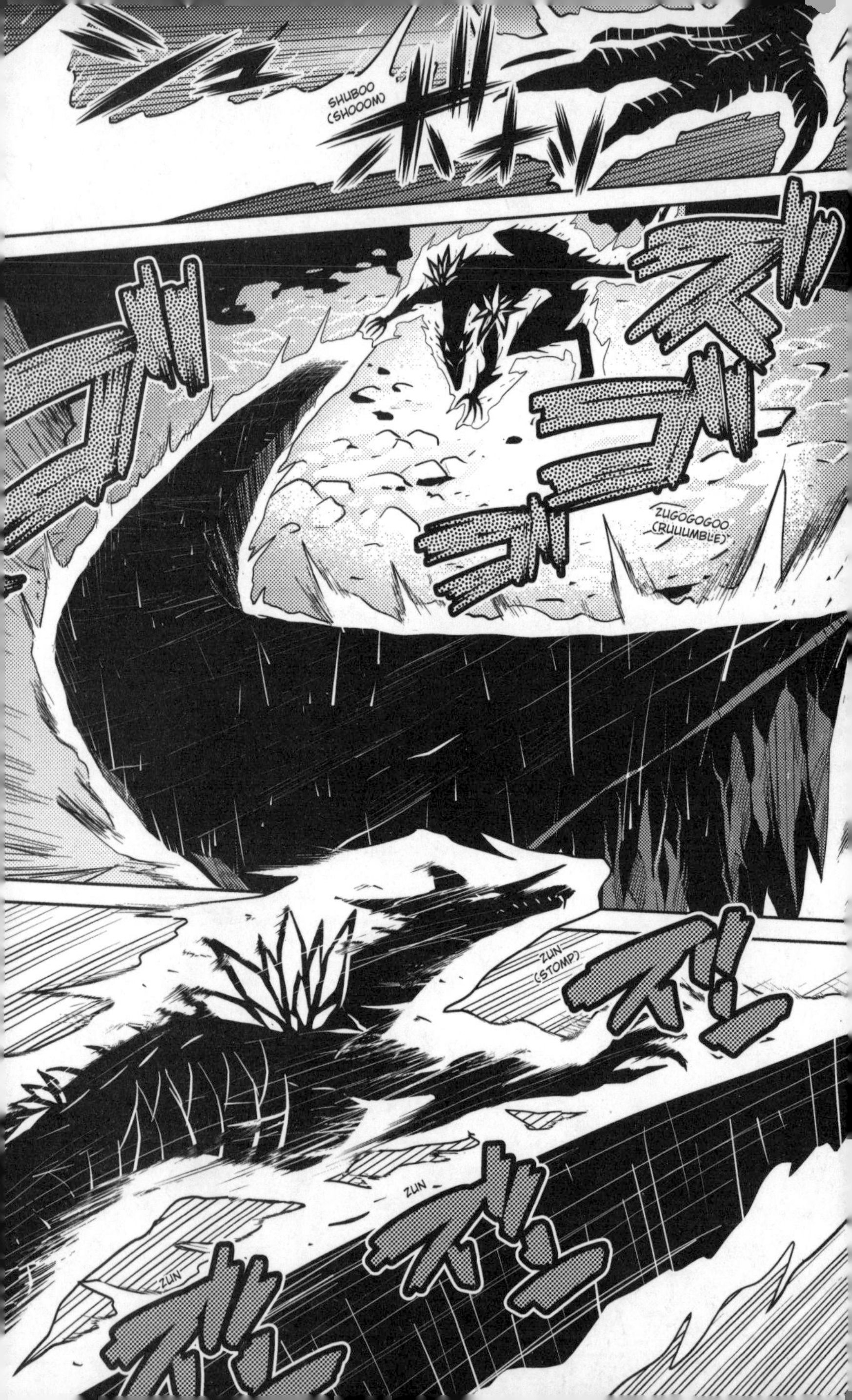
SHUBOO (SHOOOM)
ZUGOGOGOO (RUUUMBLE)
ZUN (STOMP)
ZUN
ZUN

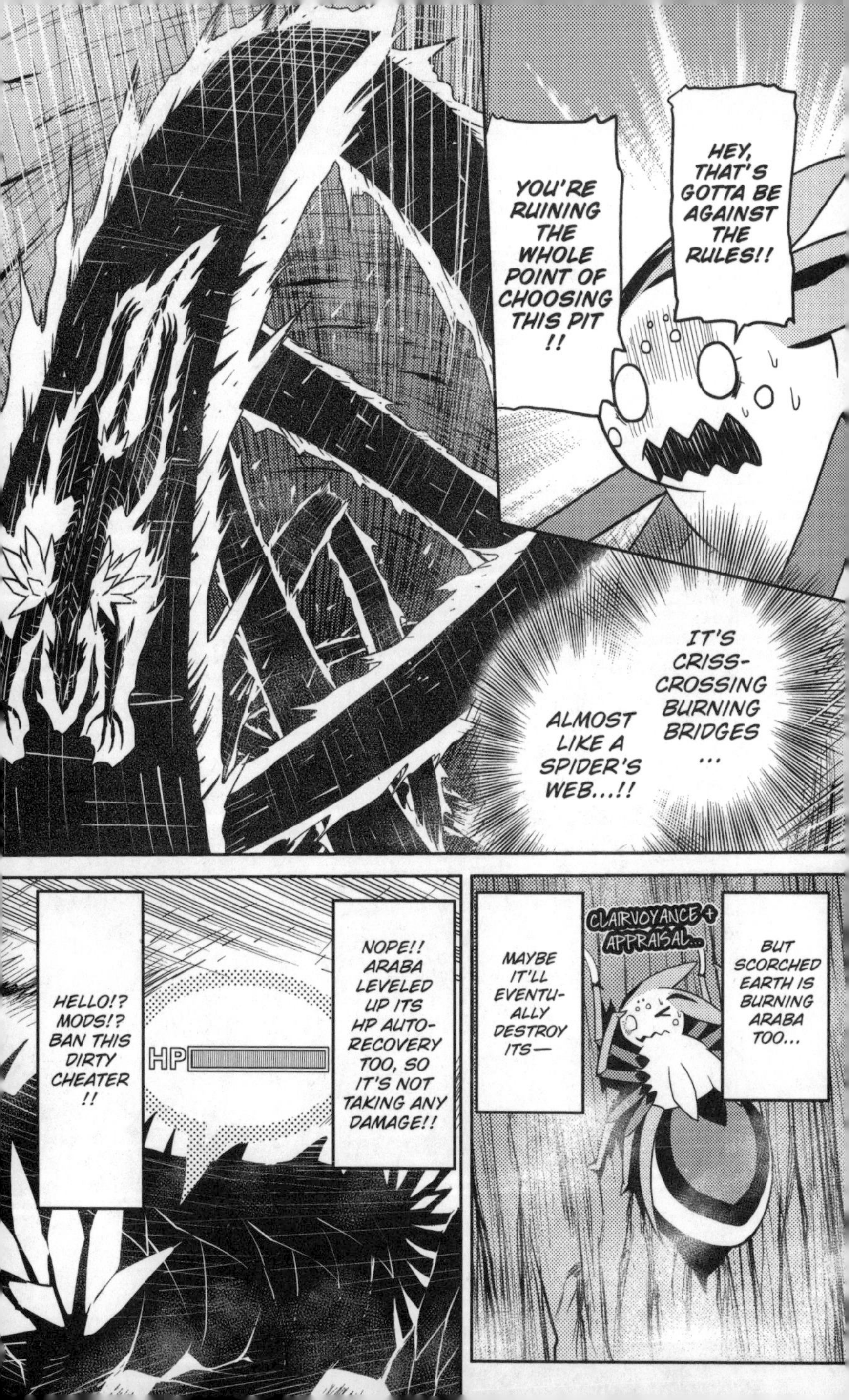
HEY, THAT'S GOTTA BE AGAINST THE RULES!!
YOU'RE RUINING THE WHOLE POINT OF CHOOSING THIS PIT!!
IT'S CRISS-CROSSING BURNING BRIDGES...
ALMOST LIKE A SPIDER'S WEB...!!
BUT SCORCHED EARTH IS BURNING ARABA TOO...
CLAIRVOYANCE + APPRAISAL...
MAYBE IT'LL EVENTUALLY DESTROY ITS—
NOPE!! ARABA LEVELED UP ITS HP AUTO-RECOVERY TOO, SO IT'S NOT TAKING ANY DAMAGE!!
HP
HELLO!? MODS!? BAN THIS DIRTY CHEATER!!

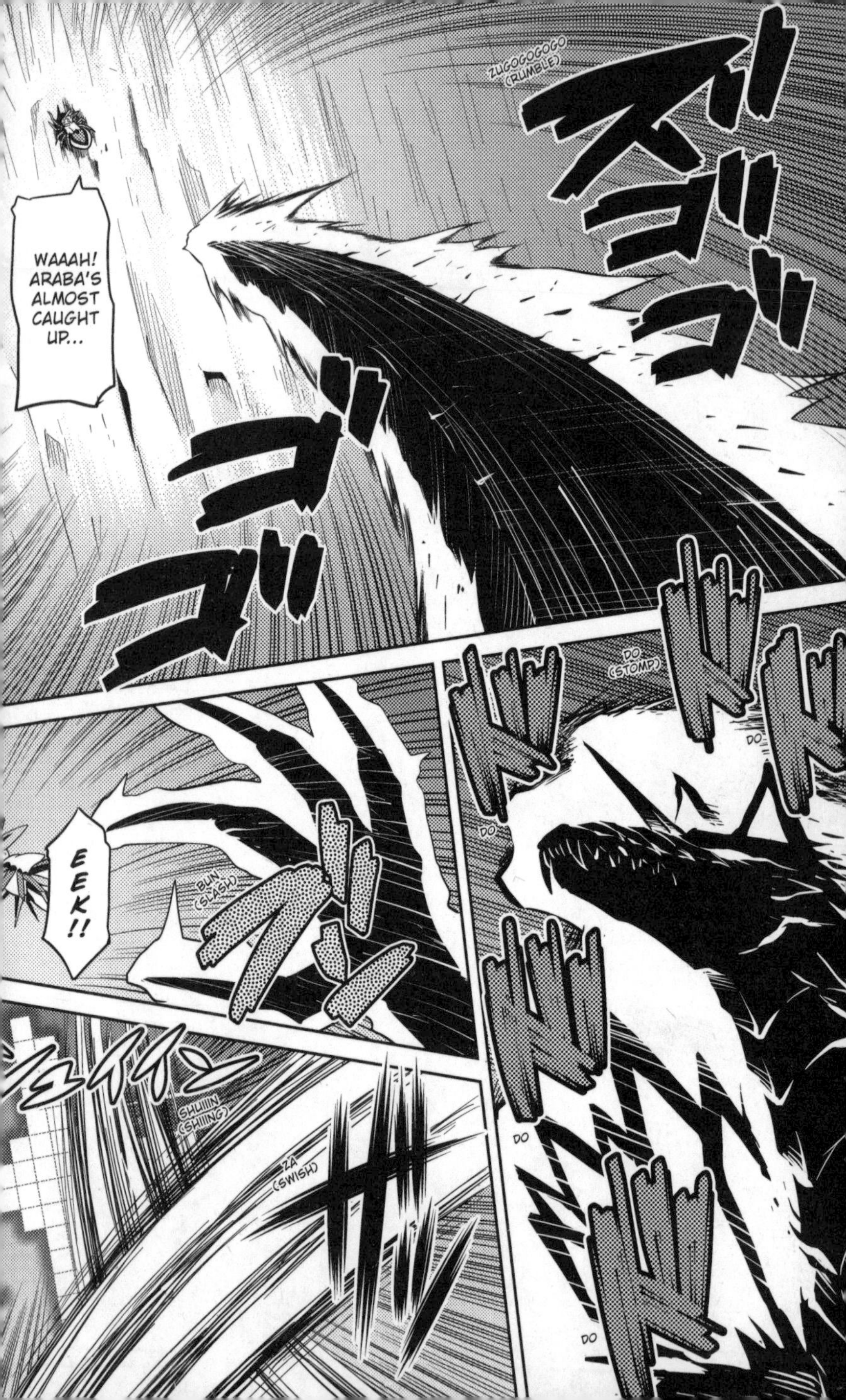
ZUGOGOGOGO (RUMBLE)
WAAAH! ARABA'S ALMOST CAUGHT UP...
DO (STOMP)
DO
DO
DO
DO
BUN (SLASH)
EEK!!
SHUIIIN (SHIIING)
ZA (SWISH)

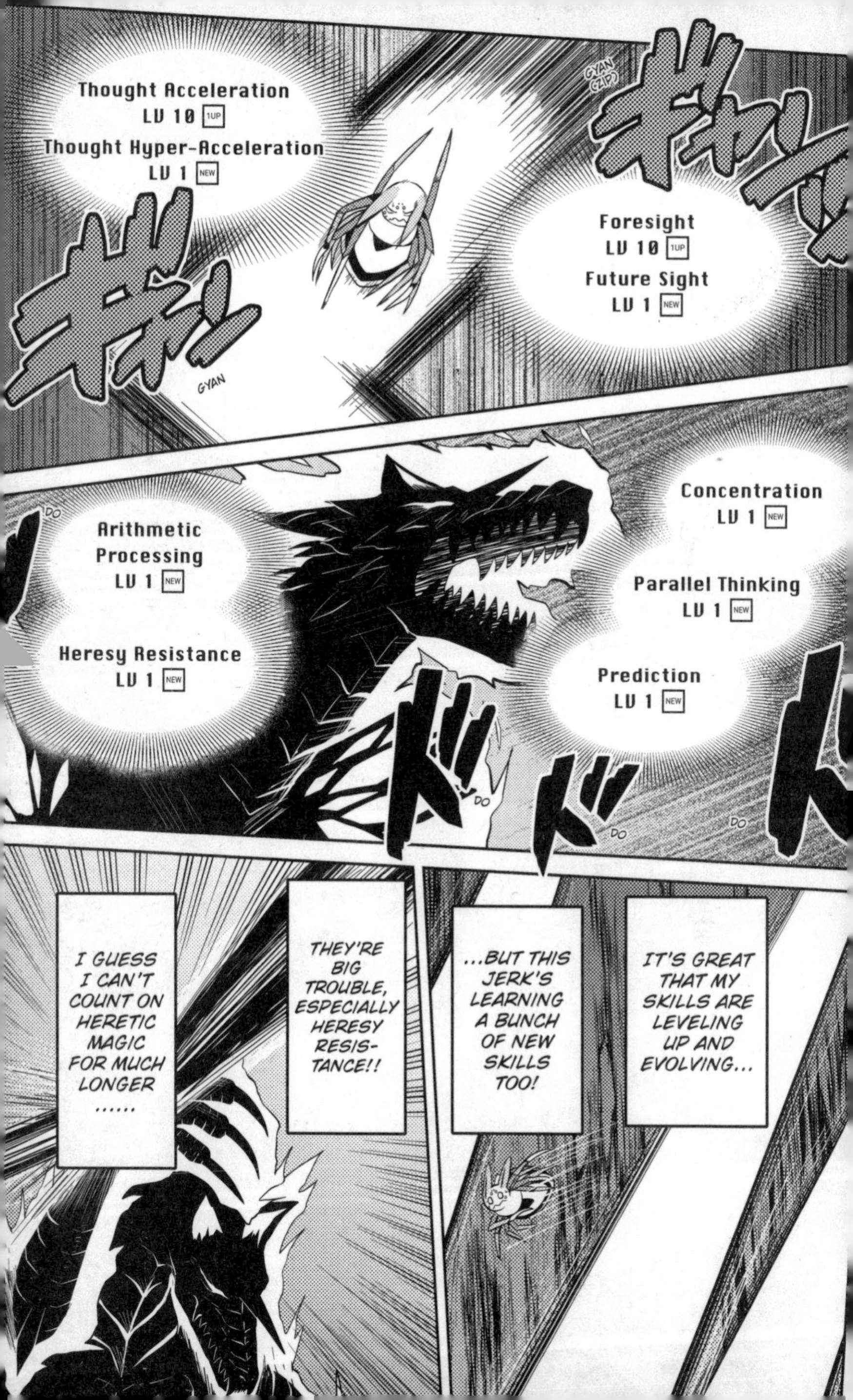
GYAN (ZIP)
Foresight LV 10 1UP
Future Sight LV 1 NEW
Thought Acceleration LV 10 1UP
Thought Hyper-Acceleration LV 1 NEW
GYAN
Concentration LV 1 NEW
Parallel Thinking LV 1 NEW
Prediction LV 1 NEW
DO
DO
DO
Arithmetic Processing LV 1 NEW
Heresy Resistance LV 1 NEW
DO
IT'S GREAT THAT MY SKILLS ARE LEVELING UP AND EVOLVING...
...BUT THIS JERK'S LEARNING A BUNCH OF NEW SKILLS TOO!
THEY'RE BIG TROUBLE, ESPECIALLY HERESY RESIS-TANCE!!
I GUESS I CAN'T COUNT ON HERETIC MAGIC FOR MUCH LONGER......

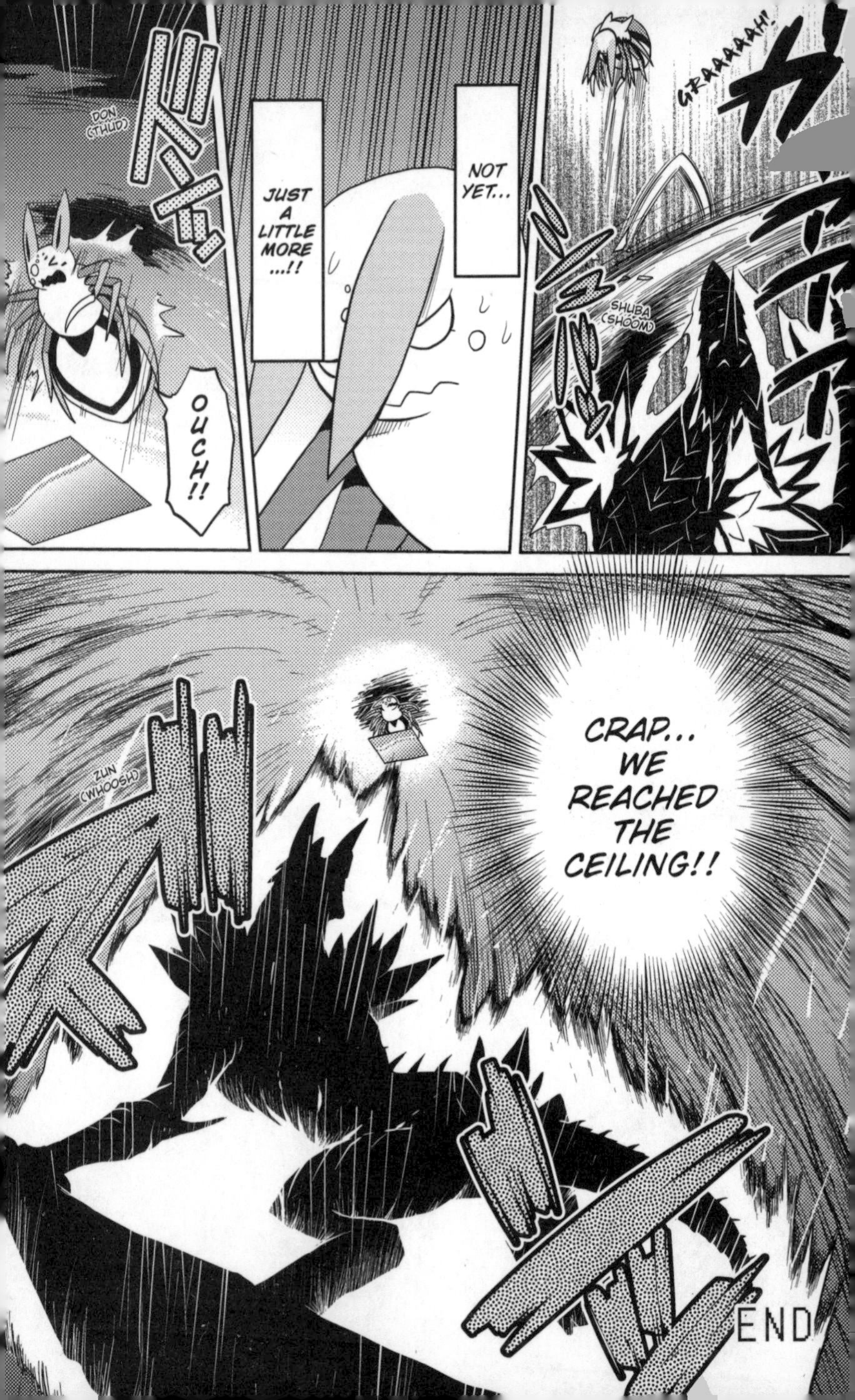
GRAAAAAH!!
SHUBA (SHOOM)
NOT YET...
JUST A LITTLE MORE ...!!
DON (THUD)
OUCH!!
CRAP... WE REACHED THE CEILING!!
ZUN (WHOOSH)
END

So I'm a Spider, So What?

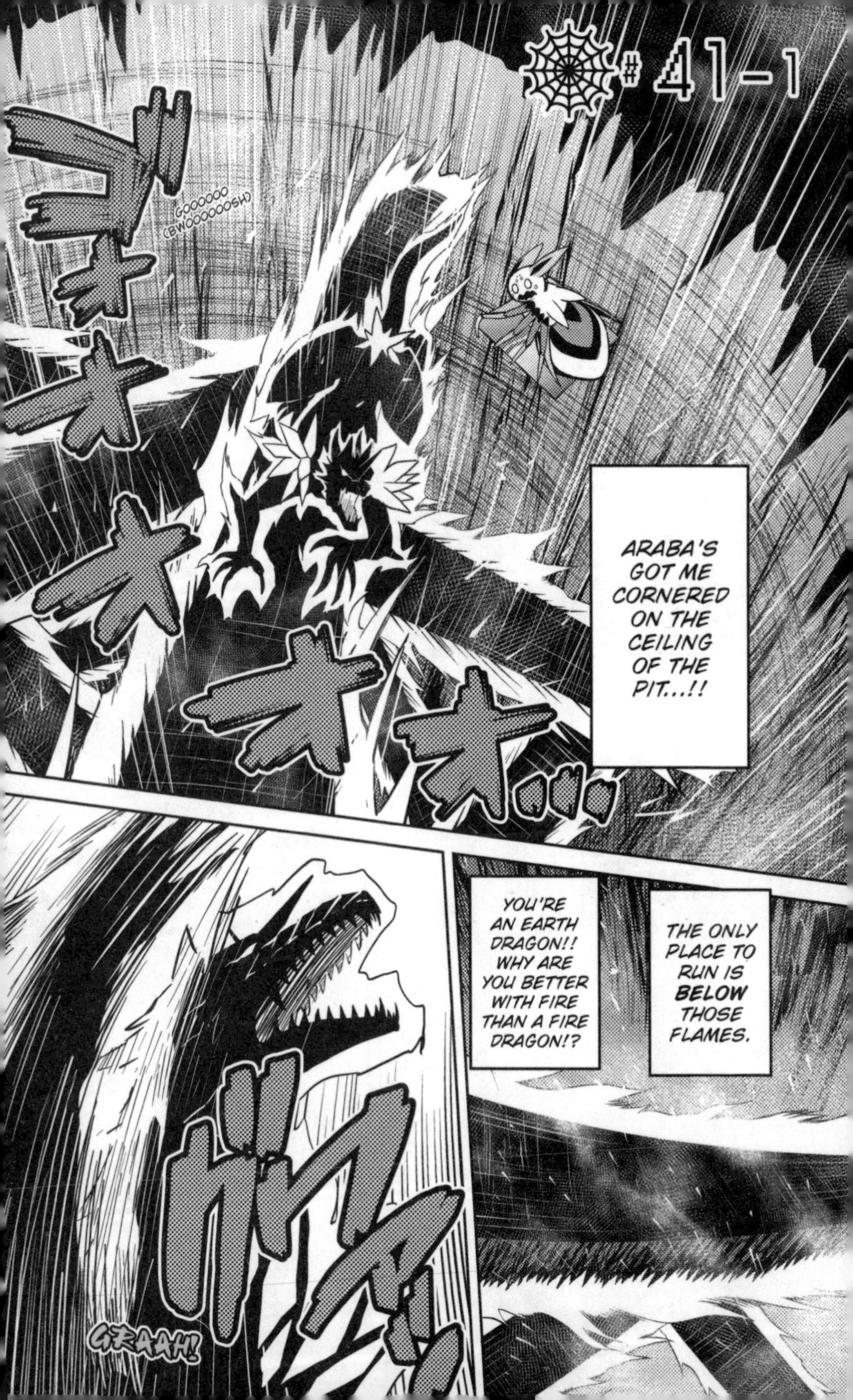
#41-1
GOOOOOO
(BWOOOOOOOSH)
ARABA'S GOT ME CORNERED ON THE CEILING OF THE PIT...!!
THE ONLY PLACE TO RUN IS **BELOW** THOSE FLAMES.
YOU'RE AN EARTH DRAGON!! WHY ARE YOU BETTER WITH FIRE THAN A FIRE DRAGON!?
GRAAH!

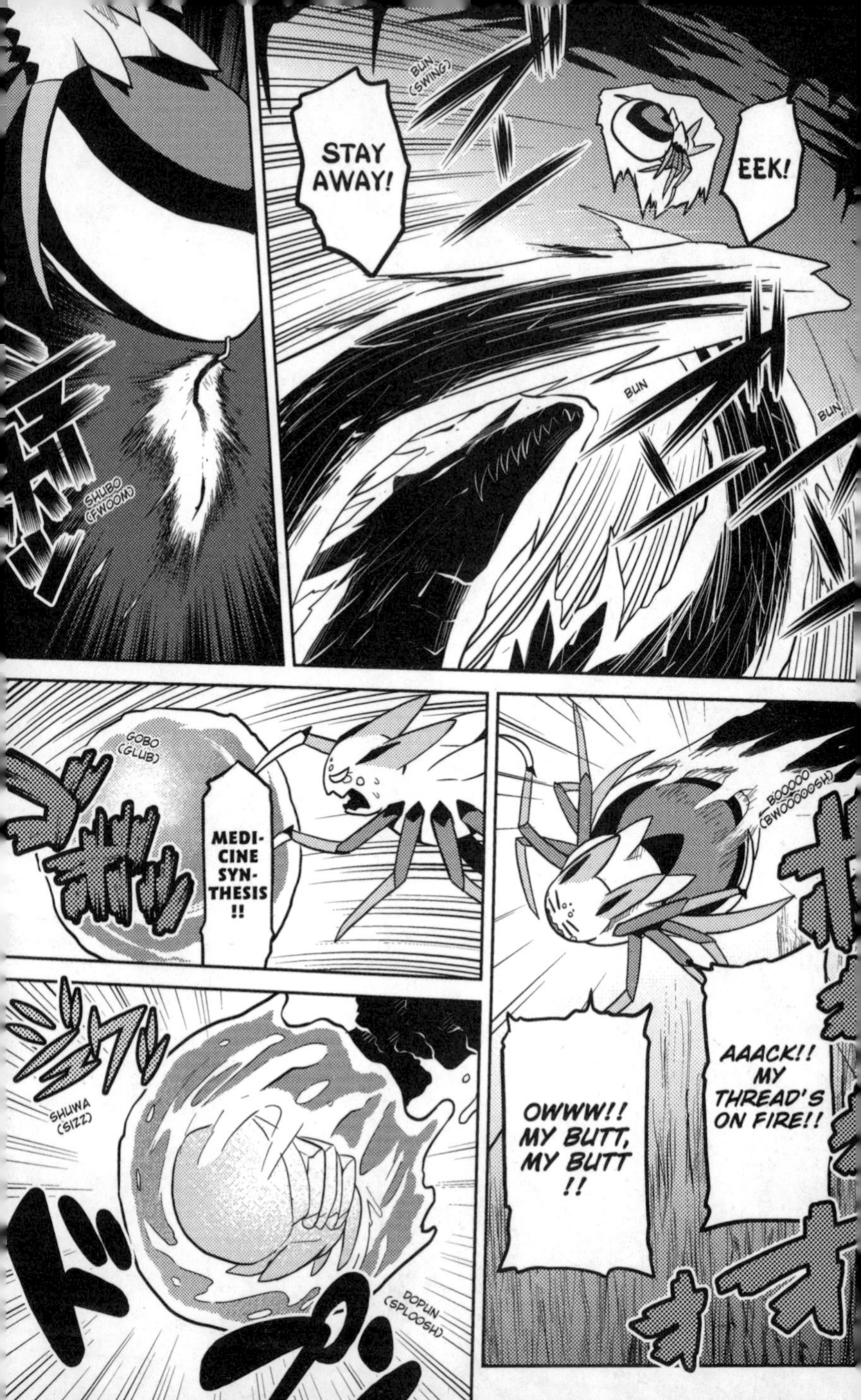
EEK!
BUN (SWING)
STAY AWAY!
BUN
BUN
SHUBO (FWOOM)
BOOOOO (BWOOOOOSH)
AAACK!! MY THREAD'S ON FIRE!!
OWWW!! MY BUTT, MY BUTT !!
MEDI-CINE SYN-THESIS !!
GOBO (GLUB)
SHUWA (SIZZ)
DOPUN (SPLOOSH)

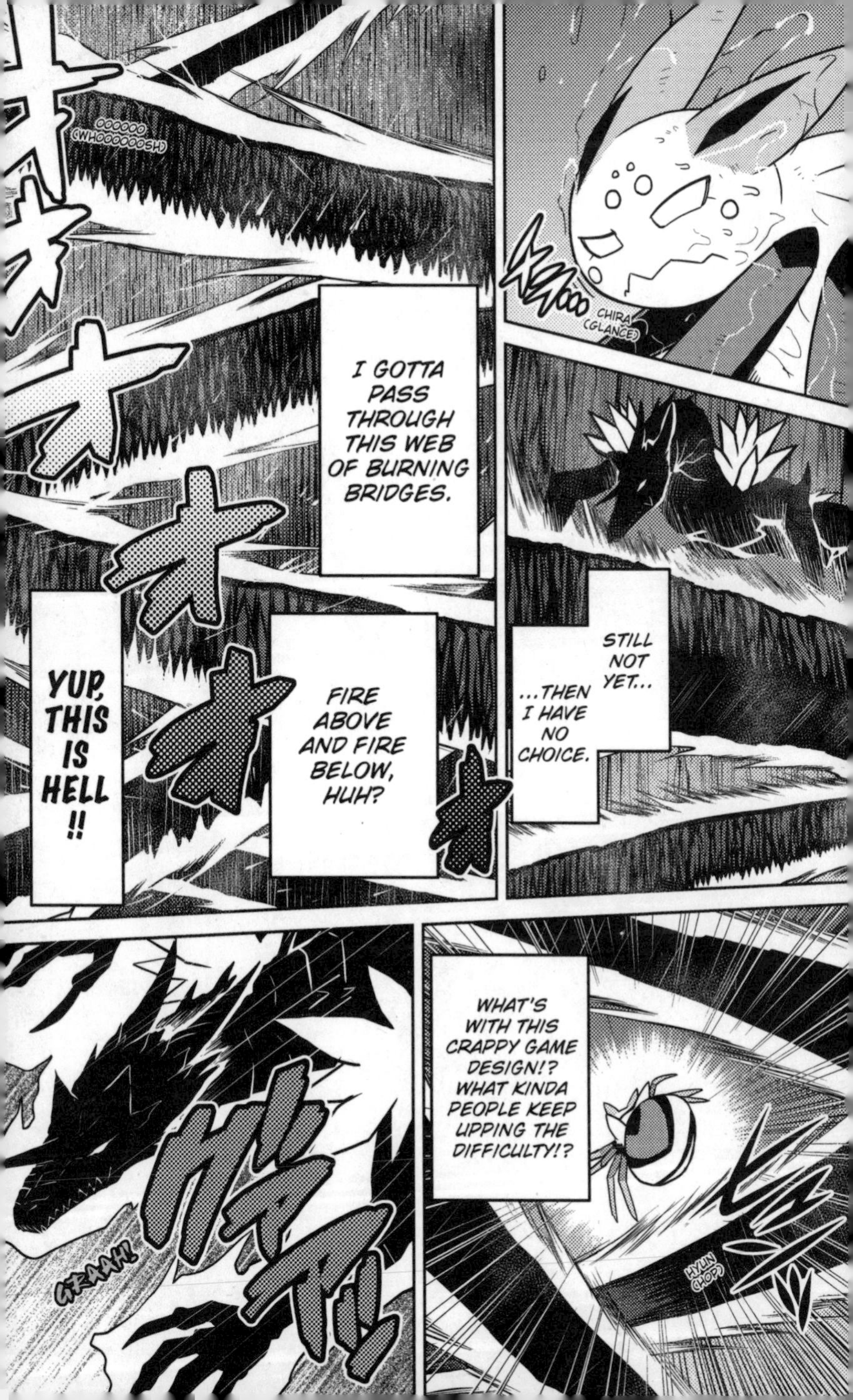

CHIRA (GLANCE)
STILL NOT YET...
...THEN I HAVE NO CHOICE.
OOOOOO (WHOOOOOOOSH)
I GOTTA PASS THROUGH THIS WEB OF BURNING BRIDGES.
FIRE ABOVE AND FIRE BELOW, HUH?
YUP, THIS IS HELL!!
WHAT'S WITH THIS CRAPPY GAME DESIGN!? WHAT KINDA PEOPLE KEEP UPPING THE DIFFICULTY!?
HYUN (HOP)
GRAAH!

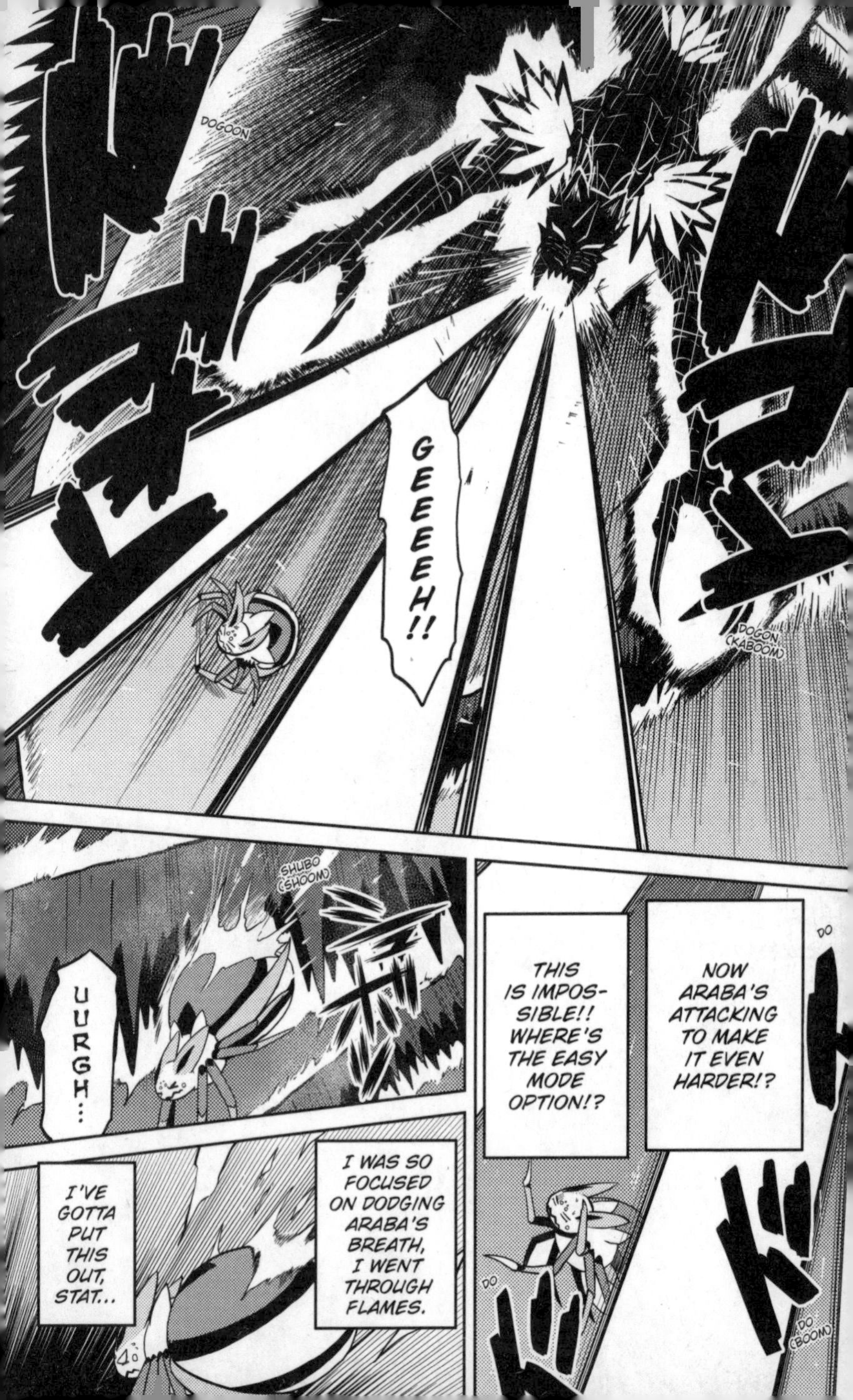
DOGOON
GEEEEEH!!
DOGON (KABOOM)
NOW ARABA'S ATTACKING TO MAKE IT EVEN HARDER!?
THIS IS IMPOSSIBLE!! WHERE'S THE EASY MODE OPTION!?
DO
DO
DO (BOOM)
SHUBO (SHOOM)
UURGH...
I WAS SO FOCUSED ON DODGING ARABA'S BREATH, I WENT THROUGH FLAMES.
I'VE GOTTA PUT THIS OUT, STAT...

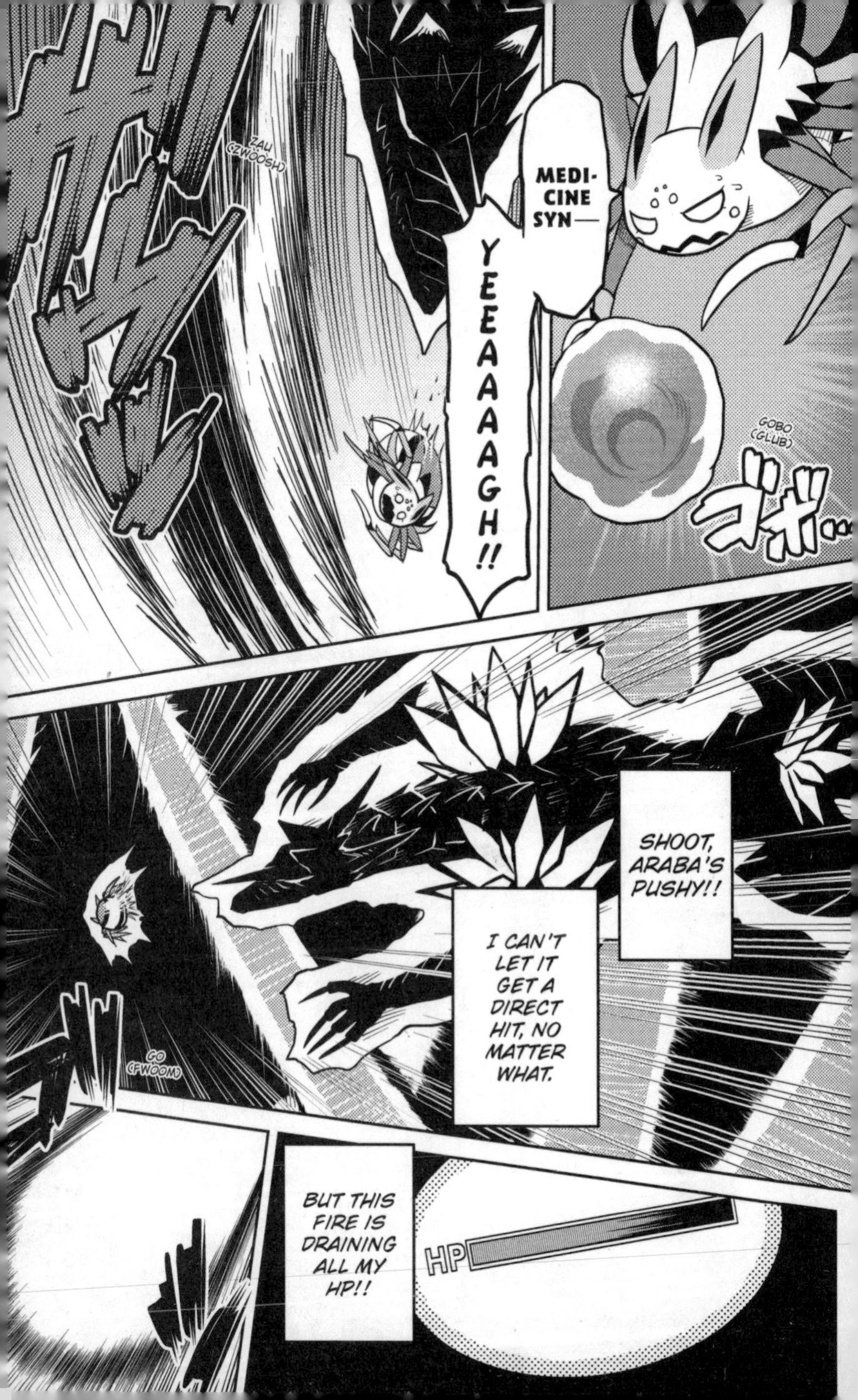
MEDI-CINE SYN—
GOBO (GLUB)
ゴボ…
YEEAAAAAGH!!
ZAU (ZWOOSH)
SHOOT, ARABA'S PUSHY!!
I CAN'T LET IT GET A DIRECT HIT, NO MATTER WHAT.
GO (FWOOM)
BUT THIS FIRE IS DRAINING ALL MY HP!!
HP

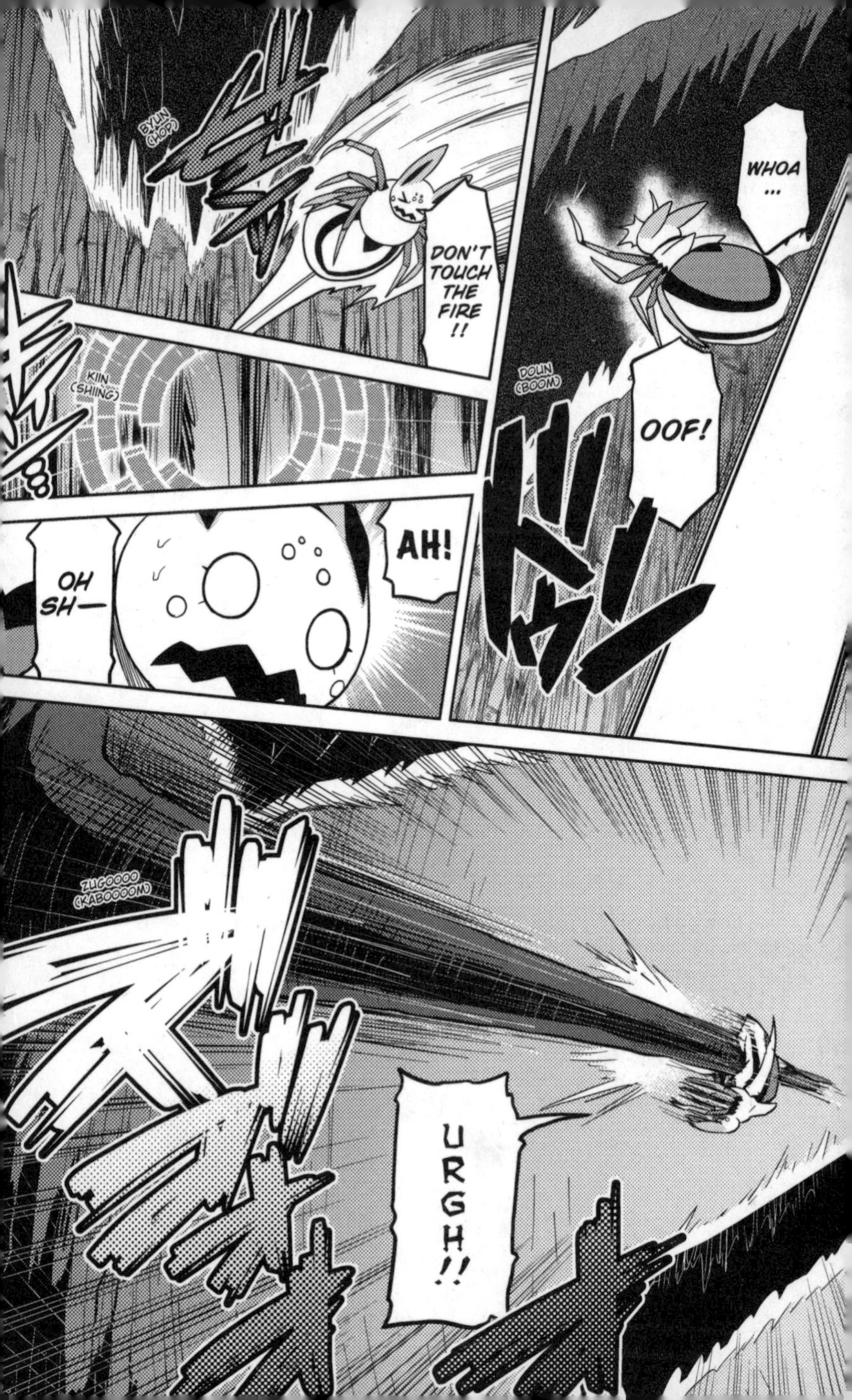
WHOA ...
DOUN (BOOM)
OOF!
BYUN (HOP)
DON'T TOUCH THE FIRE !!
KIIN (SHIING)
AH!
OH SH—
ZUGOOOO (KABOOOOM)
URGH!!

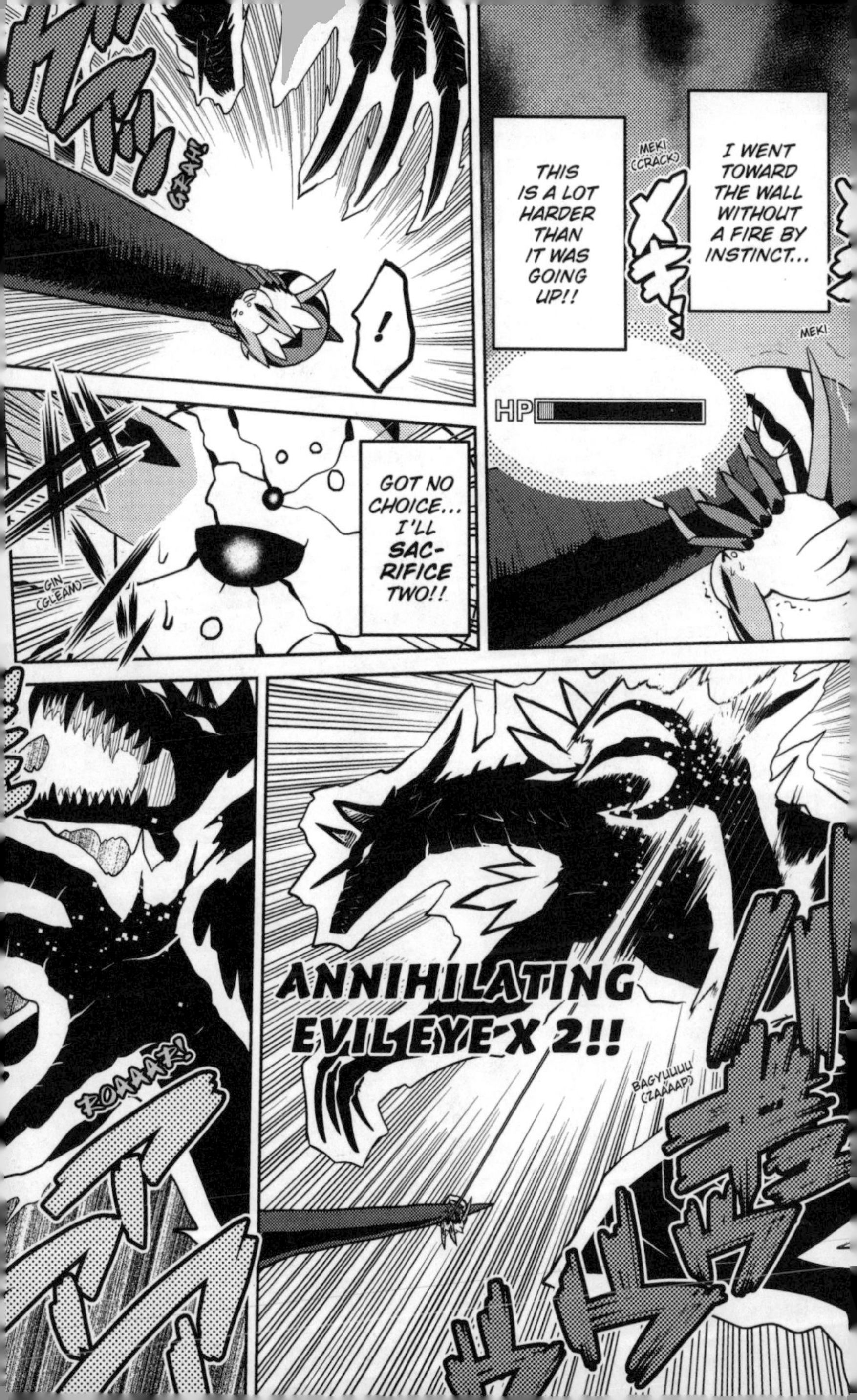
I WENT TOWARD THE WALL WITHOUT A FIRE BY INSTINCT...
MEKI (CRACK)
THIS IS A LOT HARDER THAN IT WAS GOING UP!!
MEKI
HP
!
GRAH!
GOT NO CHOICE... I'LL SACRIFICE TWO!!
GIN (GLEAM)
ANNIHILATING EVIL EYE X 2!!
BAGYUUUU (ZAAAAP)
ROAAAR!

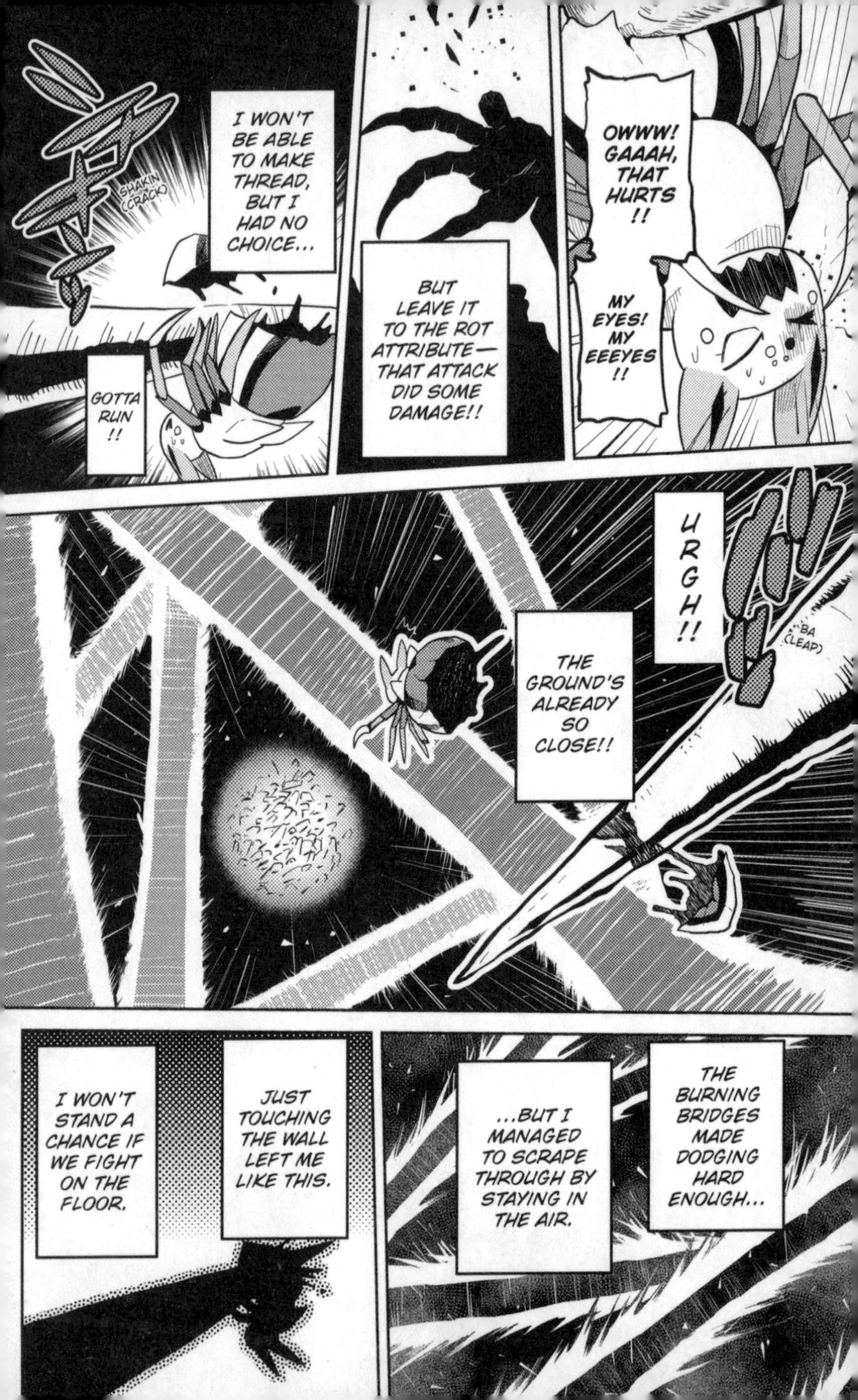
OWWW! GAAAH, THAT HURTS!!
MY EYES! MY EEEYES!!
BUT LEAVE IT TO THE ROT ATTRIBUTE— THAT ATTACK DID SOME DAMAGE!!
I WON'T BE ABLE TO MAKE THREAD, BUT I HAD NO CHOICE...
SHAKIN (CRACK)
GOTTA RUN!!
URGH!!
BA (LEAP)
THE GROUND'S ALREADY SO CLOSE!!
THE BURNING BRIDGES MADE DODGING HARD ENOUGH...
...BUT I MANAGED TO SCRAPE THROUGH BY STAYING IN THE AIR.
JUST TOUCHING THE WALL LEFT ME LIKE THIS.
I WON'T STAND A CHANCE IF WE FIGHT ON THE FLOOR.

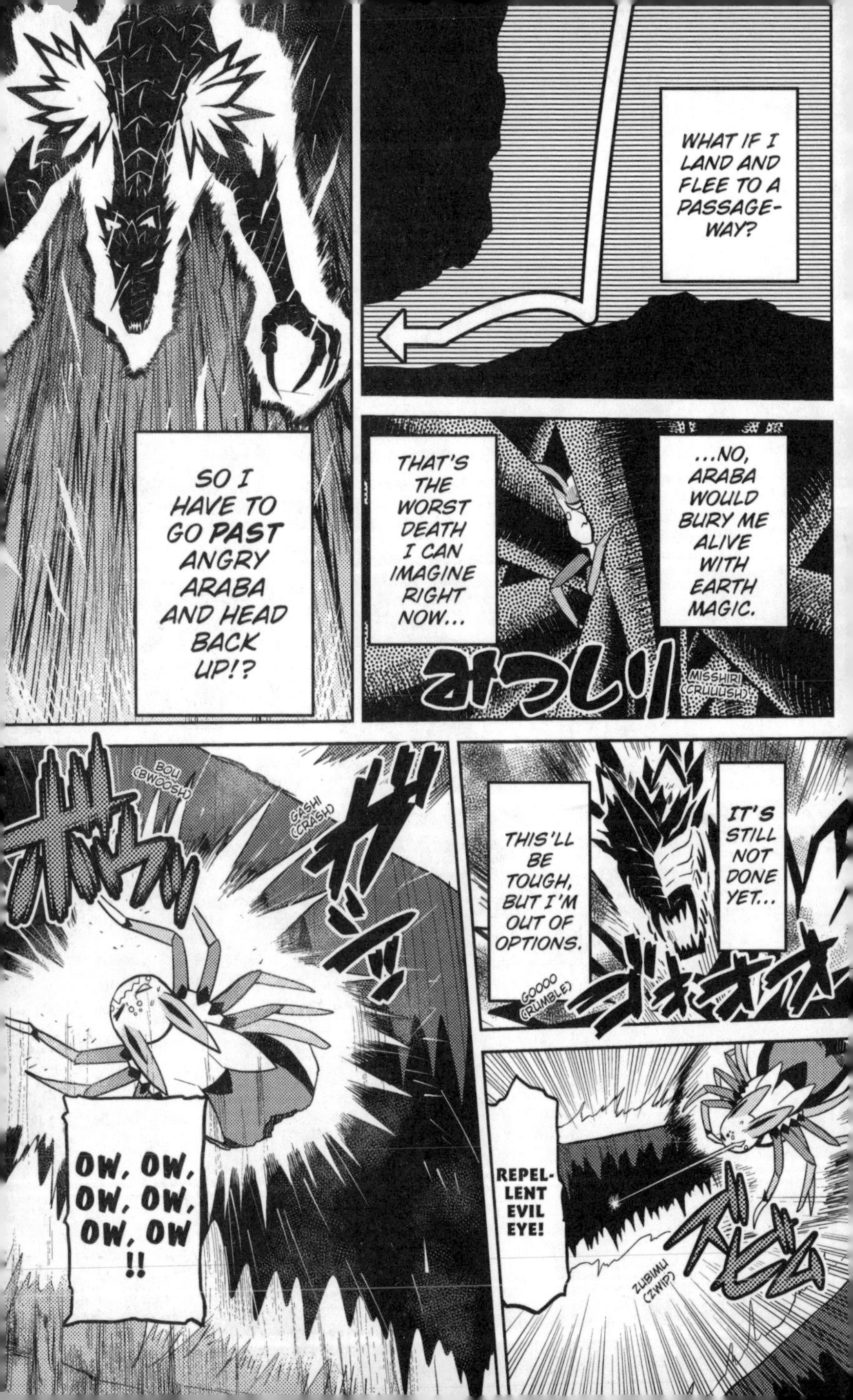
WHAT IF I LAND AND FLEE TO A PASSAGE-WAY?
...NO, ARABA WOULD BURY ME ALIVE WITH EARTH MAGIC.
THAT'S THE WORST DEATH I CAN IMAGINE RIGHT NOW...
MISSHIRI (CRUUUSH)
SO I HAVE TO GO **PAST** ANGRY ARABA AND HEAD BACK UP!?
IT'S STILL NOT DONE YET...
THIS'LL BE TOUGH, BUT I'M OUT OF OPTIONS.
GOOOO (RUMBLE)
ZUBIMU (ZWIP)
REPEL-LENT EVIL EYE!
GASHI (CRASH)
BOU (BWOOSH)
OW, OW, OW, OW, OW, OW !!

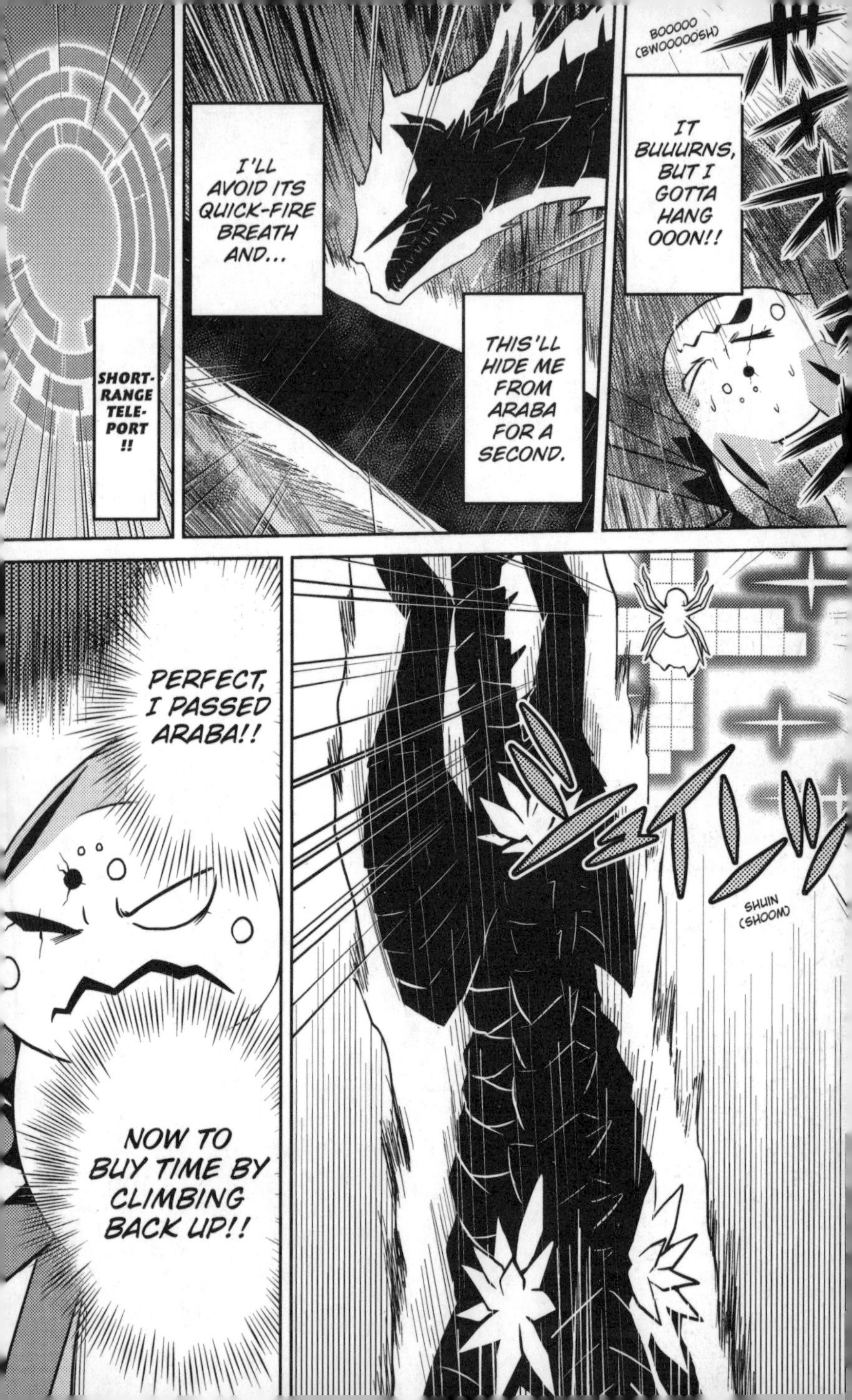
BOOOOO (BWOOOOOSH)
IT BUUURNS, BUT I GOTTA HANG OOON!!
THIS'LL HIDE ME FROM ARABA FOR A SECOND.
I'LL AVOID ITS QUICK-FIRE BREATH AND...
SHORT-RANGE TELE-PORT!!
SHUIN (SHOOM)
PERFECT, I PASSED ARABA!!
NOW TO BUY TIME BY CLIMBING BACK UP!!

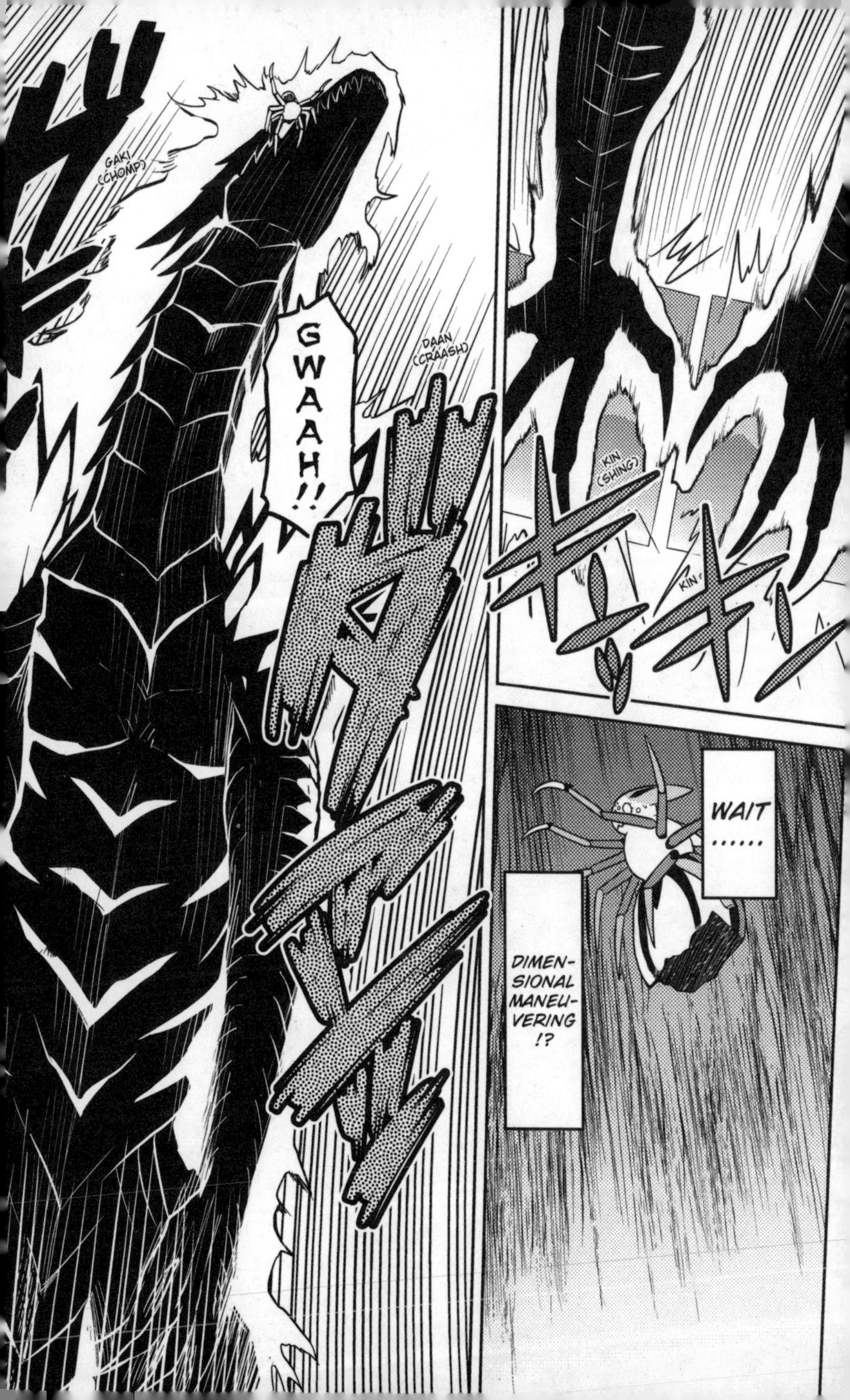
KIN (SHING)
KIN
WAIT ......
DIMEN-SIONAL MANEU-VERING !?
GAKI (CHOMP)
GWAAH!!
DAAN (CRAASH)

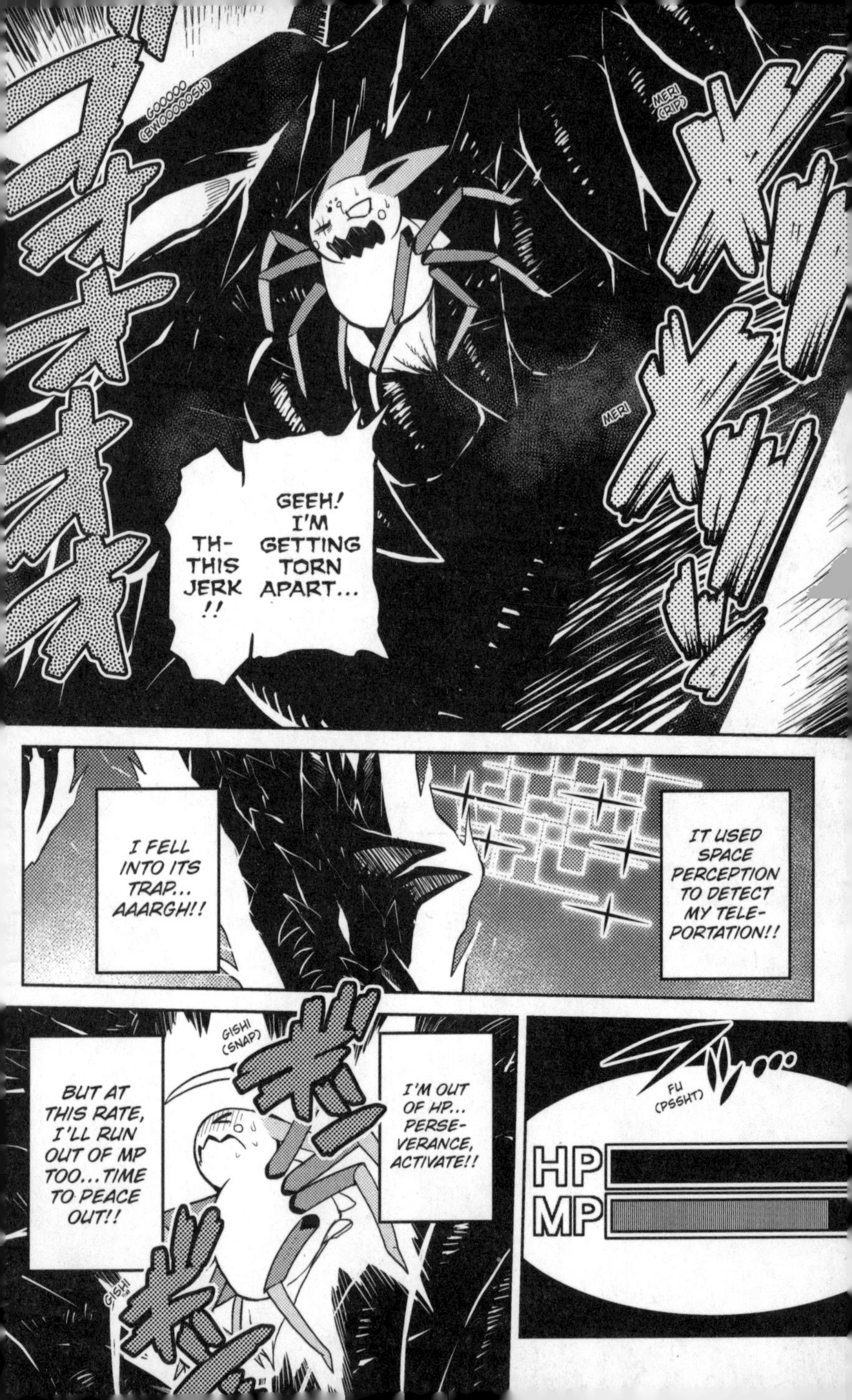
MERI (RIP)
GOOOOO (BWOOOOOSH)
MERI
GEEH! I'M GETTING TORN APART...
TH-THIS JERK!!
IT USED SPACE PERCEPTION TO DETECT MY TELEPORTATION!!
I FELL INTO ITS TRAP... AAARGH!!
FU (PSSHT)
HP
MP
GISHI (SNAP)
I'M OUT OF HP... PERSEVERANCE, ACTIVATE!!
BUT AT THIS RATE, I'LL RUN OUT OF MP TOO...TIME TO PEACE OUT!!
GISHI

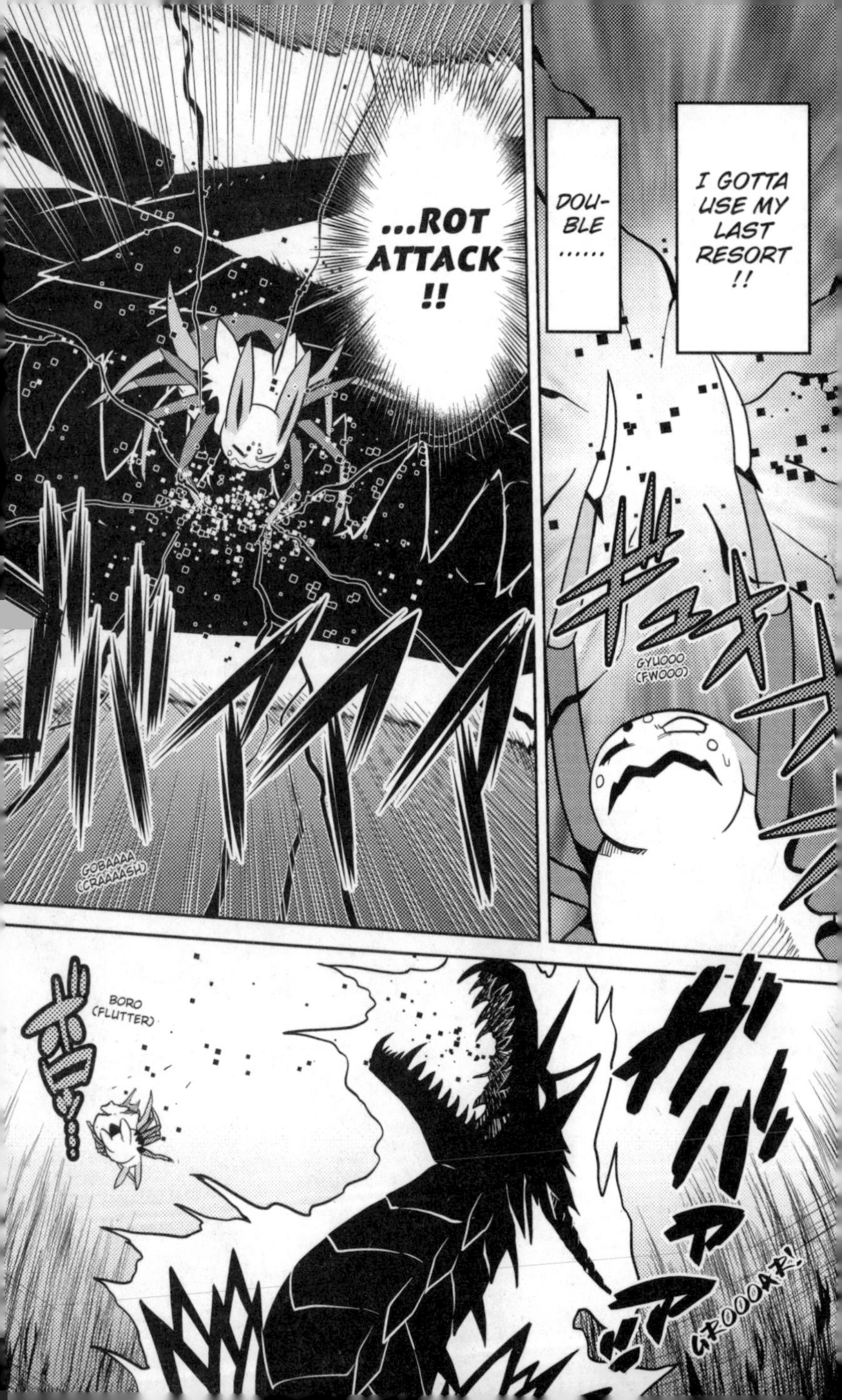
I GOTTA USE MY LAST RESORT !!
DOU-BLE ......
GYUOOO (FWOOO)
...ROT ATTACK !!
GOBAAAA (CRAAAASH)
GROOOAR!
BORO (FLUTTER)

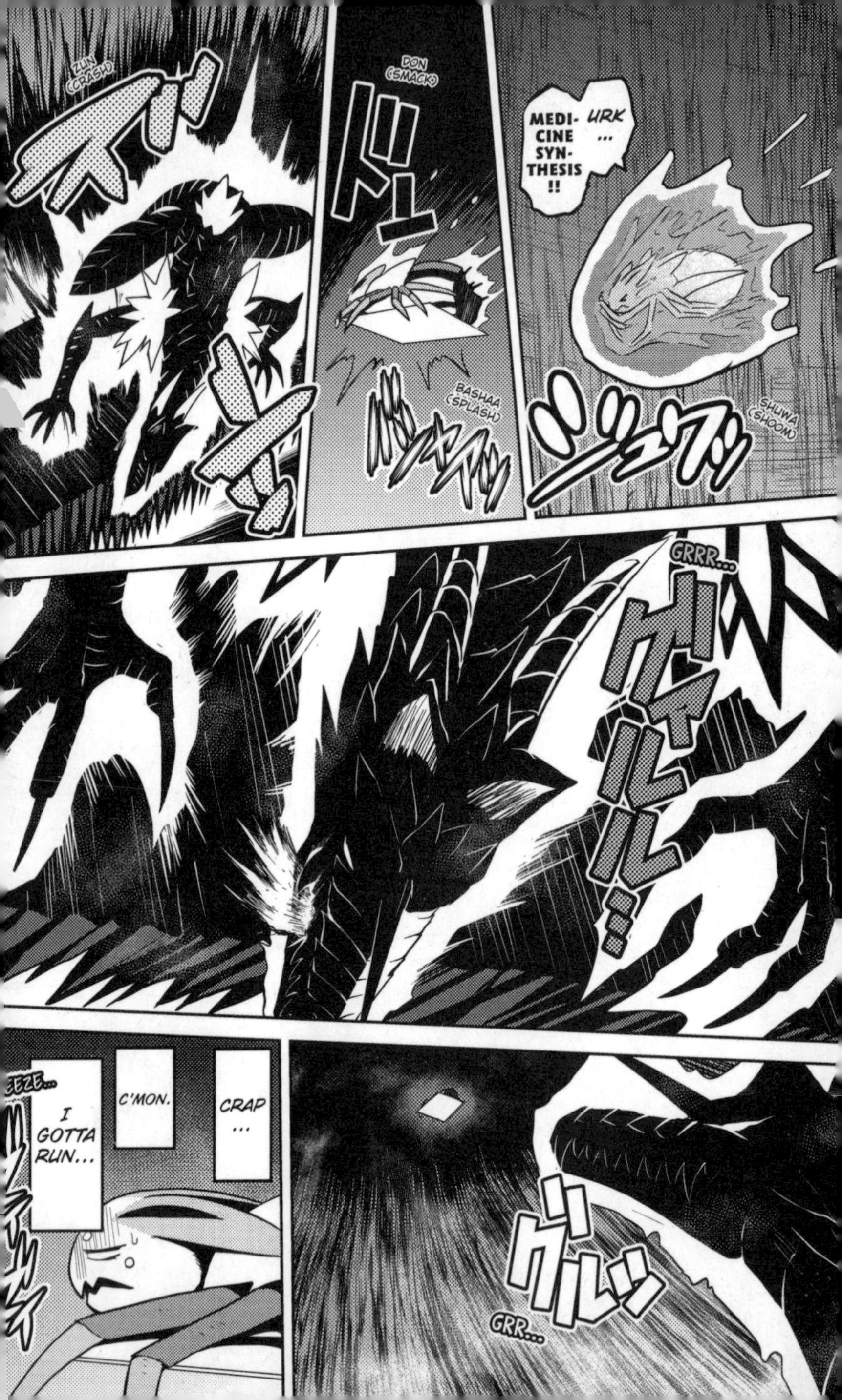
URK ...
MEDICINE SYNTHESIS!!
SHUWA (SHOOM)
DON (SMACK)
BASHAA (SPLASH)
ZUN (CRASH)
GRRR...
GRR...
CRAP ...
C'MON.
I GOTTA RUN...
EEZE...

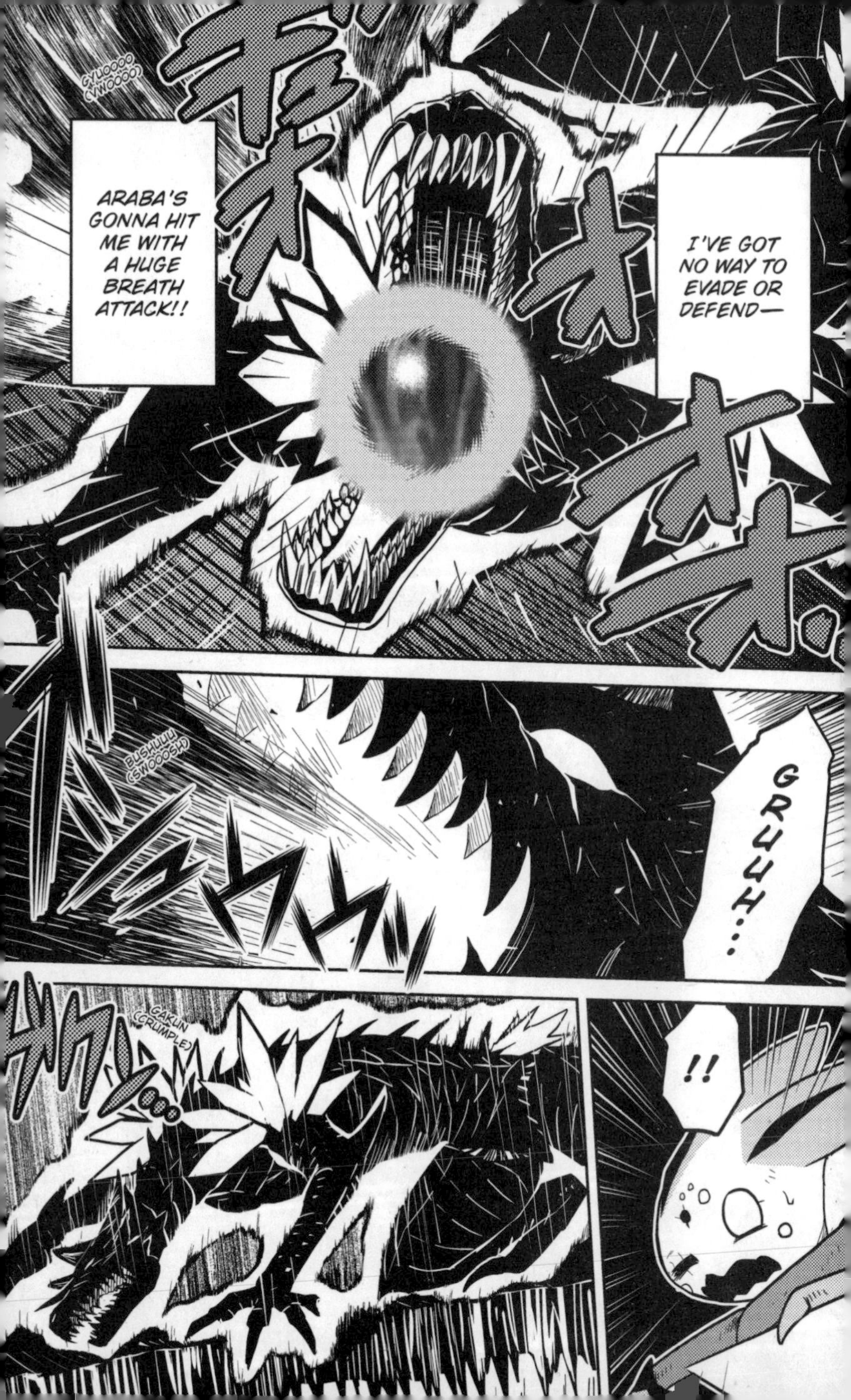
GYUOOOO (VWOOOO)
I'VE GOT NO WAY TO EVADE OR DEFEND—
ARABA'S GONNA HIT ME WITH A HUGE BREATH ATTACK!!
GRUUH...
BUSHUUU (SWOOOSH)
!!
GAKUN (CRUMPLE)

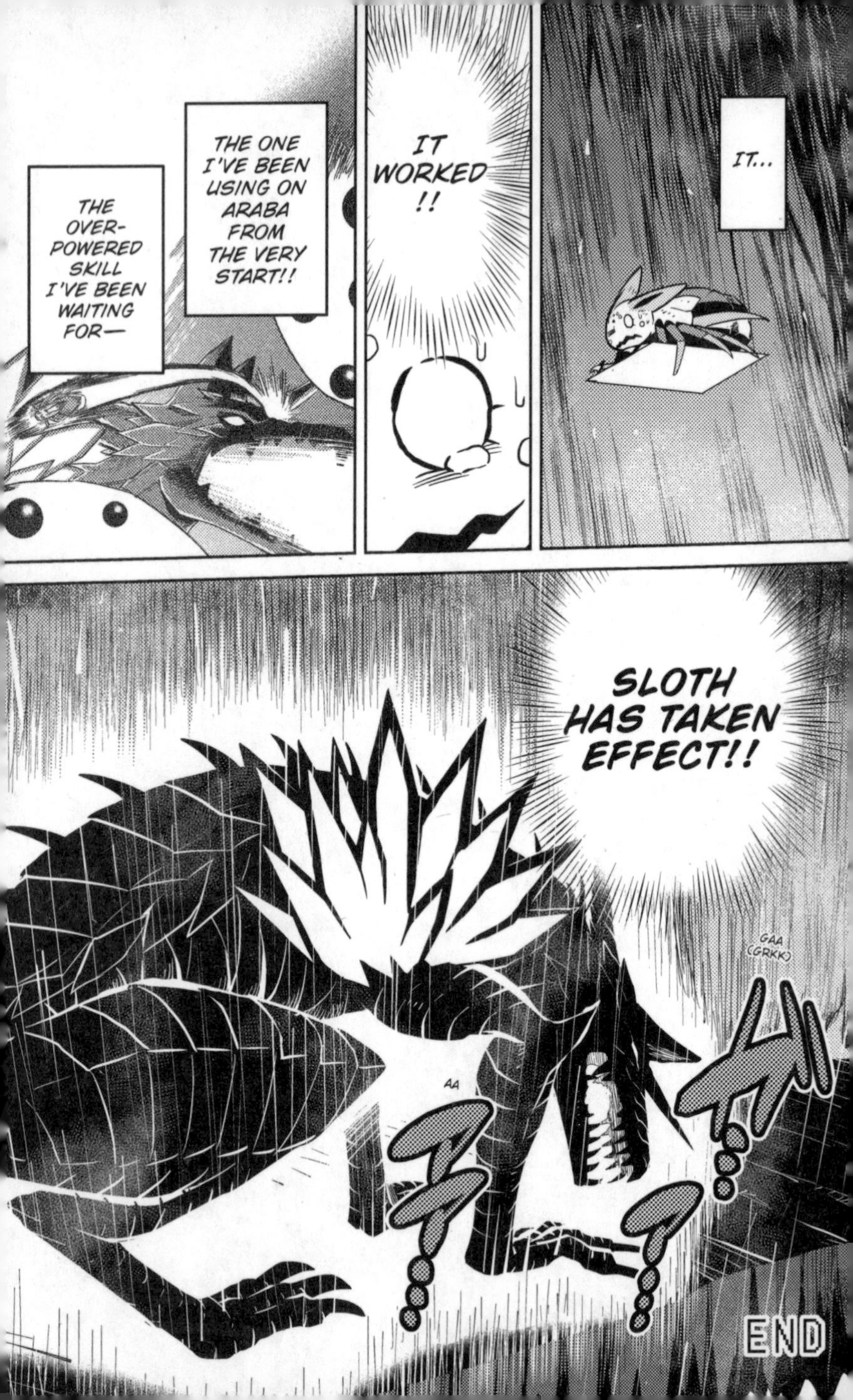
IT...
IT WORKED!!
THE ONE I'VE BEEN USING ON ARABA FROM THE VERY START!!
THE OVER-POWERED SKILL I'VE BEEN WAITING FOR—
SLOTH HAS TAKEN EFFECT!!
GAA (GRKK)
AA
END

So I'm a Spider, So What?

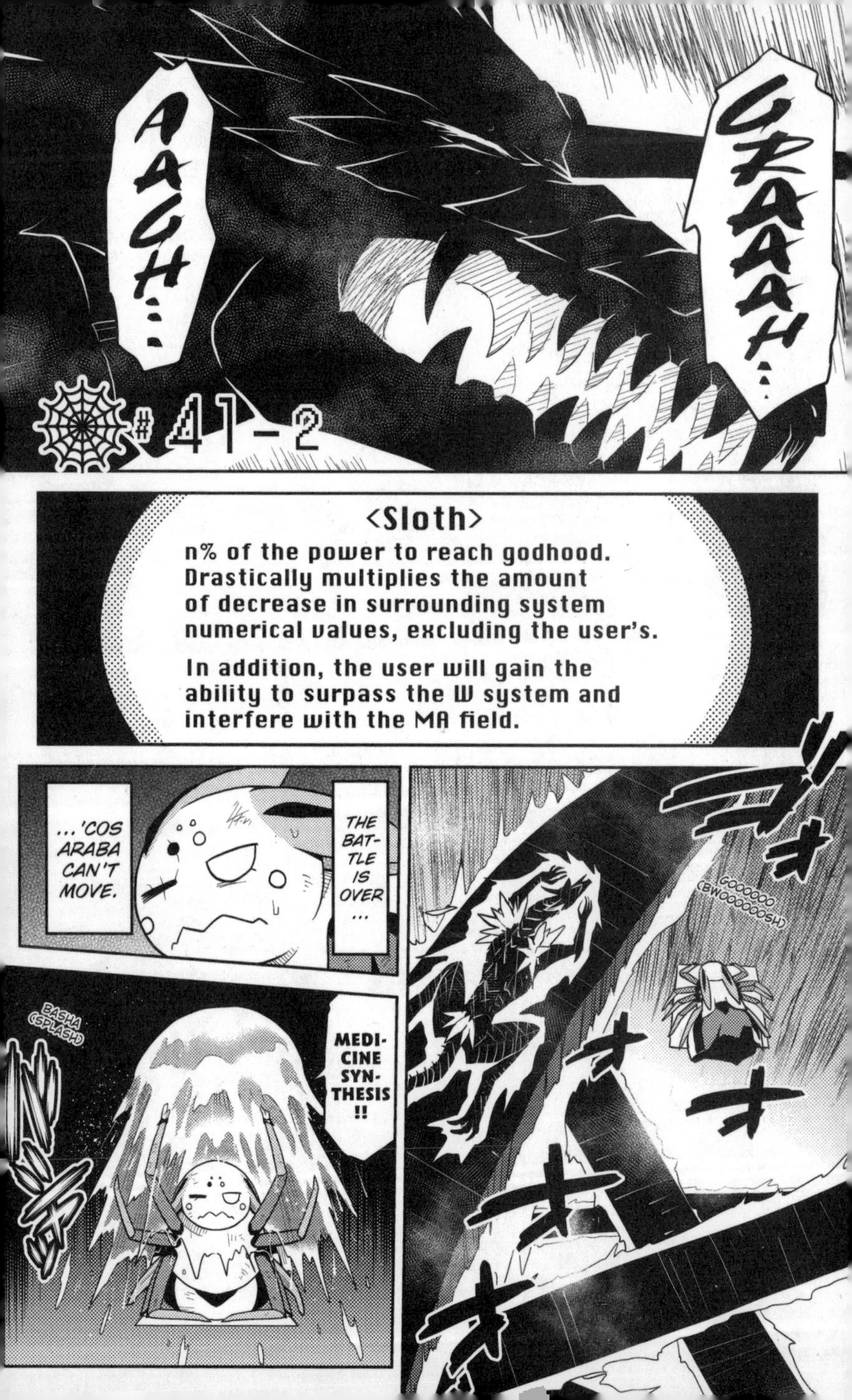
GRAAAAH...
AAGH...
#41-2
<Sloth>
n% of the power to reach godhood. Drastically multiplies the amount of decrease in surrounding system numerical values, excluding the user's.
In addition, the user will gain the ability to surpass the W system and interfere with the MA field.
GOOOOOO (BWOOOOOSH)
THE BATTLE IS OVER...
...'COS ARABA CAN'T MOVE.
MEDICINE SYNTHESIS!!
BASHA (SPLASH)

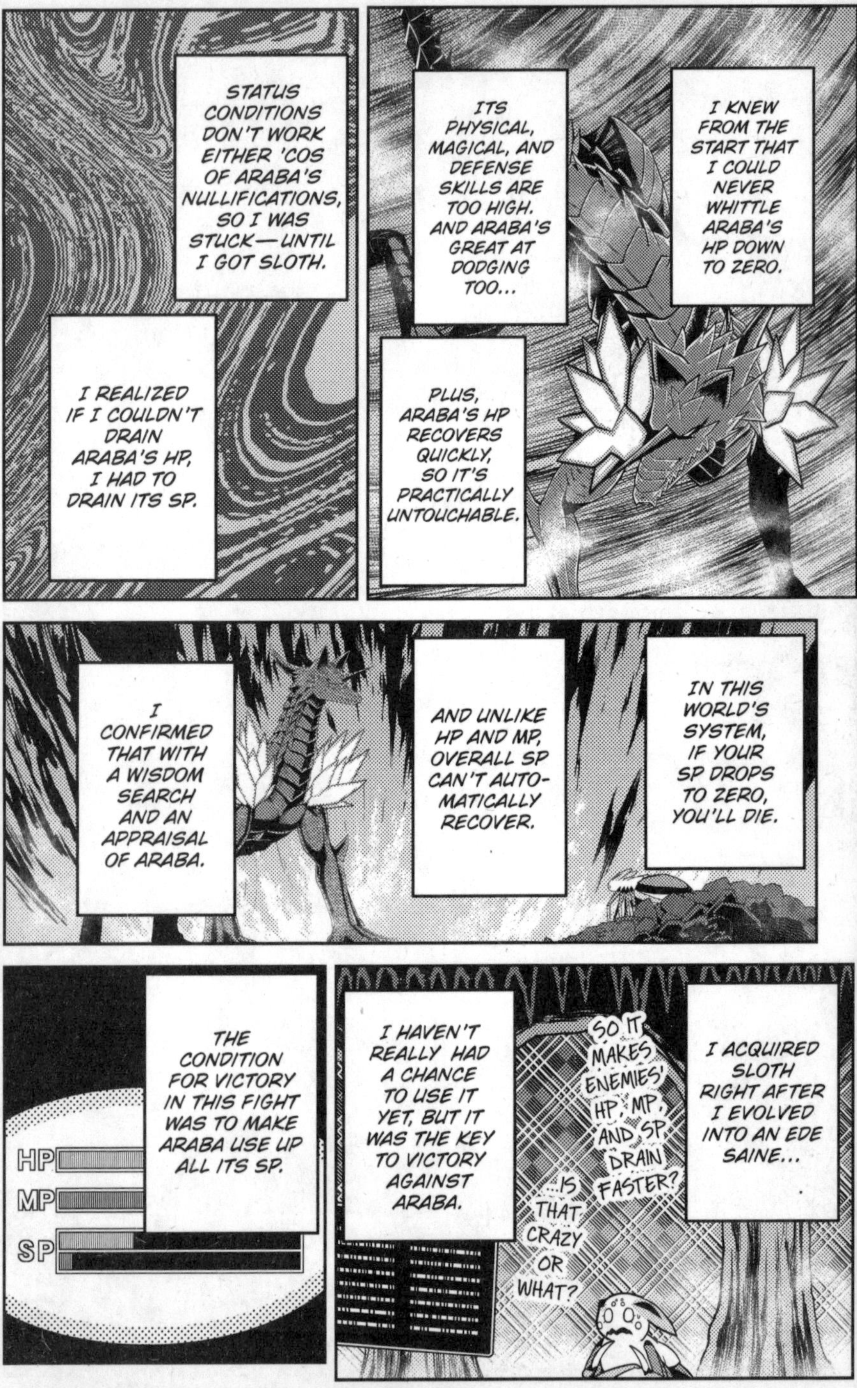
I KNEW FROM THE START THAT I COULD NEVER WHITTLE ARABA'S HP DOWN TO ZERO.
ITS PHYSICAL, MAGICAL, AND DEFENSE SKILLS ARE TOO HIGH. AND ARABA'S GREAT AT DODGING TOO…
PLUS, ARABA'S HP RECOVERS QUICKLY, SO IT'S PRACTICALLY UNTOUCHABLE.
STATUS CONDITIONS DON'T WORK EITHER 'COS OF ARABA'S NULLIFICATIONS, SO I WAS STUCK—UNTIL I GOT SLOTH.
I REALIZED IF I COULDN'T DRAIN ARABA'S HP, I HAD TO DRAIN ITS SP.
IN THIS WORLD'S SYSTEM, IF YOUR SP DROPS TO ZERO, YOU'LL DIE.
AND UNLIKE HP AND MP, OVERALL SP CAN'T AUTO-MATICALLY RECOVER.
I CONFIRMED THAT WITH A WISDOM SEARCH AND AN APPRAISAL OF ARABA.
I ACQUIRED SLOTH RIGHT AFTER I EVOLVED INTO AN EDE SAINE…
SO IT MAKES ENEMIES' HP, MP, AND SP DRAIN FASTER?
…IS THAT CRAZY OR WHAT?
I HAVEN'T REALLY HAD A CHANCE TO USE IT YET, BUT IT WAS THE KEY TO VICTORY AGAINST ARABA.
THE CONDITION FOR VICTORY IN THIS FIGHT WAS TO MAKE ARABA USE UP ALL ITS SP.
HP
MP
SP

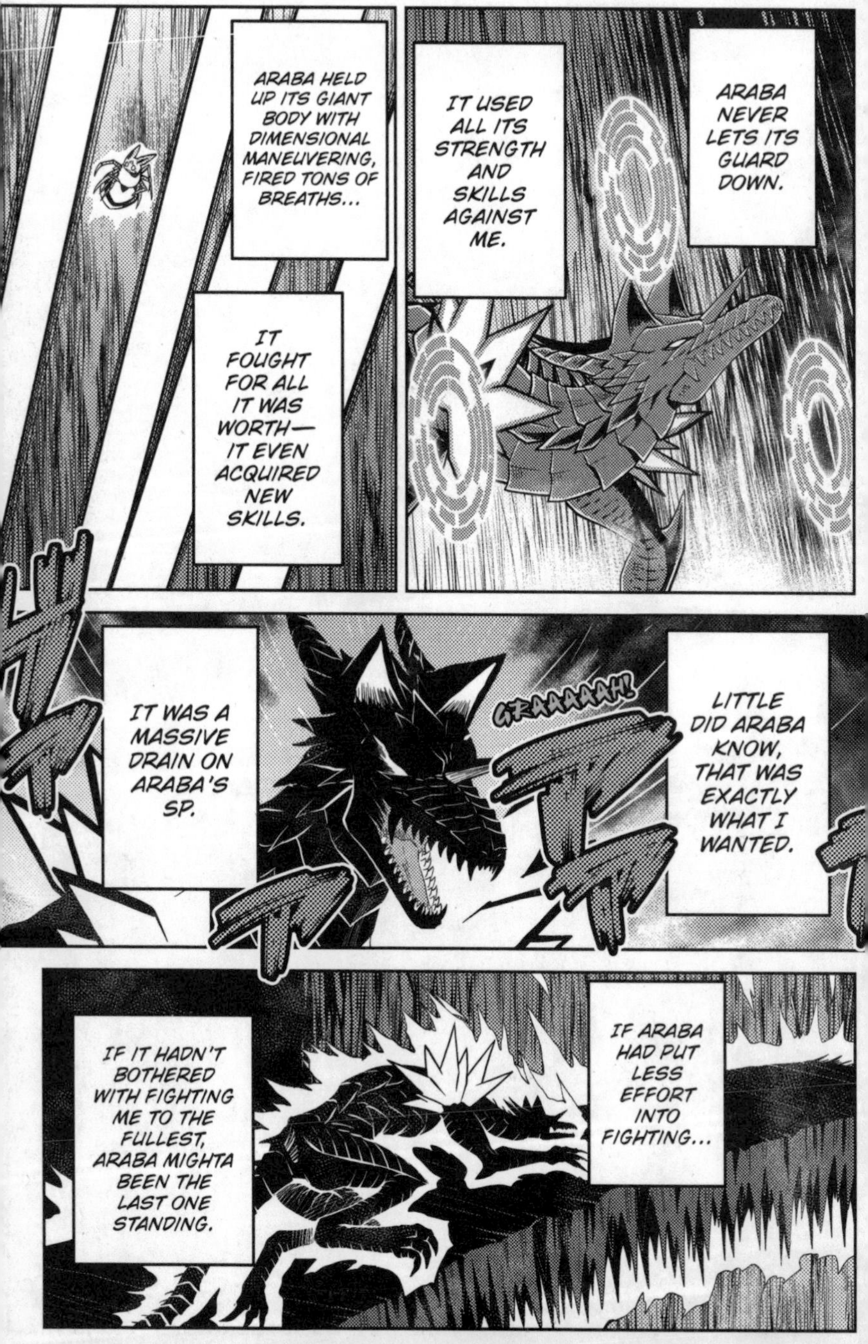
ARABA NEVER LETS ITS GUARD DOWN.
IT USED ALL ITS STRENGTH AND SKILLS AGAINST ME.
ARABA HELD UP ITS GIANT BODY WITH DIMENSIONAL MANEUVERING, FIRED TONS OF BREATHS...
IT FOUGHT FOR ALL IT WAS WORTH— IT EVEN ACQUIRED NEW SKILLS.
LITTLE DID ARABA KNOW, THAT WAS EXACTLY WHAT I WANTED.
GRAAAAAH!
IT WAS A MASSIVE DRAIN ON ARABA'S SP.
IF ARABA HAD PUT LESS EFFORT INTO FIGHTING...
IF IT HADN'T BOTHERED WITH FIGHTING ME TO THE FULLEST, ARABA MIGHTA BEEN THE LAST ONE STANDING.

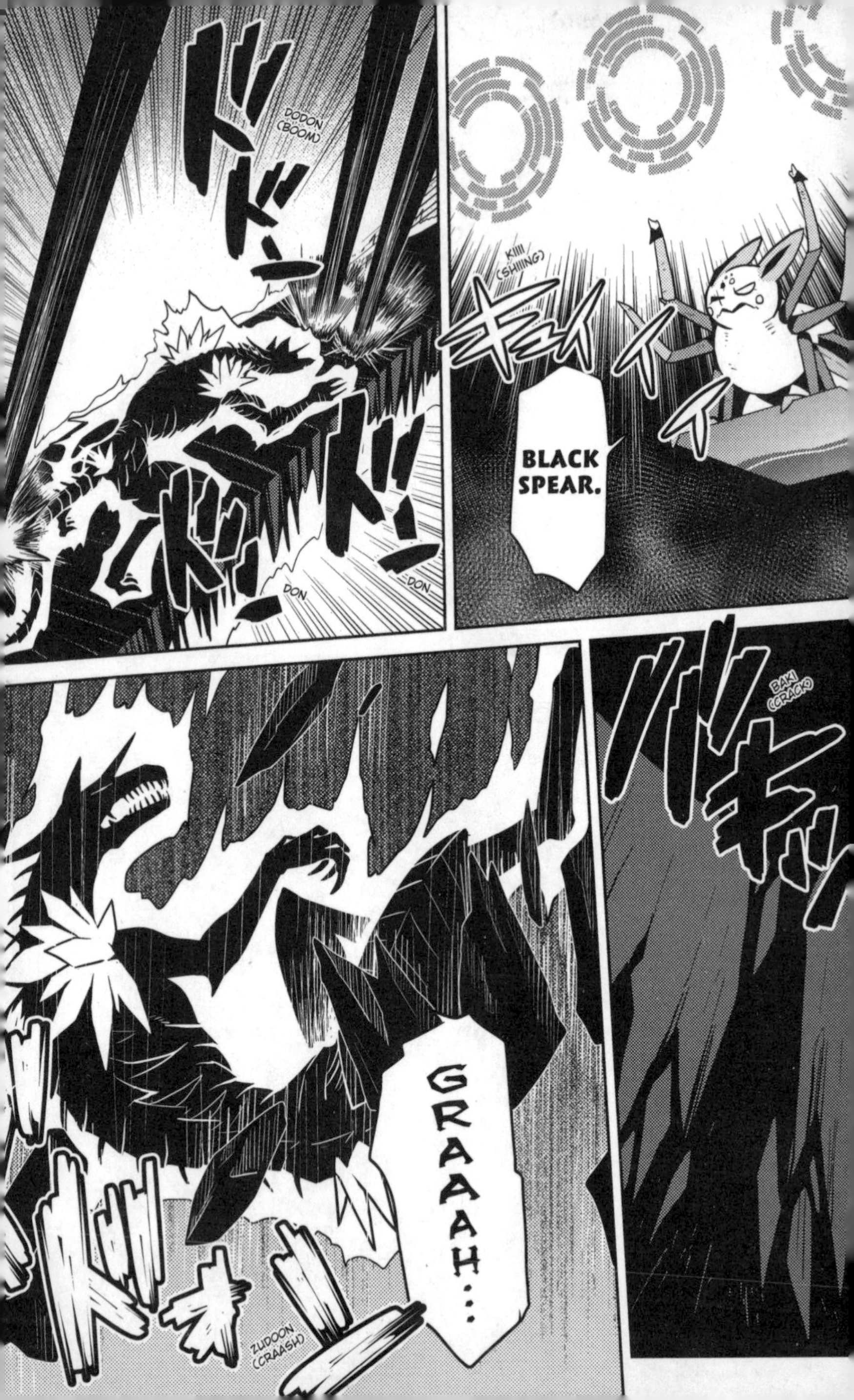
KIIII (SHIIING)
BLACK SPEAR.
DODON (BOOM)
DON
DON
BAKI (CRACK)
GRAAAH...
ZUDOON (CRAASH)

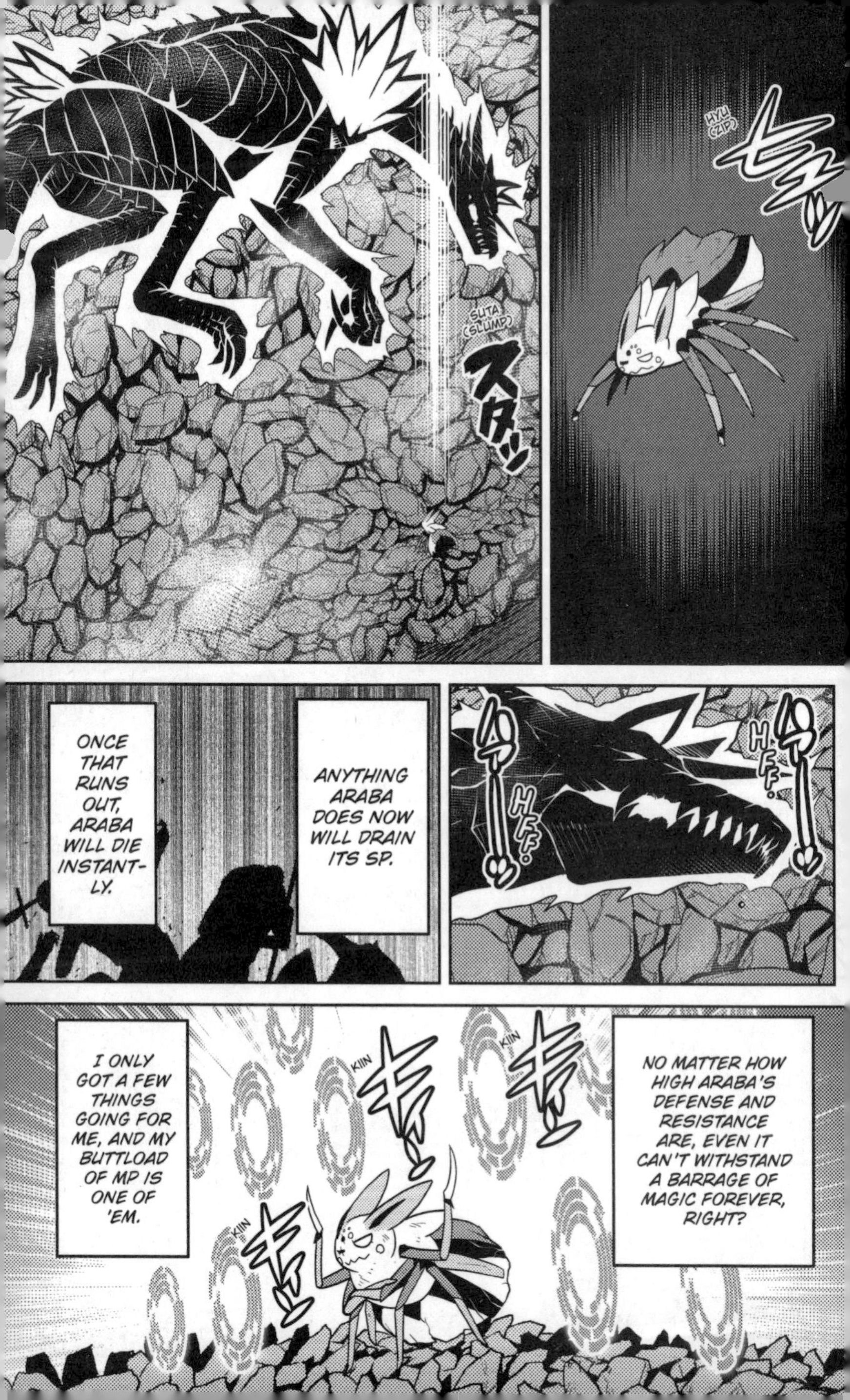
HYU (ZIP)
SUTA (SLUMP)
HFF.
HFF.
ANYTHING ARABA DOES NOW WILL DRAIN ITS SP.
ONCE THAT RUNS OUT, ARABA WILL DIE INSTANT-LY.
NO MATTER HOW HIGH ARABA'S DEFENSE AND RESISTANCE ARE, EVEN IT CAN'T WITHSTAND A BARRAGE OF MAGIC FOREVER, RIGHT?
KIIN
KIIN
KIIN
I ONLY GOT A FEW THINGS GOING FOR ME, AND MY BUTTLOAD OF MP IS ONE OF 'EM.

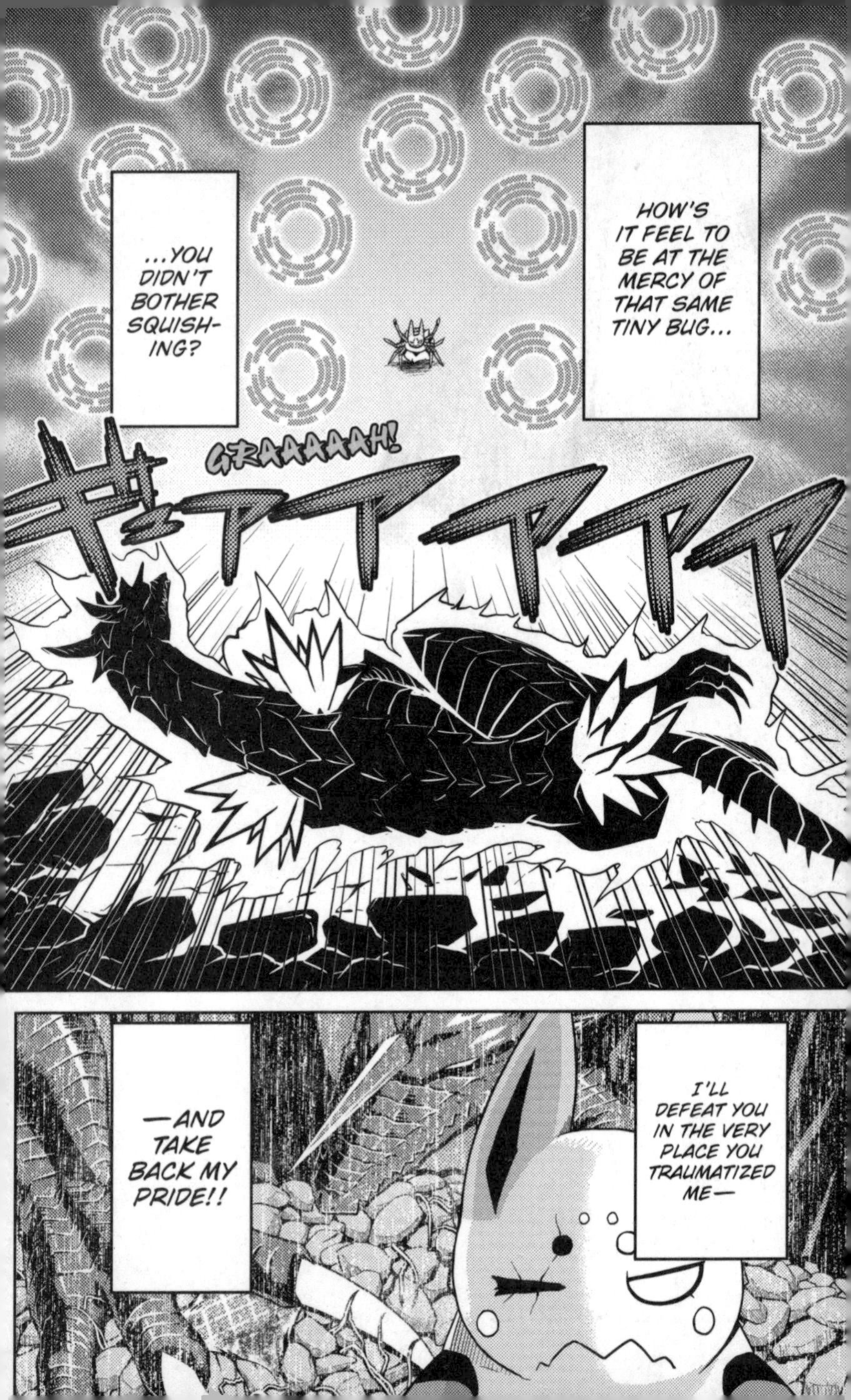
HOW'S IT FEEL TO BE AT THE MERCY OF THAT SAME TINY BUG...
...YOU DIDN'T BOTHER SQUISH-ING?
GRAAAAAAH!
I'LL DEFEAT YOU IN THE VERY PLACE YOU TRAUMATIZED ME—
—AND TAKE BACK MY PRIDE!!

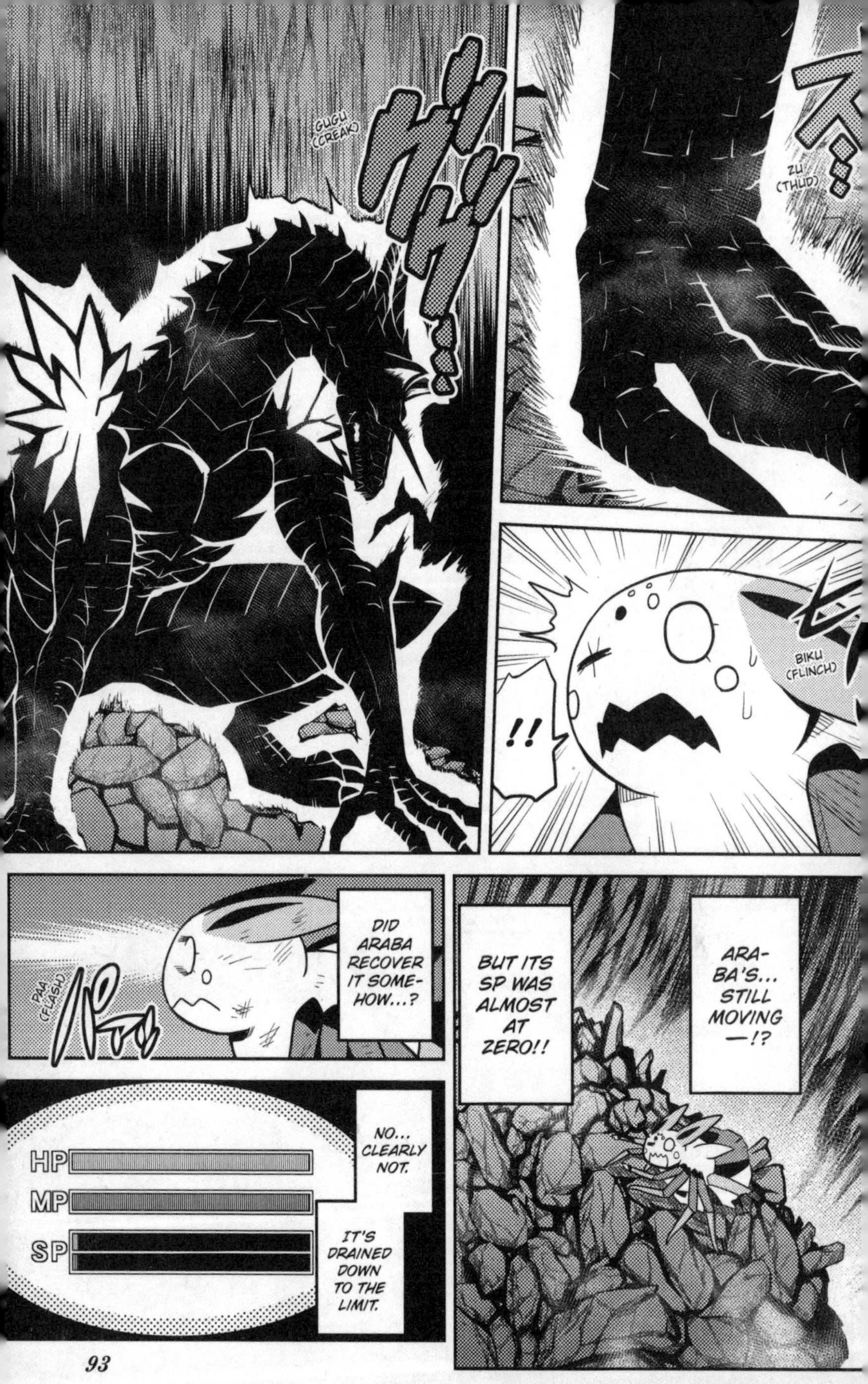
ZU (THUD)
BIKU (FLINCH)
!!
GUGU (CREAK)
ARA-BA'S... STILL MOVING—!?
BUT ITS SP WAS ALMOST AT ZERO!!
DID ARABA RECOVER IT SOMEHOW...?
PAA (FLASH)
HP
MP
SP
NO... CLEARLY NOT.
IT'S DRAINED DOWN TO THE LIMIT.

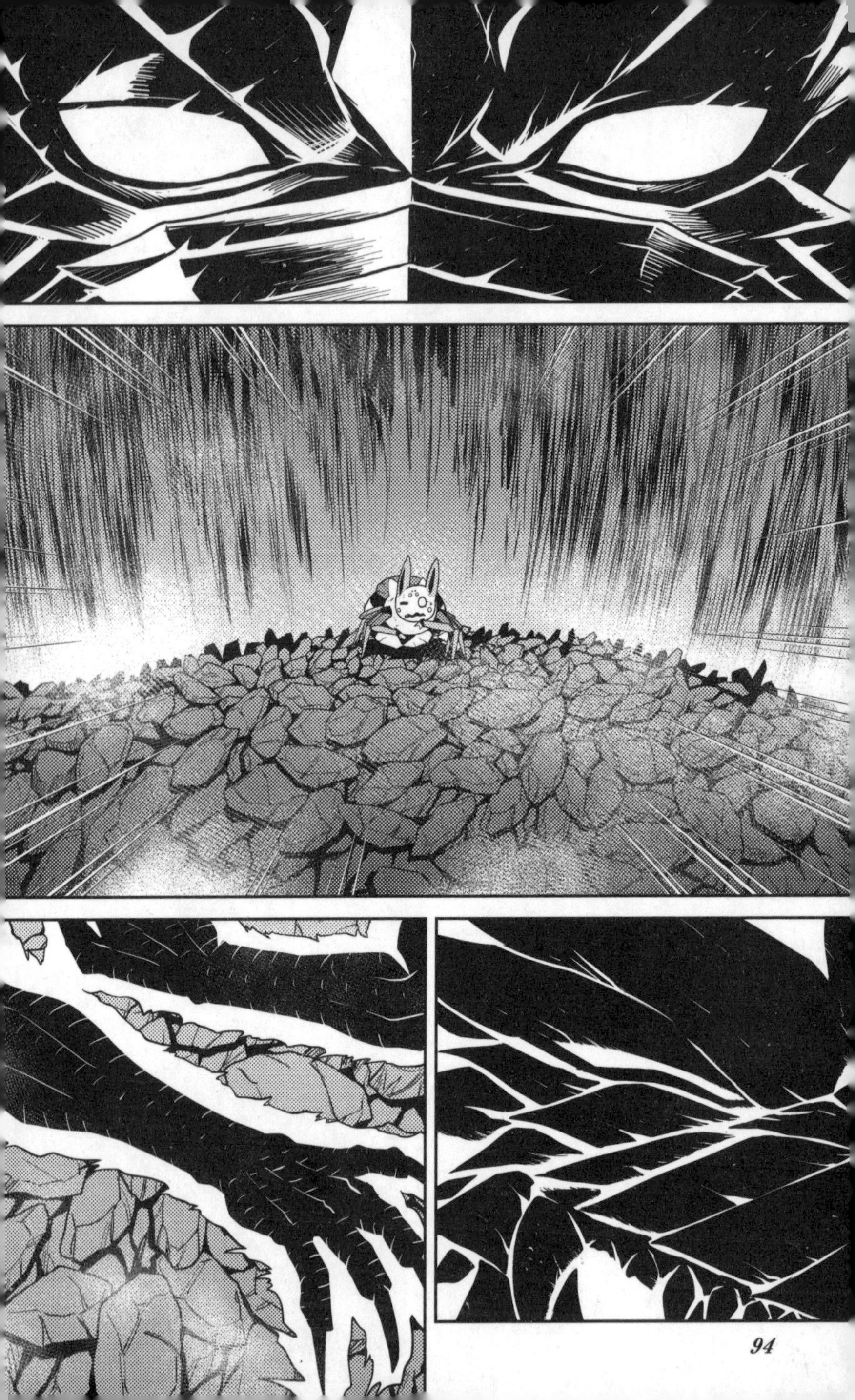

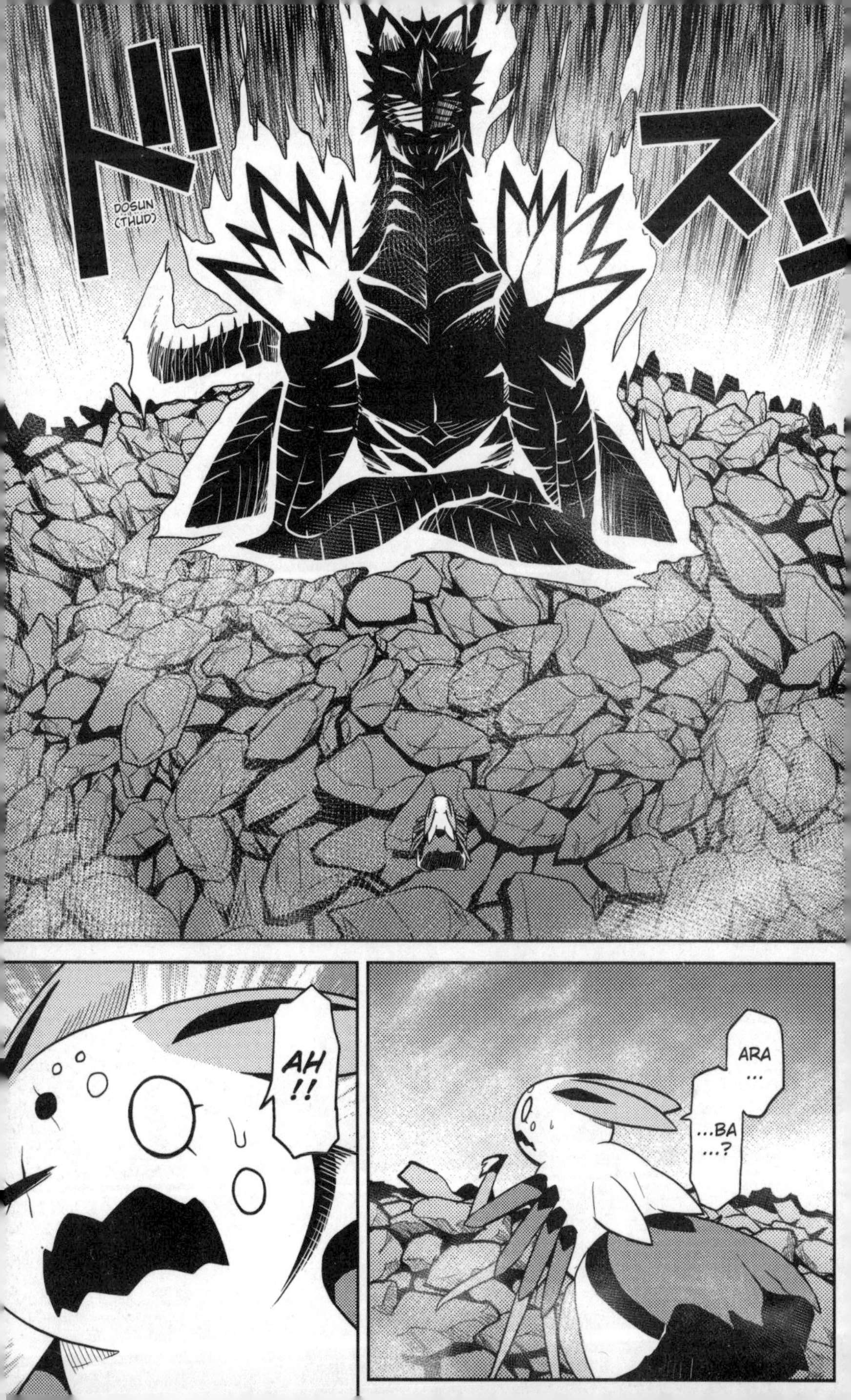
ドスン
DOSUN (THUD)
ARA ... ...BA ...?
AH !!

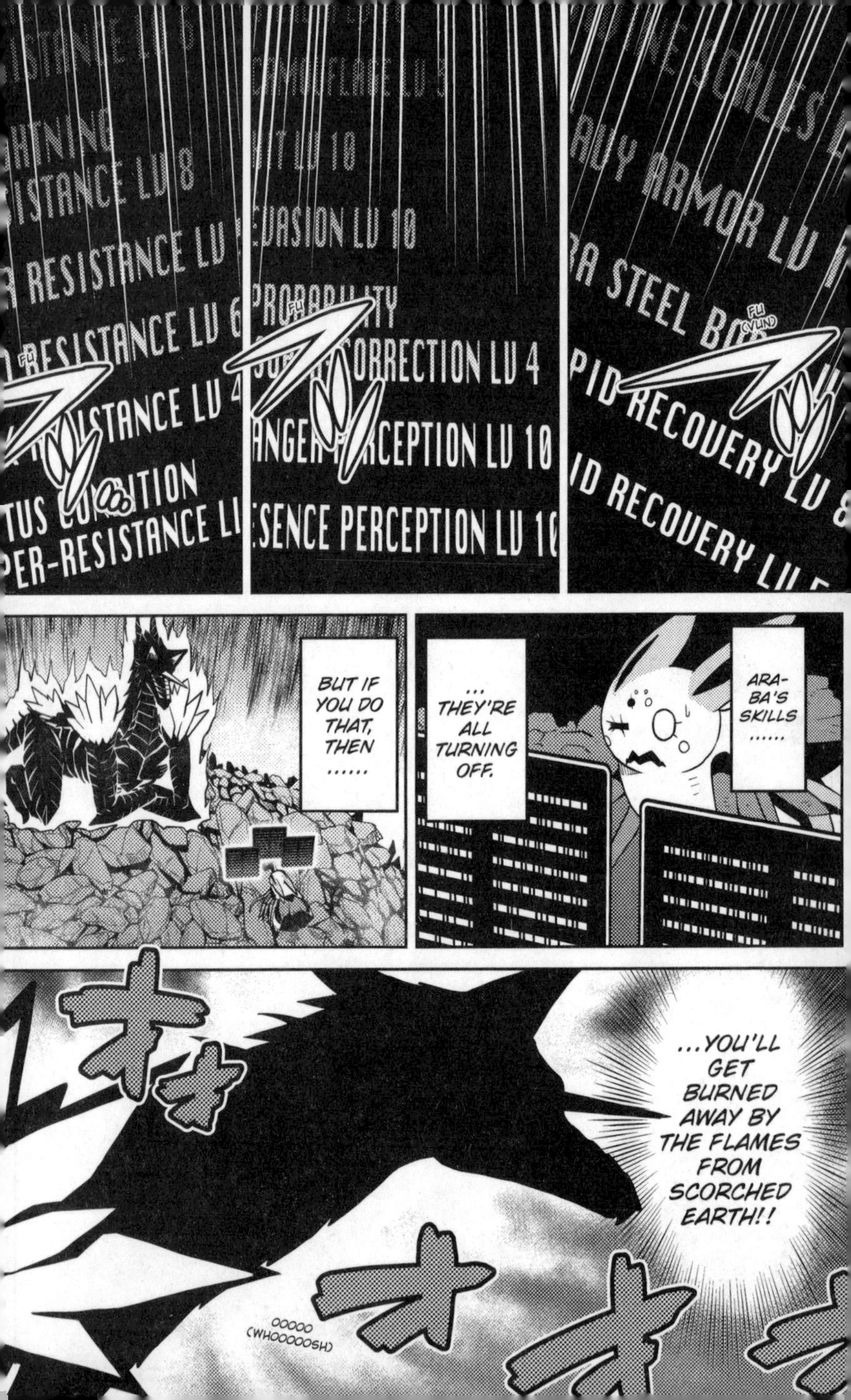
FU (VUN)
FU
FU
ARA-BA'S SKILLS......
...THEY'RE ALL TURNING OFF.
BUT IF YOU DO THAT, THEN ......
...YOU'LL GET BURNED AWAY BY THE FLAMES FROM SCORCHED EARTH!!
OOOOO (WHOOOOOSH)

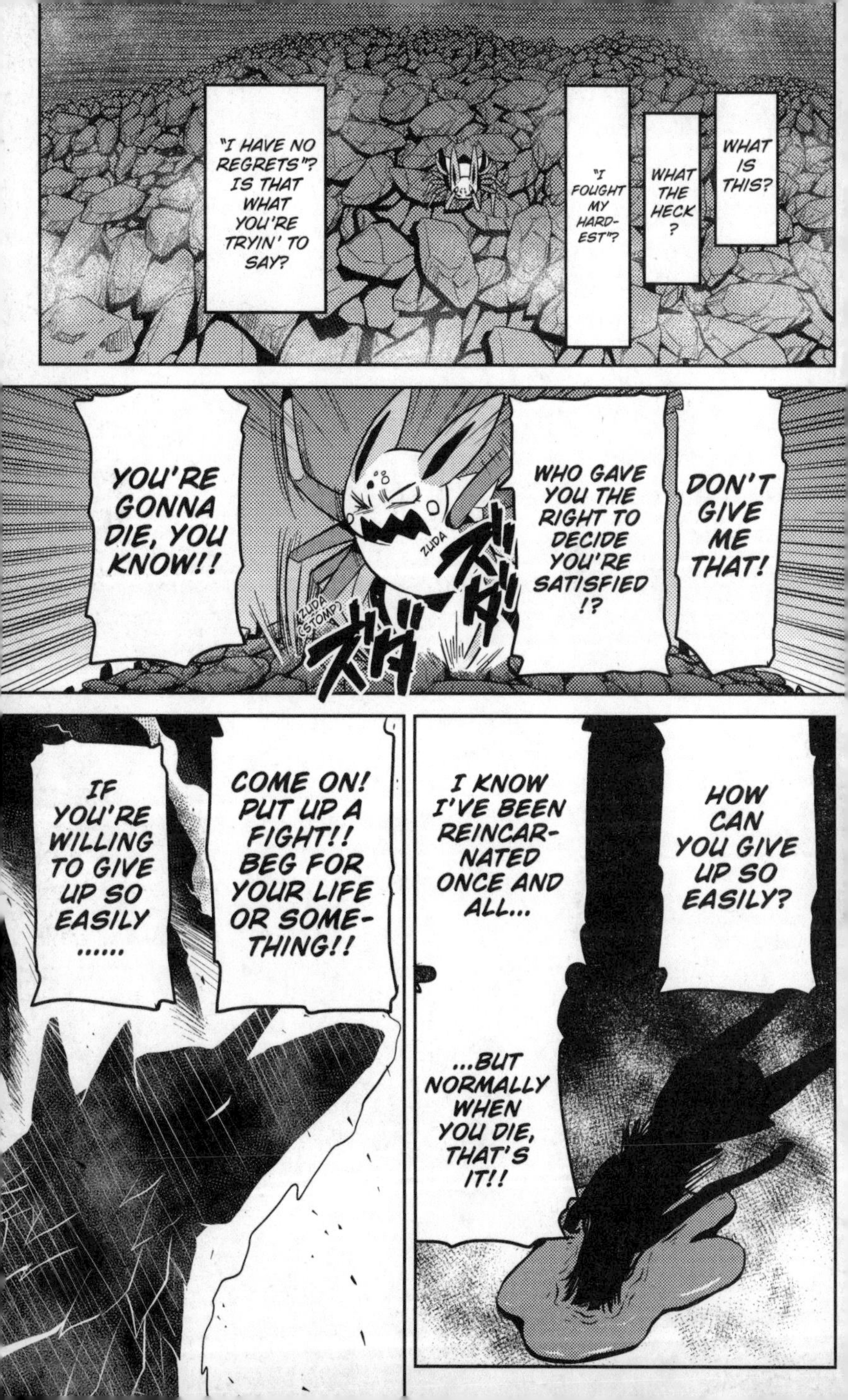
WHAT IS THIS?
WHAT THE HECK?
"I FOUGHT MY HARD-EST"?
"I HAVE NO REGRETS"? IS THAT WHAT YOU'RE TRYIN' TO SAY?
DON'T GIVE ME THAT!
WHO GAVE YOU THE RIGHT TO DECIDE YOU'RE SATISFIED!?
ZUDA
YOU'RE GONNA DIE, YOU KNOW!!
ZUDA (STOMP)
HOW CAN YOU GIVE UP SO EASILY?
I KNOW I'VE BEEN REINCAR-NATED ONCE AND ALL...
...BUT NORMALLY WHEN YOU DIE, THAT'S IT!!
COME ON! PUT UP A FIGHT!! BEG FOR YOUR LIFE OR SOME-THING!!
IF YOU'RE WILLING TO GIVE UP SO EASILY......

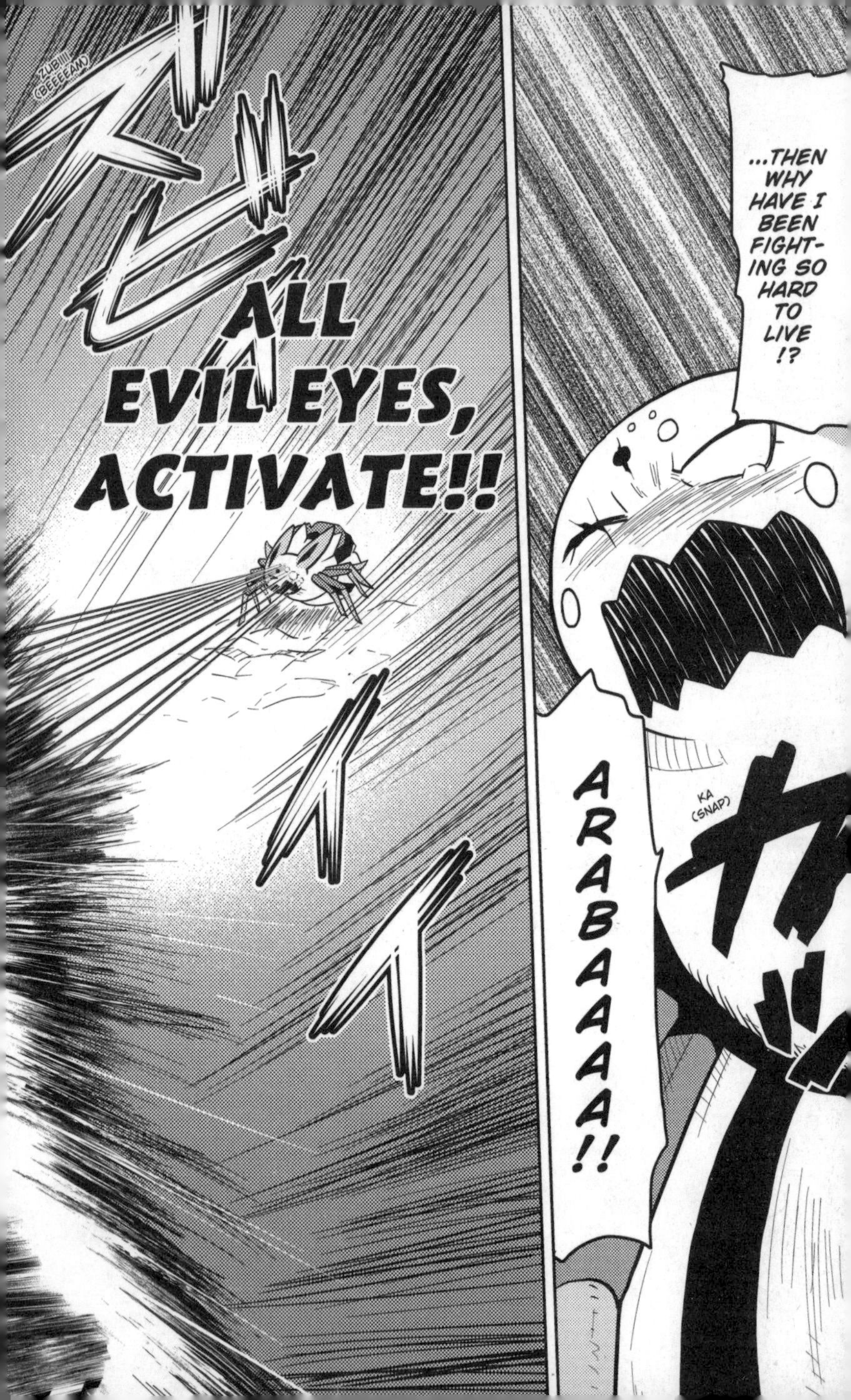
...THEN WHY HAVE I BEEN FIGHTING SO HARD TO LIVE!?
ARABAAAAAA!!
KA (SNAP)
ZUBIIIII (BEEEEEAM)
ALL EVIL EYES, ACTIVATE!!

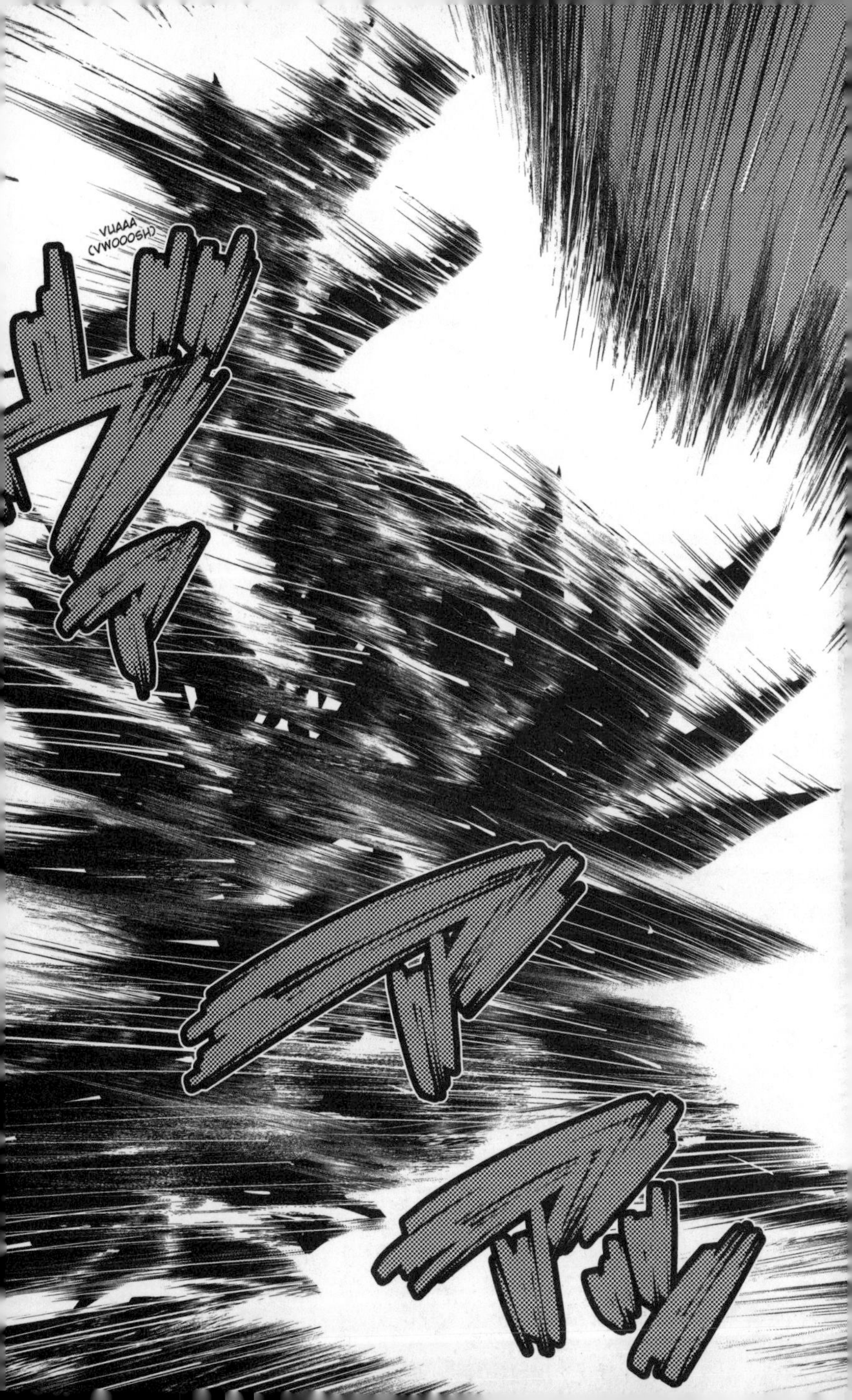
VUAAA
(VWOOOSH)

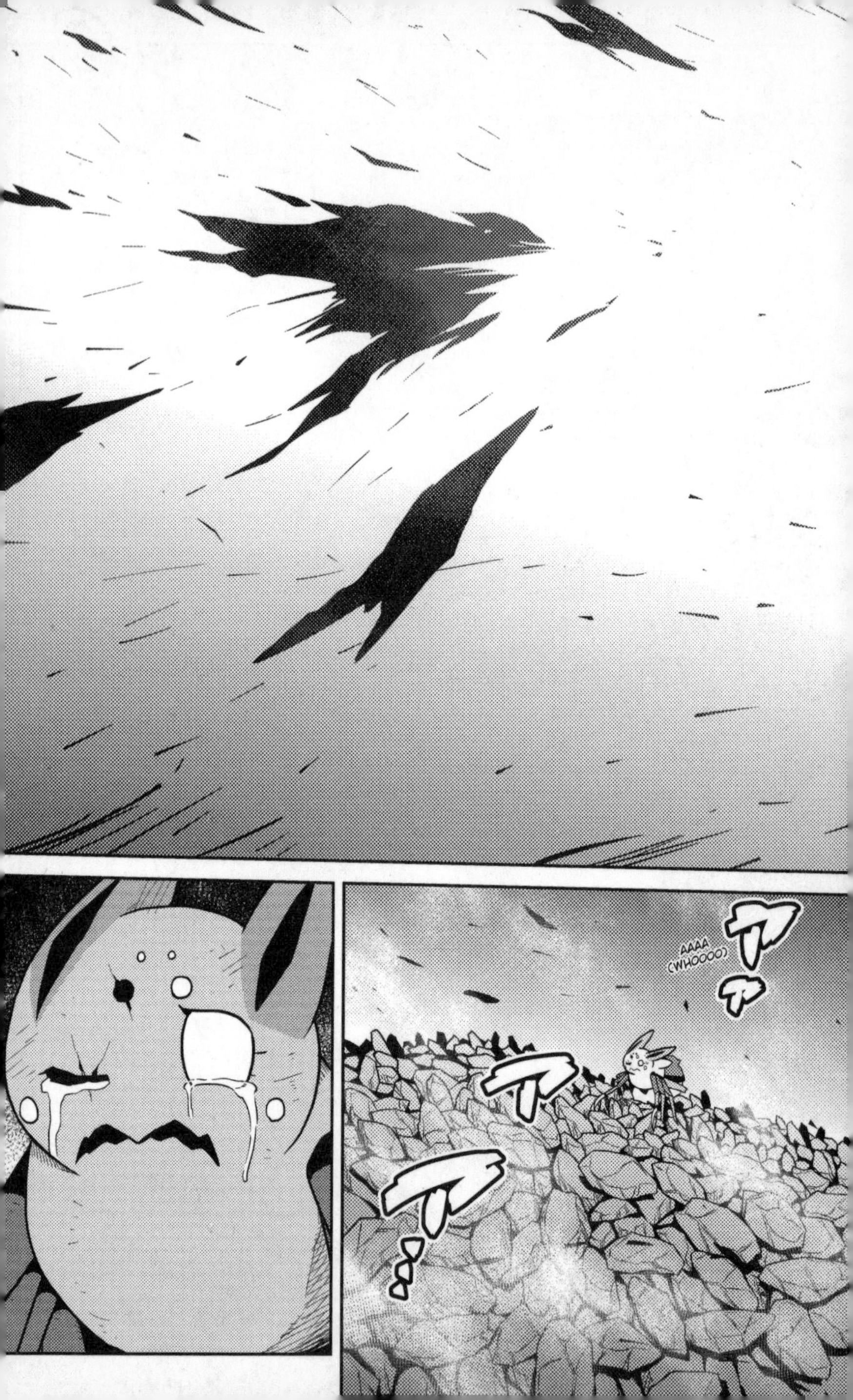
AAAA
(WHOOOO)

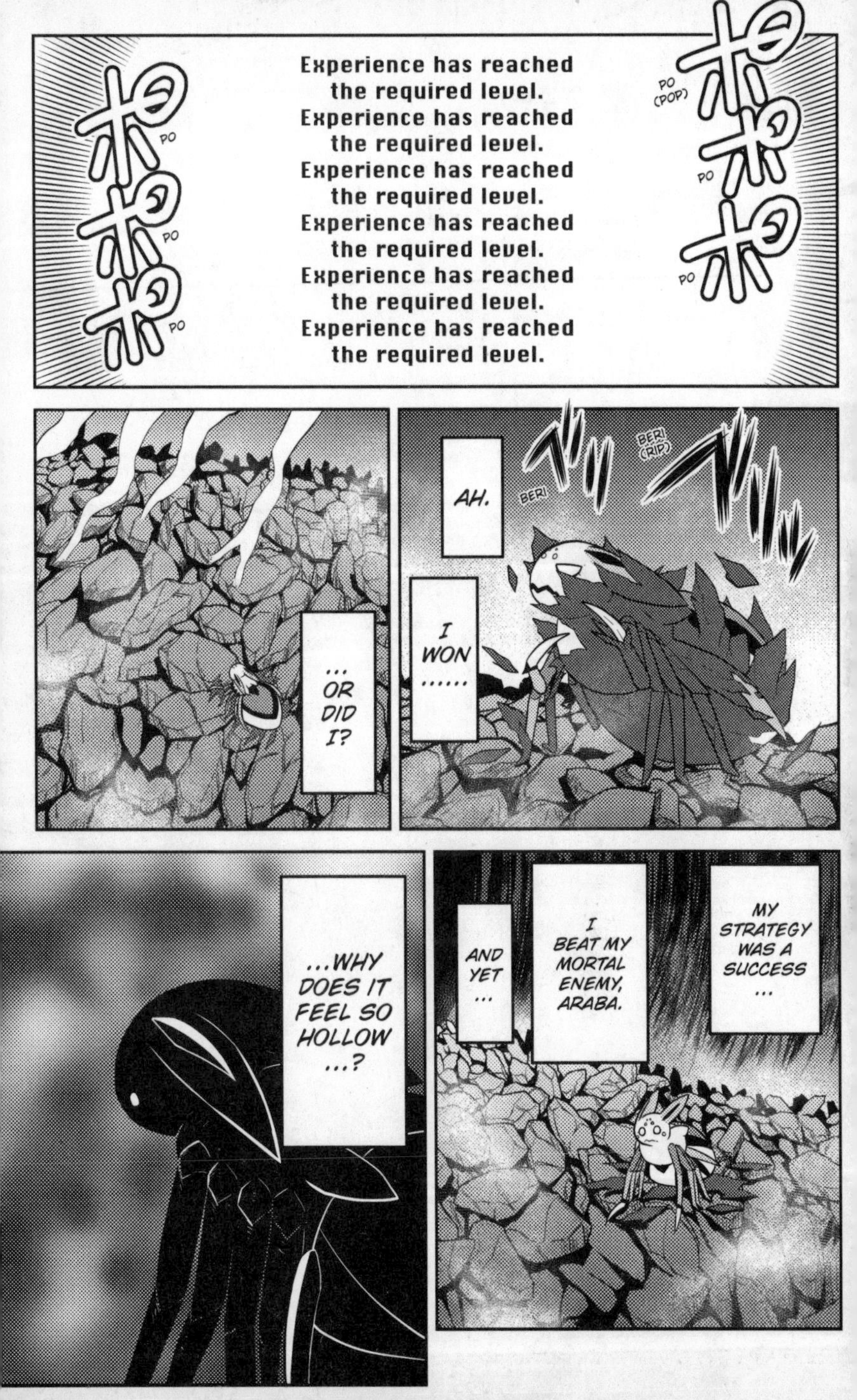
ポポポ
PO (POP)
PO
PO
Experience has reached the required level.
Experience has reached the required level.
Experience has reached the required level.
Experience has reached the required level.
Experience has reached the required level.
Experience has reached the required level.
ポポポ
PO
PO
PO
BERI (RIP)
BERI
AH.
I WON ......
... OR DID I?
MY STRATEGY WAS A SUCCESS ...
I BEAT MY MORTAL ENEMY, ARABA.
AND YET ...
...WHY DOES IT FEEL SO HOLLOW ...?

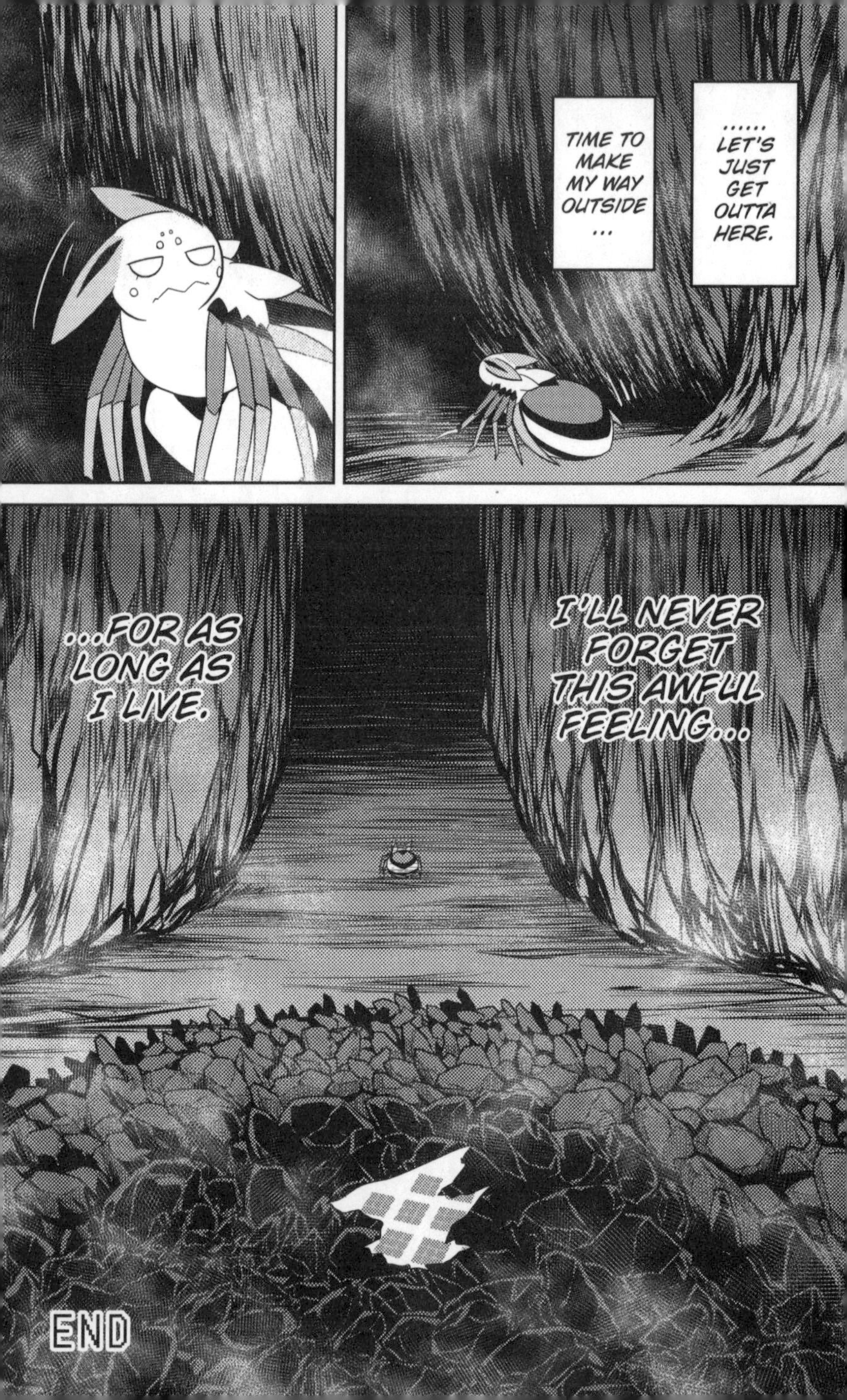

...... LET'S JUST GET OUTTA HERE.
TIME TO MAKE MY WAY OUTSIDE ...
I'LL NEVER FORGET THIS AWFUL FEELING...
...FOR AS LONG AS I LIVE.
END

so I'm a **Spider**, so What?

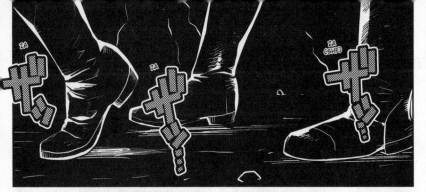

WE... WE MADE IT!

AH ......

HFF...

HFF...

IT'S THE EXIT ...!

42

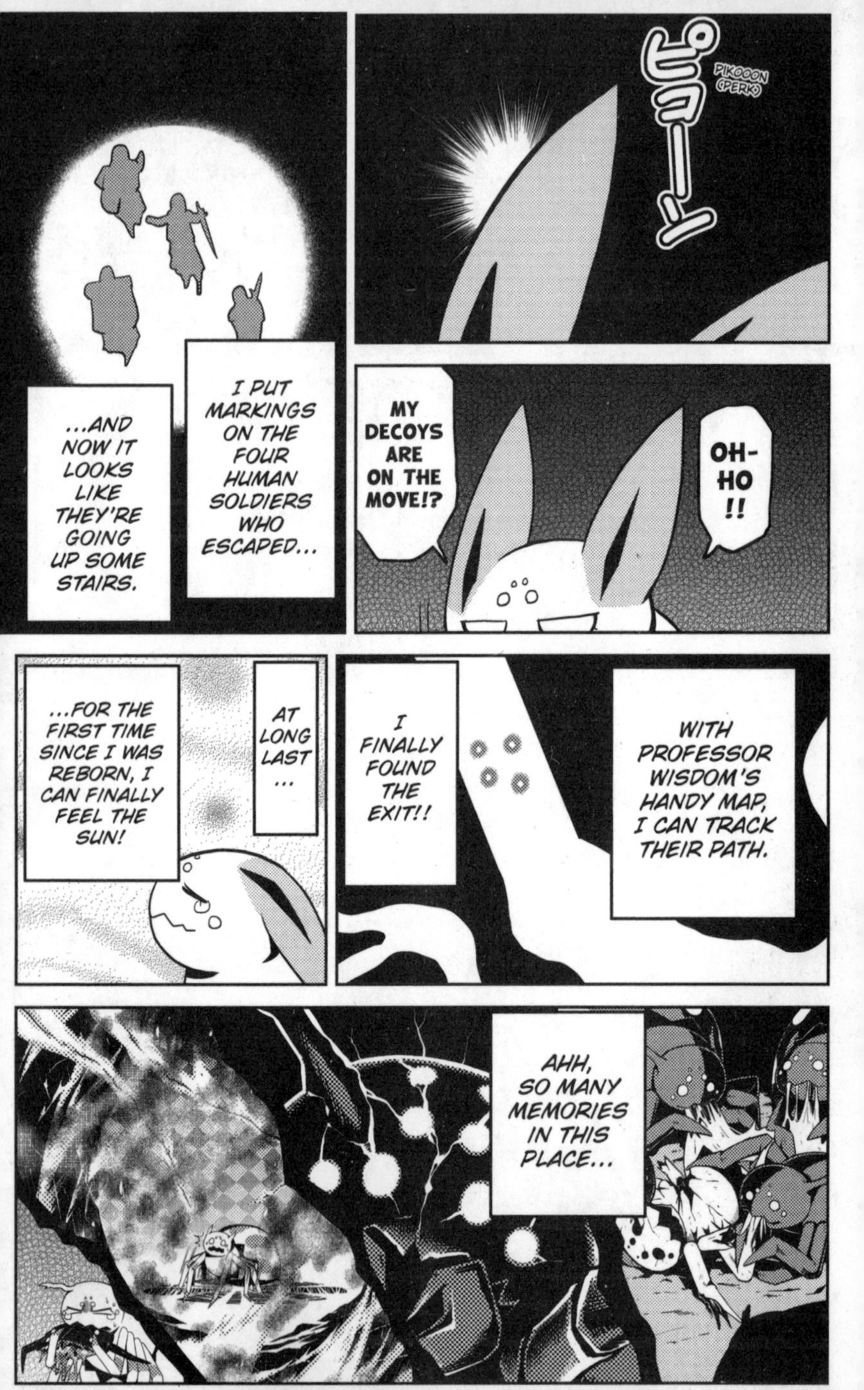
ピョーン
PIKOOON (PERK)
OH-HO !!
MY DECOYS ARE ON THE MOVE!?
I PUT MARKINGS ON THE FOUR HUMAN SOLDIERS WHO ESCAPED...
...AND NOW IT LOOKS LIKE THEY'RE GOING UP SOME STAIRS.
WITH PROFESSOR WISDOM'S HANDY MAP, I CAN TRACK THEIR PATH.
I FINALLY FOUND THE EXIT!!
AT LONG LAST...
...FOR THE FIRST TIME SINCE I WAS REBORN, I CAN FINALLY FEEL THE SUN!
AHH, SO MANY MEMORIES IN THIS PLACE...

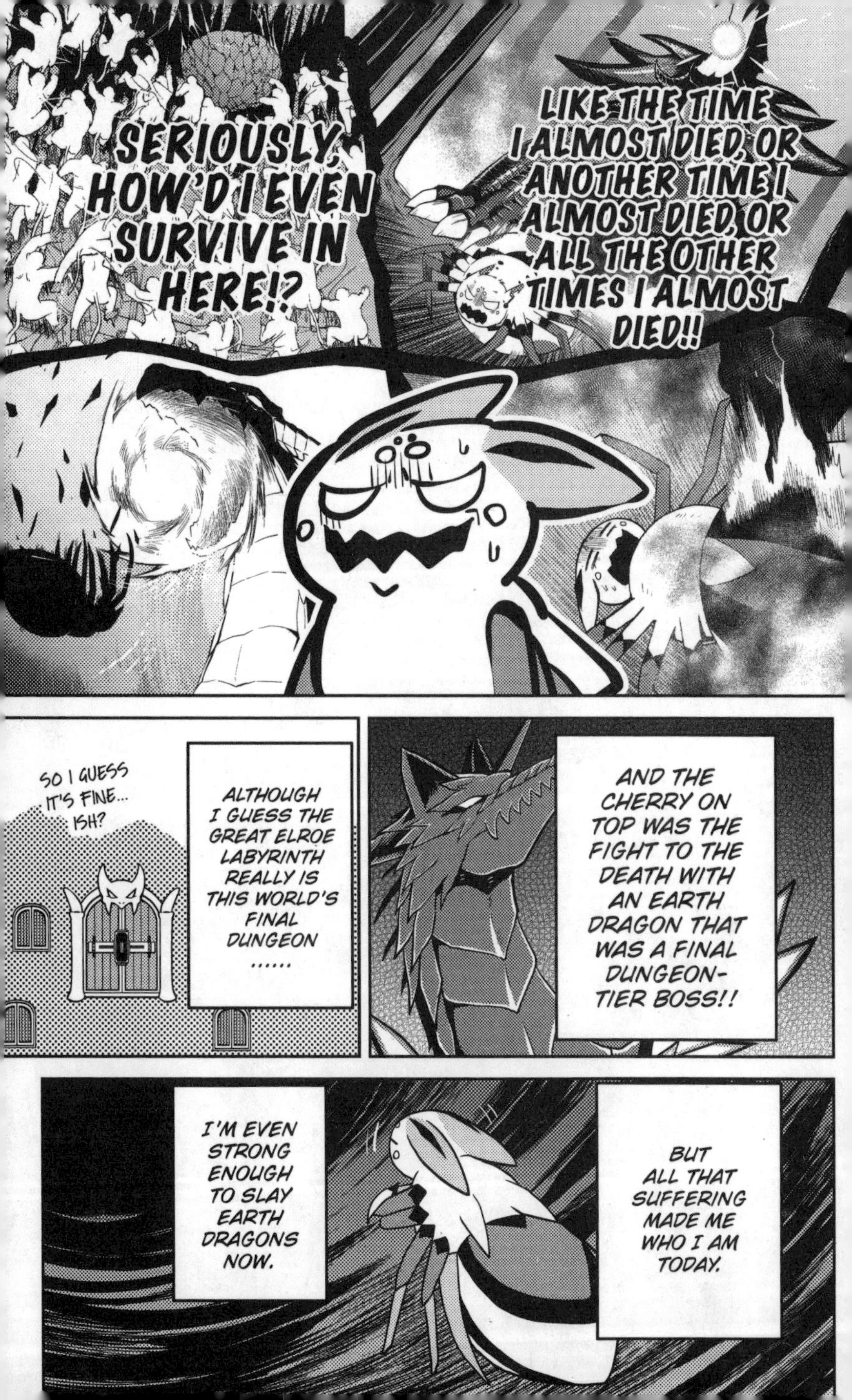
LIKE THE TIME I ALMOST DIED, OR ANOTHER TIME I ALMOST DIED, OR ALL THE OTHER TIMES I ALMOST DIED!!
SERIOUSLY, HOW'D I EVEN SURVIVE IN HERE!?
AND THE CHERRY ON TOP WAS THE FIGHT TO THE DEATH WITH AN EARTH DRAGON THAT WAS A FINAL DUNGEON-TIER BOSS!!
ALTHOUGH I GUESS THE GREAT ELROE LABYRINTH REALLY IS THIS WORLD'S FINAL DUNGEON ......
SO I GUESS IT'S FINE... ISH?
BUT ALL THAT SUFFERING MADE ME WHO I AM TODAY.
I'M EVEN STRONG ENOUGH TO SLAY EARTH DRAGONS NOW.

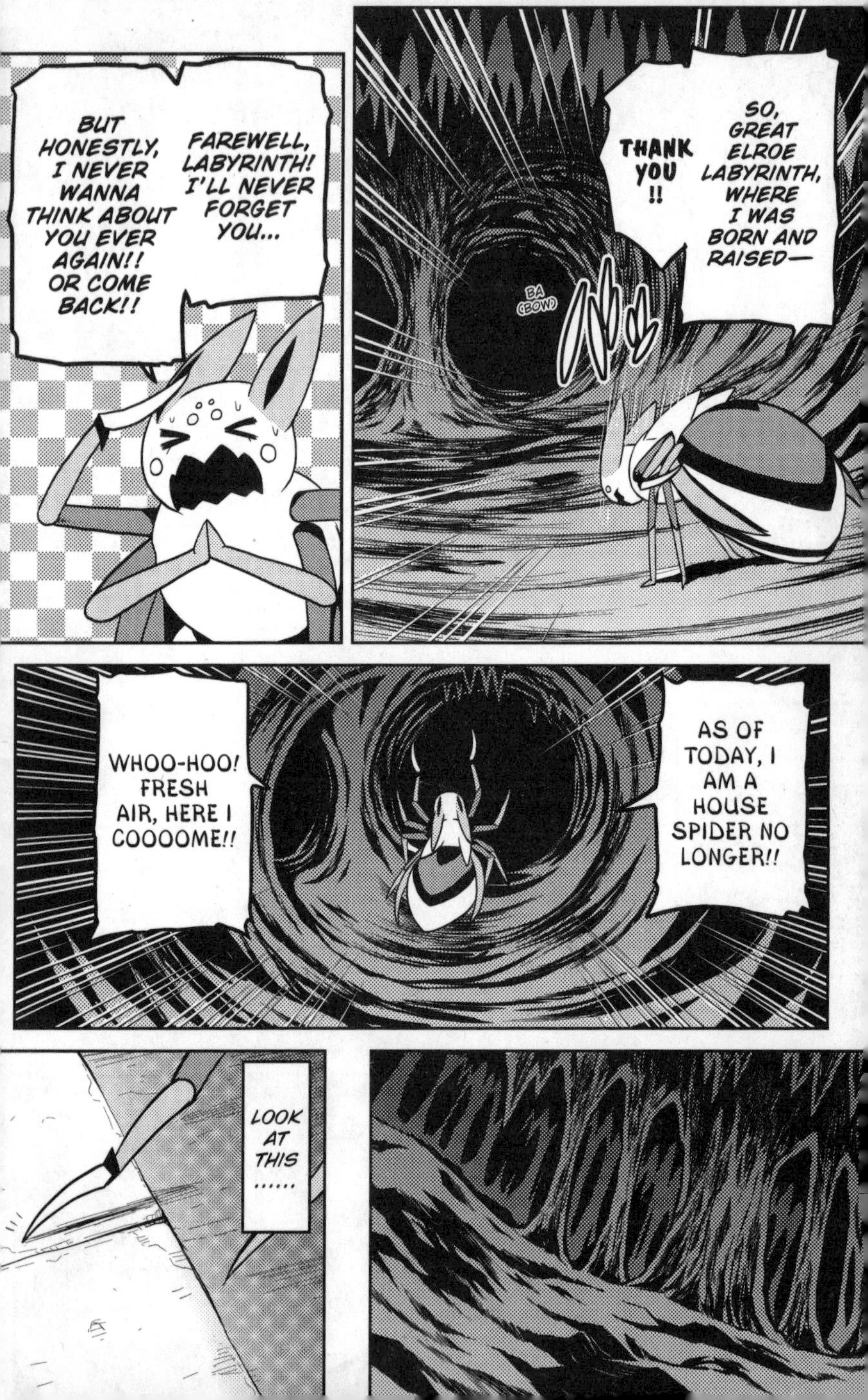
SO, GREAT ELROE LABYRINTH, WHERE I WAS BORN AND RAISED—
THANK YOU !!
BA (BOW)
FAREWELL, LABYRINTH! I'LL NEVER FORGET YOU...
BUT HONESTLY, I NEVER WANNA THINK ABOUT YOU EVER AGAIN!! OR COME BACK!!
AS OF TODAY, I AM A HOUSE SPIDER NO LONGER!!
WHOO-HOO! FRESH AIR, HERE I COOOOME!!
LOOK AT THIS ......

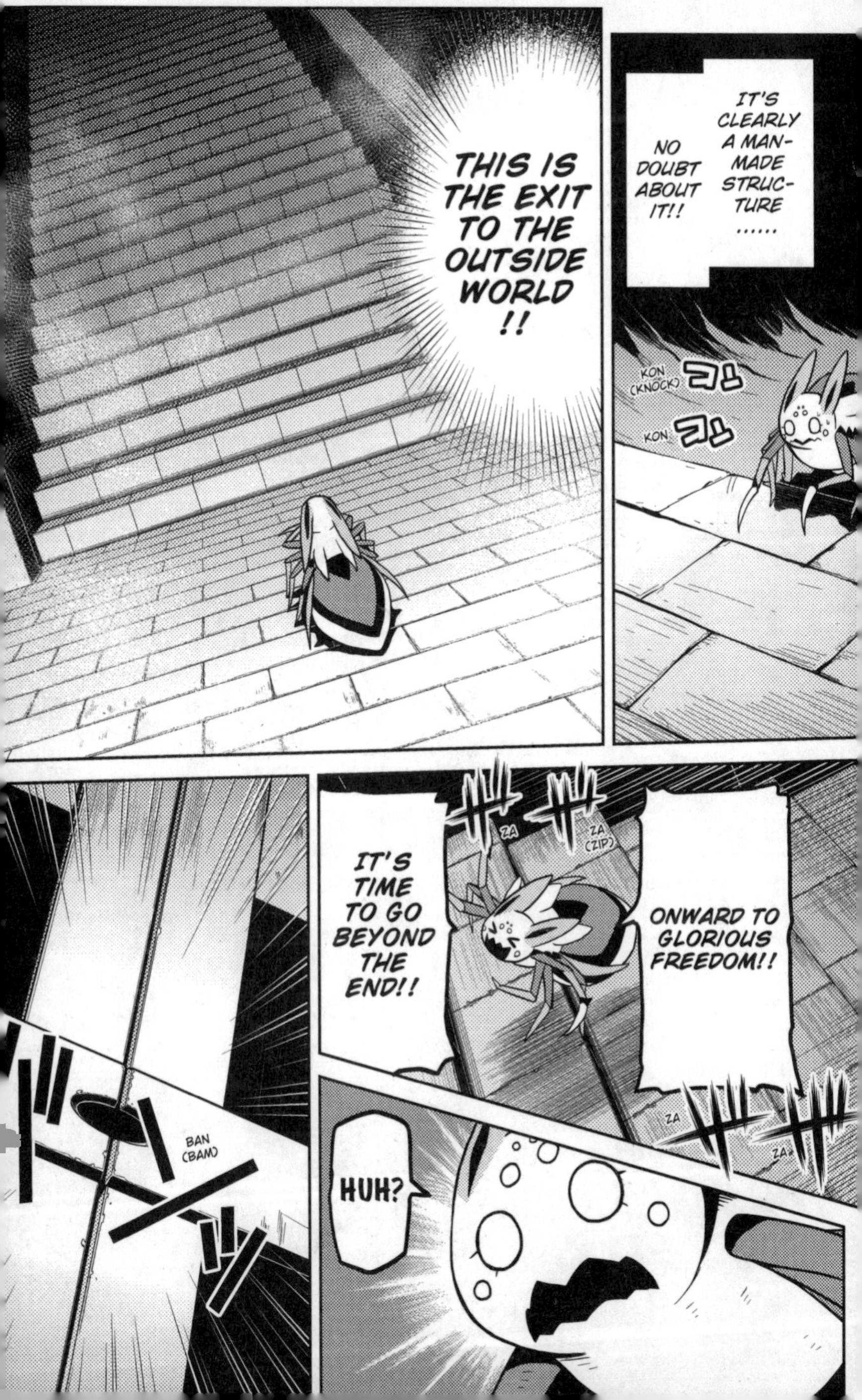
IT'S CLEARLY A MAN-MADE STRUCTURE......
NO DOUBT ABOUT IT!!
KON (KNOCK)
KON
THIS IS THE EXIT TO THE OUTSIDE WORLD !!
ZA (ZIP)
ZA
ONWARD TO GLORIOUS FREEDOM!!
IT'S TIME TO GO BEYOND THE END!!
ZA
ZA
HUH?
BAN (BAM)

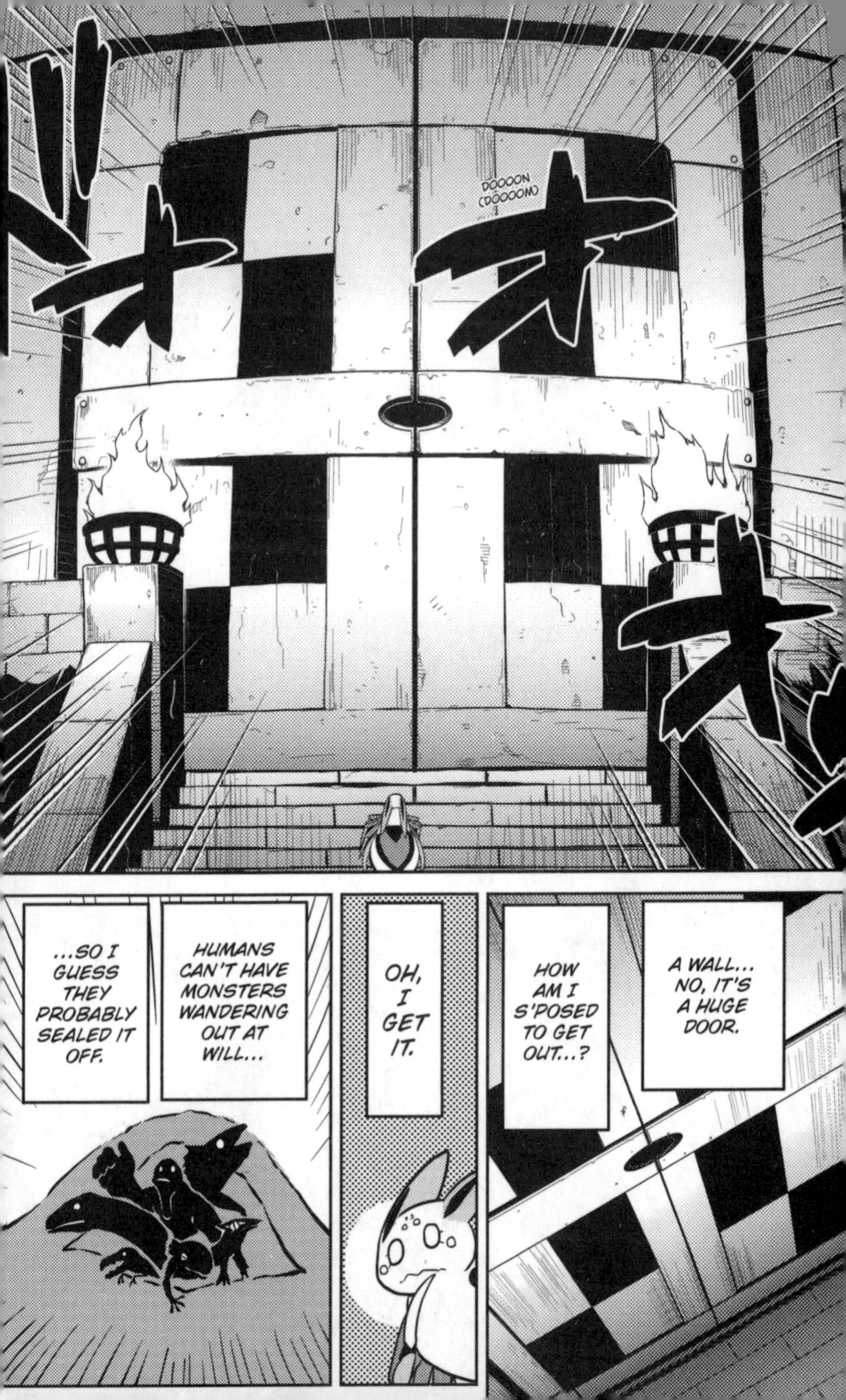
DOOOON
(DOOOOM)
A WALL... NO, IT'S A HUGE DOOR.
HOW AM I S'POSED TO GET OUT...?
OH, I GET IT.
HUMANS CAN'T HAVE MONSTERS WANDERING OUT AT WILL...
...SO I GUESS THEY PROBABLY SEALED IT OFF.

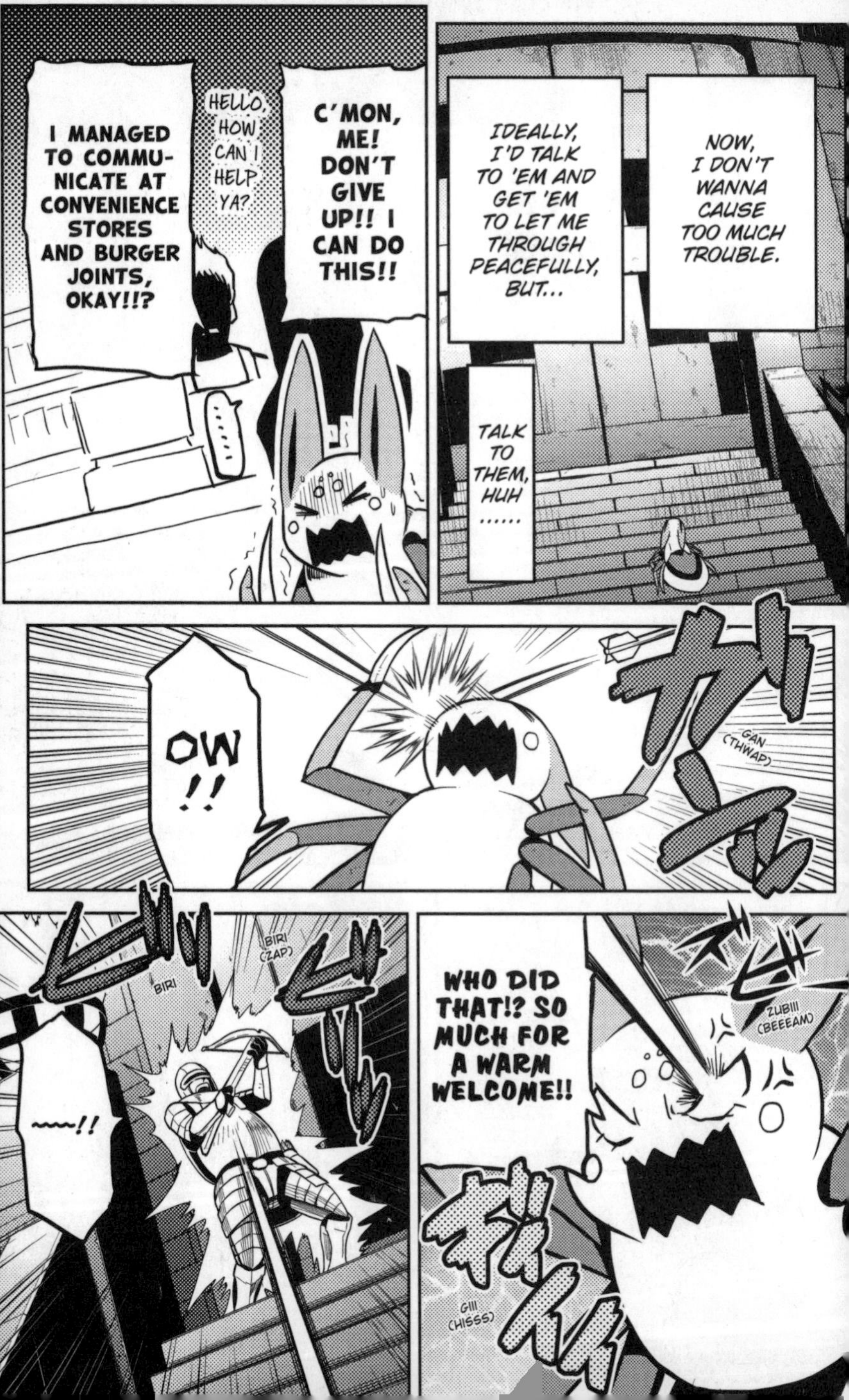
NOW, I DON'T WANNA CAUSE TOO MUCH TROUBLE.
IDEALLY, I'D TALK TO 'EM AND GET 'EM TO LET ME THROUGH PEACEFULLY, BUT...
TALK TO THEM, HUH ......
C'MON, ME! DON'T GIVE UP!! I CAN DO THIS!!
HELLO, HOW CAN I HELP YA?
I MANAGED TO COMMUNICATE AT CONVENIENCE STORES AND BURGER JOINTS, OKAY!!?
......
GAN (THWAP)
OW!!
ZUBIII (BEEEAM)
WHO DID THAT!? SO MUCH FOR A WARM WELCOME!!
GIII (HISSS)
BIRI (ZAP)
BIRI
~~~!!
~~~

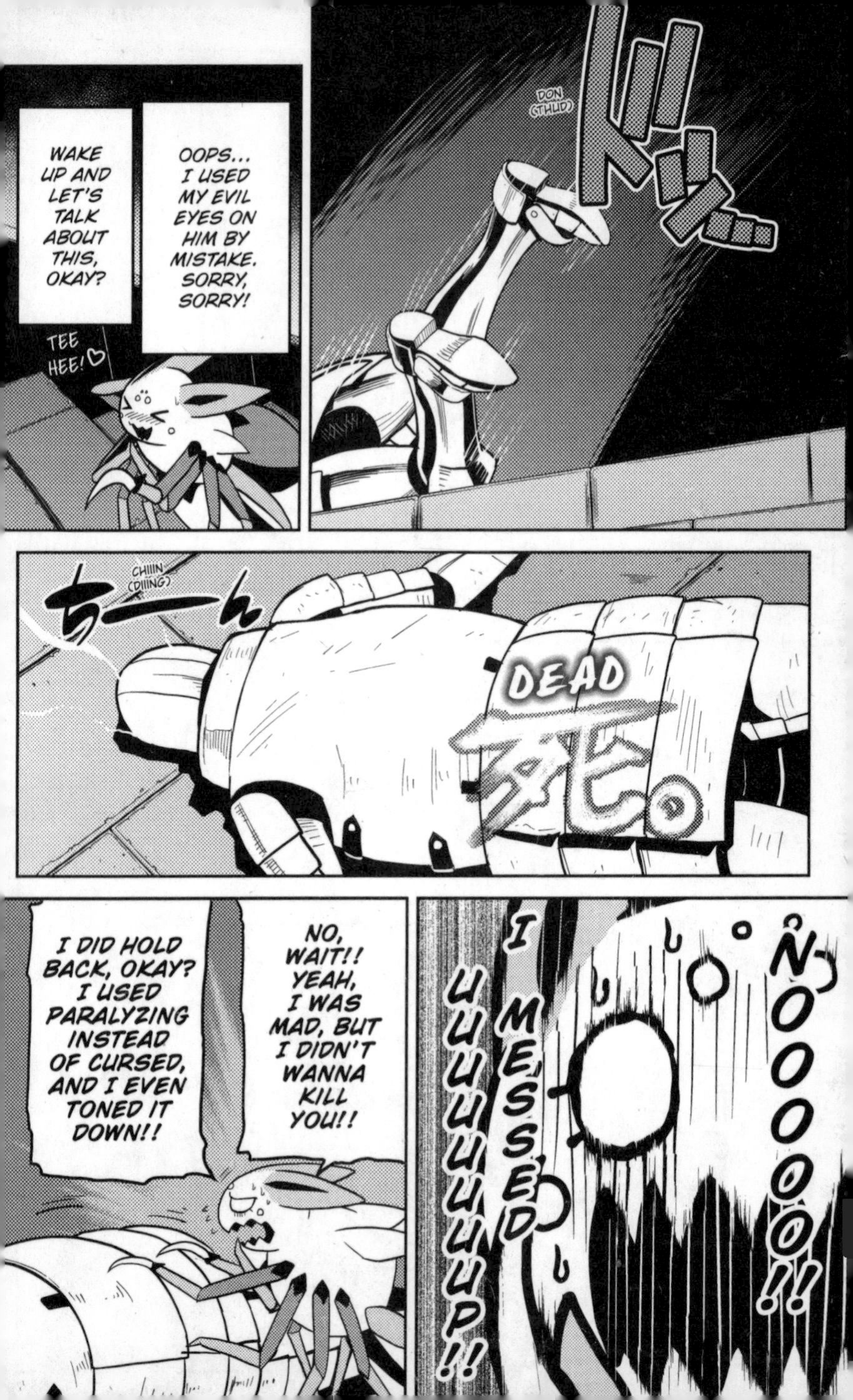

DON (THUD)
OOPS... I USED MY EVIL EYES ON HIM BY MISTAKE. SORRY, SORRY!
WAKE UP AND LET'S TALK ABOUT THIS, OKAY?
TEE HEE!♡
CHIIN (DIIING)
ちーん
DEAD
死。
NOOOOOOOO!!
I MESSED UUUUUUUUP!!
NO, WAIT!! YEAH, I WAS MAD, BUT I DIDN'T WANNA KILL YOU!!
I DID HOLD BACK, OKAY? I USED PARALYZING INSTEAD OF CURSED, AND I EVEN TONED IT DOWN!!

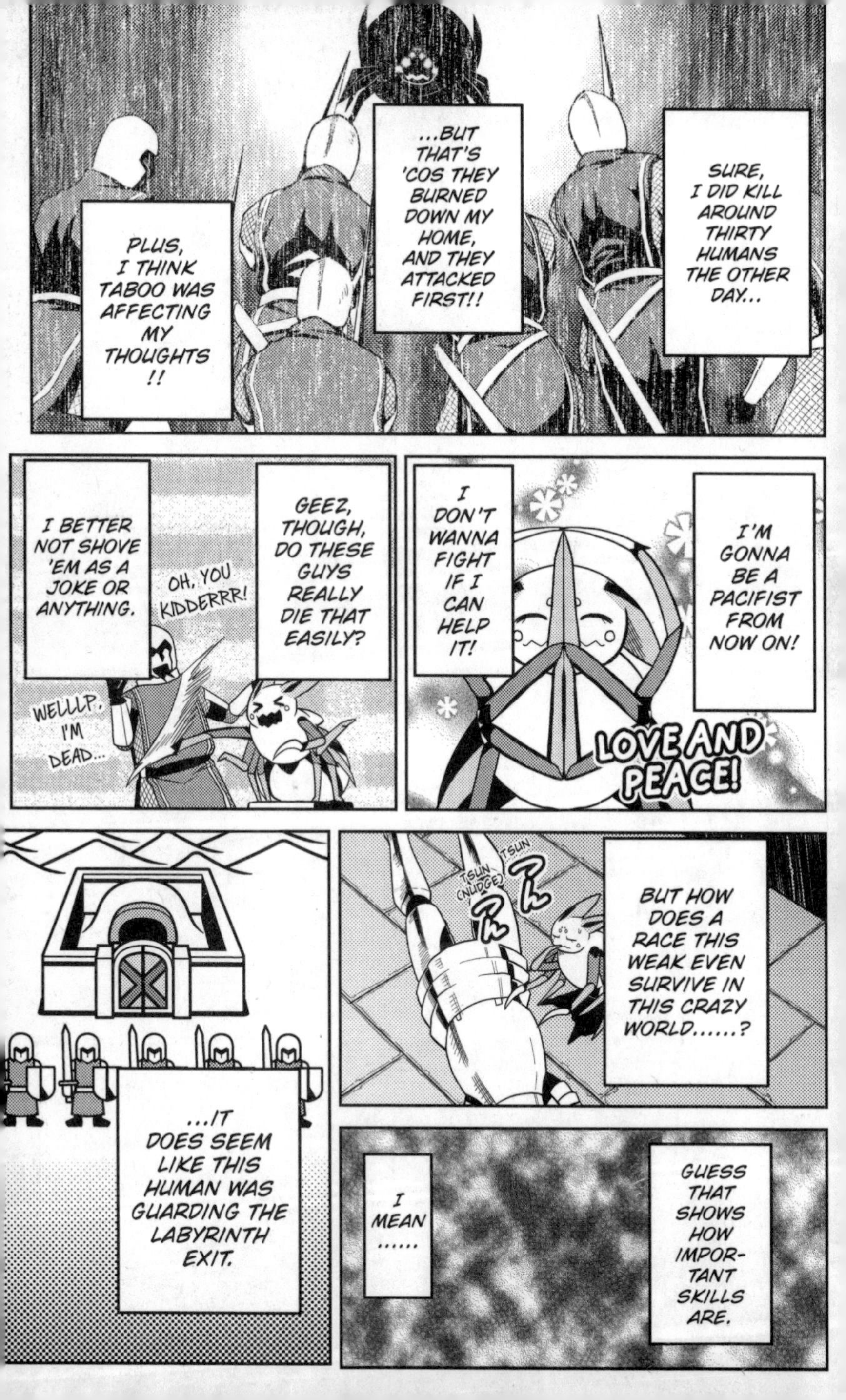
SURE, I DID KILL AROUND THIRTY HUMANS THE OTHER DAY...
...BUT THAT'S 'COS THEY BURNED DOWN MY HOME, AND THEY ATTACKED FIRST!!
PLUS, I THINK TABOO WAS AFFECTING MY THOUGHTS!!
I'M GONNA BE A PACIFIST FROM NOW ON!
I DON'T WANNA FIGHT IF I CAN HELP IT!
LOVE AND PEACE!
GEEZ, THOUGH, DO THESE GUYS REALLY DIE THAT EASILY?
OH, YOU KIDDERRR!
I BETTER NOT SHOVE 'EM AS A JOKE OR ANYTHING.
WELLLP, I'M DEAD...
TSUN
TSUN (NUDGE)
BUT HOW DOES A RACE THIS WEAK EVEN SURVIVE IN THIS CRAZY WORLD......?
GUESS THAT SHOWS HOW IMPORTANT SKILLS ARE.
I MEAN......
...IT DOES SEEM LIKE THIS HUMAN WAS GUARDING THE LABYRINTH EXIT.

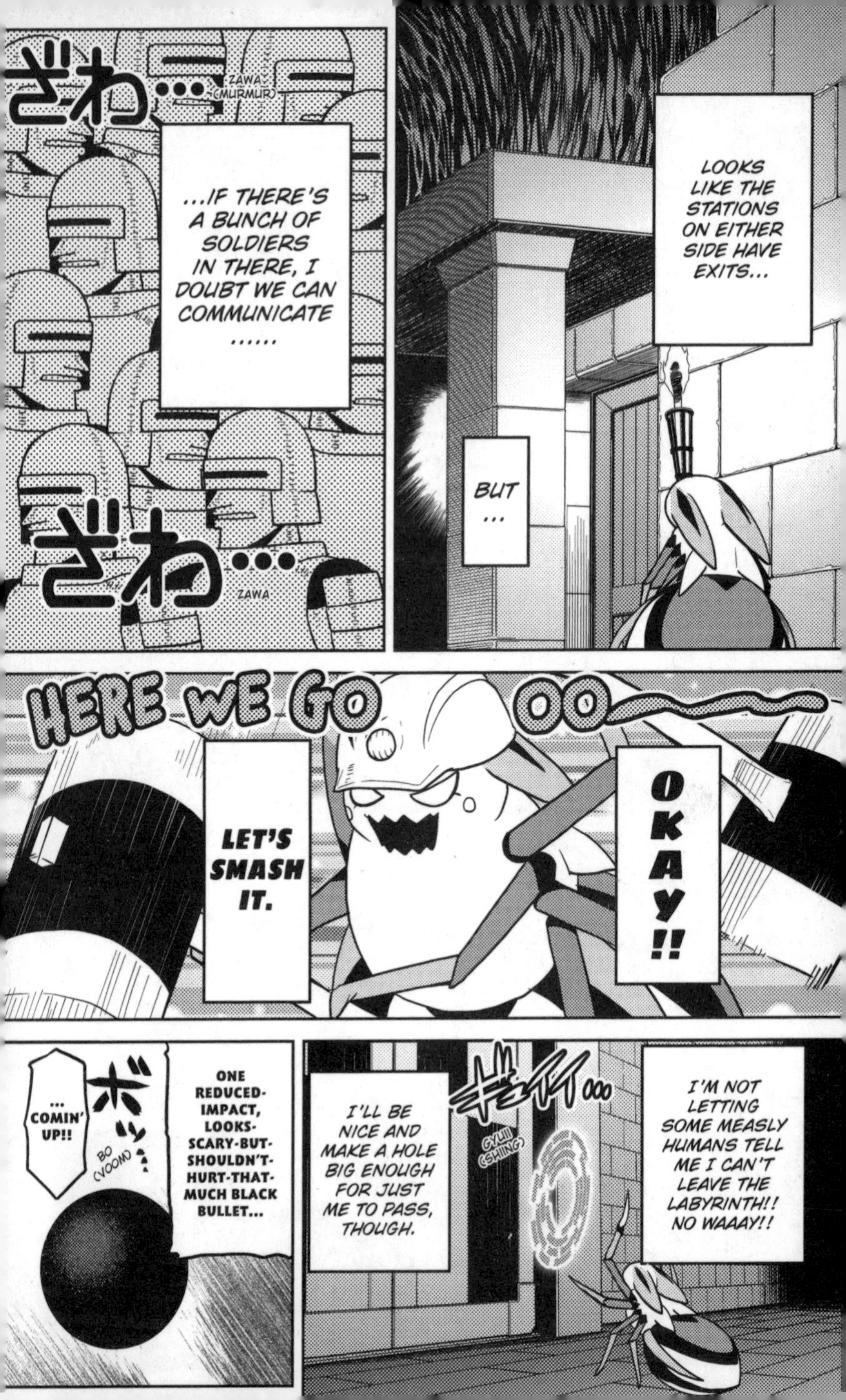
LOOKS LIKE THE STATIONS ON EITHER SIDE HAVE EXITS...
BUT...
ざわ…
ZAWA (MURMUR)
...IF THERE'S A BUNCH OF SOLDIERS IN THERE, I DOUBT WE CAN COMMUNICATE ......
ざわ…
ZAWA
HERE WE GO OO~~~
OKAY!!
LET'S SMASH IT.
I'M NOT LETTING SOME MEASLY HUMANS TELL ME I CAN'T LEAVE THE LABYRINTH!! NO WAAAY!!
GYUII (SHING)
I'LL BE NICE AND MAKE A HOLE BIG ENOUGH FOR JUST ME TO PASS, THOUGH.
ONE REDUCED-IMPACT, LOOKS-SCARY-BUT-SHOULDN'T-HURT-THAT-MUCH BLACK BULLET...
ボッ
BO (VOOM)
...COMIN' UP!!

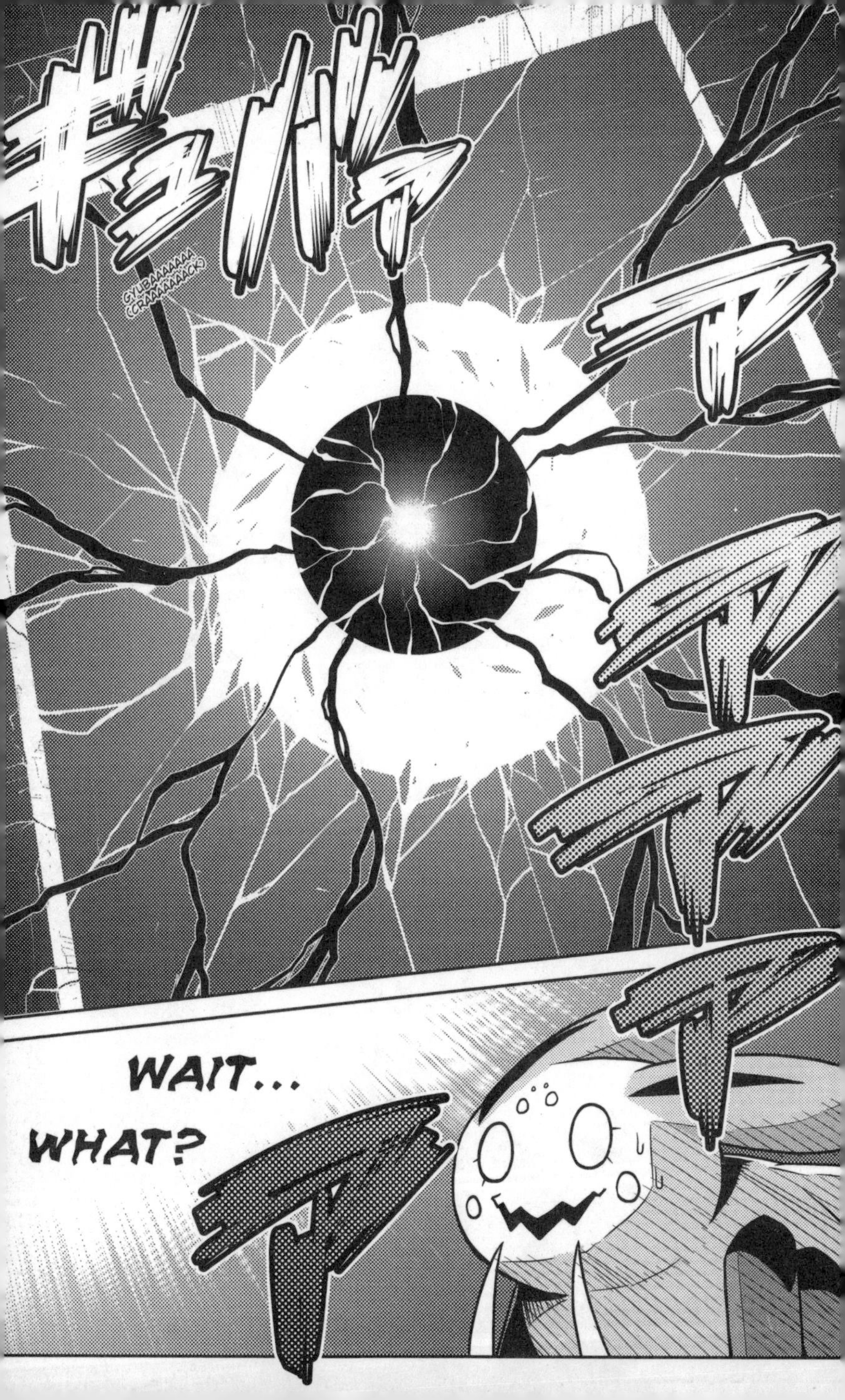
GYUBAAAAAAA
(CRAAAAAAACK)
WAIT...
WHAT?

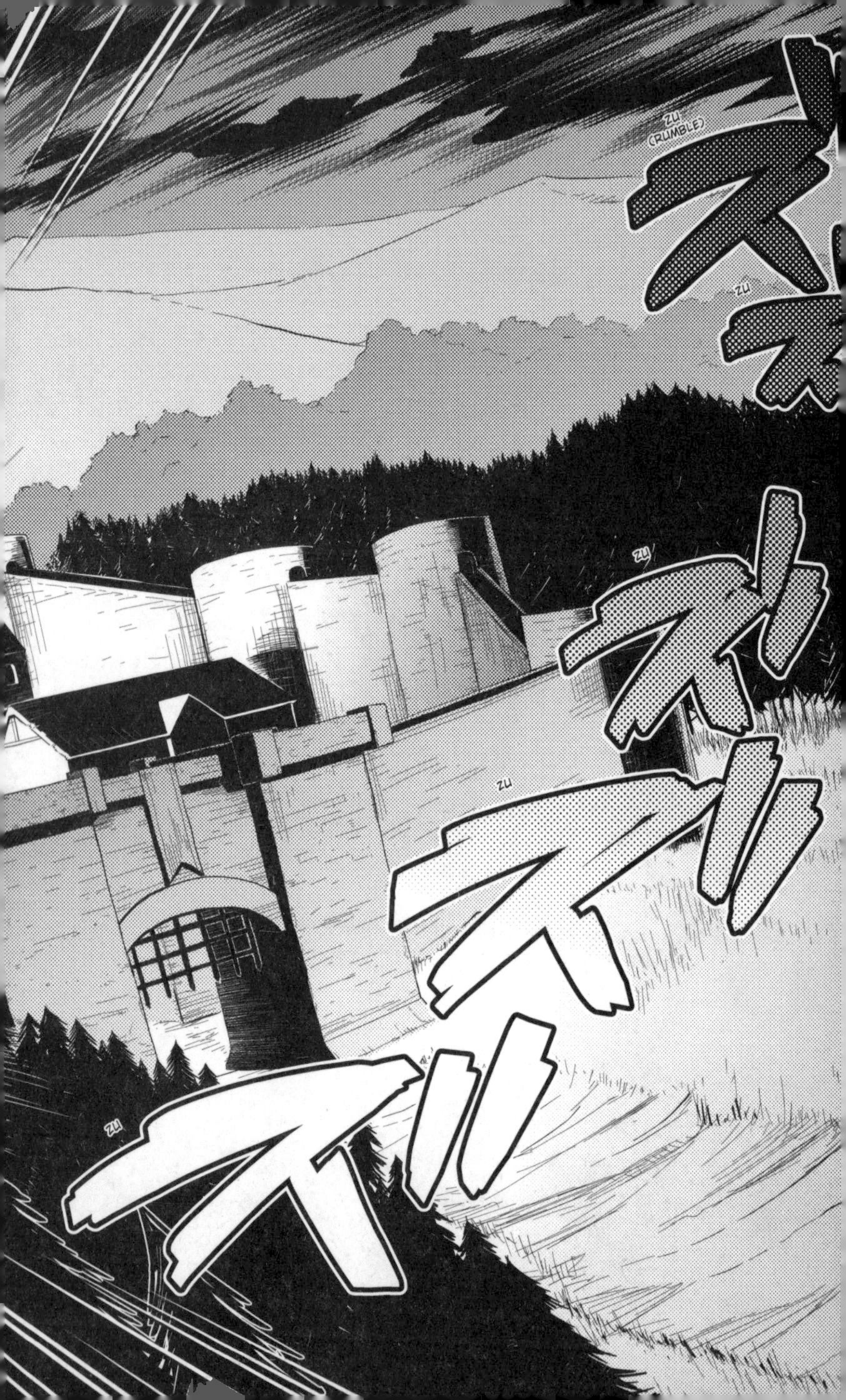
ZU
(RUMBLE)
ZU
ZU
ZU
ZU

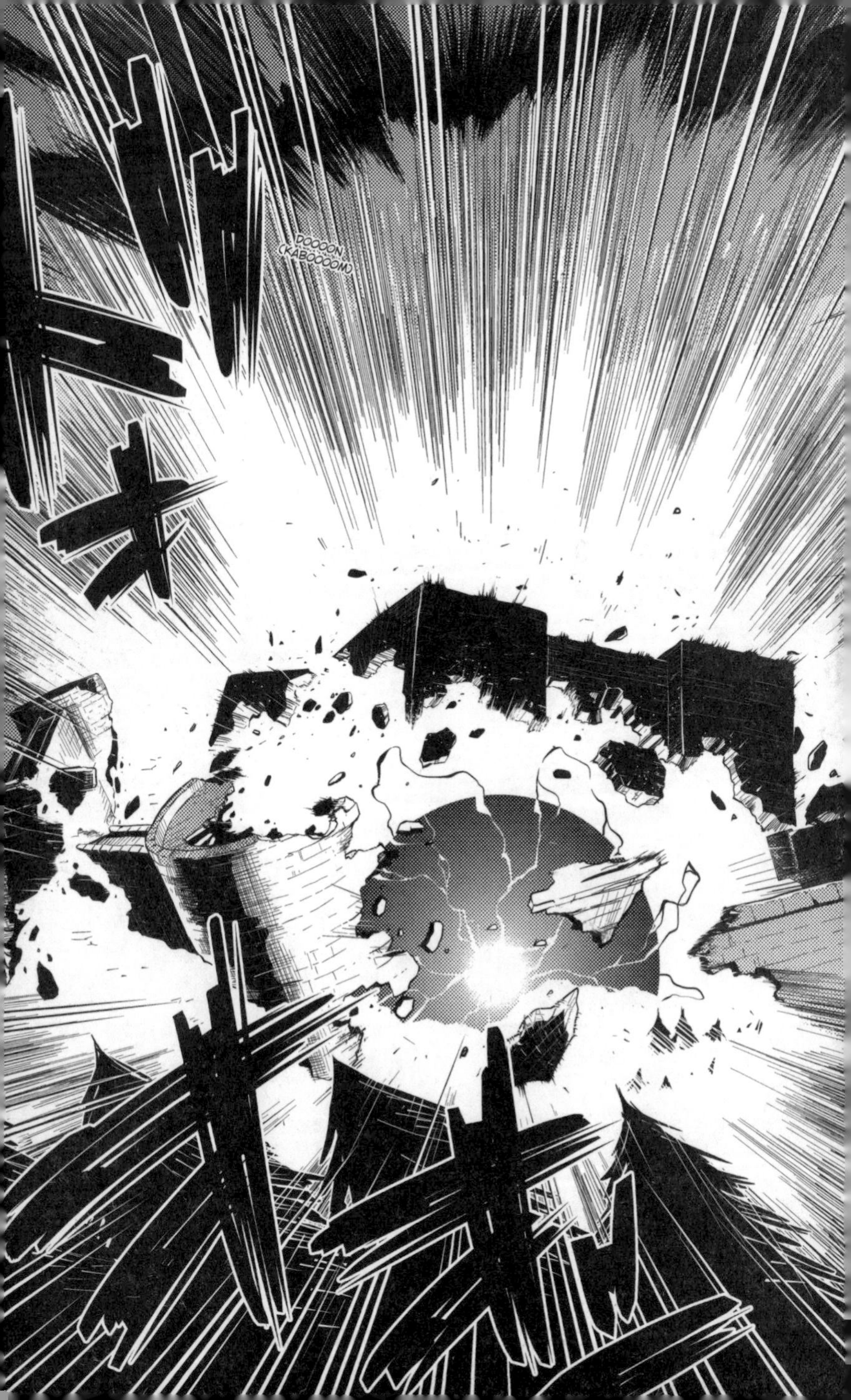
DOOOON
(KABOOOOM)

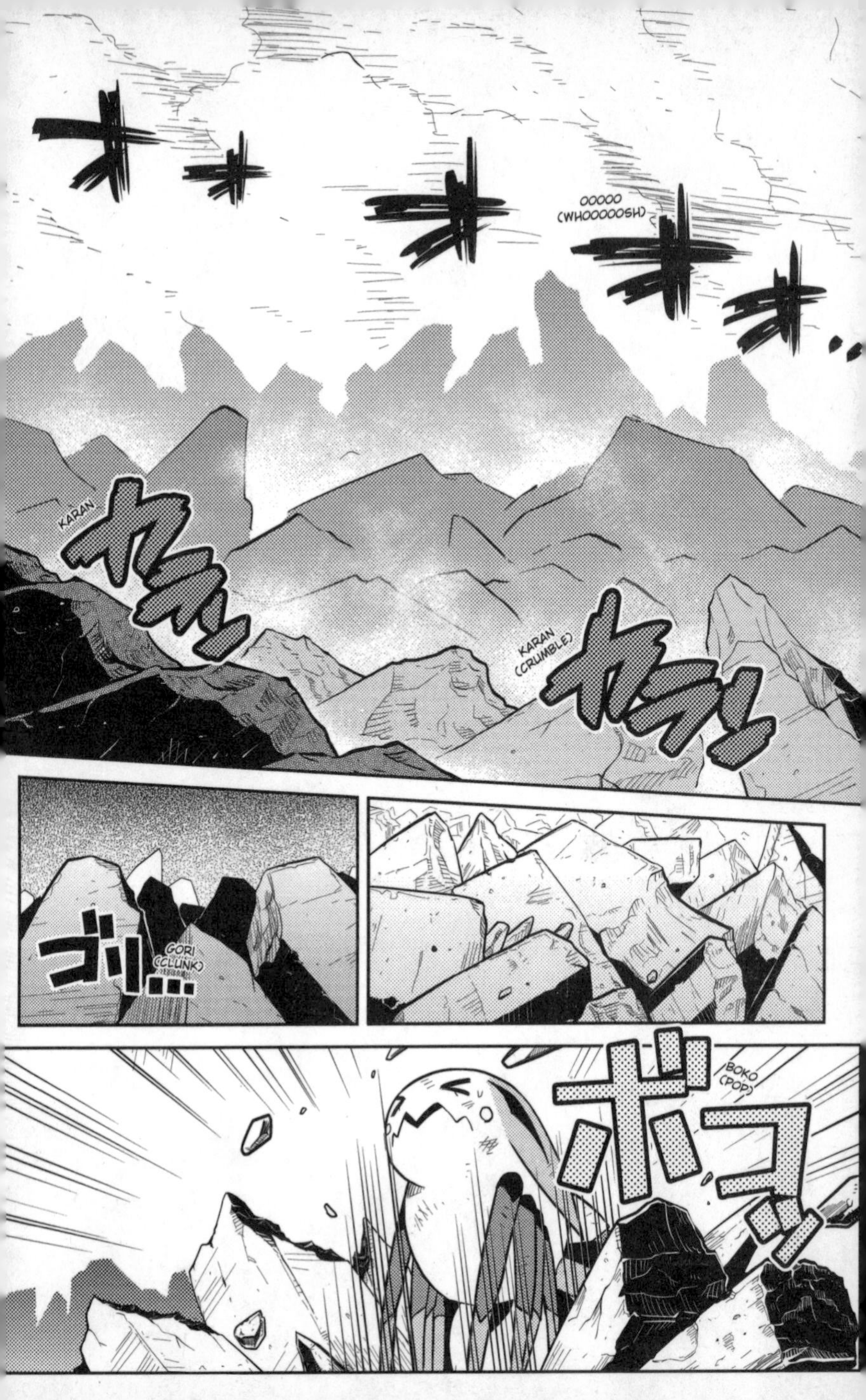
OOOOO (WHOOOOOSH)
KARAN (CRUMBLE)
KARAN
GORI (CLUNK)
BOKO (POP)

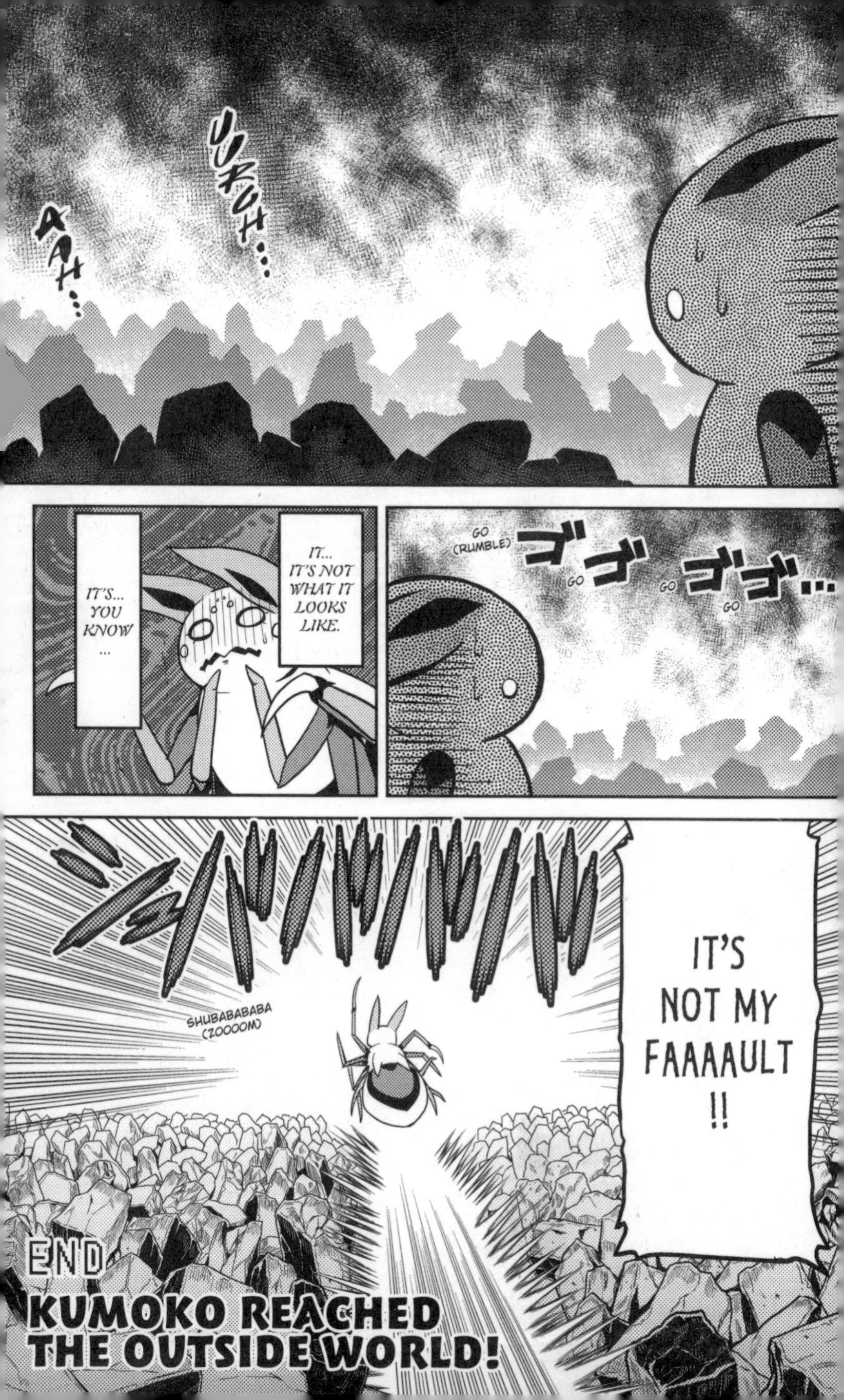
UURUH...
AAH...
GO (RUMBLE) ゴゴ
GO GO
ゴゴ...
GO GO
IT... IT'S NOT WHAT IT LOOKS LIKE.
IT'S... YOU KNOW ...
IT'S NOT MY FAAAAULT !!
SHUBABABABA (ZOOOOM)
END
KUMOKO REACHED THE OUTSIDE WORLD!

So I'm a Spider, So What?

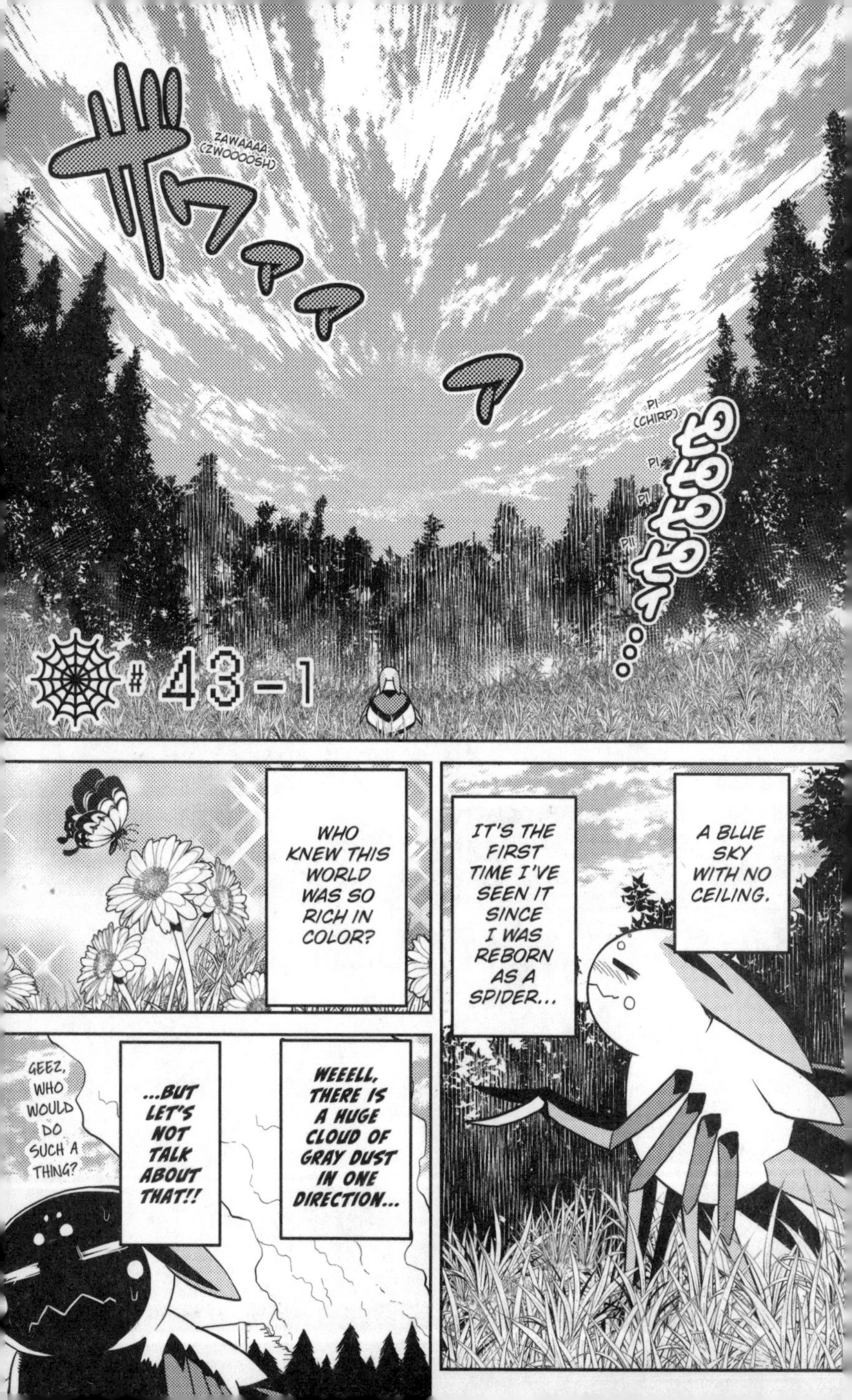
ZAWAAAA
(ZWOOOOSH)
PI
(CHIRP)
PI
PI
PI!
#43-1
A BLUE SKY WITH NO CEILING.
IT'S THE FIRST TIME I'VE SEEN IT SINCE I WAS REBORN AS A SPIDER...
WHO KNEW THIS WORLD WAS SO RICH IN COLOR?
WEEELL, THERE IS A HUGE CLOUD OF GRAY DUST IN ONE DIRECTION...
...BUT LET'S NOT TALK ABOUT THAT!!
GEEZ, WHO WOULD DO SUCH A THING?

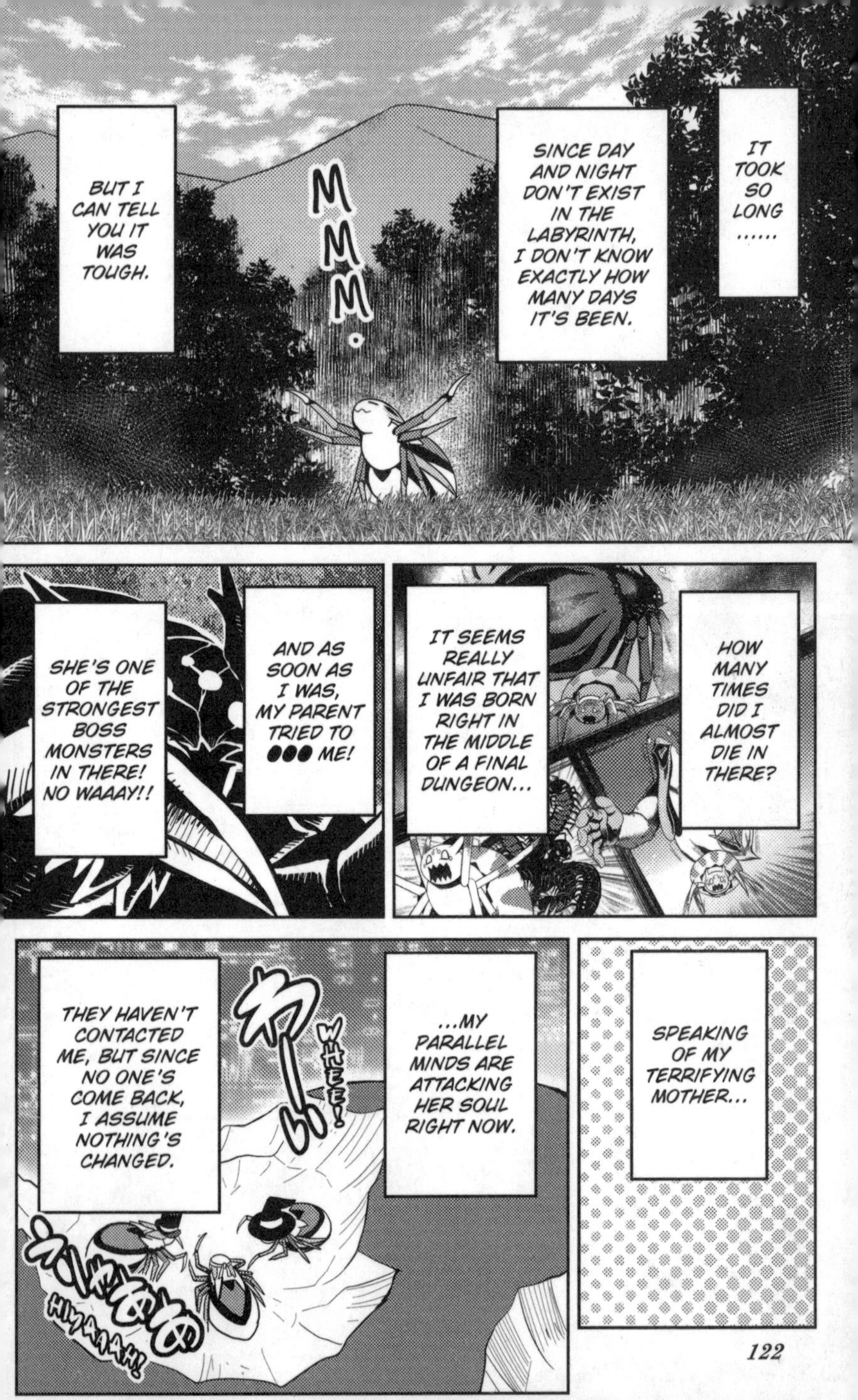
IT TOOK SO LONG......
SINCE DAY AND NIGHT DON'T EXIST IN THE LABYRINTH, I DON'T KNOW EXACTLY HOW MANY DAYS IT'S BEEN.
MMM.
BUT I CAN TELL YOU IT WAS TOUGH.
HOW MANY TIMES DID I ALMOST DIE IN THERE?
IT SEEMS REALLY UNFAIR THAT I WAS BORN RIGHT IN THE MIDDLE OF A FINAL DUNGEON...
AND AS SOON AS I WAS, MY PARENT TRIED TO ●●● ME!
SHE'S ONE OF THE STRONGEST BOSS MONSTERS IN THERE! NO WAAAY!!
SPEAKING OF MY TERRIFYING MOTHER...
...MY PARALLEL MINDS ARE ATTACKING HER SOUL RIGHT NOW.
WHEEE!
THEY HAVEN'T CONTACTED ME, BUT SINCE NO ONE'S COME BACK, I ASSUME NOTHING'S CHANGED.
HIYAAAAH!

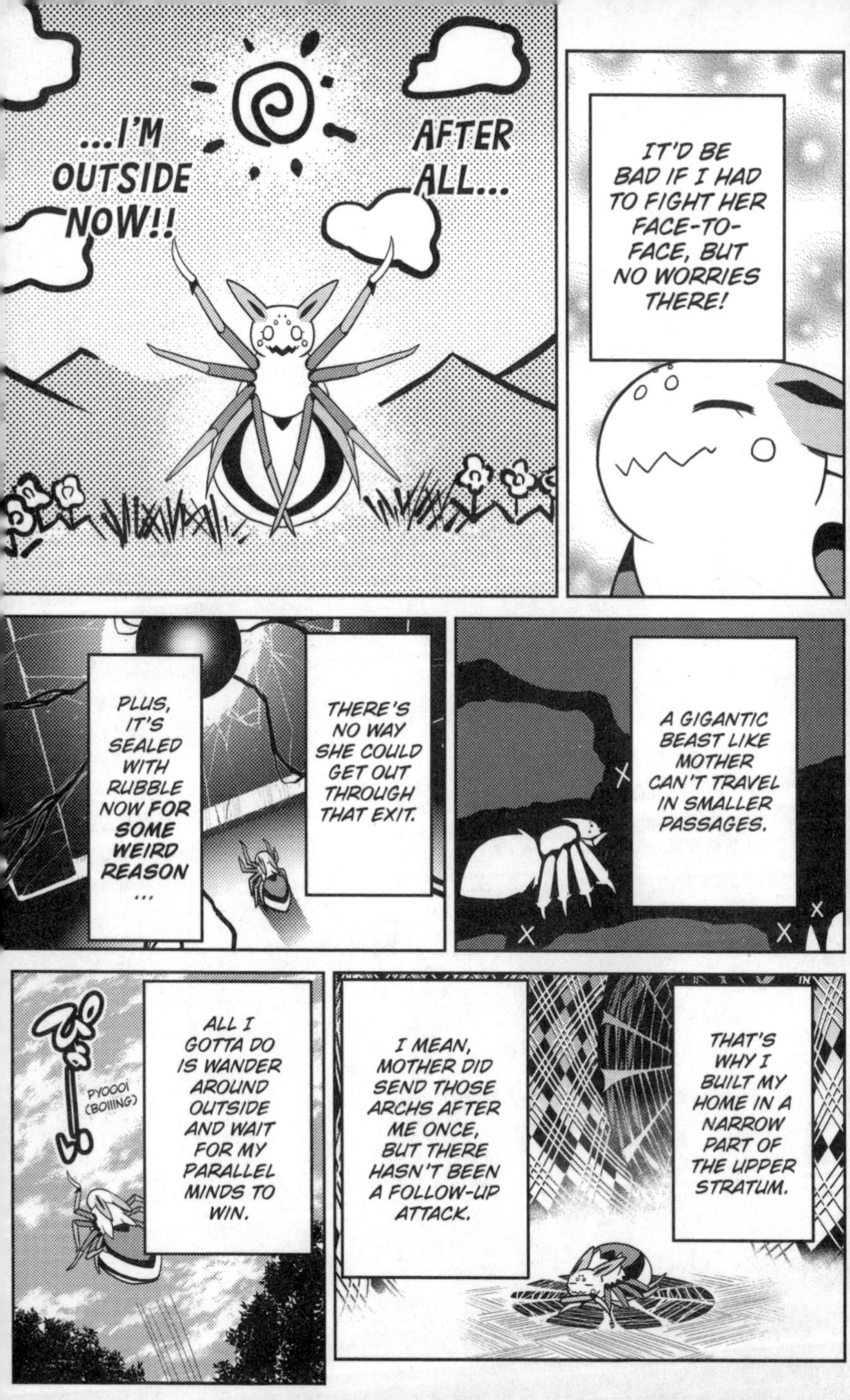
IT'D BE BAD IF I HAD TO FIGHT HER FACE-TO-FACE, BUT NO WORRIES THERE!
AFTER ALL...
...I'M OUTSIDE NOW!!
A GIGANTIC BEAST LIKE MOTHER CAN'T TRAVEL IN SMALLER PASSAGES.
THERE'S NO WAY SHE COULD GET OUT THROUGH THAT EXIT.
PLUS, IT'S SEALED WITH RUBBLE NOW FOR SOME WEIRD REASON...
THAT'S WHY I BUILT MY HOME IN A NARROW PART OF THE UPPER STRATUM.
I MEAN, MOTHER DID SEND THOSE ARCHS AFTER ME ONCE, BUT THERE HASN'T BEEN A FOLLOW-UP ATTACK.
ALL I GOTTA DO IS WANDER AROUND OUTSIDE AND WAIT FOR MY PARALLEL MINDS TO WIN.
PYOOOI (BOIIING)

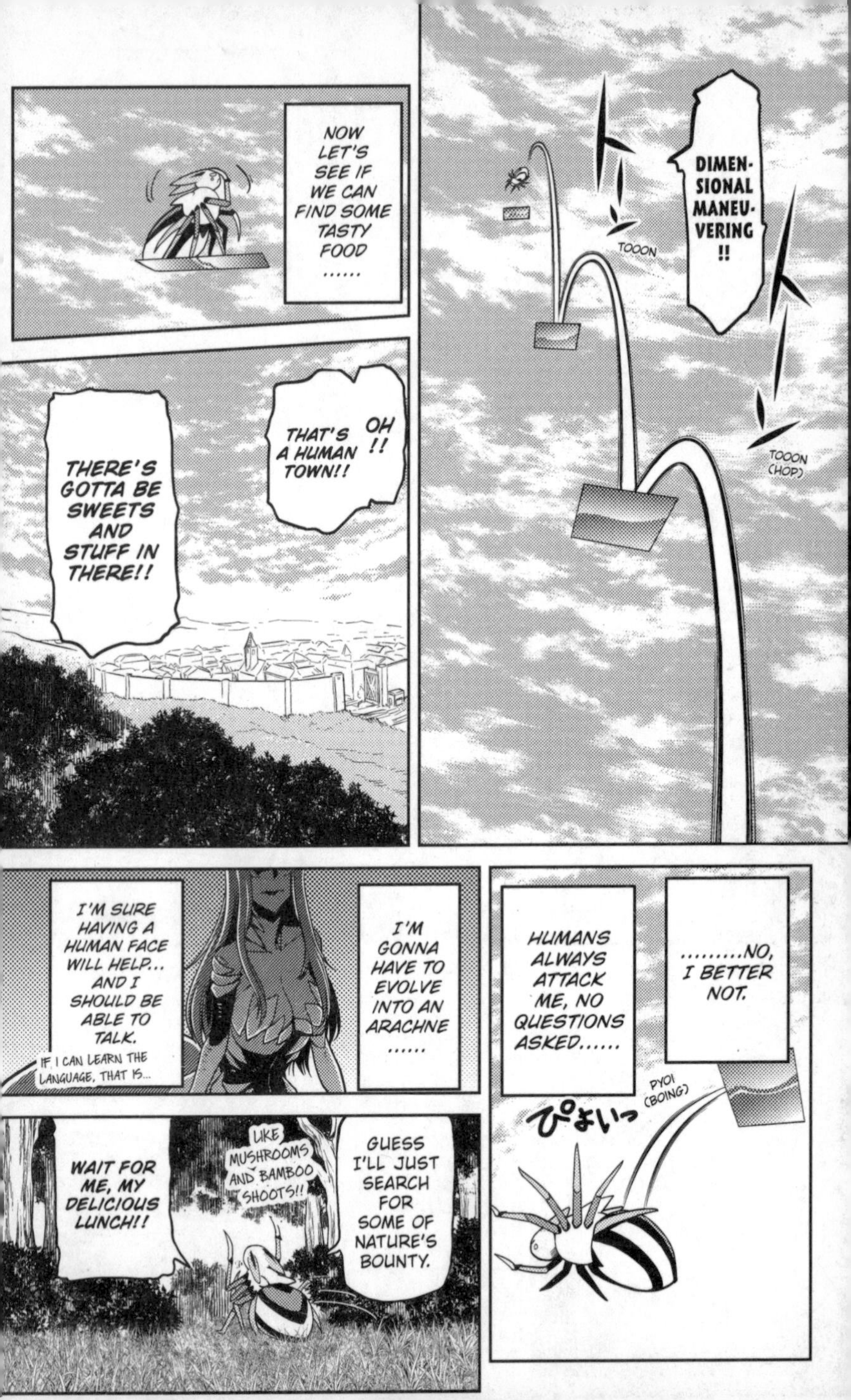
DIMEN-SIONAL MANEU-VERING!!
TOOON
TOOON (HOP)
NOW LET'S SEE IF WE CAN FIND SOME TASTY FOOD ......
OH!!
THAT'S A HUMAN TOWN!!
THERE'S GOTTA BE SWEETS AND STUFF IN THERE!!
........NO, I BETTER NOT.
HUMANS ALWAYS ATTACK ME, NO QUESTIONS ASKED......
ぴょいっ
PYOI (BOING)
I'M GONNA HAVE TO EVOLVE INTO AN ARACHNE ......
I'M SURE HAVING A HUMAN FACE WILL HELP... AND I SHOULD BE ABLE TO TALK.
IF I CAN LEARN THE LANGUAGE, THAT IS...
GUESS I'LL JUST SEARCH FOR SOME OF NATURE'S BOUNTY.
LIKE MUSHROOMS AND BAMBOO SHOOTS!!
WAIT FOR ME, MY DELICIOUS LUNCH!!

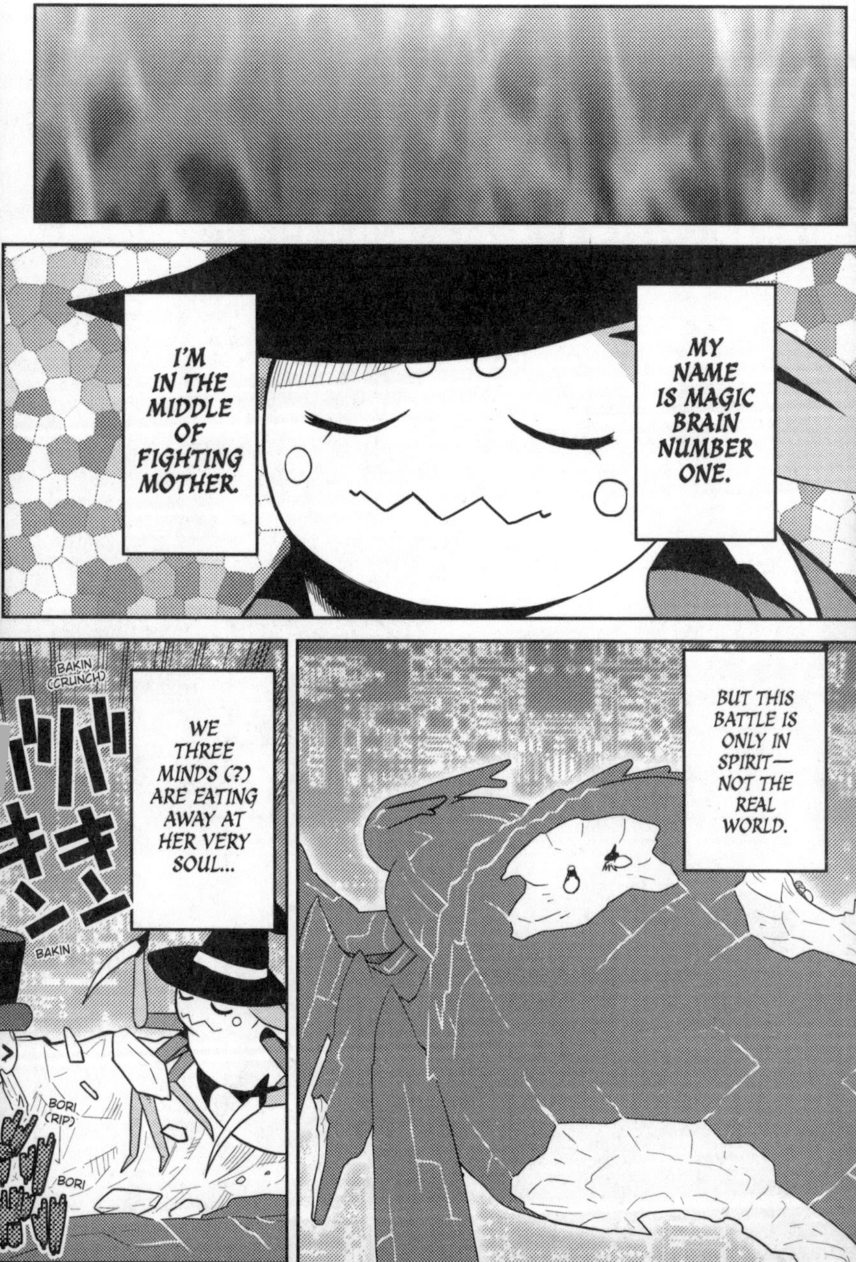
MY NAME IS MAGIC BRAIN NUMBER ONE.
I'M IN THE MIDDLE OF FIGHTING MOTHER.
BUT THIS BATTLE IS ONLY IN SPIRIT— NOT THE REAL WORLD.
WE THREE MINDS (?) ARE EATING AWAY AT HER VERY SOUL...
BAKIN (CRUNCH)
BAKIN
BORI (RIP)
BORI

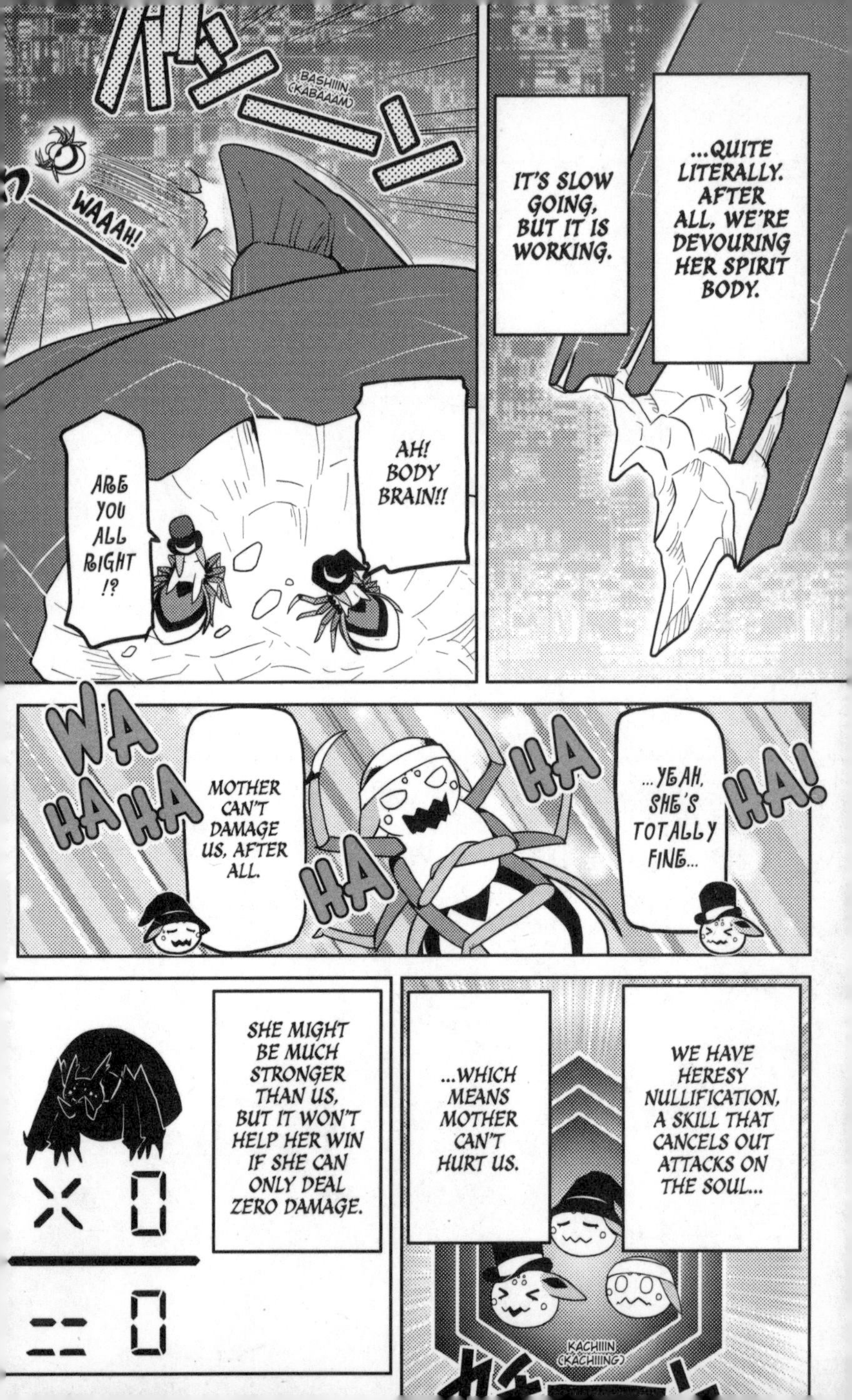
...QUITE LITERALLY. AFTER ALL, WE'RE DEVOURING HER SPIRIT BODY.
IT'S SLOW GOING, BUT IT IS WORKING.
BASHIIIN (KABAAAM)
WAAAH!
AH! BODY BRAIN!!
ARE YOU ALL RIGHT!?
...YEAH, SHE'S TOTALLY FINE...
HA HA HA!
MOTHER CAN'T DAMAGE US, AFTER ALL.
WA HA HA HA HA
WE HAVE HERESY NULLIFICATION, A SKILL THAT CANCELS OUT ATTACKS ON THE SOUL...
...WHICH MEANS MOTHER CAN'T HURT US.
KACHIIIN (KACHIIING)
SHE MIGHT BE MUCH STRONGER THAN US, BUT IT WON'T HELP HER WIN IF SHE CAN ONLY DEAL ZERO DAMAGE.
× 0
= 0

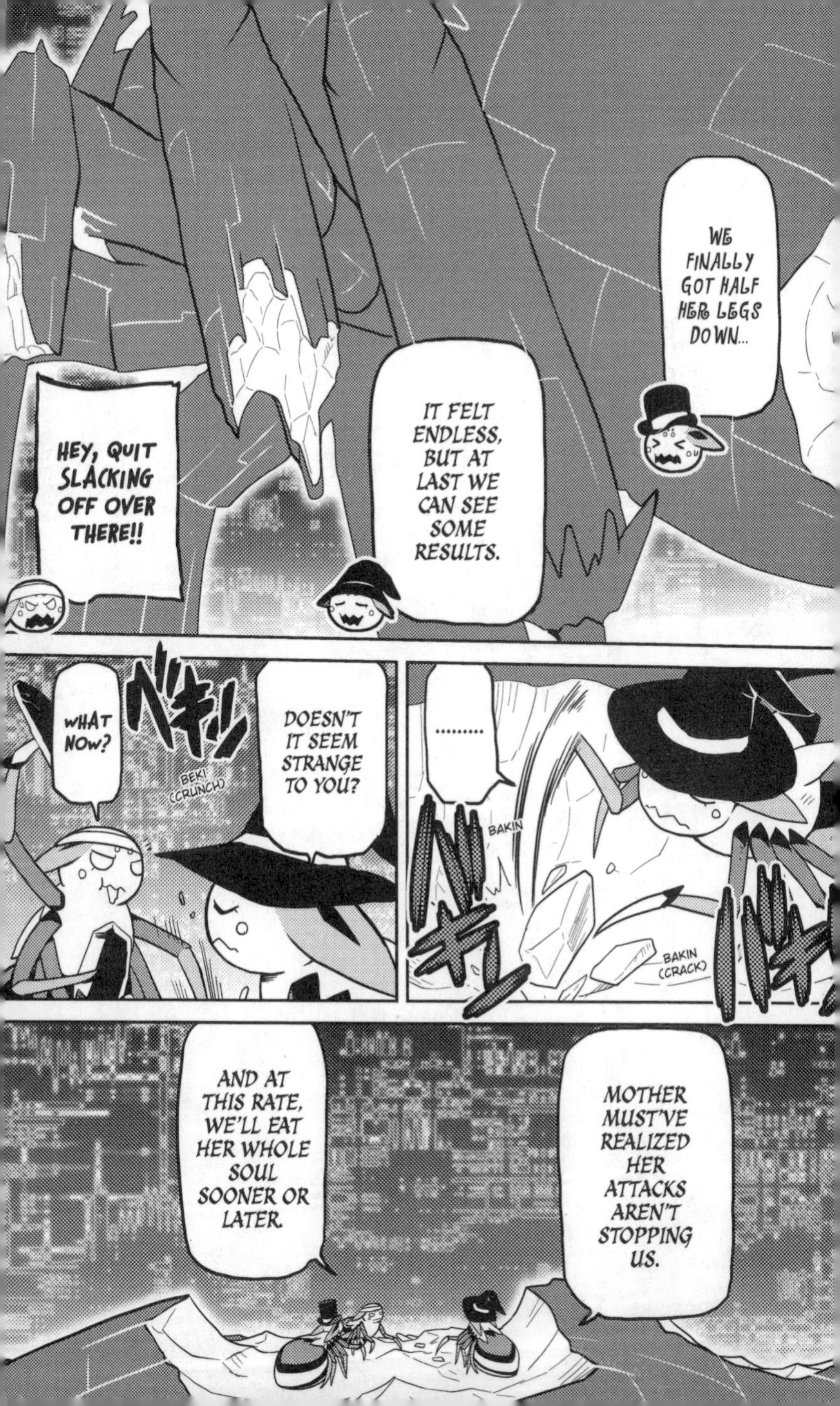
WE FINALLY GOT HALF HER LEGS DOWN...
IT FELT ENDLESS, BUT AT LAST WE CAN SEE SOME RESULTS.
HEY, QUIT SLACKING OFF OVER THERE!!
....
BAKIN
BAKIN (CRACK)
DOESN'T IT SEEM STRANGE TO YOU?
ベキッ
BEKI (CRUNCH)
WHAT NOW?
MOTHER MUST'VE REALIZED HER ATTACKS AREN'T STOPPING US.
AND AT THIS RATE, WE'LL EAT HER WHOLE SOUL SOONER OR LATER.

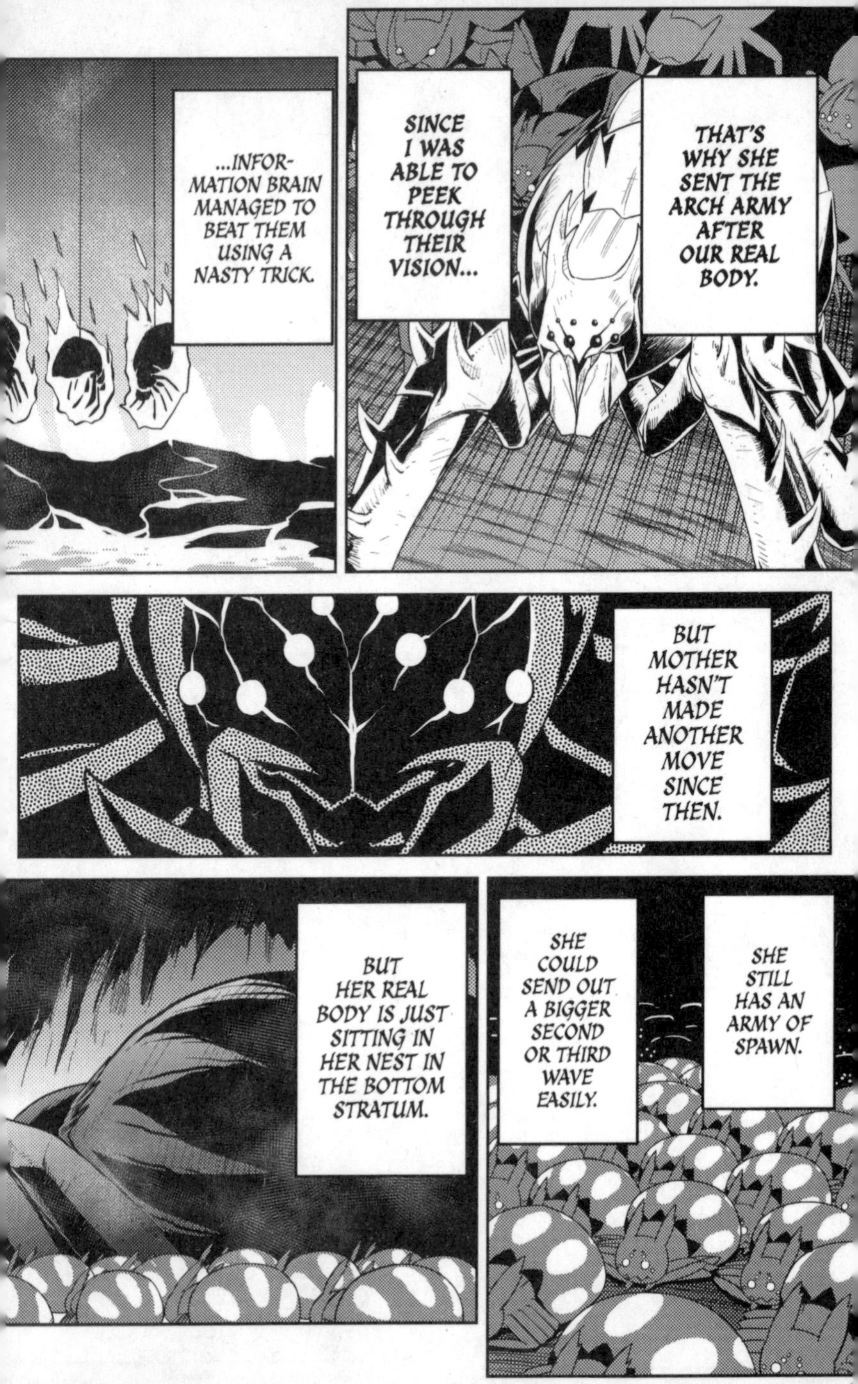
THAT'S WHY SHE SENT THE ARCH ARMY AFTER OUR REAL BODY.
SINCE I WAS ABLE TO PEEK THROUGH THEIR VISION...
...INFOR-MATION BRAIN MANAGED TO BEAT THEM USING A NASTY TRICK.
BUT MOTHER HASN'T MADE ANOTHER MOVE SINCE THEN.
SHE STILL HAS AN ARMY OF SPAWN.
SHE COULD SEND OUT A BIGGER SECOND OR THIRD WAVE EASILY.
BUT HER REAL BODY IS JUST SITTING IN HER NEST IN THE BOTTOM STRATUM.

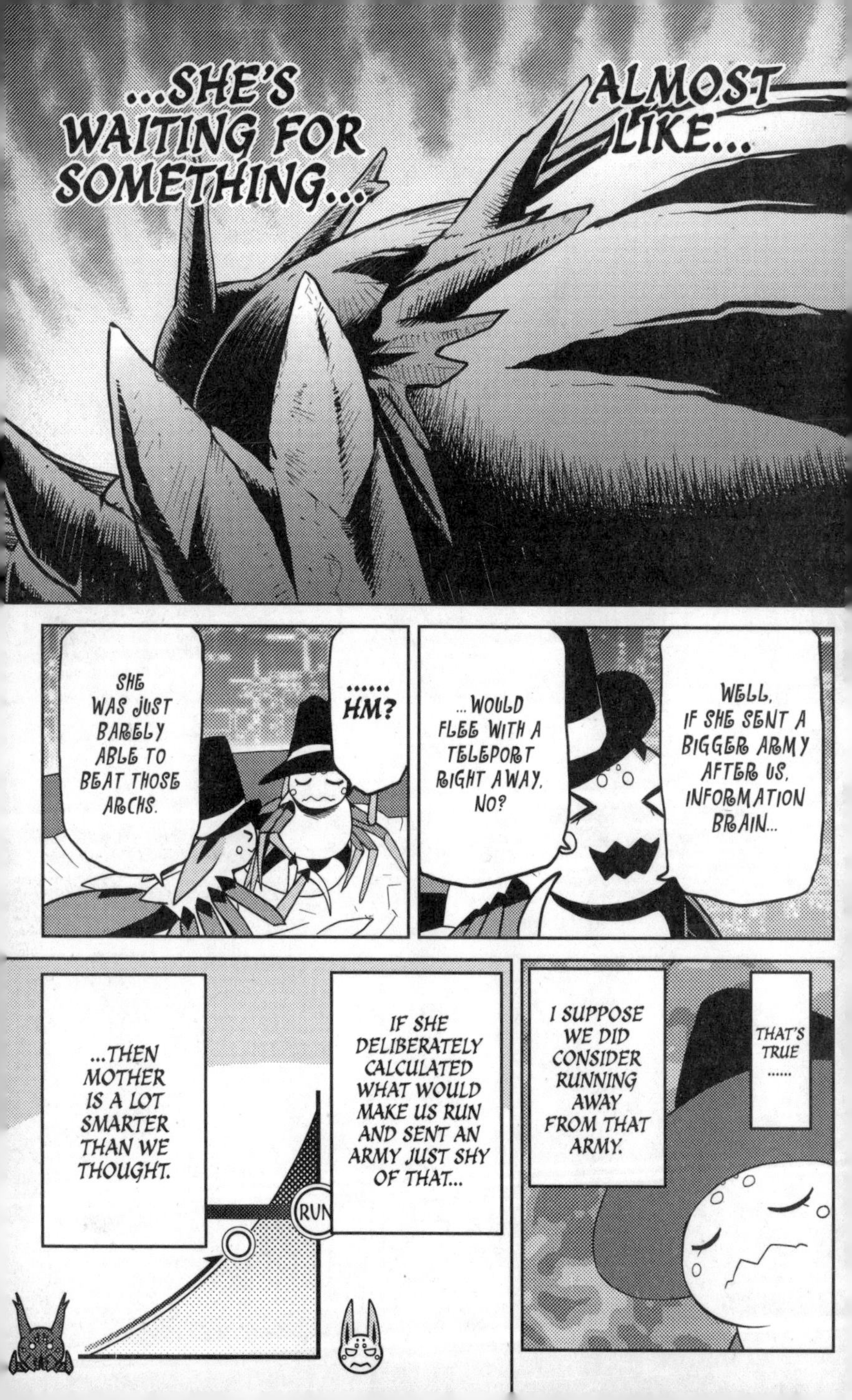
ALMOST LIKE...
...SHE'S WAITING FOR SOMETHING...
WELL, IF SHE SENT A BIGGER ARMY AFTER US, INFORMATION BRAIN...
...WOULD FLEE WITH A TELEPORT RIGHT AWAY, NO?
......HM?
SHE WAS JUST BARELY ABLE TO BEAT THOSE ARCHS.
THAT'S TRUE......
I SUPPOSE WE DID CONSIDER RUNNING AWAY FROM THAT ARMY.
IF SHE DELIBERATELY CALCULATED WHAT WOULD MAKE US RUN AND SENT AN ARMY JUST SHY OF THAT...
RUN
...THEN MOTHER IS A LOT SMARTER THAN WE THOUGHT.

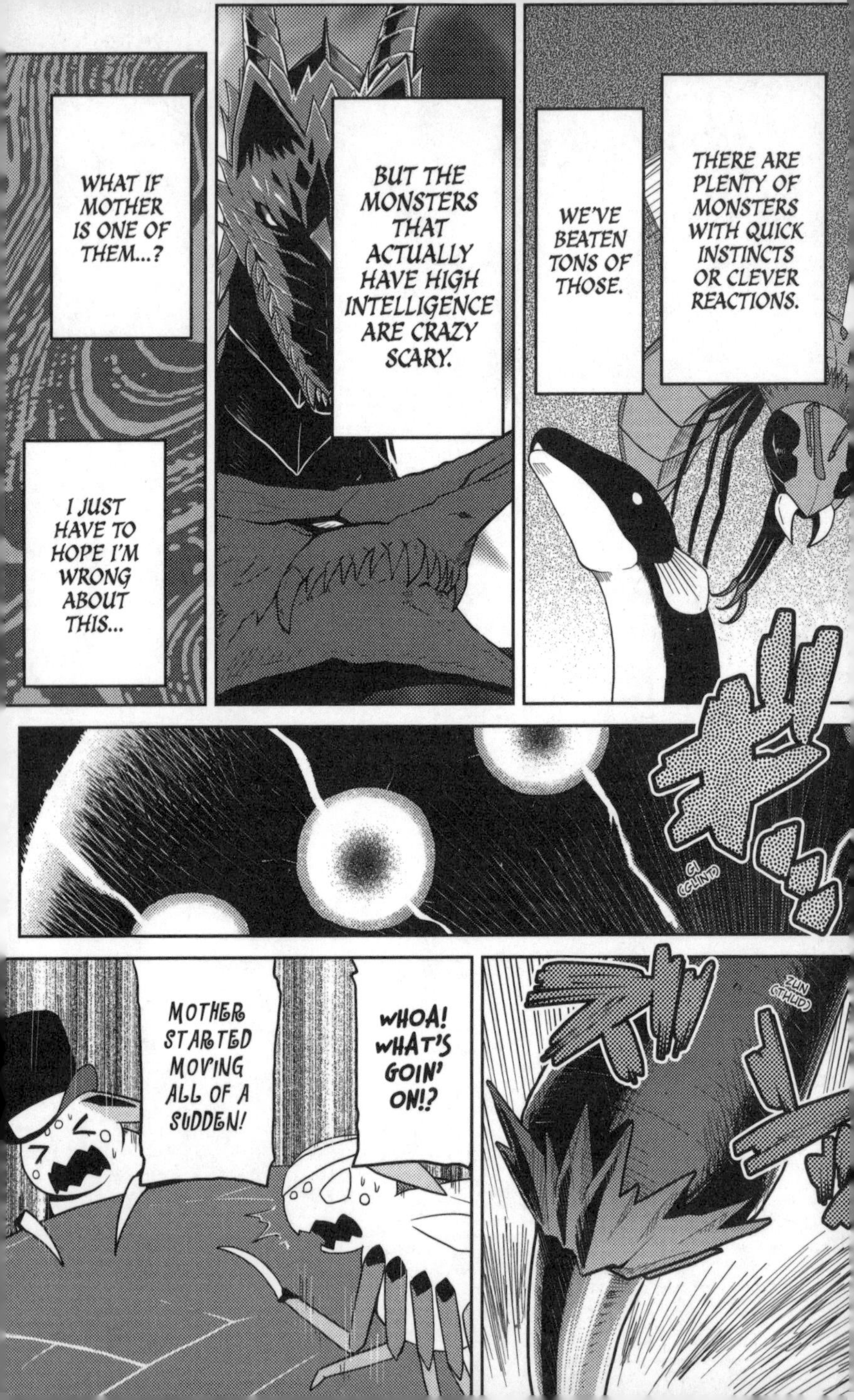
THERE ARE PLENTY OF MONSTERS WITH QUICK INSTINCTS OR CLEVER REACTIONS.
WE'VE BEATEN TONS OF THOSE.
BUT THE MONSTERS THAT ACTUALLY HAVE HIGH INTELLIGENCE ARE CRAZY SCARY.
WHAT IF MOTHER IS ONE OF THEM...?
I JUST HAVE TO HOPE I'M WRONG ABOUT THIS...
GI (GLINT)
ZUN (THUD)
WHOA! WHAT'S GOIN' ON!?
MOTHER STARTED MOVING ALL OF A SUDDEN!

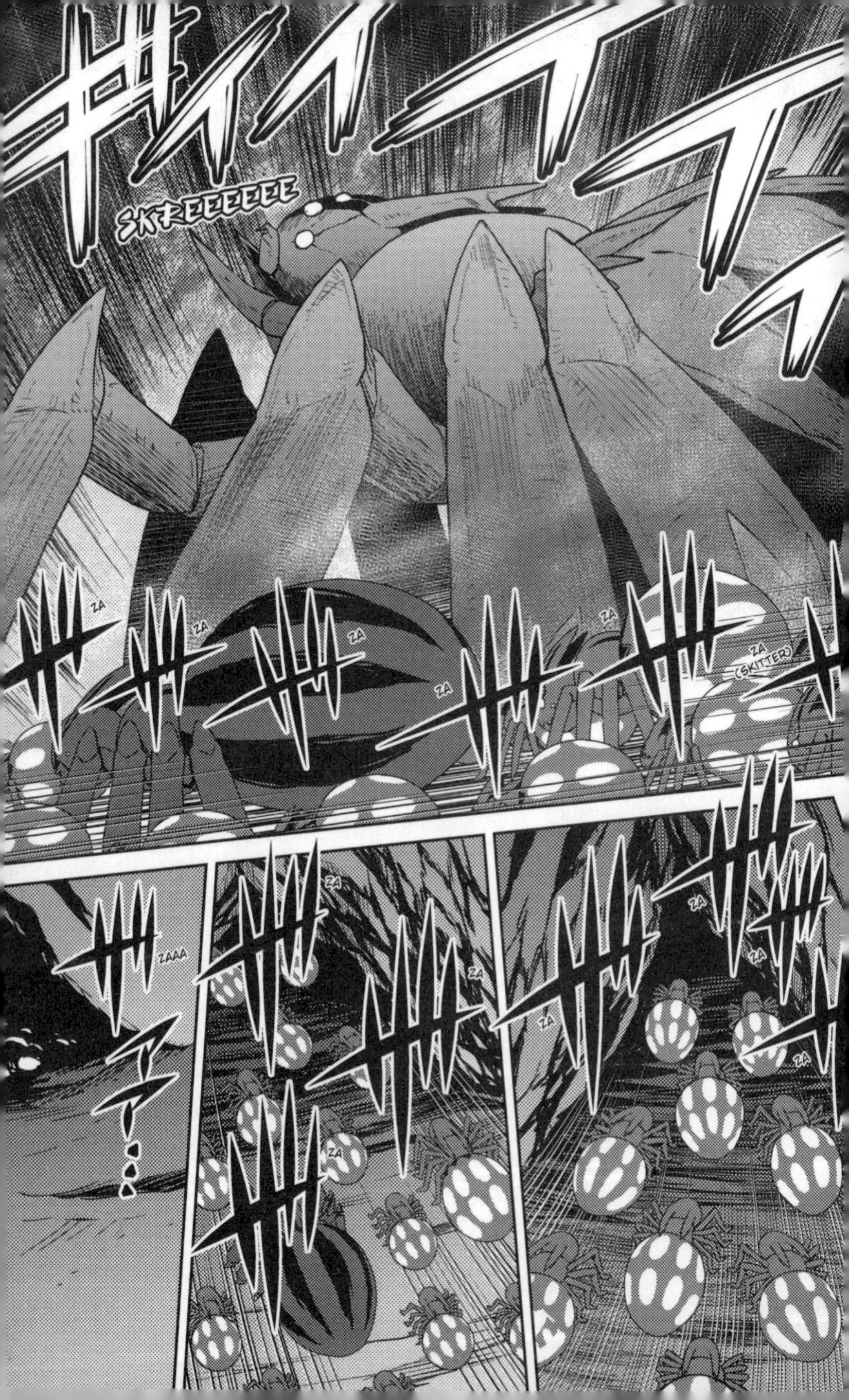
SKREEEEEEE
ZA
(SKITTER)
ZA
ZA
ZA
ZA
ZA
ZA
ZA
ZA
ZA
ZA
ZA
ZA
ZAAA

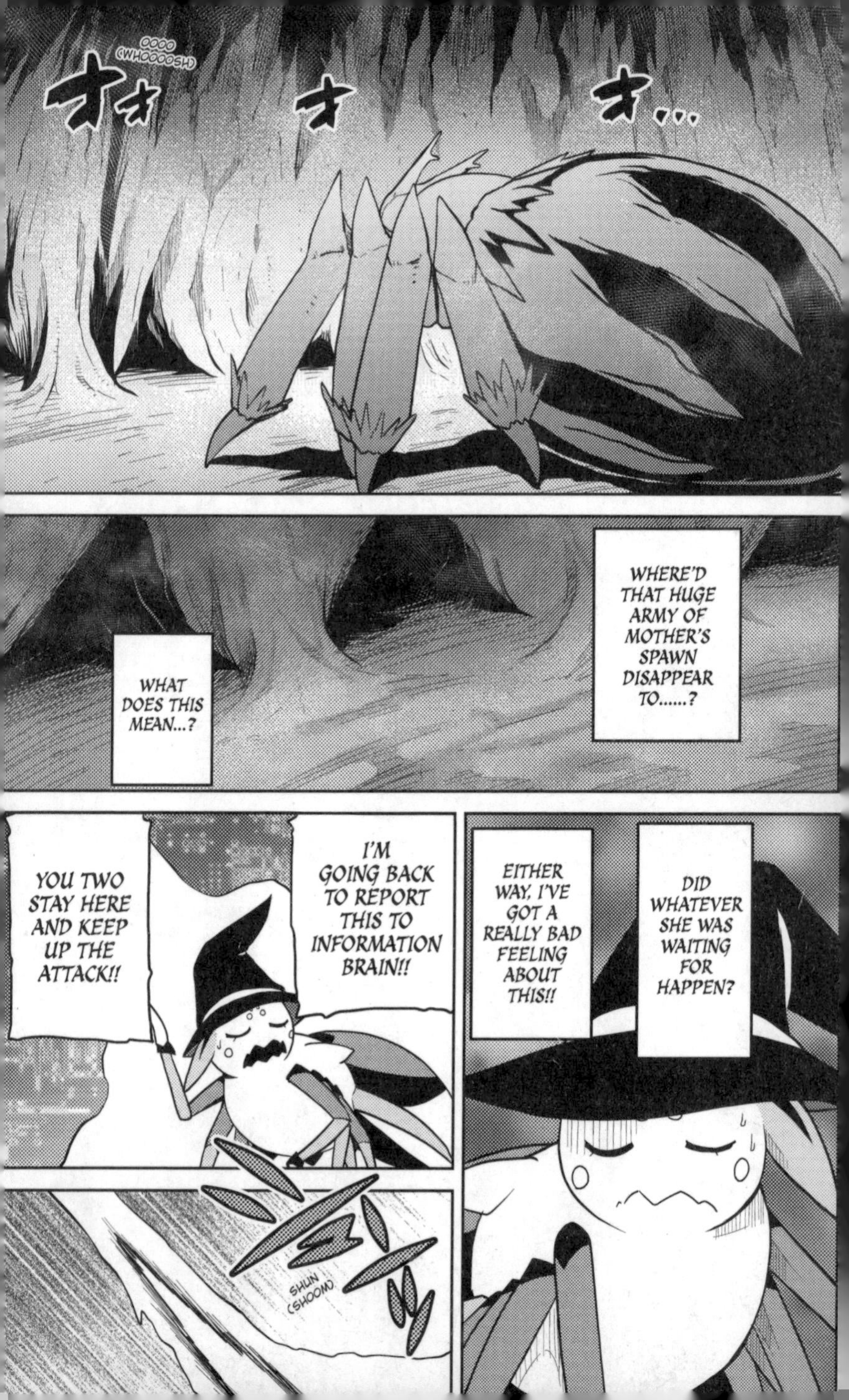
OOOO (WHOOOOSH)
オォ オ ォ...
WHERE'D THAT HUGE ARMY OF MOTHER'S SPAWN DISAPPEAR TO......?
WHAT DOES THIS MEAN...?
DID WHATEVER SHE WAS WAITING FOR HAPPEN?
EITHER WAY, I'VE GOT A REALLY BAD FEELING ABOUT THIS!!
I'M GOING BACK TO REPORT THIS TO INFORMATION BRAIN!!
YOU TWO STAY HERE AND KEEP UP THE ATTACK!!
SHUN (SHOOM)

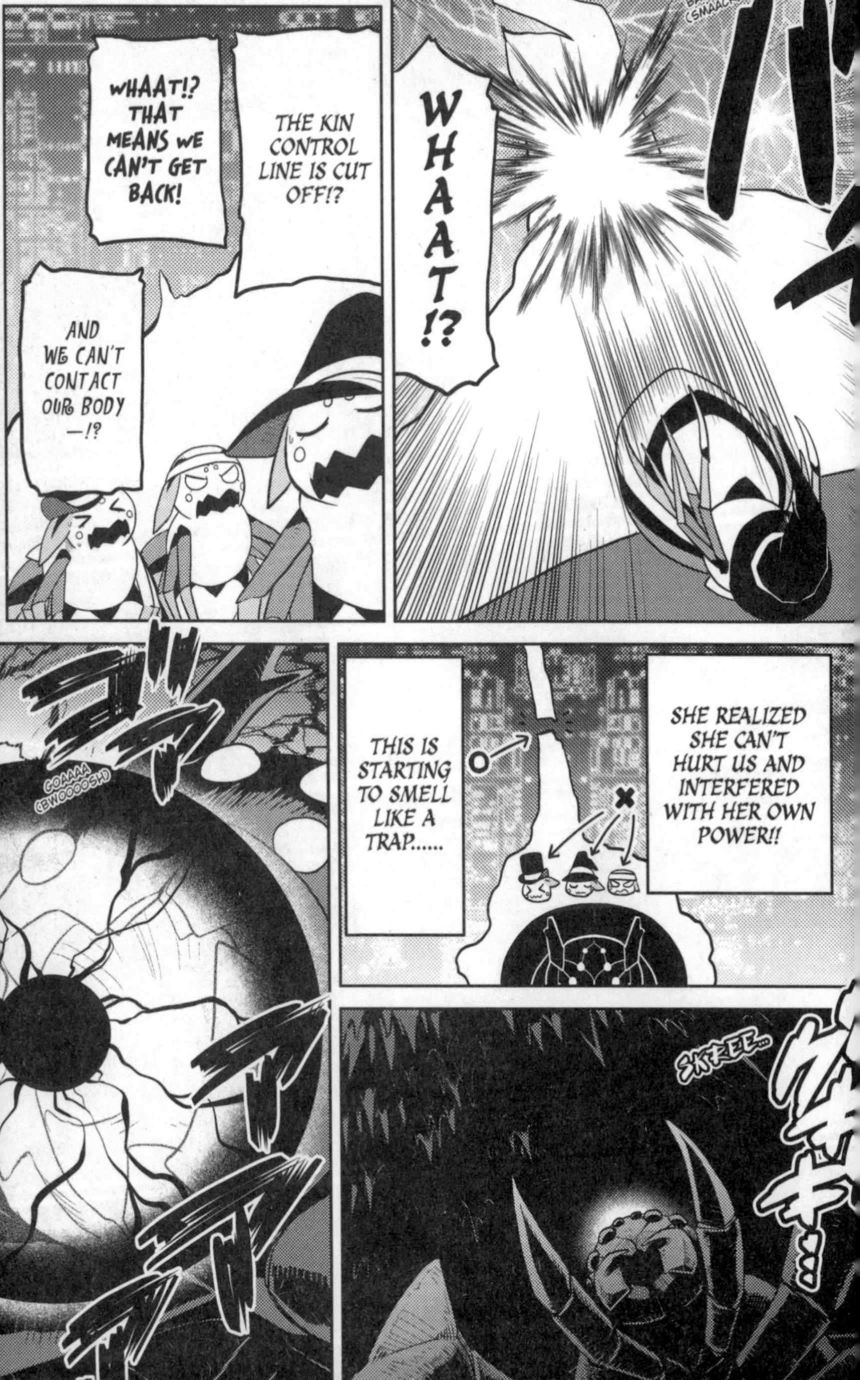
BACHAA (SMAACK)
WHAAAT!?
THE KIN CONTROL LINE IS CUT OFF!?
WHAAT!? THAT MEANS WE CAN'T GET BACK!
AND WE CAN'T CONTACT OUR BODY—!?
SHE REALIZED SHE CAN'T HURT US AND INTERFERED WITH HER OWN POWER!!
THIS IS STARTING TO SMELL LIKE A TRAP......
SKREE...
GOAAAA (BWOOOOSH)

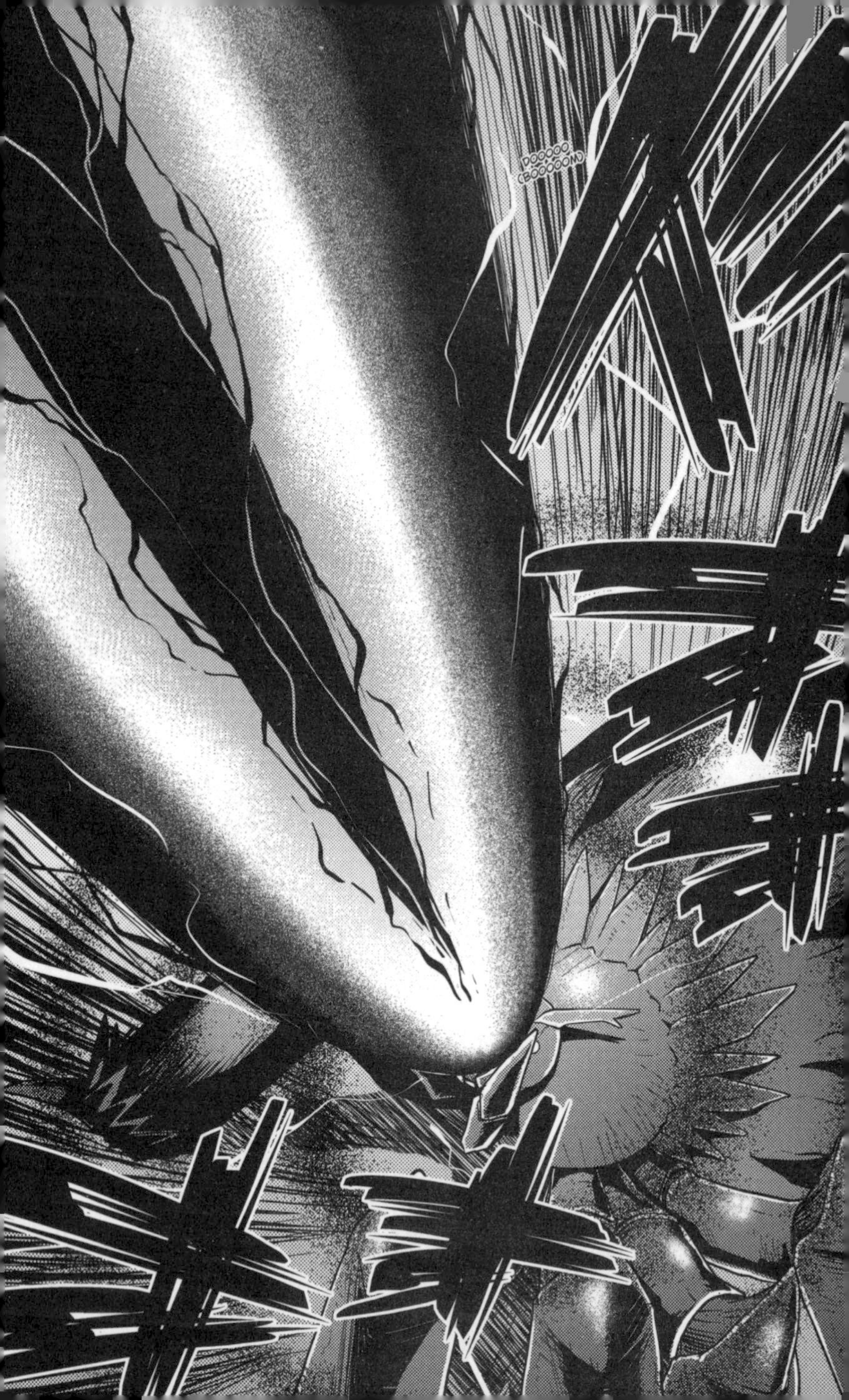
DOOOOO
(BOOOOOM)

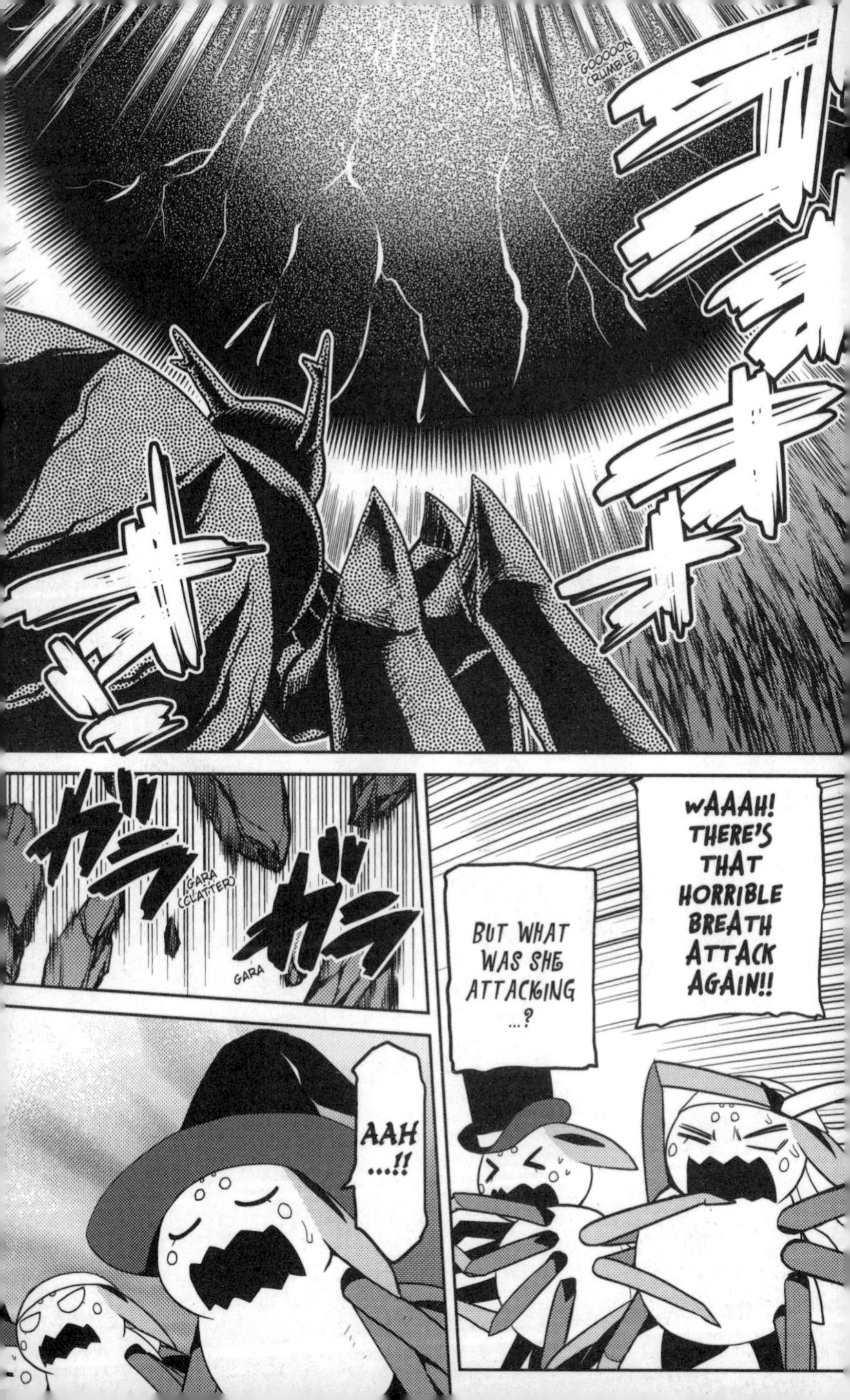
GOOOOON (RUMBLE)
WAAAH! THERE'S THAT HORRIBLE BREATH ATTACK AGAIN!!
BUT WHAT WAS SHE ATTACKING ...?
GARA (CLATTER)
GARA
AAH ...!!

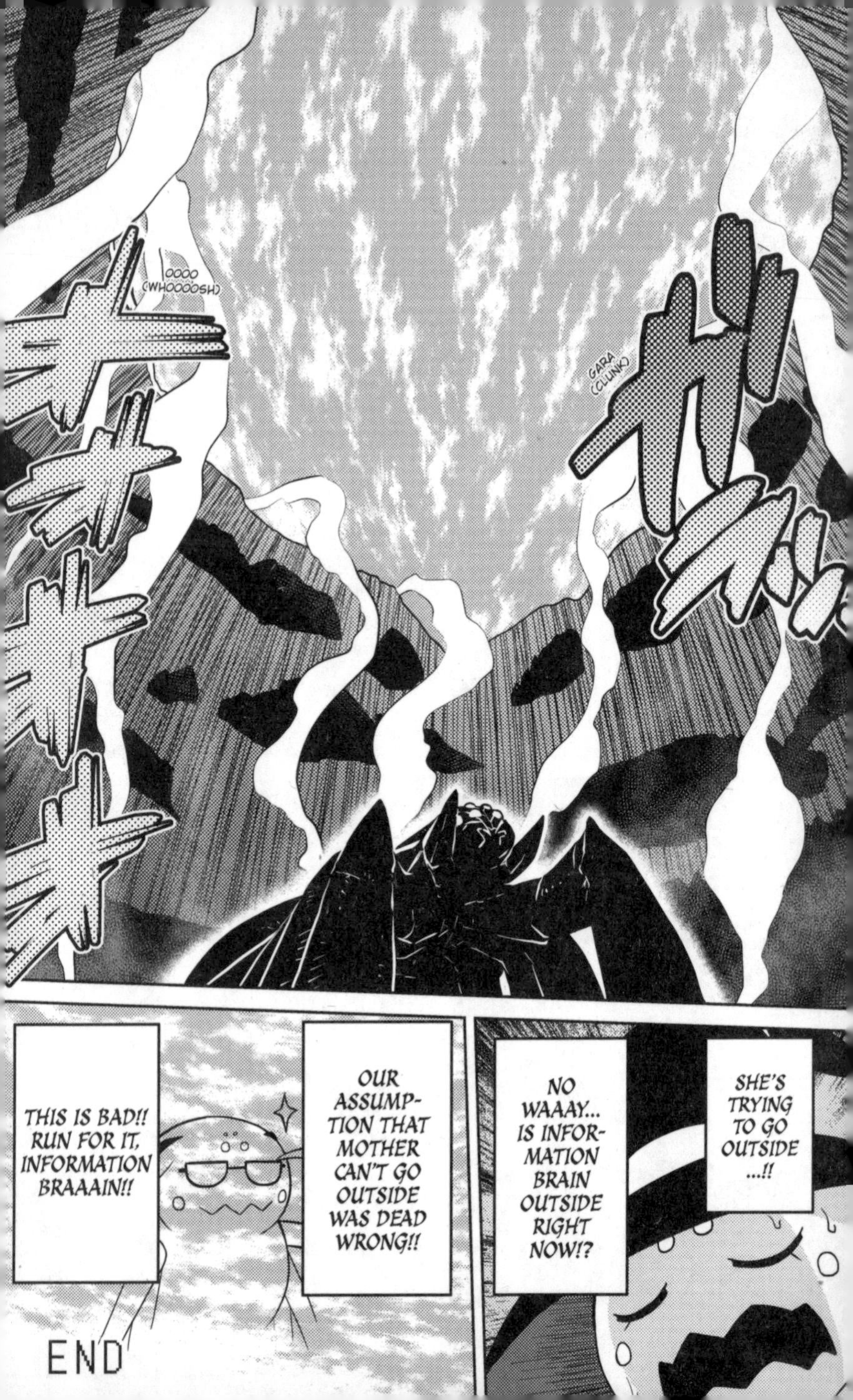
GARA (CLUNK)
OOOO (WHOOOOSH)
SHE'S TRYING TO GO OUTSIDE ...!!
NO WAAAY... IS INFOR-MATION BRAIN OUTSIDE RIGHT NOW!?
OUR ASSUMP-TION THAT MOTHER CAN'T GO OUTSIDE WAS DEAD WRONG!!
THIS IS BAD!! RUN FOR IT, INFORMATION BRAAAIN!!
END

So I'm a Spider, So What?

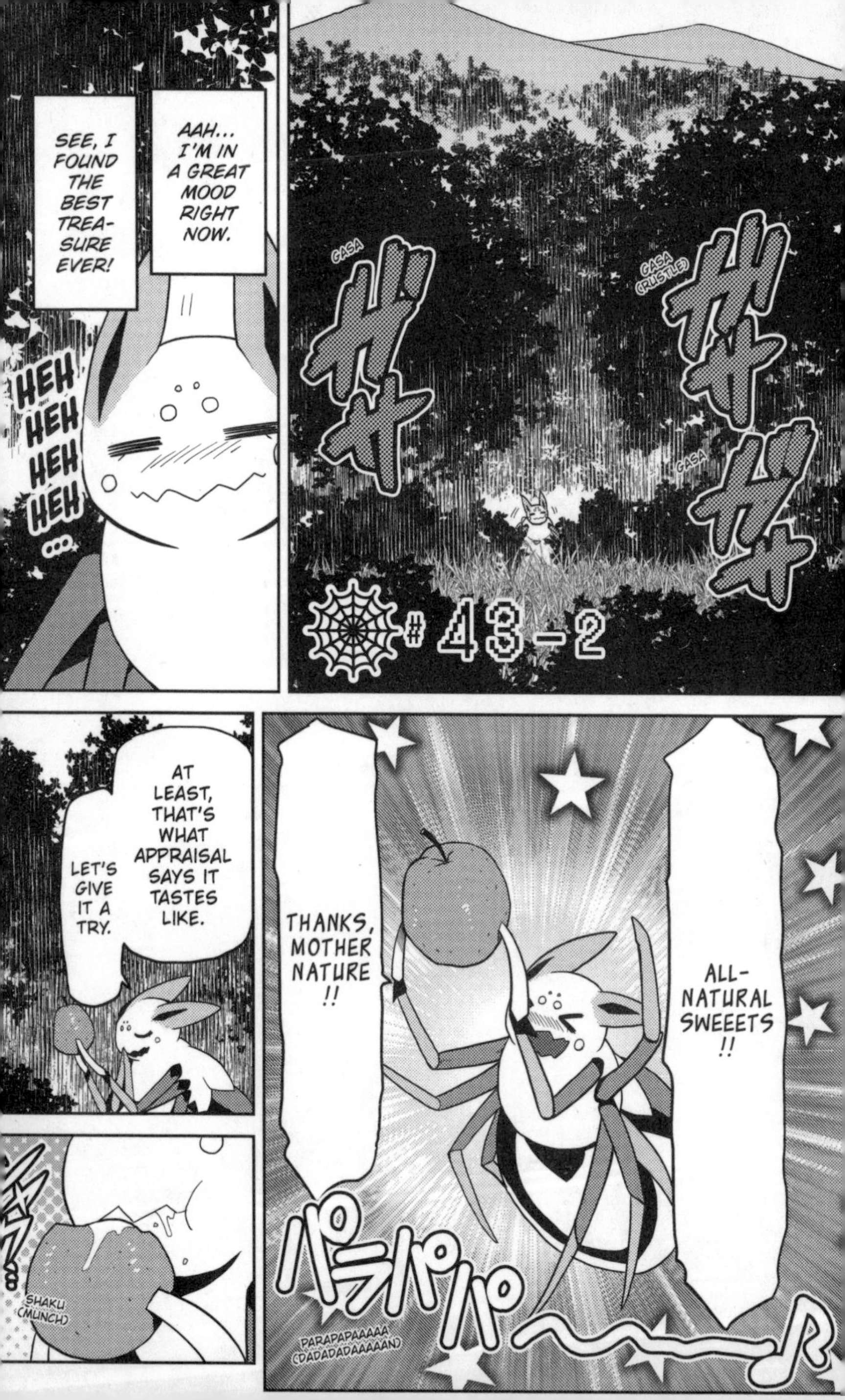
GASA (RUSTLE)
GASA
GASA
#43-2
AAH... I'M IN A GREAT MOOD RIGHT NOW.
SEE, I FOUND THE BEST TREASURE EVER!
HEH HEH HEH HEH...
ALL-NATURAL SWEEETS!!
THANKS, MOTHER NATURE!!
PARAPAPAAAAA (DADADADAAAAAN)
AT LEAST, THAT'S WHAT APPRAISAL SAYS IT TASTES LIKE.
LET'S GIVE IT A TRY.
SHAKU (MUNCH)

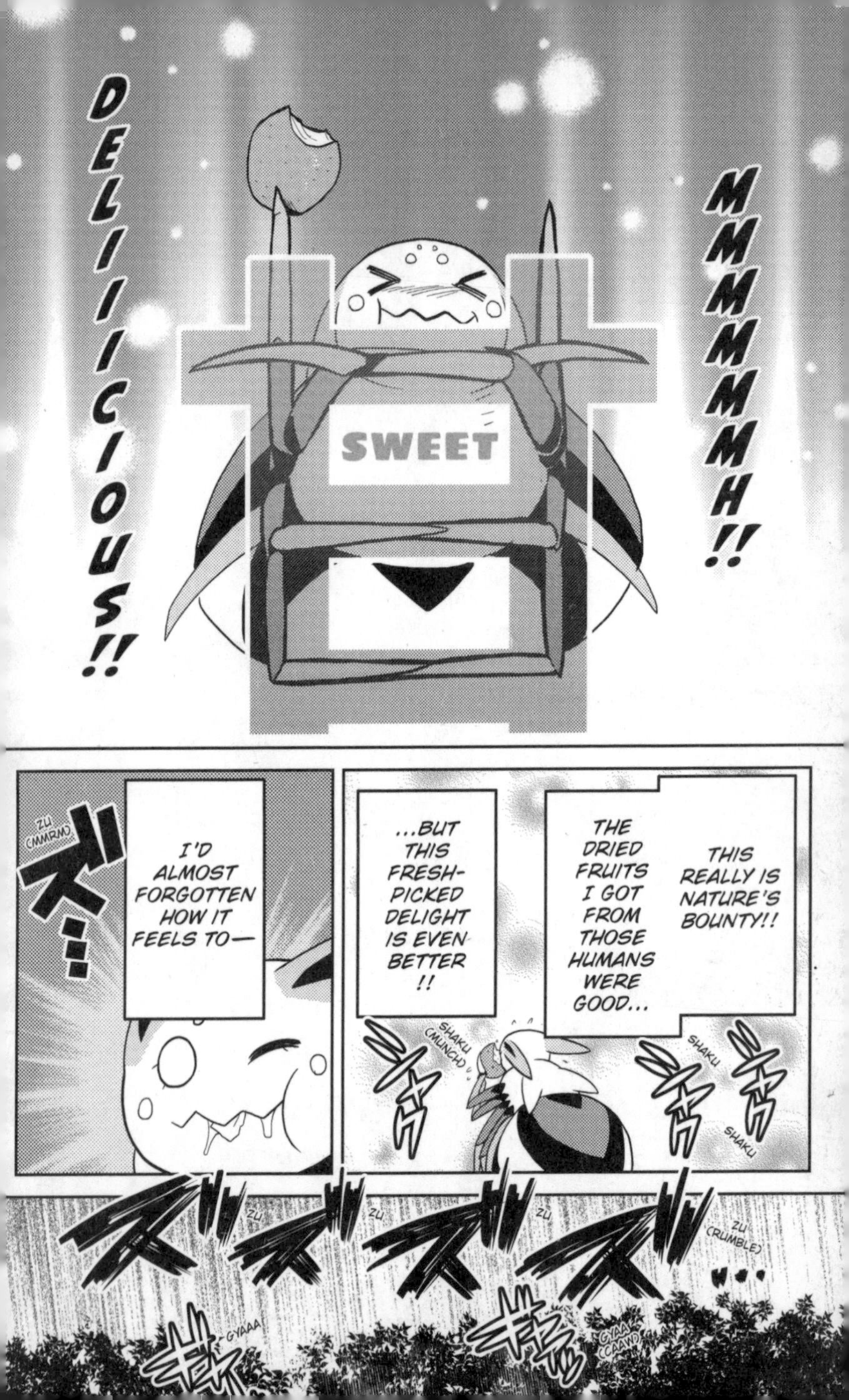
MMMMMMMH!!
DELIIIICIOUS!!
SWEET
THIS REALLY IS NATURE'S BOUNTY!!
THE DRIED FRUITS I GOT FROM THOSE HUMANS WERE GOOD...
...BUT THIS FRESH-PICKED DELIGHT IS EVEN BETTER!!
SHAKU
SHAKU
SHAKU (MUNCH)
ZU (MMRM)
I'D ALMOST FORGOTTEN HOW IT FEELS TO—
ZU (RUMBLE)
ZU
ZU
ZU
GYAA (CAAW)
GYAAA

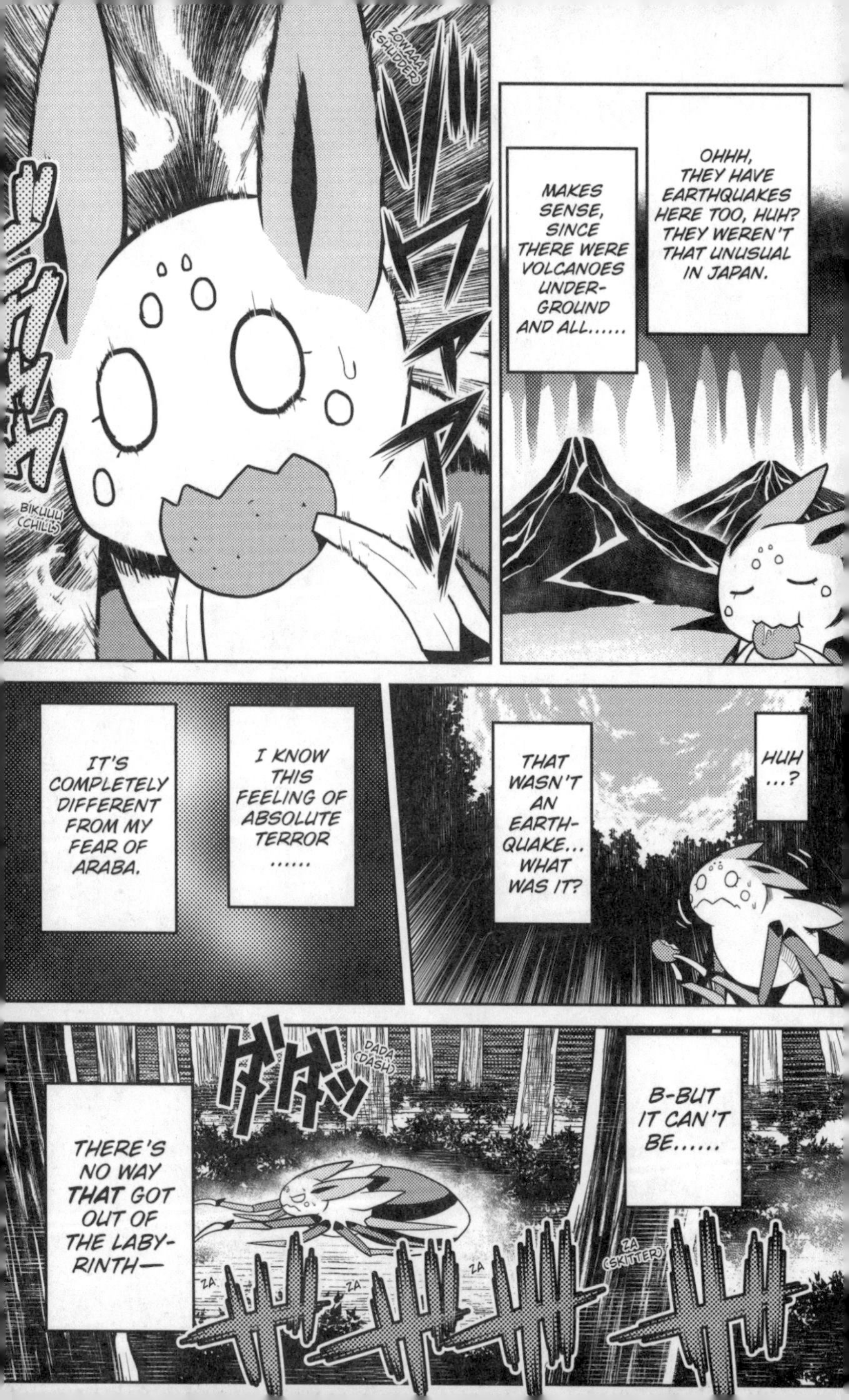
OHHH, THEY HAVE EARTHQUAKES HERE TOO, HUH? THEY WEREN'T THAT UNUSUAL IN JAPAN.
MAKES SENSE, SINCE THERE WERE VOLCANOES UNDER-GROUND AND ALL......
ZOWAAA (SHUDDER)
BIKUUU (CHILLS)
HUH ...?
THAT WASN'T AN EARTH-QUAKE... WHAT WAS IT?
I KNOW THIS FEELING OF ABSOLUTE TERROR ......
IT'S COMPLETELY DIFFERENT FROM MY FEAR OF ARABA.
B-BUT IT CAN'T BE......
DADA (DASH)
ZA (SKITTER)
ZA
ZA
ZA
THERE'S NO WAY THAT GOT OUT OF THE LABY-RINTH—

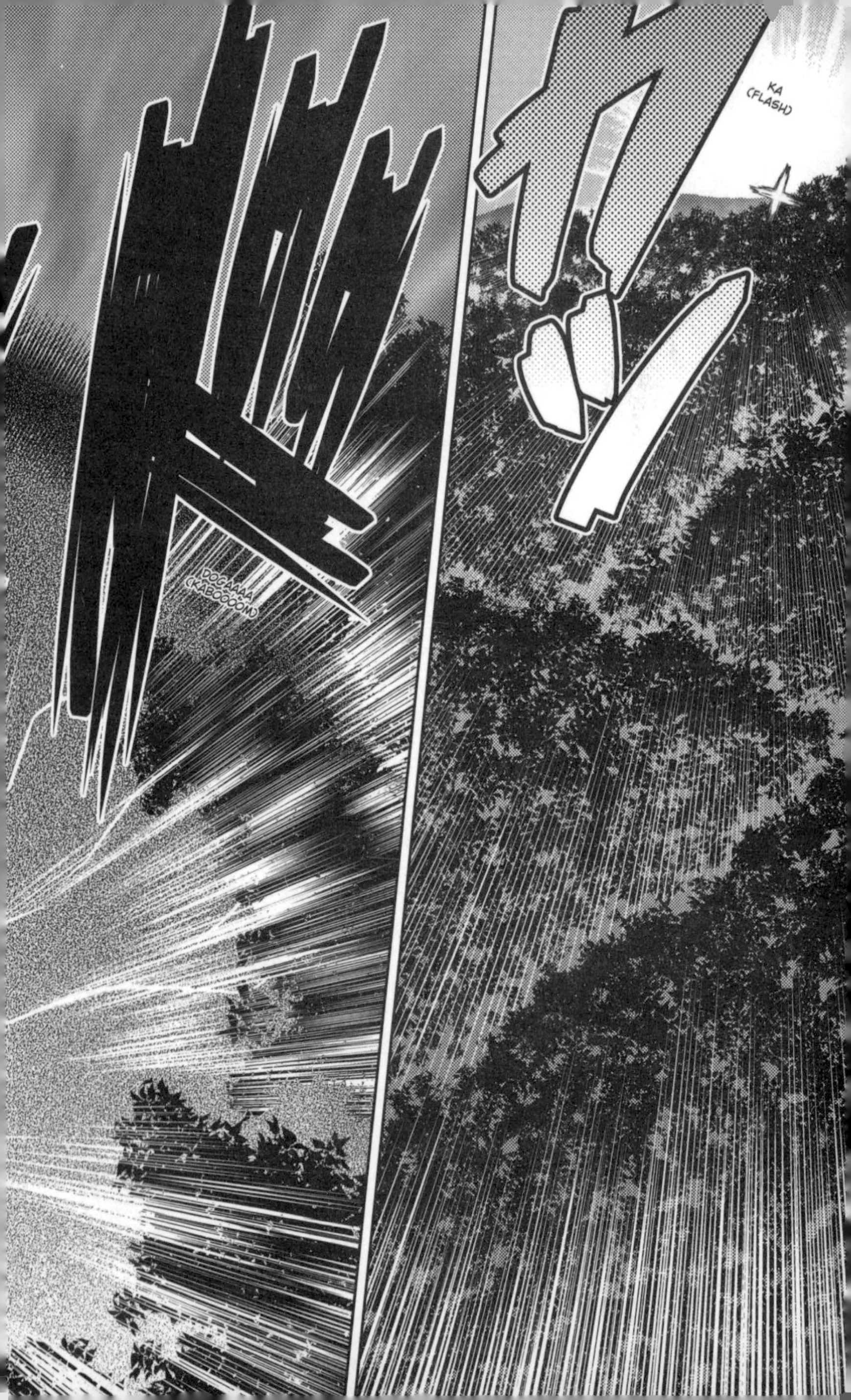
KA (FLASH)
DOGAAAA (KABOOOOM)

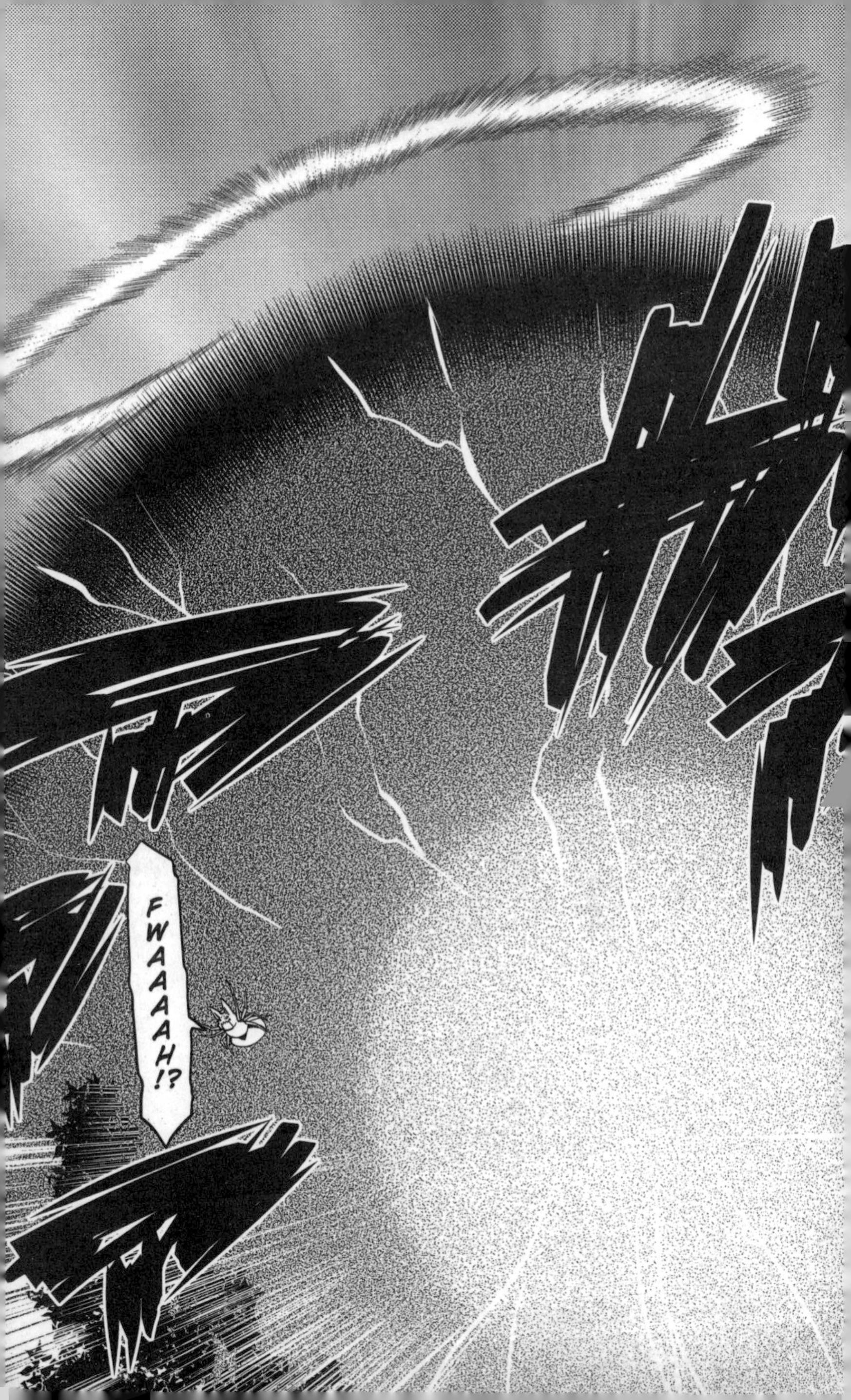
FWAAAAAH!?

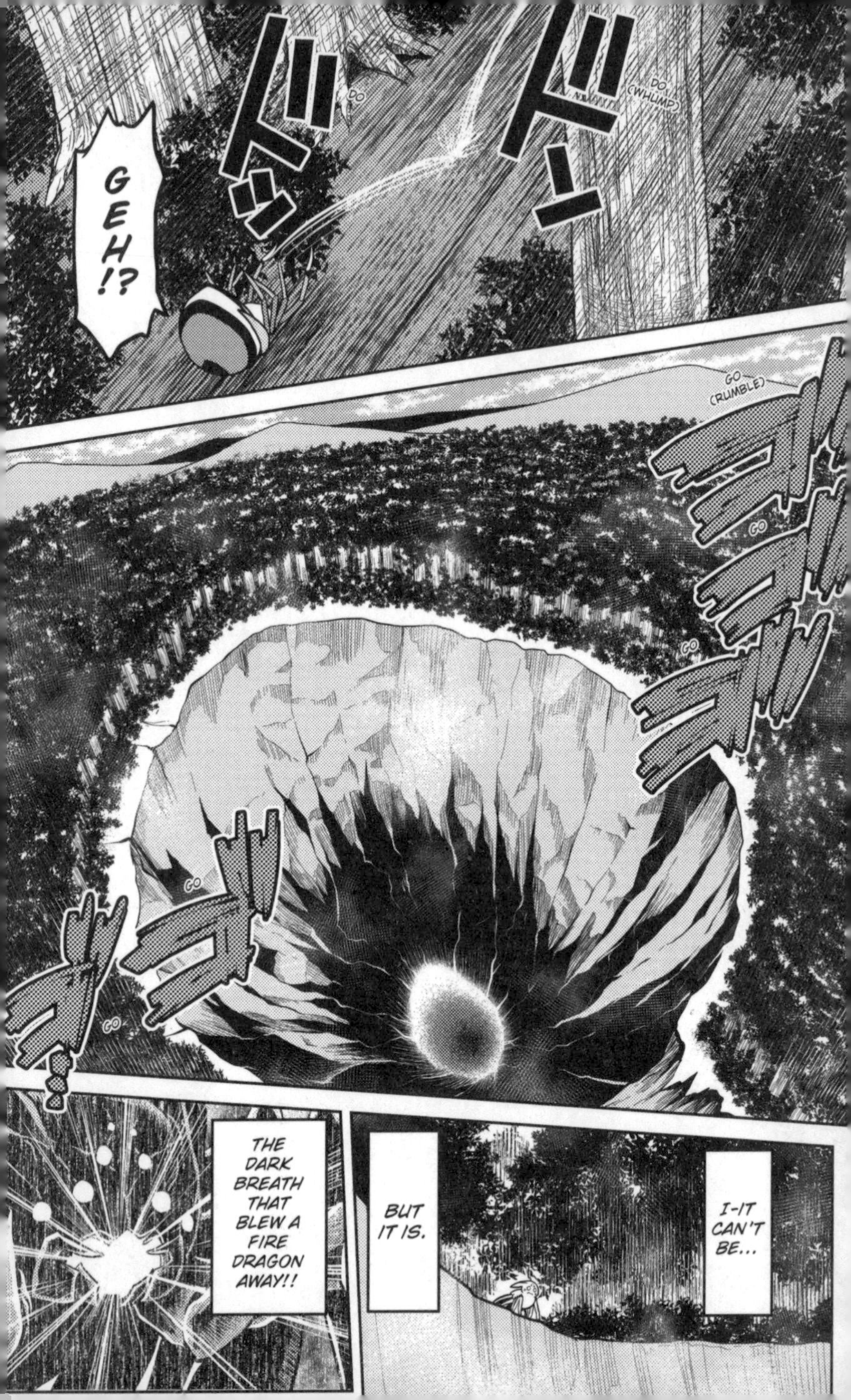
DO (WHUMP)
DO
GEH!?
GO (RUMBLE)
GO
GO
GO
GO
I-IT CAN'T BE...
BUT IT IS.
THE DARK BREATH THAT BLEW A FIRE DRAGON AWAY!!

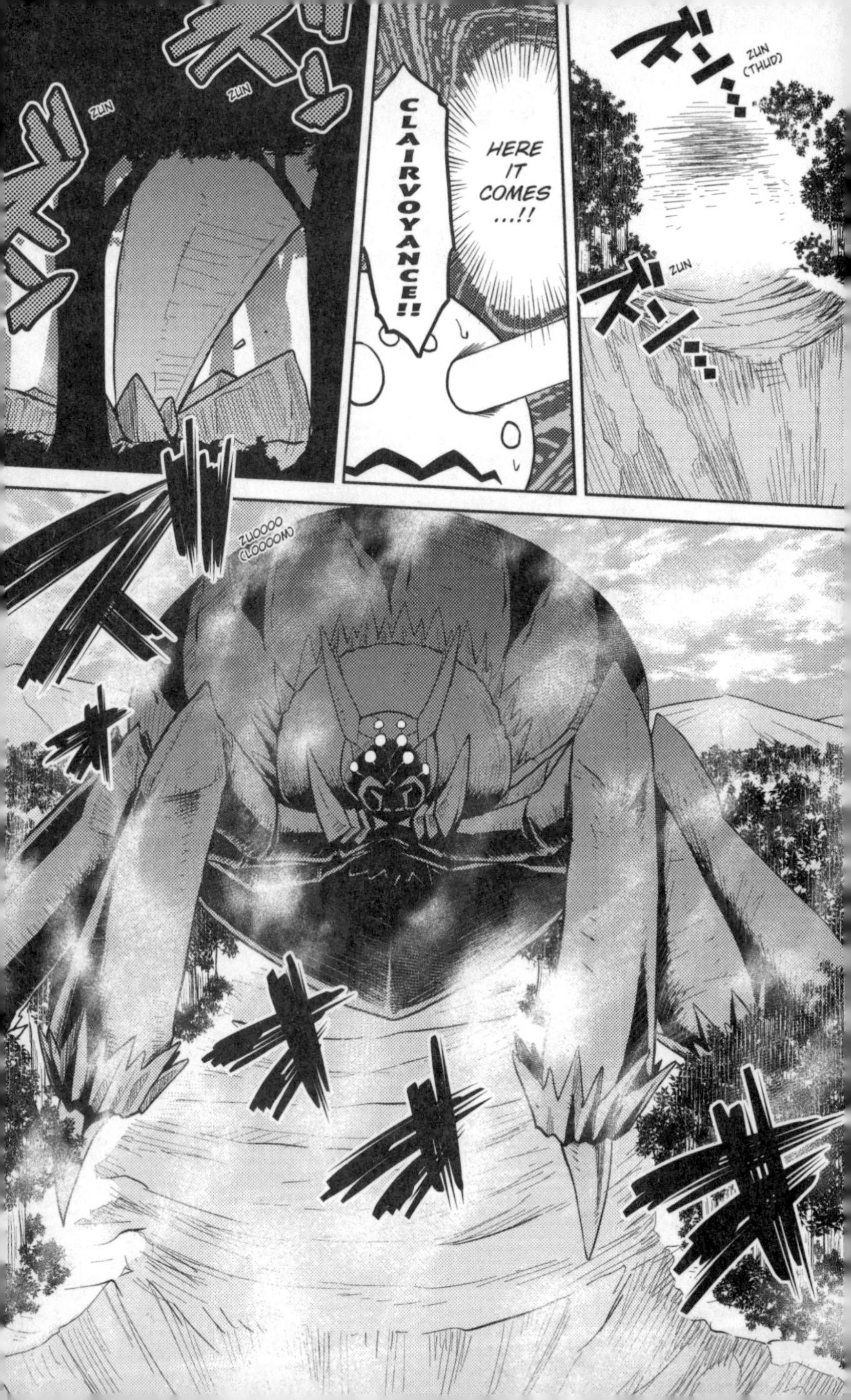
ZUN (THUD)
ZUN
HERE IT COMES ...!!
CLAIRVOYANCE!!
ZUN
ZUN
ZUOOOO (WOOOOM)

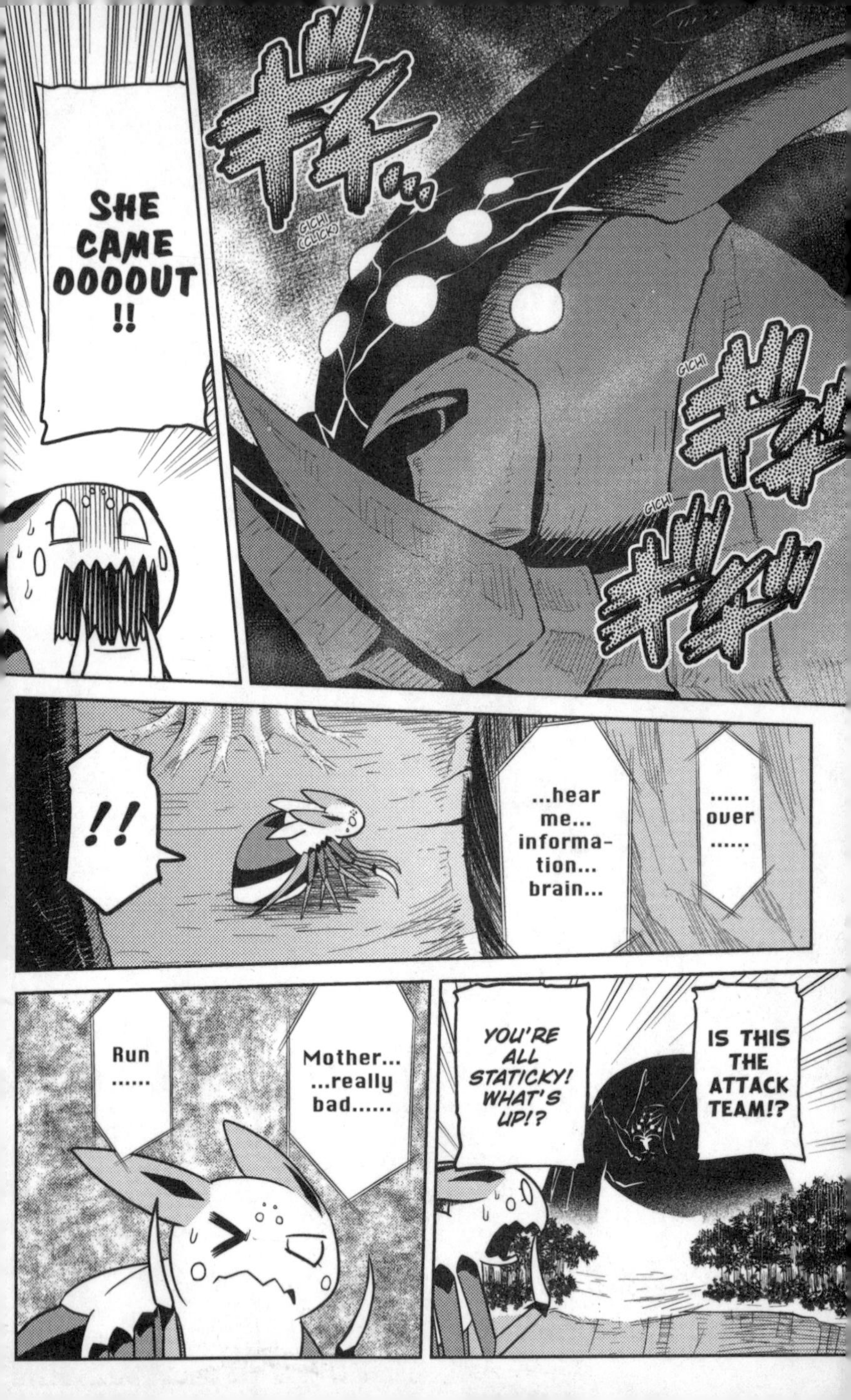
GICHI
GICHI
GICHI (CLICK)
SHE CAME OOOOUT !!
...... over ......
...hear me... information-tion... brain...
!!
IS THIS THE ATTACK TEAM!?
YOU'RE ALL STATICKY! WHAT'S UP!?
Mother... ...really bad......
Run ......

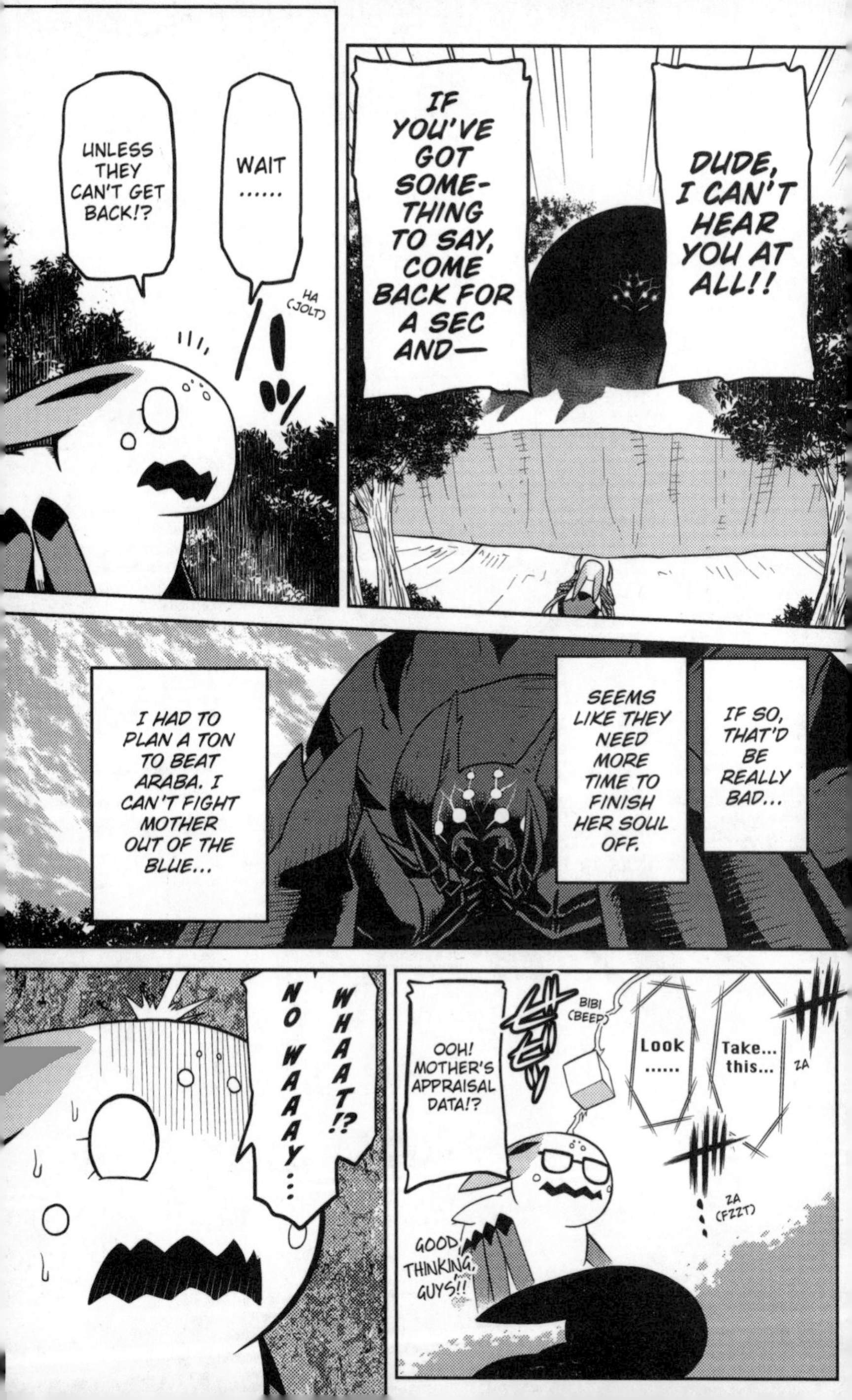
DUDE, I CAN'T HEAR YOU AT ALL!!
IF YOU'VE GOT SOME-THING TO SAY, COME BACK FOR A SEC AND—
WAIT ......
HA (JOLT)
UNLESS THEY CAN'T GET BACK!?
IF SO, THAT'D BE REALLY BAD...
SEEMS LIKE THEY NEED MORE TIME TO FINISH HER SOUL OFF.
I HAD TO PLAN A TON TO BEAT ARABA. I CAN'T FIGHT MOTHER OUT OF THE BLUE...
ZA
Take... this...
Look ......
BIBI (BEEP)
OOH! MOTHER'S APPRAISAL DATA!?
ZA (FZZT)
GOOD THINKING, GUYS!!
WHAAAT!? NO WAAAAY...

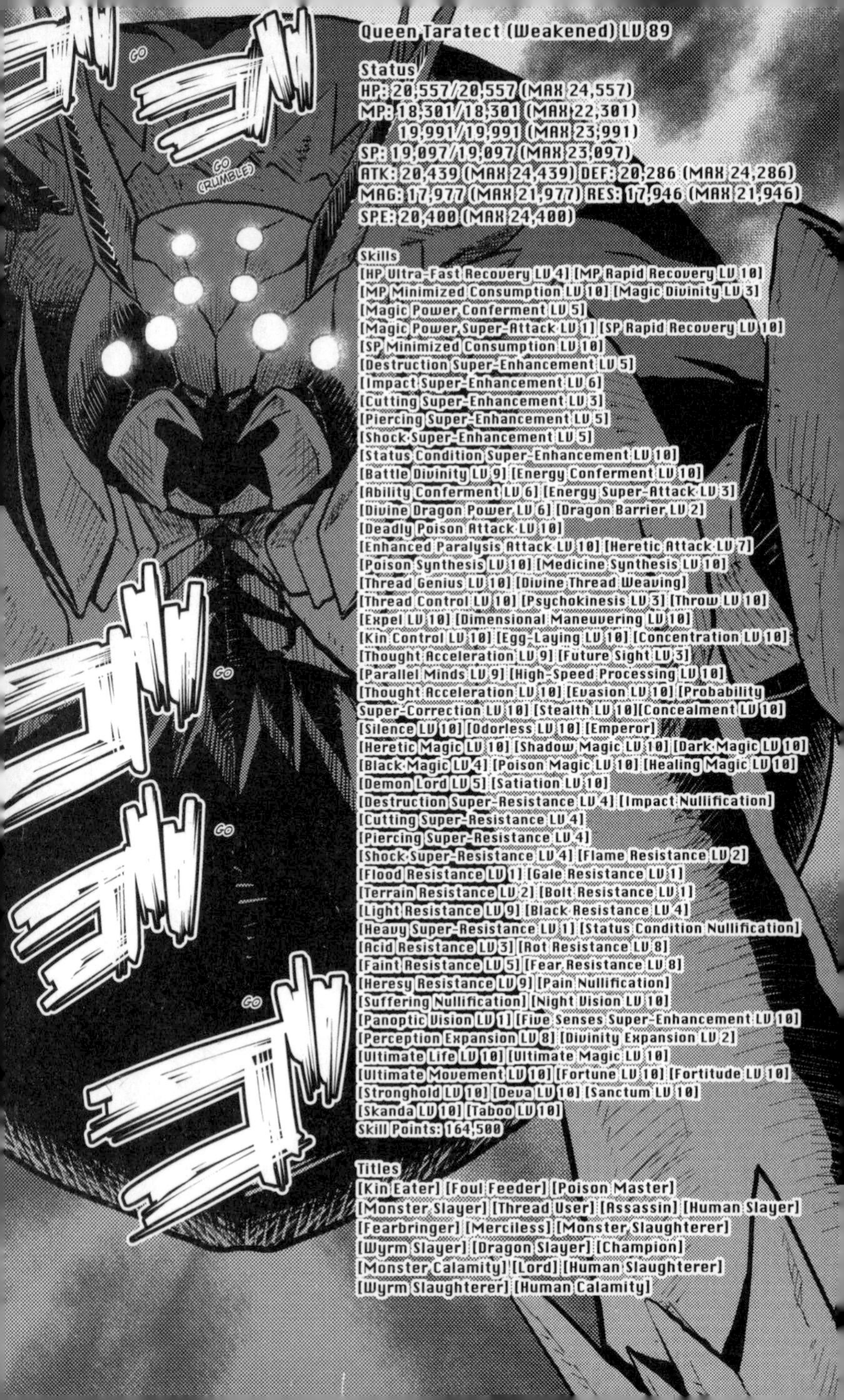
Queen Taratect (Weakened) LV 89
Status
HP: 20,557/20,557 (MAX 24,557)
MP: 18,301/18,301 (MAX 22,301)
19,991/19,991 (MAX 23,991)
SP: 19,097/19,097 (MAX 23,097)
ATK: 20,439 (MAX 24,439) DEF: 20,286 (MAX 24,286)
MAG: 17,977 (MAX 21,977) RES: 17,946 (MAX 21,946)
SPE: 20,400 (MAX 24,400)
Skills
[HP Ultra-Fast Recovery LV 4] [MP Rapid Recovery LV 10]
[MP Minimized Consumption LV 10] [Magic Divinity LV 3]
[Magic Power Conferment LV 5]
[Magic Power Super-Attack LV 1] [SP Rapid Recovery LV 10]
[SP Minimized Consumption LV 10]
[Destruction Super-Enhancement LV 5]
[Impact Super-Enhancement LV 6]
[Cutting Super-Enhancement LV 3]
[Piercing Super-Enhancement LV 5]
[Shock Super-Enhancement LV 5]
[Status Condition Super-Enhancement LV 10]
[Battle Divinity LV 9] [Energy Conferment LV 10]
[Ability Conferment LV 6] [Energy Super-Attack LV 3]
[Divine Dragon Power LV 6] [Dragon Barrier LV 2]
[Deadly Poison Attack LV 10]
[Enhanced Paralysis Attack LV 10] [Heretic Attack LV 7]
[Poison Synthesis LV 10] [Medicine Synthesis LV 10]
[Thread Genius LV 10] [Divine Thread Weaving]
[Thread Control LV 10] [Psychokinesis LV 3] [Throw LV 10]
[Expel LV 10] [Dimensional Maneuvering LV 10]
[Kin Control LV 10] [Egg-Laying LV 10] [Concentration LV 10]
[Thought Acceleration LV 9] [Future Sight LV 3]
[Parallel Minds LV 9] [High-Speed Processing LV 10]
[Thought Acceleration LV 10] [Evasion LV 10] [Probability Super-Correction LV 10] [Stealth LV 10][Concealment LV 10]
[Silence LV 10] [Odorless LV 10] [Emperor]
[Heretic Magic LV 10] [Shadow Magic LV 10] [Dark Magic LV 10]
[Black Magic LV 4] [Poison Magic LV 10] [Healing Magic LV 10]
[Demon Lord LV 5] [Satiation LV 10]
[Destruction Super-Resistance LV 4] [Impact Nullification]
[Cutting Super-Resistance LV 4]
[Piercing Super-Resistance LV 4]
[Shock Super-Resistance LV 4] [Flame Resistance LV 2]
[Flood Resistance LV 1] [Gale Resistance LV 1]
[Terrain Resistance LV 2] [Bolt Resistance LV 1]
[Light Resistance LV 9] [Black Resistance LV 4]
[Heavy Super-Resistance LV 1] [Status Condition Nullification]
[Acid Resistance LV 3] [Rot Resistance LV 8]
[Faint Resistance LV 5] [Fear Resistance LV 8]
[Heresy Resistance LV 9] [Pain Nullification]
[Suffering Nullification] [Night Vision LV 10]
[Panoptic Vision LV 1] [Five Senses Super-Enhancement LV 10]
[Perception Expansion LV 8] [Divinity Expansion LV 2]
[Ultimate Life LV 10] [Ultimate Magic LV 10]
[Ultimate Movement LV 10] [Fortune LV 10] [Fortitude LV 10]
[Stronghold LV 10] [Deva LV 10] [Sanctum LV 10]
[Skanda LV 10] [Taboo LV 10]
Skill Points: 164,500
Titles
[Kin Eater] [Foul Feeder] [Poison Master]
[Monster Slayer] [Thread User] [Assassin] [Human Slayer]
[Fearbringer] [Merciless] [Monster Slaughterer]
[Wyrm Slayer] [Dragon Slayer] [Champion]
[Monster Calamity] [Lord] [Human Slaughterer]
[Wyrm Slaughterer] [Human Calamity]
GO
GO (RUMBLE)
GO
GO
GO

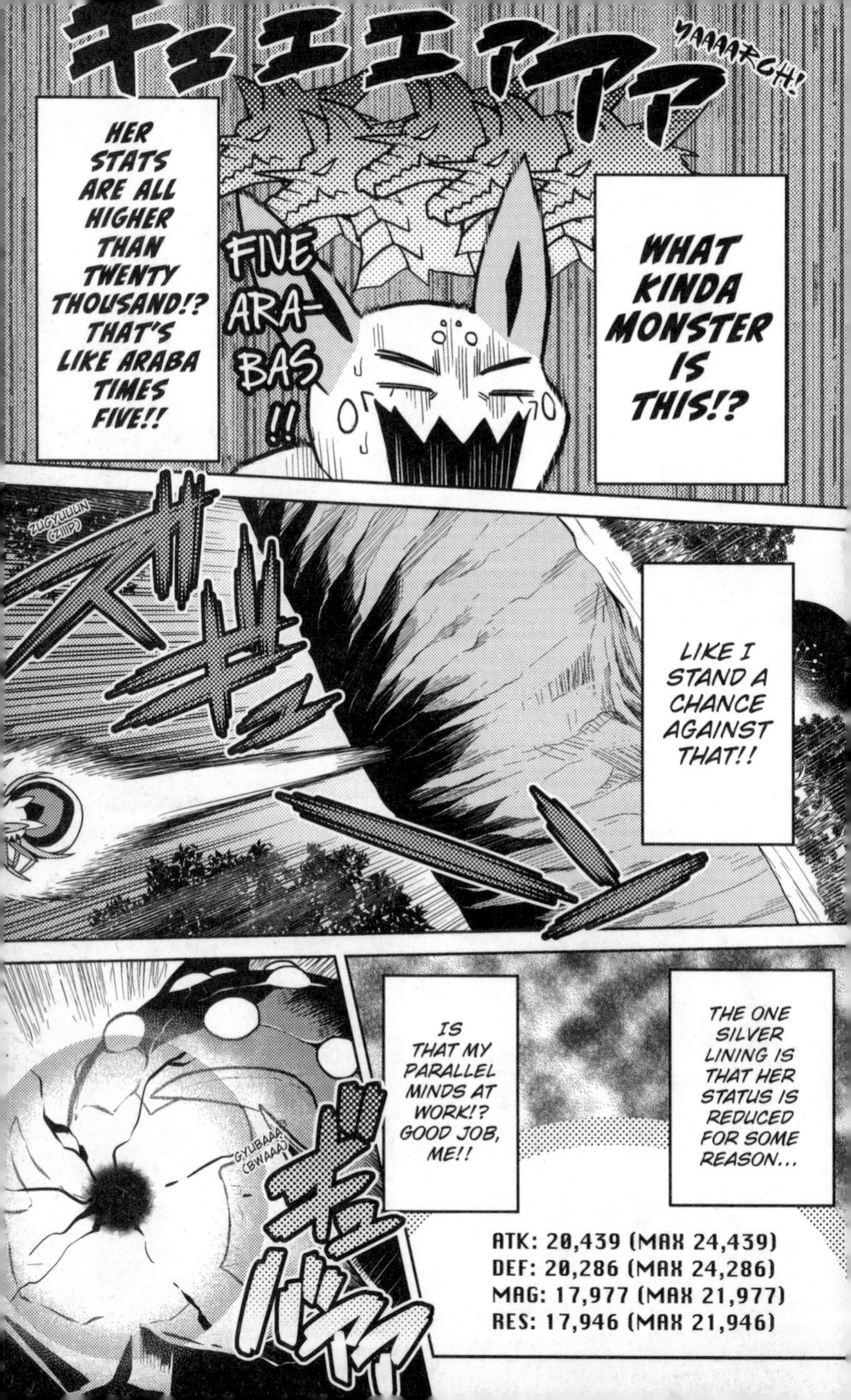
キェエエアアア
YAAAARGH!
WHAT KINDA MONSTER IS THIS!?
FIVE ARABAS!!
HER STATS ARE ALL HIGHER THAN TWENTY THOUSAND!? THAT'S LIKE ARABA TIMES FIVE!!
LIKE I STAND A CHANCE AGAINST THAT!!
ZUGYUUUN (ZIIIP)
THE ONE SILVER LINING IS THAT HER STATUS IS REDUCED FOR SOME REASON...
ATK: 20,439 (MAX 24,439)
DEF: 20,286 (MAX 24,286)
MAG: 17,977 (MAX 21,977)
RES: 17,946 (MAX 21,946)
IS THAT MY PARALLEL MINDS AT WORK!? GOOD JOB, ME!!
GYUBAAA (BWAAA)

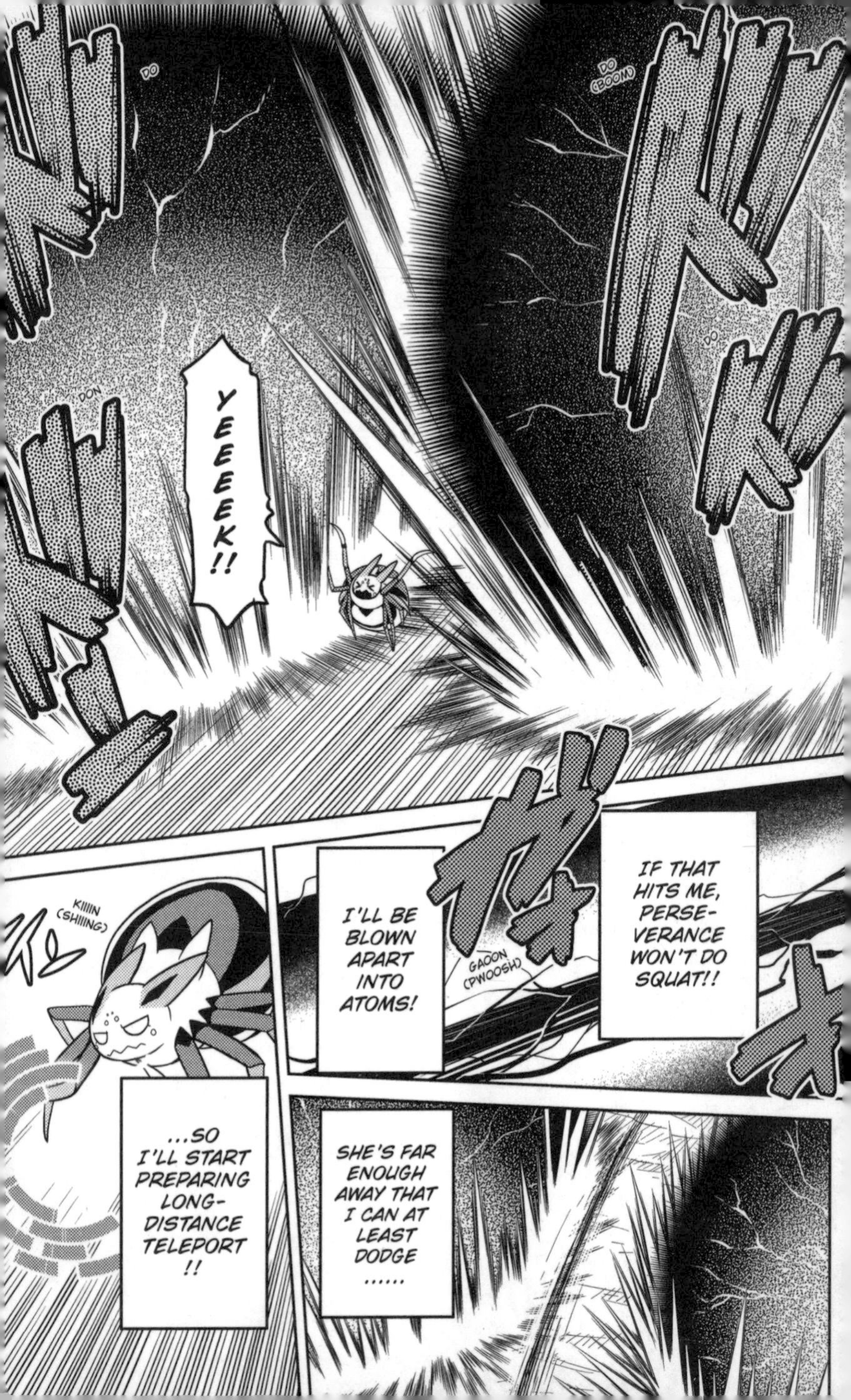
DO (BOOM)
DO
DO
YEEEEEK!!
DON
IF THAT HITS ME, PERSE-VERANCE WON'T DO SQUAT!!
I'LL BE BLOWN APART INTO ATOMS!
GAOON (PWOOSH)
SHE'S FAR ENOUGH AWAY THAT I CAN AT LEAST DODGE ......
KIIIN (SHIIING)
...SO I'LL START PREPARING LONG-DISTANCE TELEPORT !!

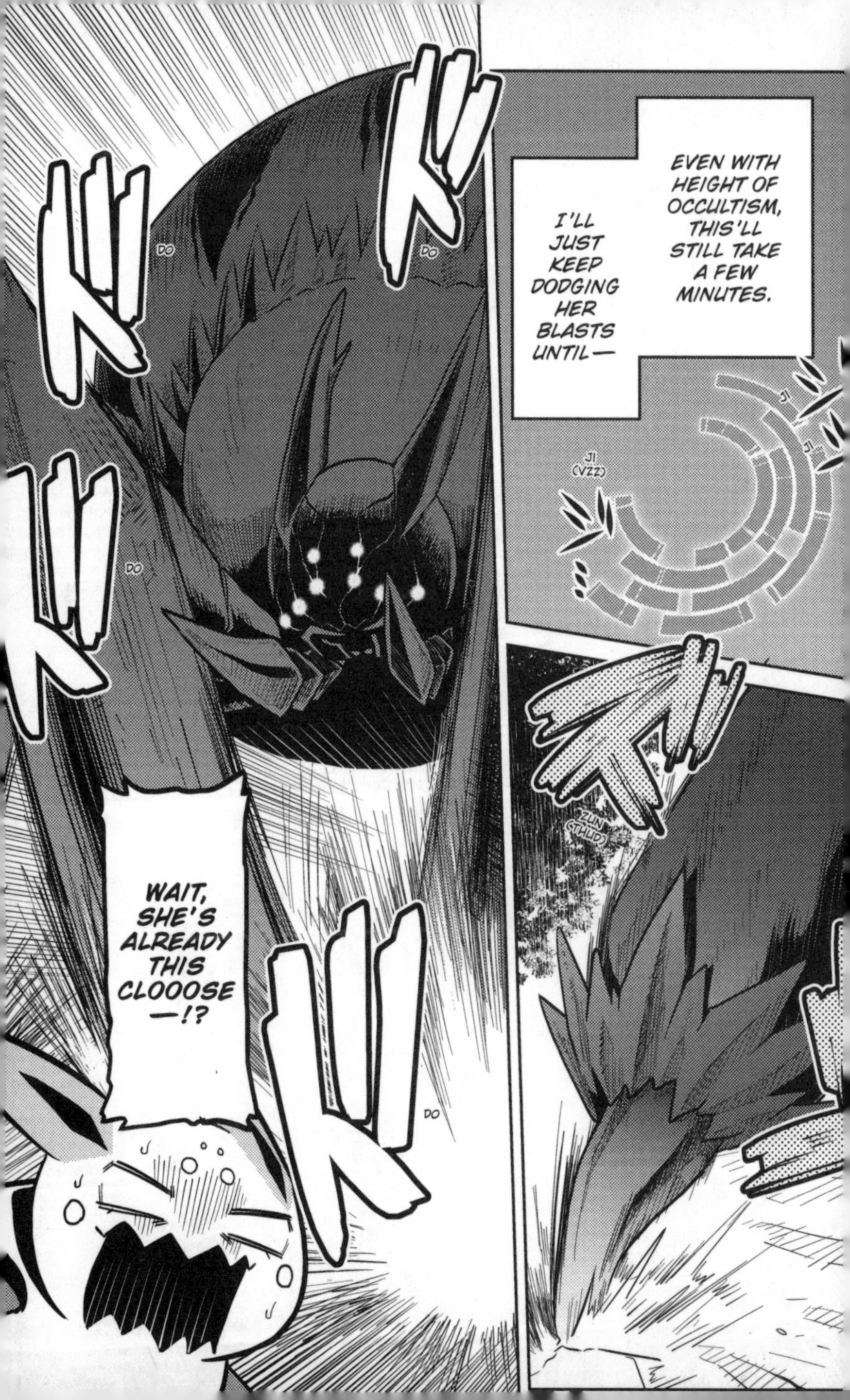
EVEN WITH HEIGHT OF OCCULTISM, THIS'LL STILL TAKE A FEW MINUTES.
I'LL JUST KEEP DODGING HER BLASTS UNTIL—
JI
JI
JI (VZZ)
ZUN (THUD)
DO
DO
DO
WAIT, SHE'S ALREADY THIS CLOOOSE—!?
DO

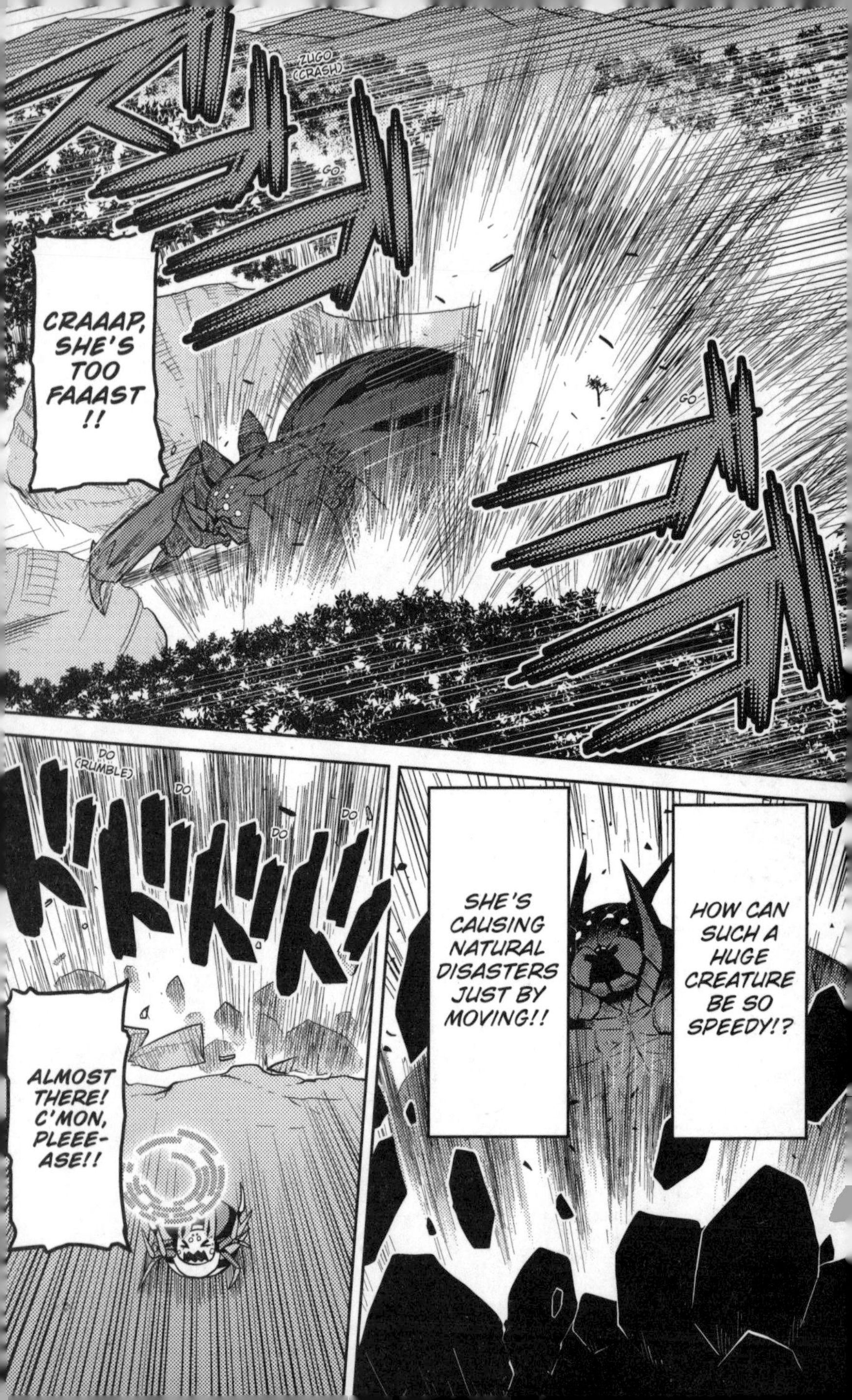
ZUGO (CRASH)
GO
CRAAAP, SHE'S TOO FAAAST!!
GO
GO
HOW CAN SUCH A HUGE CREATURE BE SO SPEEDY!?
SHE'S CAUSING NATURAL DISASTERS JUST BY MOVING!!
DO (RUMBLE)
DO
DO
DO
ALMOST THERE! C'MON, PLEEE-ASE!!

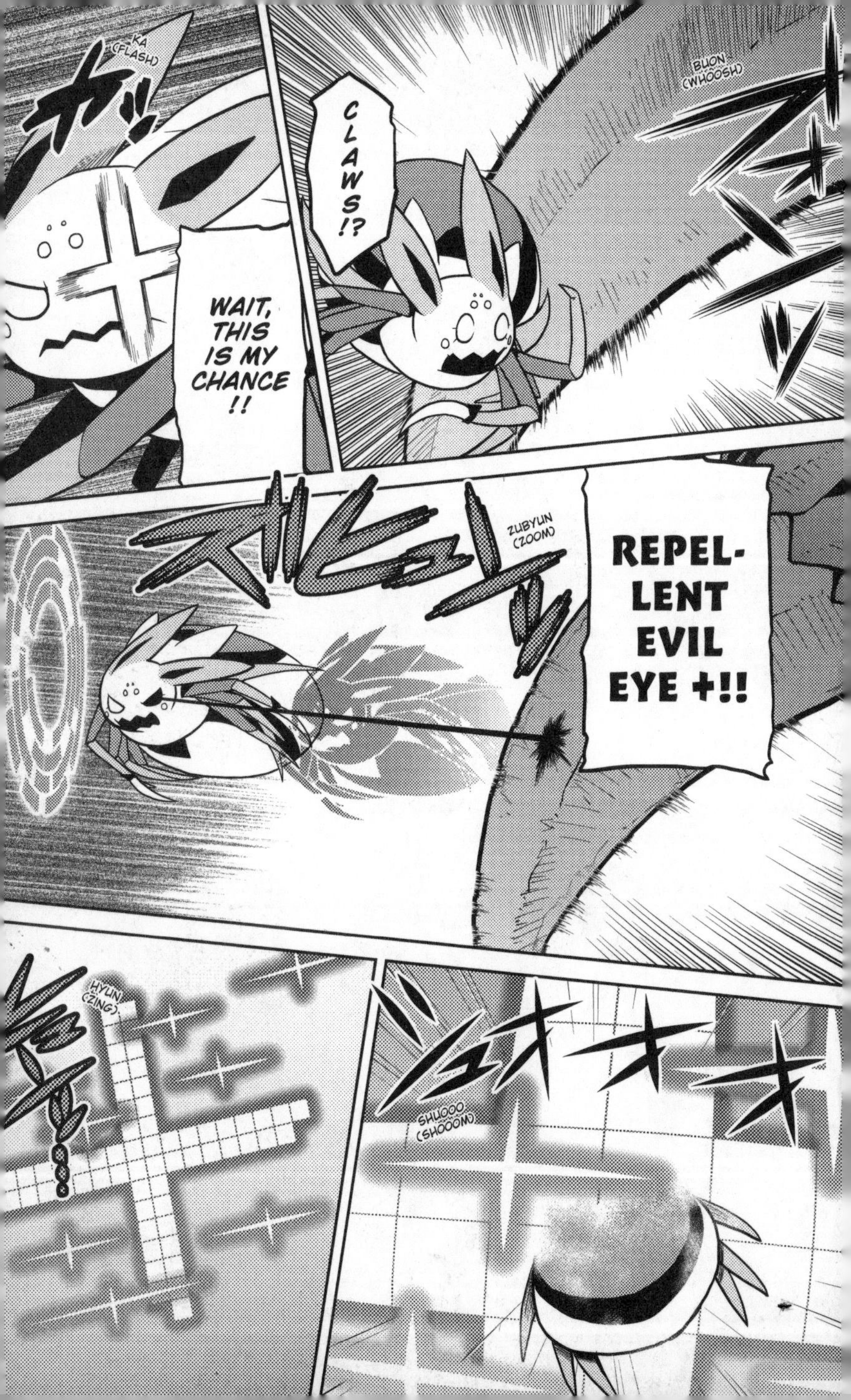
BUON
(WHOOSH)
CLAWS!?
KA
(FLASH)
WAIT, THIS IS MY CHANCE!!
REPEL-LENT EVIL EYE +!!
ZUBYUN
(ZOOM)
SHUOOO
(SHOOOM)
HYUN
(ZING)

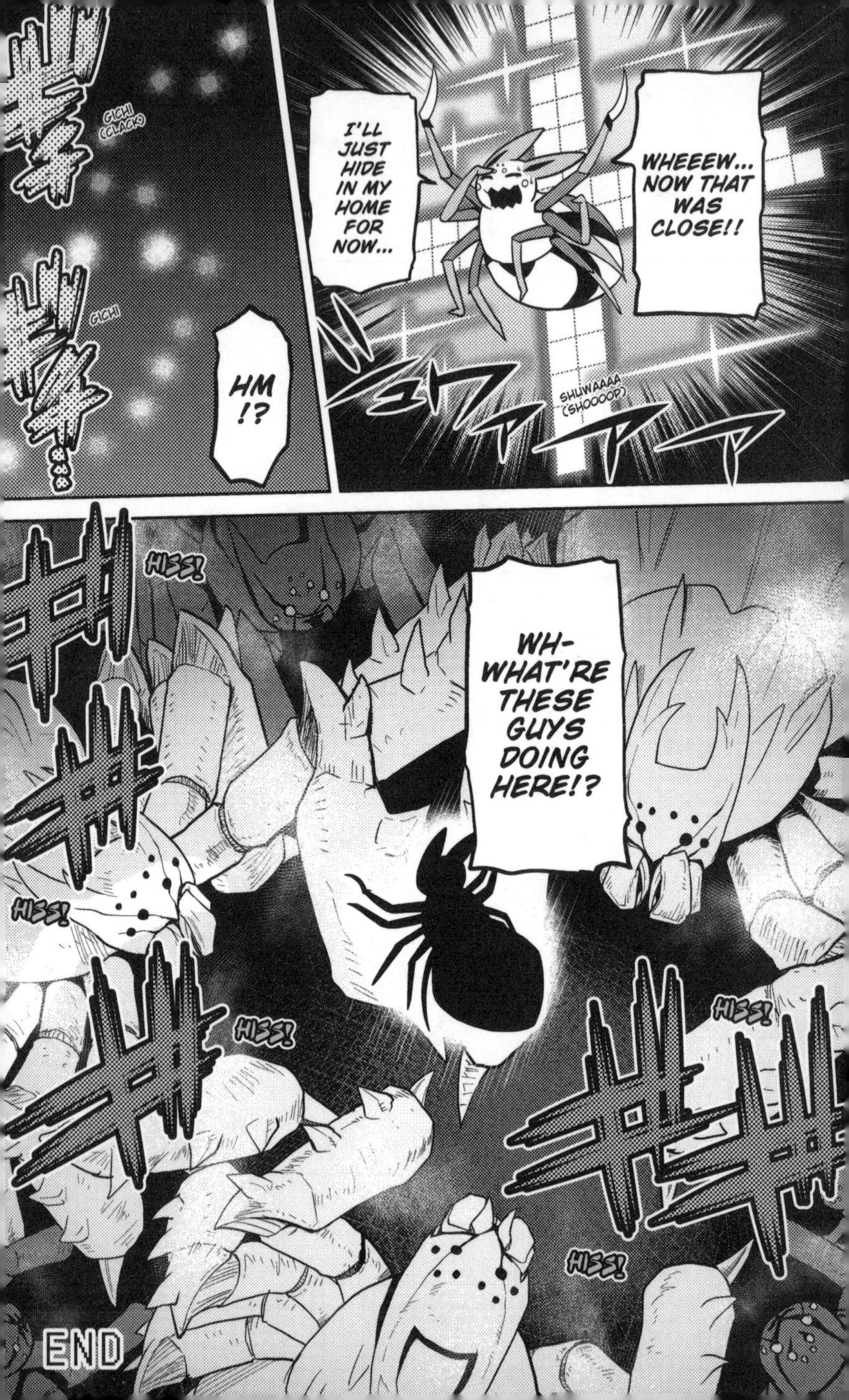
WHEEEW... NOW THAT WAS CLOSE!!
I'LL JUST HIDE IN MY HOME FOR NOW...
SHUWAAAA (SHOOOOP)
GICHI (CLACK)
GICHI
HM!?
HISS!
WH-WHAT'RE THESE GUYS DOING HERE!?
HISS!
HISS!
HISS!
HISS!
END

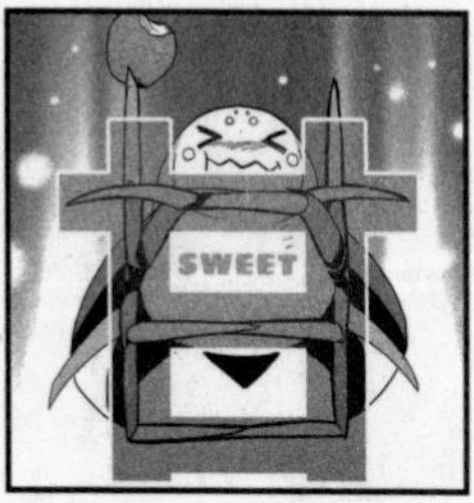
SWEET

So I'm a Spider, so What?

Bonus Short Comic

ANOTHER REINCARNATION #4

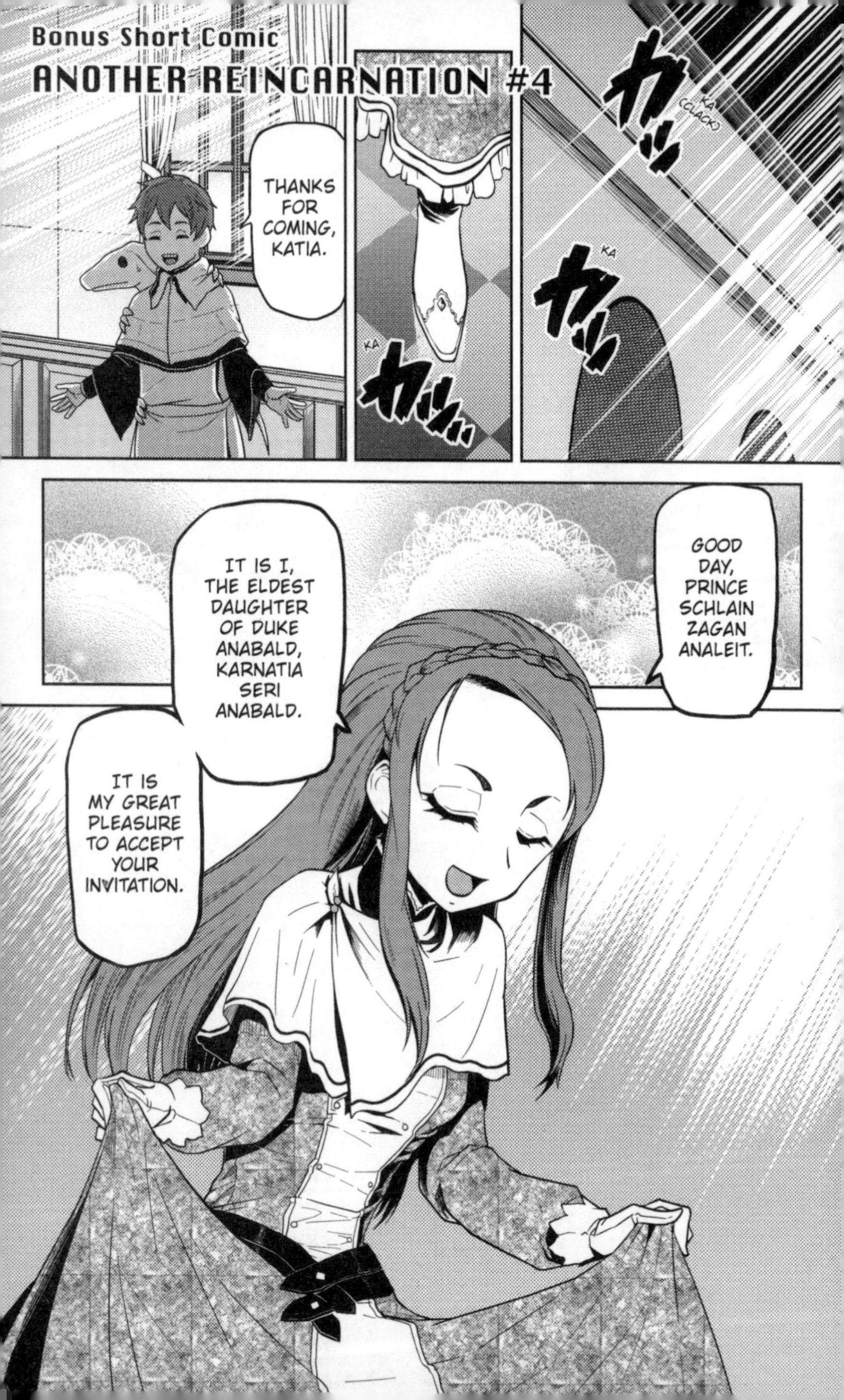
KA (CLACK)
KA
KA
THANKS FOR COMING, KATIA.
GOOD DAY, PRINCE SCHLAIN ZAGAN ANALEIT.
IT IS I, THE ELDEST DAUGHTER OF DUKE ANABALD, KARNATIA SERI ANABALD.
IT IS MY GREAT PLEASURE TO ACCEPT YOUR INVITATION.

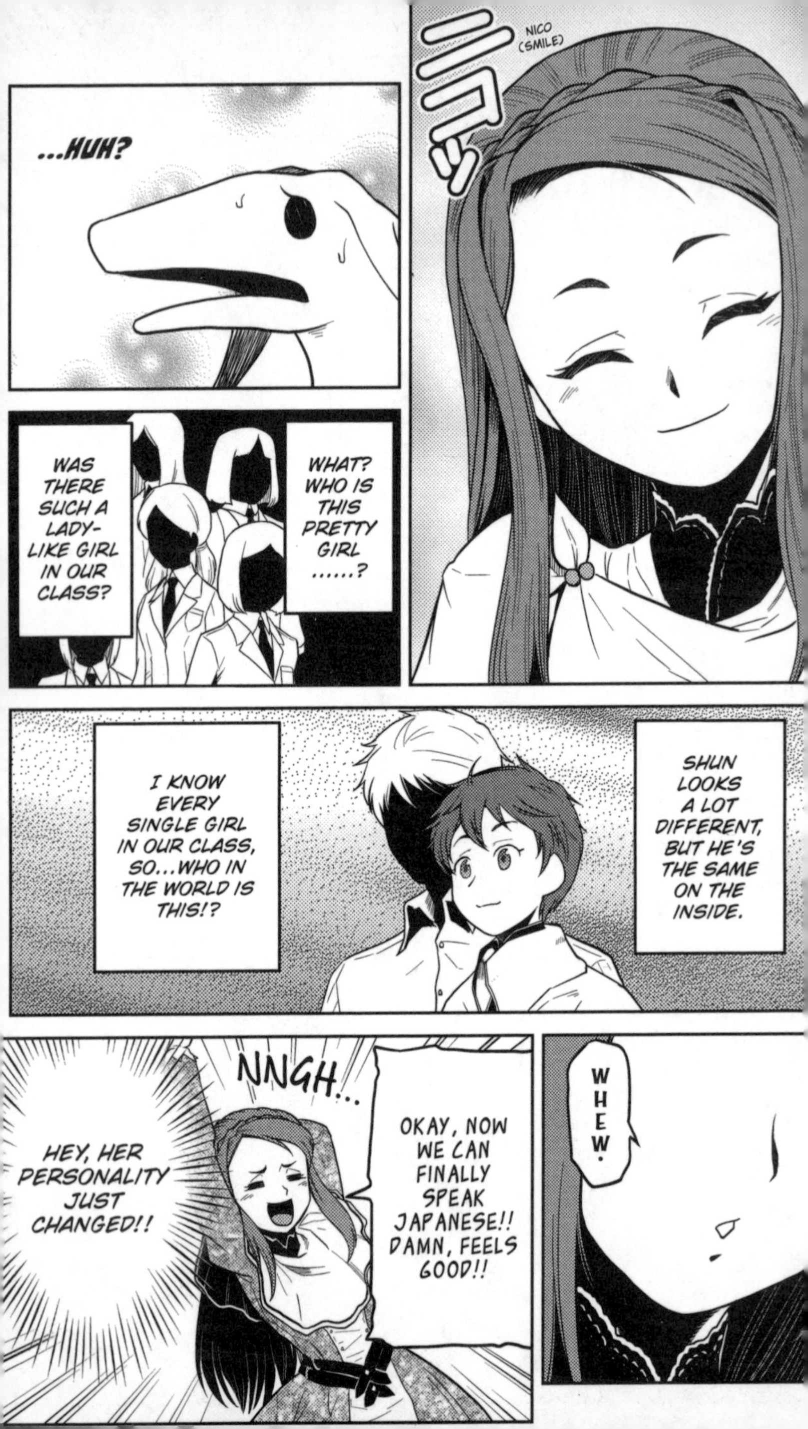
ニコッ
NICO (SMILE)
...HUH?
WHAT? WHO IS THIS PRETTY GIRL......?
WAS THERE SUCH A LADY-LIKE GIRL IN OUR CLASS?
SHUN LOOKS A LOT DIFFERENT, BUT HE'S THE SAME ON THE INSIDE.
I KNOW EVERY SINGLE GIRL IN OUR CLASS, SO...WHO IN THE WORLD IS THIS!?
WHEW.
NNGH...
OKAY, NOW WE CAN FINALLY SPEAK JAPANESE!! DAMN, FEELS GOOD!!
HEY, HER PERSONALITY JUST CHANGED!!

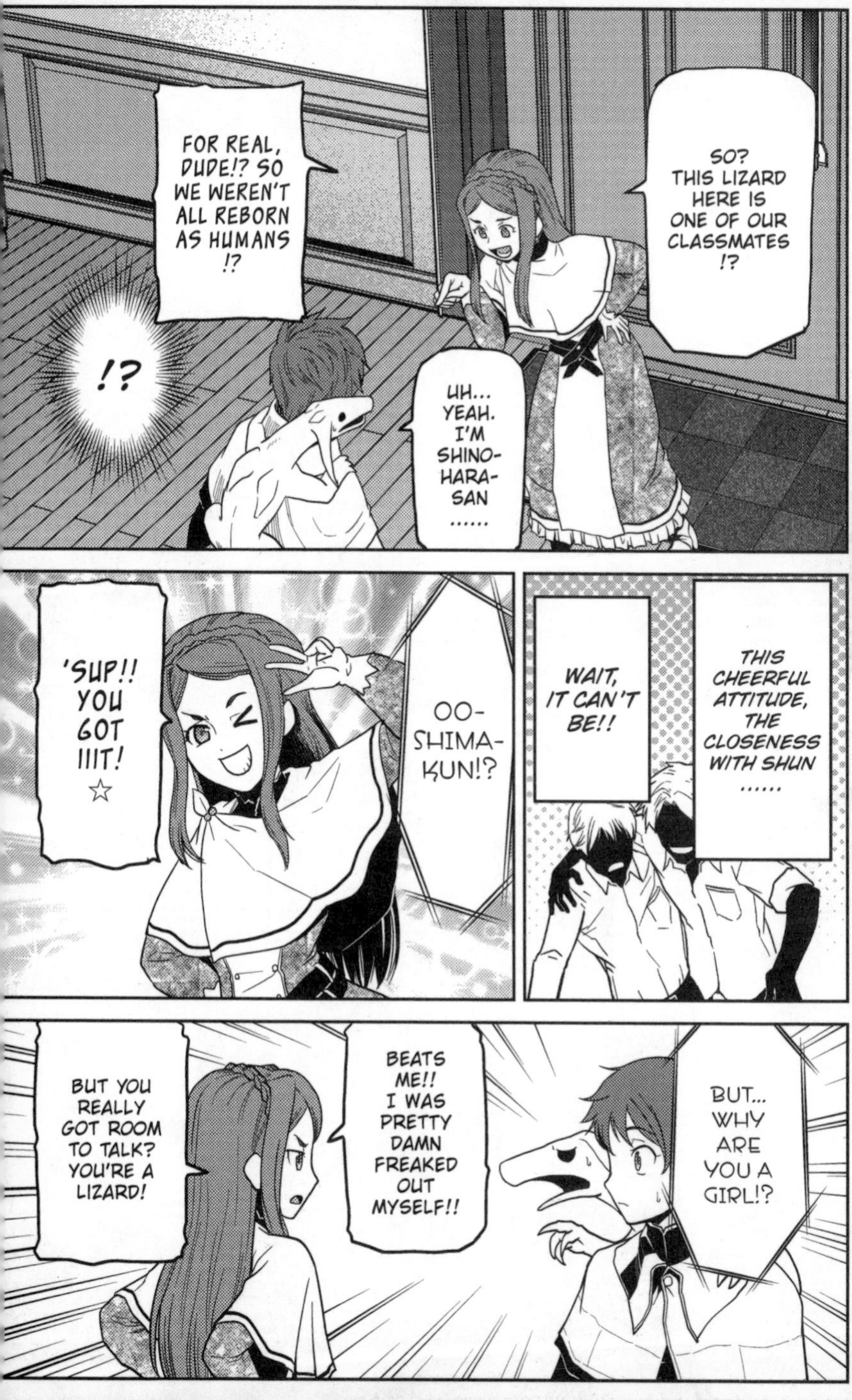
SO? THIS LIZARD HERE IS ONE OF OUR CLASSMATES!?
FOR REAL, DUDE!? SO WE WEREN'T ALL REBORN AS HUMANS!?
UH... YEAH. I'M SHINOHARA-SAN......
!?
THIS CHEERFUL ATTITUDE, THE CLOSENESS WITH SHUN......
WAIT, IT CAN'T BE!!
OO-SHIMA-KUN!?
'SUP!! YOU GOT IIIIT! ☆
BUT... WHY ARE YOU A GIRL!?
BEATS ME!! I WAS PRETTY DAMN FREAKED OUT MYSELF!!
BUT YOU REALLY GOT ROOM TO TALK? YOU'RE A LIZARD!

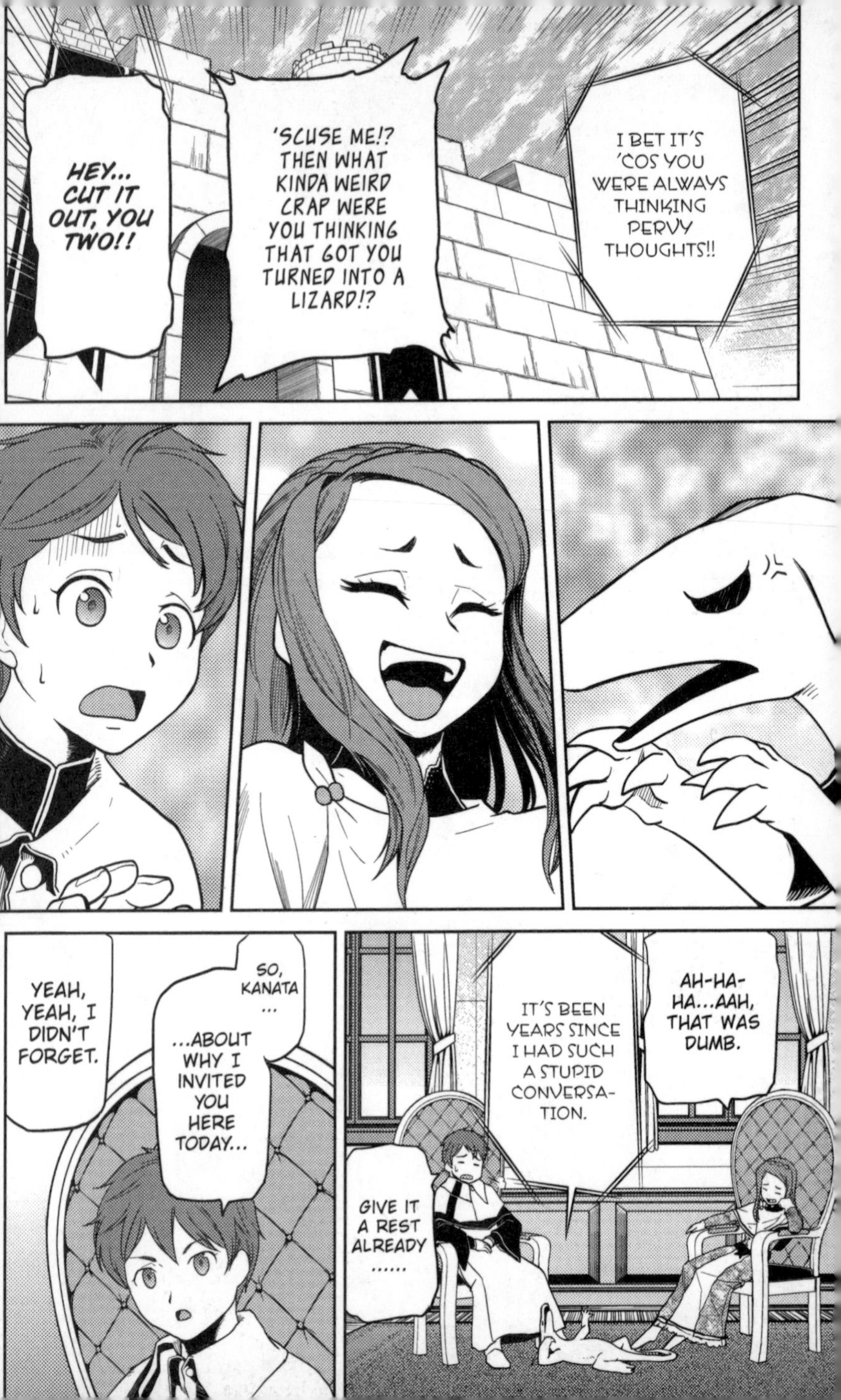
I BET IT'S 'COS YOU WERE ALWAYS THINKING PERVY THOUGHTS!!
'SCUSE ME!? THEN WHAT KINDA WEIRD CRAP WERE YOU THINKING THAT GOT YOU TURNED INTO A LIZARD!?
HEY... CUT IT OUT, YOU TWO!!
AH-HA-HA...AAH, THAT WAS DUMB.
IT'S BEEN YEARS SINCE I HAD SUCH A STUPID CONVERSA-TION.
GIVE IT A REST ALREADY ......
SO, KANATA ...
...ABOUT WHY I INVITED YOU HERE TODAY...
YEAH, YEAH, I DIDN'T FORGET.

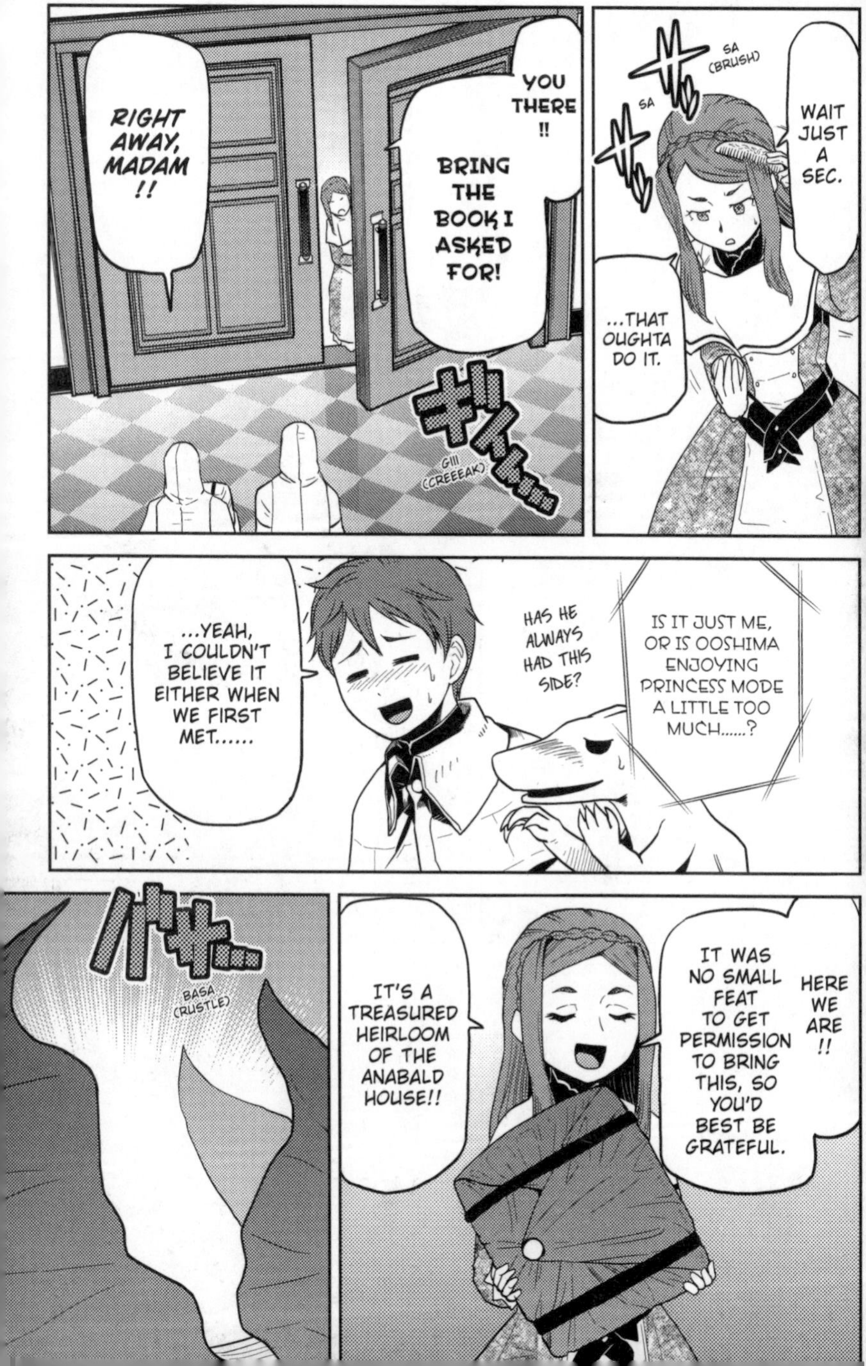
SA (BRUSH)
SA
WAIT JUST A SEC.
...THAT OUGHTA DO IT.
YOU THERE!!
BRING THE BOOK I ASKED FOR!
RIGHT AWAY, MADAM!!
GIII (CREEEAK)
IS IT JUST ME, OR IS OOSHIMA ENJOYING PRINCESS MODE A LITTLE TOO MUCH......?
HAS HE ALWAYS HAD THIS SIDE?
...YEAH, I COULDN'T BELIEVE IT EITHER WHEN WE FIRST MET......
HERE WE ARE!!
IT WAS NO SMALL FEAT TO GET PERMISSION TO BRING THIS, SO YOU'D BEST BE GRATEFUL.
IT'S A TREASURED HEIRLOOM OF THE ANABALD HOUSE!!
BASA (RUSTLE)

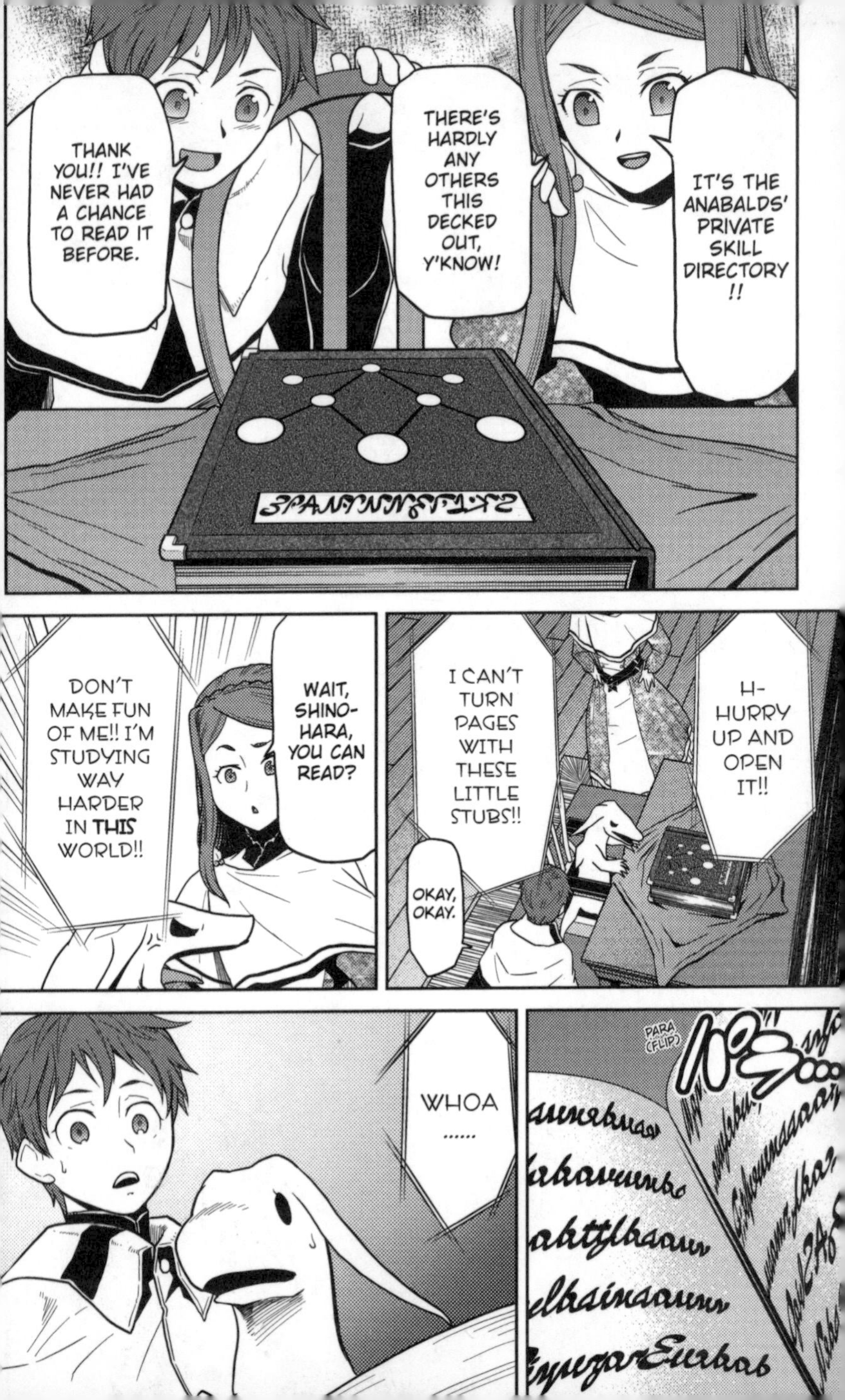
IT'S THE ANABALDS' PRIVATE SKILL DIRECTORY!!
THERE'S HARDLY ANY OTHERS THIS DECKED OUT, Y'KNOW!
THANK YOU!! I'VE NEVER HAD A CHANCE TO READ IT BEFORE.
H-HURRY UP AND OPEN IT!!
I CAN'T TURN PAGES WITH THESE LITTLE STUBS!!
OKAY, OKAY.
WAIT, SHINOHARA, YOU CAN READ?
DON'T MAKE FUN OF ME!! I'M STUDYING WAY HARDER IN **THIS** WORLD!!
PARA (FLIP)
WHOA ......

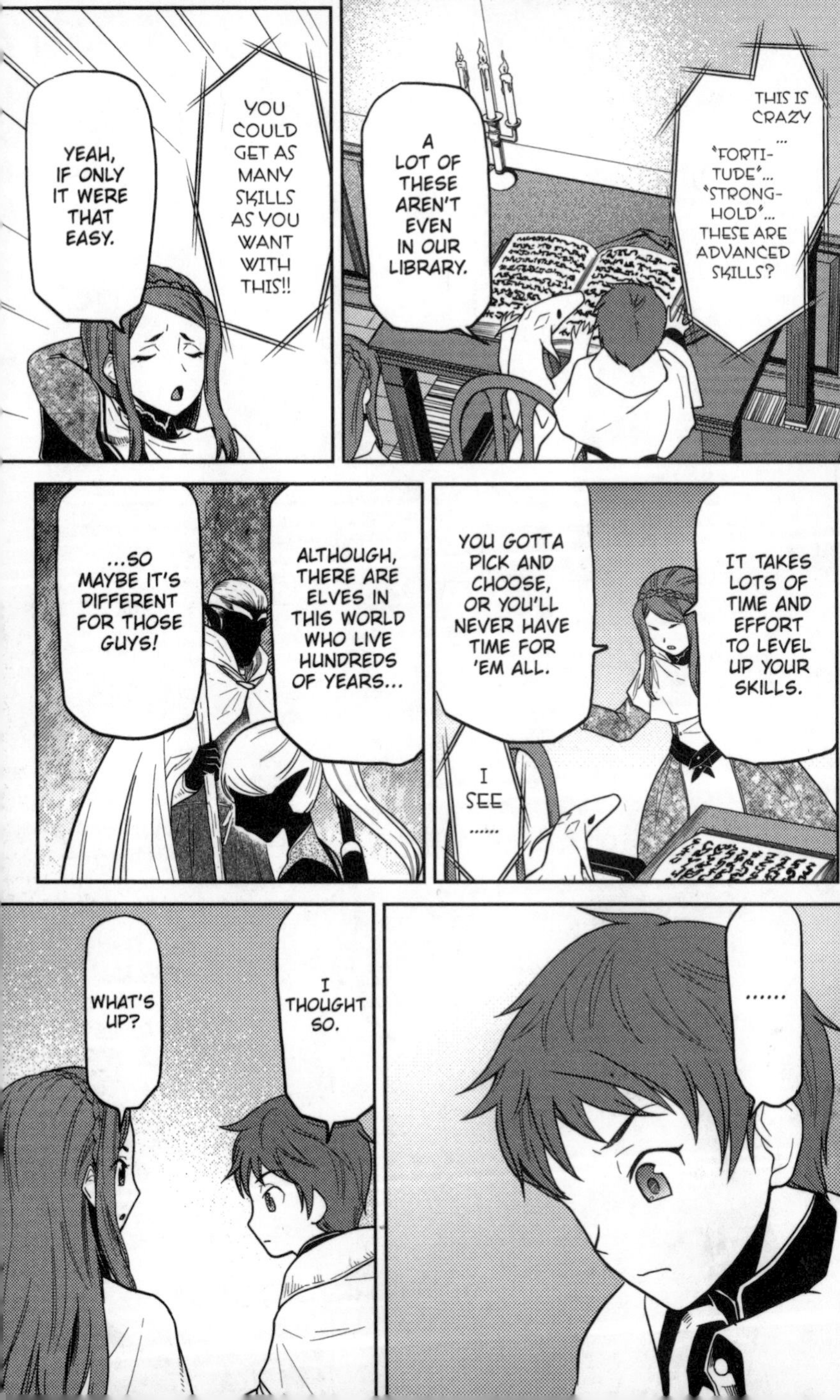
THIS IS CRAZY ... "FORTITUDE"... "STRONGHOLD"... THESE ARE ADVANCED SKILLS?
A LOT OF THESE AREN'T EVEN IN OUR LIBRARY.
YOU COULD GET AS MANY SKILLS AS YOU WANT WITH THIS!!
YEAH, IF ONLY IT WERE THAT EASY.
IT TAKES LOTS OF TIME AND EFFORT TO LEVEL UP YOUR SKILLS.
YOU GOTTA PICK AND CHOOSE, OR YOU'LL NEVER HAVE TIME FOR 'EM ALL.
I SEE ......
ALTHOUGH, THERE ARE ELVES IN THIS WORLD WHO LIVE HUNDREDS OF YEARS...
...SO MAYBE IT'S DIFFERENT FOR THOSE GUYS!
......
I THOUGHT SO.
WHAT'S UP?

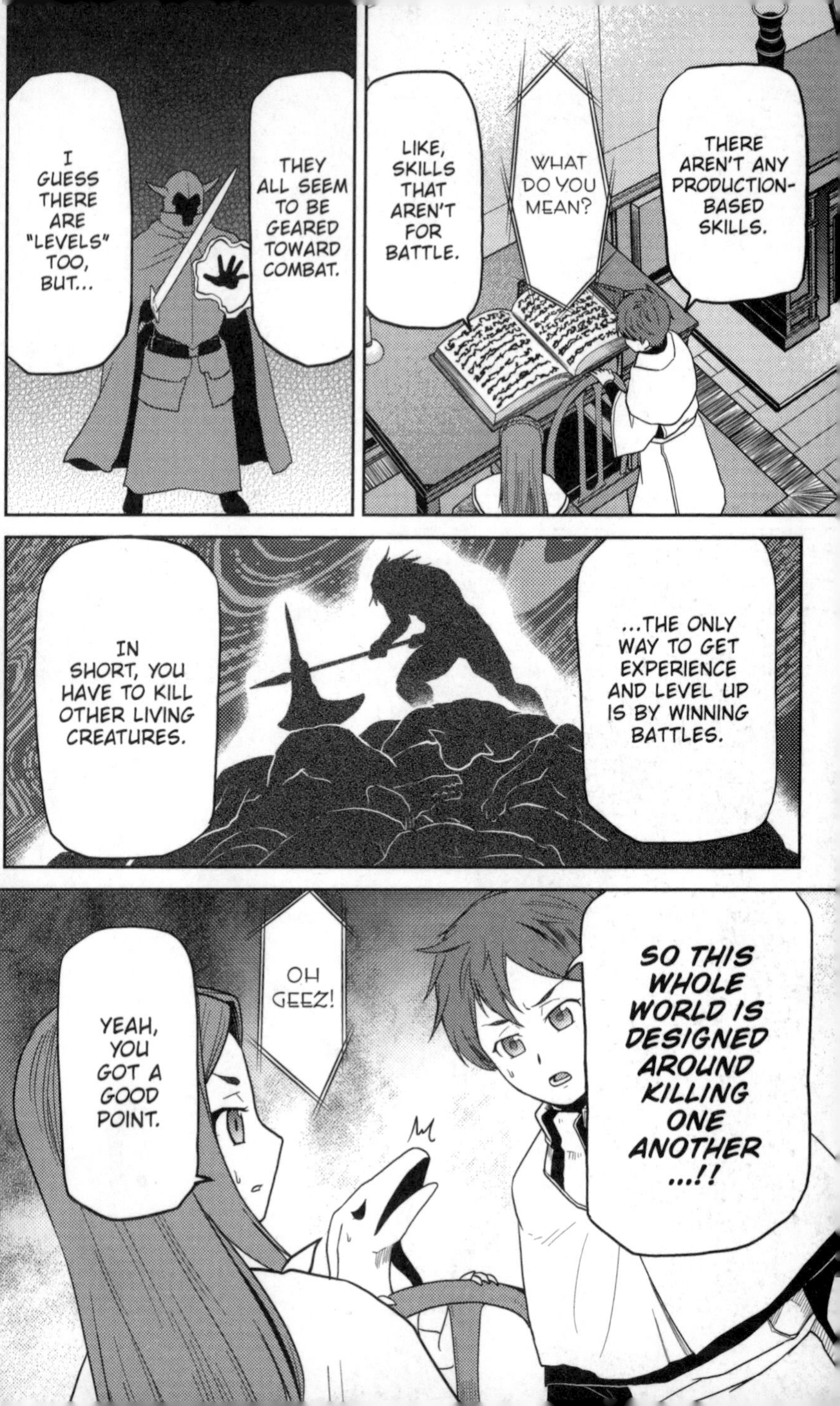
THERE AREN'T ANY PRODUCTION-BASED SKILLS.
WHAT DO YOU MEAN?
LIKE, SKILLS THAT AREN'T FOR BATTLE.
THEY ALL SEEM TO BE GEARED TOWARD COMBAT.
I GUESS THERE ARE "LEVELS" TOO, BUT...
...THE ONLY WAY TO GET EXPERIENCE AND LEVEL UP IS BY WINNING BATTLES.
IN SHORT, YOU HAVE TO KILL OTHER LIVING CREATURES.
SO THIS WHOLE WORLD IS DESIGNED AROUND KILLING ONE ANOTHER ...!!
OH GEEZ!
YEAH, YOU GOT A GOOD POINT.

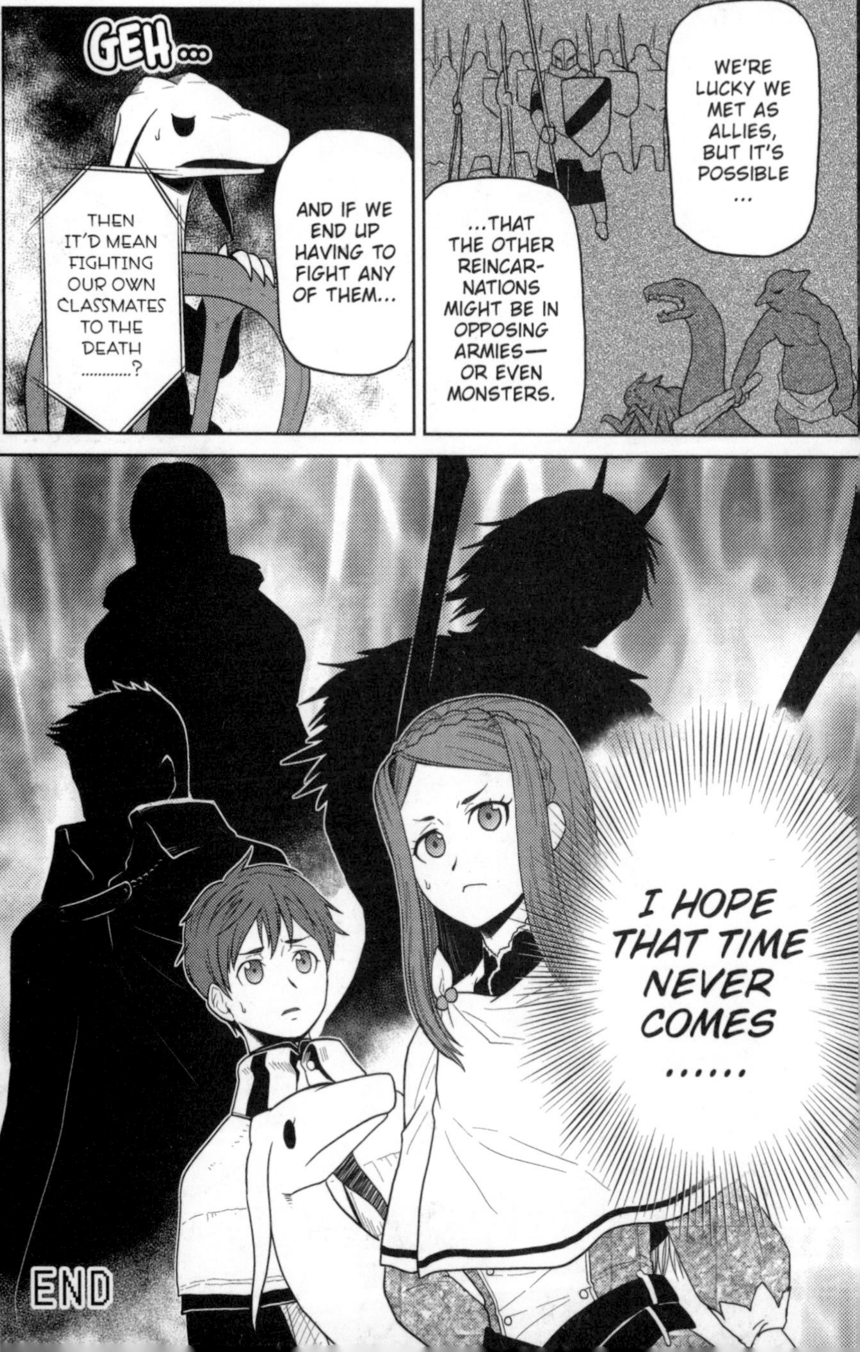
WE'RE LUCKY WE MET AS ALLIES, BUT IT'S POSSIBLE ...
...THAT THE OTHER REINCAR-NATIONS MIGHT BE IN OPPOSING ARMIES— OR EVEN MONSTERS.
AND IF WE END UP HAVING TO FIGHT ANY OF THEM...
GEH...
THEN IT'D MEAN FIGHTING OUR OWN CLASSMATES TO THE DEATH ....?
I HOPE THAT TIME NEVER COMES ......
END

So I'm a Spider, so What?

AFTERWORD

ORIGINAL CREATOR: OKINA BABA

HELLO, HELLO. IT'S ME, THE ORIGINAL CREATOR, OKINA BABA.

THE TIME HAS FINALLY COME!

THE FATEFUL SHOWDOWN WITH ARABA!

MOST OF THIS VOLUME IS ABOUT THAT FIGHT, AS BEFITS SUCH A MAJOR EVENT.

I DON'T THINK THERE'S BEEN SUCH A LONG BATTLE SCENE SINCE THE MANGA VERSION STARTED.

EVEN THAT BATTLE WITH THE HUGE ARMY OF MONKEYS DIDN'T LAST AS LONG AS THIS BATTLE WITH ARABA.

TALK ABOUT A TOUGH FIGHT.

BY THE WAY, THIS WAS APPARENTLY A TOUGH FIGHT FOR KAKASHI-SENSEI TOO.

I MEAN, DRAWING IT MUST HAVE BEEN HELL.

AFTER ALL, ARABA IS SUPER-DETAILED.

AND THERE'S TONS OF MOVEMENT.

AND A CRAZY AMOUNT OF SFX.

BUT THAT'S JUST HOW IT IS!

FOR A NOVEL, ALL YOU HAVE TO DO IS WRITE. SO FOR ME, BATTLE SCENES AND CONVERSATIONAL SCENES TAKE THE SAME AMOUNT OF CALORIES, BUT CLEARLY THAT'S NOT THE CASE FOR MANGA.

BUT THANKS TO KAKASHI-SENSEI'S HARD WORK IN THE FACE OF ALL THIS PRESSURE, THE RESULT IS A BATTLE SCENE THAT'S EVEN MORE INTENSE THAN THE ORIGINAL!

THAT'S KAKASHI-SENSEI FOR YOU.

BUT THERE'S NO TIME FOR HER TO REST, BECAUSE UP NEXT IS A NEW LEVEL OF HELL, THE BATTLE AGAINST MOTHER...

D-DON'T LOOK AT ME LIKE THAT!

IT'S NOT MY FAULT AS THE CREATOR, OKAY!?

I'M SURE THE GODS OF MANGA ARE JUST GIVING KAKASHI-SENSEI A SERIES OF TESTS!

SO DON'T BLAME ME!

AND PLEASE, CONTINUE TO SUPPORT THE HELLISH CREATION THAT IS THE SO I'M A SPIDER, SO WHAT? MANGA.

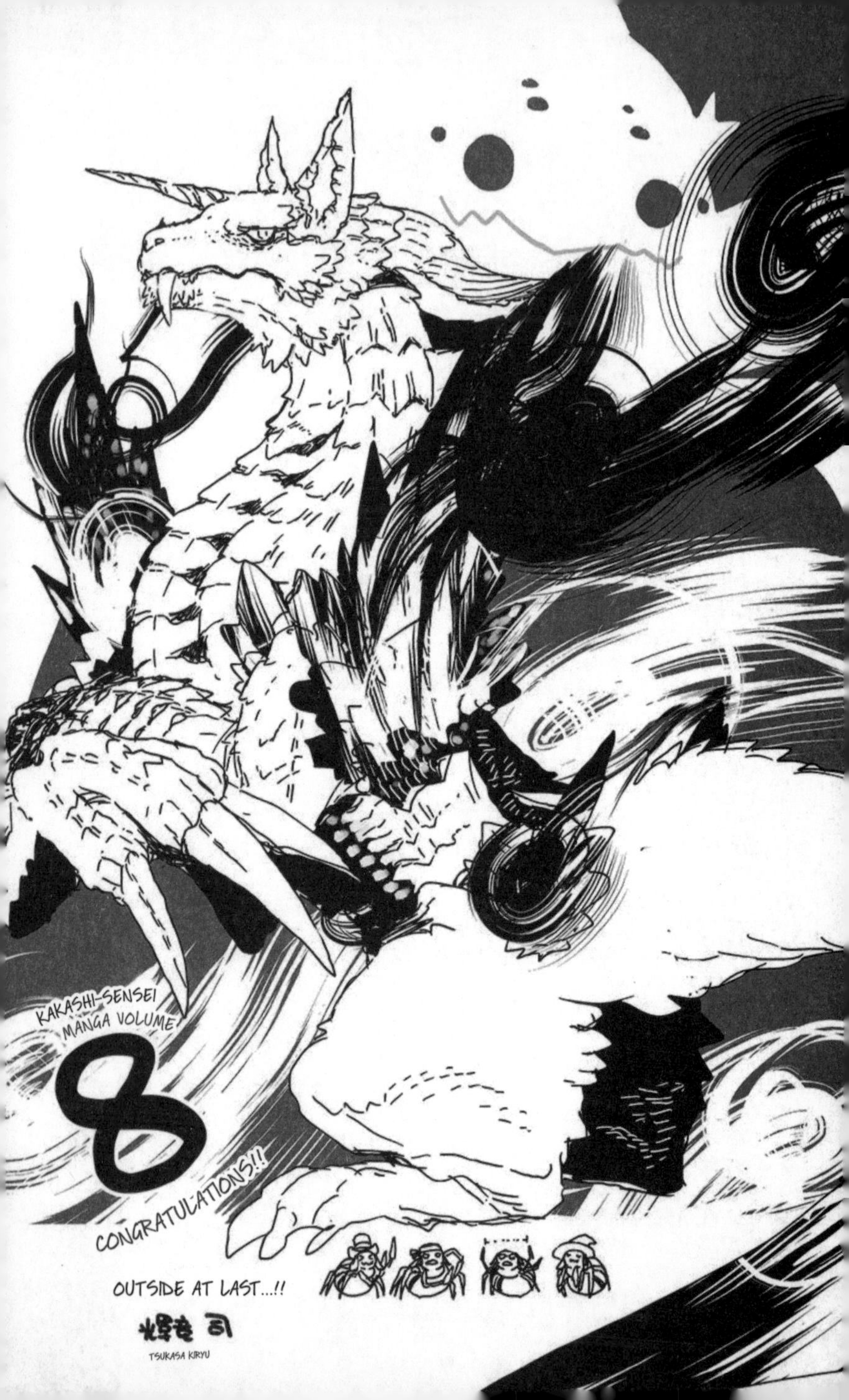
KAKASHI-SENSEI MANGA VOLUME 8
CONGRATULATIONS!!
OUTSIDE AT LAST...!!
TSUKASA KIRYU

STAFF LIST

The author

ASAHIRO KAKASHI

Assistant

TERUO HATANAKA

Design

R design studio

(Shinji Yamaguchi)

You're reading
the wrong way!
Turn the page to read
a bonus short story by
So I'm a Spider, So What?
original creator,
Okina Baba!

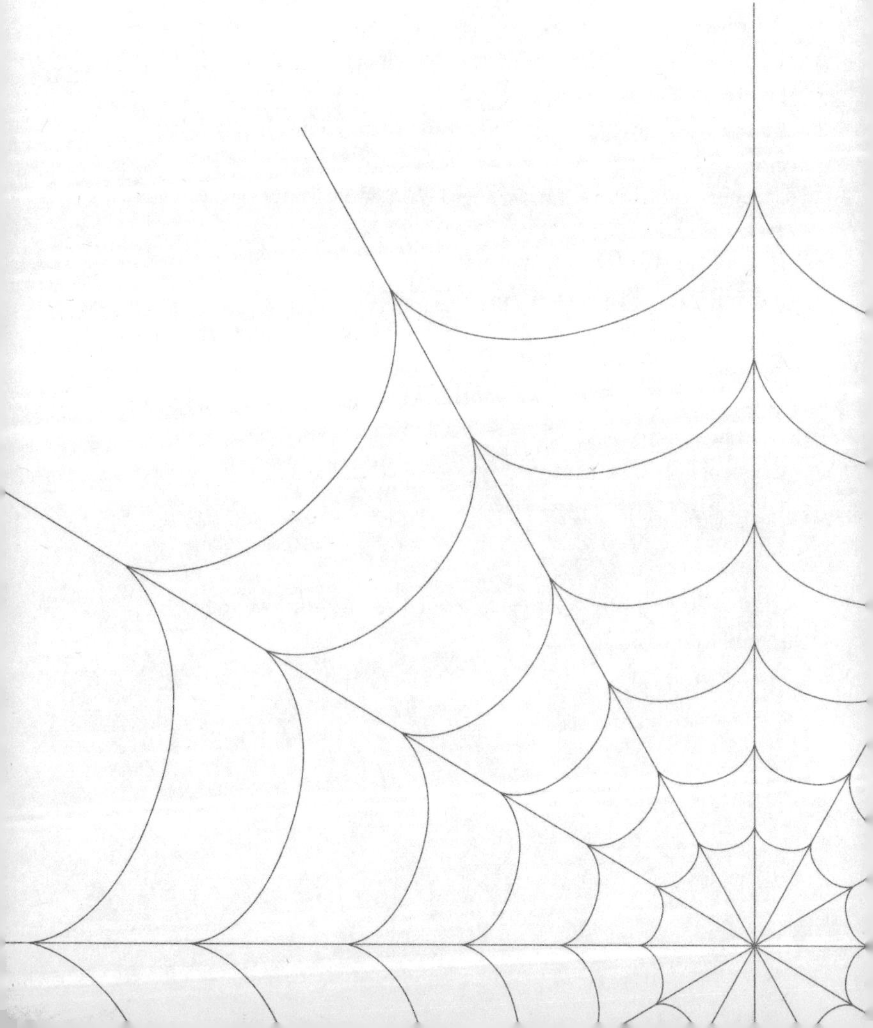

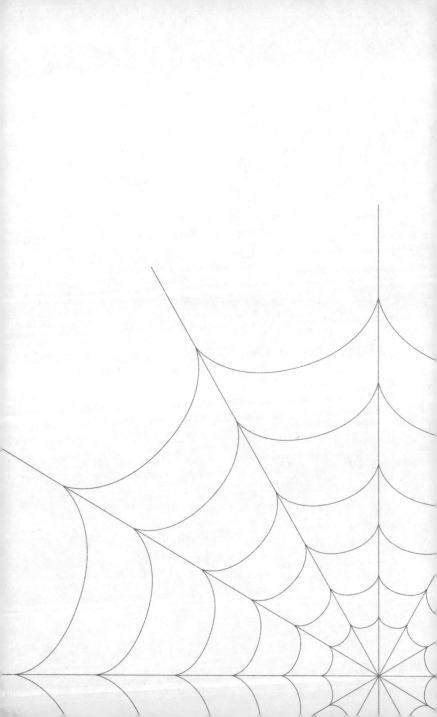

Hmph. But still!

All that is about to change!

I'll be a good, upstanding member of the outside world!

Starting NOW!

I'm taking my first step forward!

Into this unknown country!

And the unknown world's nature!

And the unknown world's FOOD!

Sweets! Meat dishes! Seafood! Protein! Candy! DESSEEEEERT!

I'll take anything at this point!

Whatever tasty food you've got, just put it in my mouuuuuth!

I don't wanna eat poisonous monsters anymore.

I've had it up to here with gross food.

Since I was fighting to survive in the dungeon, I didn't have much of a choice, but things are gonna be different from here on out!

I'm gonna eat whatever tasty things I want, when I want, as much as I want!

Heh. Heh-heh. Bwa-ha-ha-ha!

Just you wait, delicious new foods!

I wonder what the cuisine in this world is like. Western food? Japanese? Chinese?

Since it's another world, maybe it'll be a whole new kind of cooking that defies any categories I know!

Oh man! I can't even imagine!

I don't have to live in the dungeon anymore!

Yahoooo!

......Now, shortly after getting all excited about this, I wound up back in the dungeon again.

Why, life? Whyyy?

[The End]

Bonus Short Story

So I'm a Spider, So What?
The Outside Food I Crave
Okina Baba

Hooray! I escaped the Great Elroe Labyrinth!

Yes! Yes! YESSSS!

Frickin' finally!

It was a long road, that's for sure!

But now I've finally escaped that awful place!

Man, what kind of hellish fate was it to be born in a last-level-tier dungeon?

It's basically like, *Hello, go die.*

I can't believe I got out alive...

But since I survived that special circle of hell, I've gotten a lot stronger.

Besides, having basically started out in the last dungeon, I've seen a lot of this world's secrets and hidden routes...

I'm not entirely sure that's a good thing.

I guess it's better to know than to not know, if it might help me solve problems in the future or something?

Well, nothing I can do about it now.

A little extra knowledge never hurt anyone—or at least, let's pretend that's the case.

Well, and let's be honest, I don't actually know all that much about this world.

I mean, I've never been outside the labyrinth before!

Sure, I talked big about knowing lots of secrets and hidden routes a second ago, but I don't really know anything else.

I still have no idea what it's like here in the outside world.

I'm like a shut-in with no knowledge of society!

Come on! That's practically no different from my previous life!

So I'm a Spider, So What?

8

Art: **Asahiro Kakashi**

Original Story: **Okina Baba**

Character Design: **Tsukasa Kiryu**

Translation: Jenny McKeon ✖ Lettering: Bianca Pistillo

KUMO DESUGA, NANIKA? Volume 8
© Asahiro Kakashi 2020
© Okina Baba, Tsukasa Kiryu 2020
First published in Japan in 2020 by KADOKAWA CORPORATION, Tokyo.
English translation rights arranged with KADOKAWA CORPORATION, Tokyo, through TUTTLE-MORI AGENCY, INC.

English translation © 2020 by Yen Press, LLC

Yen Press
150 West 30th Street, 19th Floor
New York, NY 10001

Visit us at yenpress.com
facebook.com/yenpress
twitter.com/yenpress
yenpress.tumblr.com
instagram.com/yenpress

First Yen Press Edition: August 2020

Yen Press is an imprint of Yen Press, LLC.
The Yen Press name and logo are trademarks of Yen Press, LLC.

Library of Congress Control Number: 2017954138

ISBNs: 978-1-9753-1555-9 (paperback)
978-1-9753-1556-6 (ebook)

10 9 8 7 6 5 4 3 2 1

WOR

Printed in the United States of America

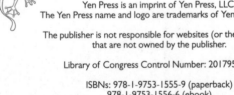

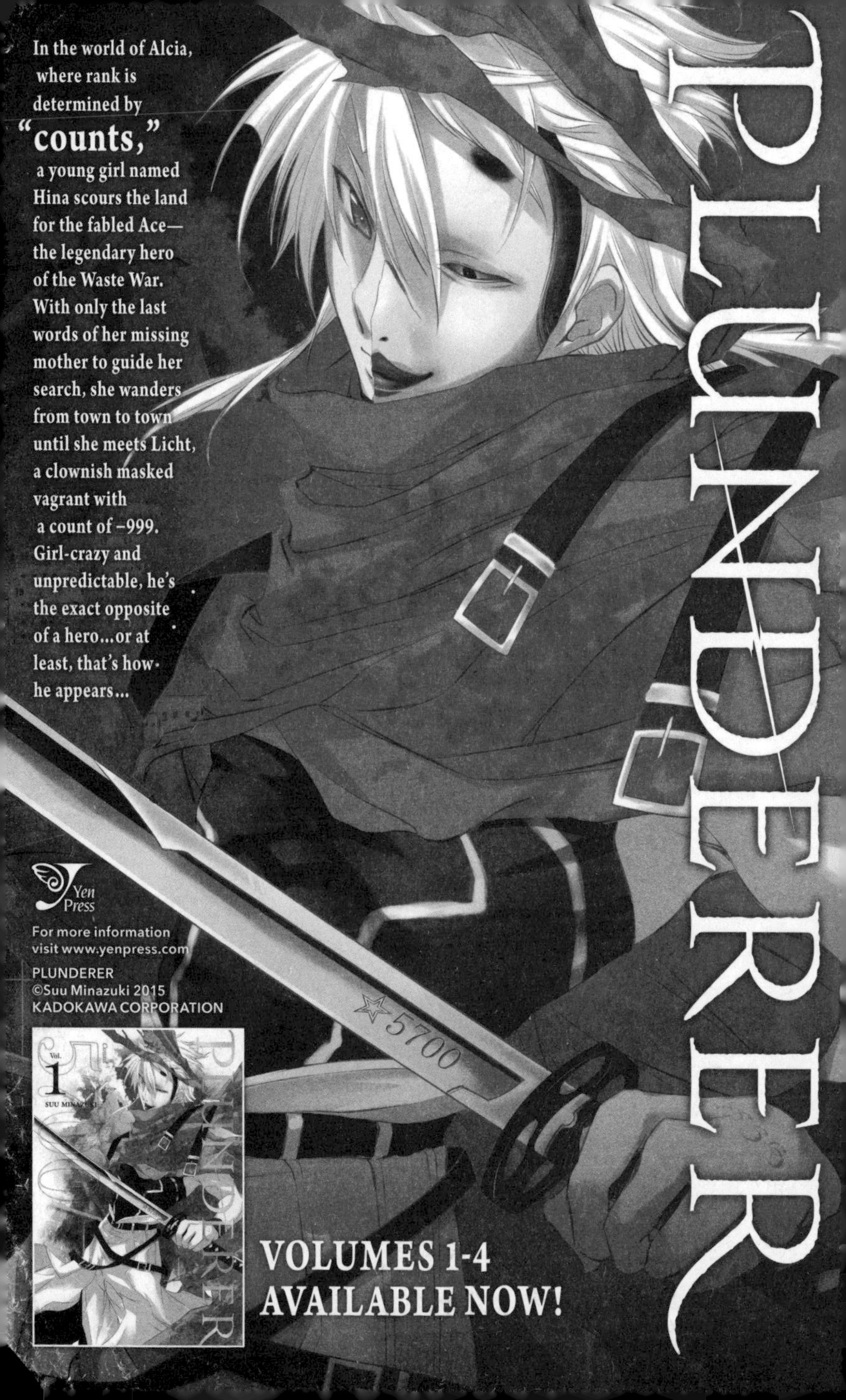
PLUNDERER
In the world of Alcia, where rank is determined by "counts," a young girl named Hina scours the land for the fabled Ace—the legendary hero of the Waste War. With only the last words of her missing mother to guide her search, she wanders from town to town until she meets Licht, a clownish masked vagrant with a count of −999. Girl-crazy and unpredictable, he's the exact opposite of a hero...or at least, that's how he appears...
Yen Press
For more information visit www.yenpress.com
PLUNDERER
©Suu Minazuki 2015
KADOKAWA CORPORATION
VOLUMES 1-4
AVAILABLE NOW!
5700